THE OVERSEAS DEPARTMENT
THE PROVISIONAL IRA ON ACTIVE SERVICE IN EUROPE

Steven J. Farr

Copyright © 2020 Steven J. Farr

All rights reserved.

ISBN: 9798572196658

FOR

Smita Islania; Melanie Anan & Clive Hazell; Rosalind, Dillon-Lee and family; Tina Smith and family; Irene Heakin and family; Lyndal Melrose & Vicky Coss; Andy Kelly; TP; SC: may your heavy sacrifices not be in vain.

My parents; thank you for everything, but especially for teaching me the difference between right and wrong.

My wife, daughter and brothers for their love and support.

C, M, E, J, D and M for distracting me from the writing of this book with beer, Bratwurst and Bundesliga.

Written in the hope that there is no return to the dark days and that both communities in the northern part of the island of Ireland see a day where they can both peacefully co-exist on the same piece of land.

CONTENTS

KEENWIND RED 7
NOTE FROM THE AUTHOR 15
INTRO: 1969-1980 21

1 THE PADRE 41
2 THE RATTLE OF HEAVY STUFF 74
3 BUTTON JOB 101
4 546, FALLS ROAD 121
5 THE POPE 132
6 THE NEWRY CONNECTION 147
7 DESSIE 167
8 FIREBALL 179
9 FERMDOWN 195
10 THE GERMAN 222
11 FIREBREAK 237
12 AFTERMATH 253
13 SAFE HOUSES 268
14 SITTING DUCKS 283
15 HEERLE 302
16 THE SURGEON 314
17 THE MUSHROOM SHED 326
18 CITY OF DIAMONDS 335
19 „GOOD LUCK" 346
20 720 DAYS IN THE BUNKER 363
21 HOLIDAY IN SANDHATTEN 374
22 EPILOGUE 395

BIBLIOGRAPHY 423
   BOOKS 423
   PRESS & ONLINE 426
   LEGAL & SECURITY SERVICES DOCUMENTS 442
   TV & MISCELLANEOUS 446
INDEX 449

THE OVERSEAS DEPARTEMENT

KEENWIND RED

It is around 6.50pm: the clocks moved back to daylight-saving time a few weeks ago and it has been dark for a while. It is a murky, overcast autumn darkness – a reasonably mild evening for October but the developing mist indicates a cold snap is on the way. A young man with closely-cropped hair, in his early twenties, sits in the front driver's seat of a beige Ford station wagon with a brown vinyl roof, parked at the side of the tree-lined stretch of road that runs through the small village situated in the very west of West Germany. About fifty metres away, a BP petrol station glows eerily in the gloom; adjacent to it a squat building - a *Schnellimbiss* snack bar – from whose window emanates a bright light, reflecting onto the petrol station forecourt.

The man has been sitting there for a while; barring a short stop at a petrol station in Reuver just the other side of the border in the Netherlands, where he had the chance to stretch his legs, he has been at the wheel of the car since he left The Hague a few hours ago. He has had time to think about the wide range of people who have assisted him on his journey to this non-descript village on the border between Germany and the Netherlands; aside from people back home, acquaintances in Mainz, Göttingen, Hamburg, Hannover, Düsseldorf, Berlin, Nijmegen, Venlo, The Hague, Maastricht, the naive girl in Amsterdam – all have played their part in getting him here. For them, for his colleagues, but mainly for himself, he is anxious to get things right this time. He watches the intermittent arrival and departure of cars at the petrol station from the distance; mainly Germans who live locally, people on the way home from work. The attention of the man in the station wagon is drawn to a car with British registration plates; straining to look at the occupants of the vehicle, he notices that both driver and passenger are women and he looks away briefly, disinterested. As the car drives off the forecourt, he looks up to see a dark Volkswagen Jetta arriving at the petrol station; in the driver's seat a small Asian woman, next to her in the passenger seat a man of sub-Saharan ethnicity in his mid-thirties, dressed in green camouflage military fatigues. The vehicle number plate also catches his eye: FBR 790 Y. British-registered. The senses of the man in the station wagon heighten once again.

Two other men have also been watching the car, and more importantly its occupants, arrive at the filling station with a strong sense of interest. These two men are, to all intents and purposes, invisible; for they are hidden behind a bush at the side of the snack bar, wearing camouflage jackets, black balaclavas, black military berets. They watch and wait as the man enters the snack bar, exiting a short time later with piping-hot food, heading in short strides back to the Jetta. They watch with coiled intent through eyeholes cut into the black woollen masks, as the man opens the front left-hand side door and climbs in.

Suddenly the two men burst into action. They emerge from behind the bushes and run the few steps towards the car. One is around 1.85m in height, holding a dark gun metal grey Ruger magnum revolver in his right hand. The other, shorter and stockier, holds in his left hand a menacing-looking black Kalashnikov AK-47 assault rifle; in the dull glow of the forecourt lights, the serial number NK-8441 engraved on one side of the firearm glints faintly and briefly; on the other, the safety lever is set at halfway to "FA": full automatic fire mode. Once the trigger is squeezed, the gun will continue to fire until the trigger is released. The man with the assault rifle runs towards the driver's door, stops still and, holding the AK-47 away from him in his left hand, arm outstretched, aims at the door. His fingers squeeze the trigger, letting off a burst of gunfire at the closed window, the muzzle flash for an instant seemingly setting the night air on fire. The hail of bullets smash through the front and rear windows, hitting the man in the passenger seat in the chest, shoulder and head, the automatically ejected ammunition cartridges bouncing off the tarmac and forming a shallow pool of metal around the gunman. Panicking, the driver puts her foot on the pedal in a vain attempt to escape – she wildly veers the Jetta off the concourse, across the road and towards the front garden of the yellow brick guest house opposite the petrol station, narrowly missing a large oak tree, but instead hitting a wooden fence and coming to an abrupt standstill. In a split-second, the other gunman runs from the station forecourt across the road towards the car from behind, takes aim with his right hand and fires a single shot through the back windscreen. The glass shatters.

Meanwhile, the driver has started the engine of the beige Ford station wagon and accelerates, covering the short distance to the petrol station in a matter of seconds before screeching to a halt. This is a signal for the two gunmen; they run to the station wagon, fling open the doors, jump in and slam the doors shut; the car does a sharp U-turn, picks up speed and races away from the scene at breakneck speed, heading out of the village towards the border with the Netherlands.

In the Jetta, the man is slumped face-down on the glove box covered in blood; the woman, clearly under severe shock, frantically gets out of the car and scrabbles to open the rear passenger door. As people living in the houses adjacent to and across the road from the petrol station emerge from their front doors and into their gardens to see the source of the unusual noises, employees from the snack bar and petrol station - as well as the occupants of cars that had pulled into the petrol station behind the Jetta – also spill onto the forecourt; disturbed by the gunfire, the screeching tyres, the gruesome scene just played out before their eyes. The driver of the bullet-ridden Jetta leans into the car and struggles to pull something out of the back seat. She clutches it tightly to her chest and begins to walk around in circles in the middle of the road. A siren gradually pierces the silence, growing louder by the second. As the station wagon nears the border from Germany into the Netherlands, a police car with horn blaring and lights flashing, closely followed by an ambulance, pulls to a halt and men in uniform jump out. Oblivious to the uniforms and the concerned faces of onlookers coming to her aid, to the pool of blood spreading across her clothing, to the paramedic guiding her out of the middle of the road to sit in a chair borrowed from a nearby house and wrapping a blanket around her shoulders, the woman continues to cling to the bundle of cloth in her arms. After what seems like an eternity, a figure in uniform gently puts an arm around her, all the while talking to her softly and - as if asking for permission - hesitantly and carefully prises out of her hands the lifeless body of her six-month old baby daughter.

As the severely shocked woman and her dead baby are taken away to hospital, and a long stream of crime scene tape pulled around the crashed Jetta, the local police are joined by members of the Royal Air Force Police (RAFP) from the nearby RAF base in Wildenrath. Shortly after their arrival, Inspector Bodo Strickstrock from the local German police force, based in the nearby town of Heinsberg, appears on the scene to coordinate; his first call on the radio is to *Heine*, the central command point of his Heinsberg police team, requesting further assistance to be sent from Aachen, around 35 kilometres away. Aware that police communications may be being monitored by both the press and possibly also the perpetrators, he borrows a secure mobile communications unit from the RAF Police officers to fire off a "W.E." message ("Wichtiges Ereignis" or "Important Event") to the central coordination service of the *LKA NRW* (Landeskriminalamt NRW, the German Police Service of the State of North Rhine Westphalia) and to the NRW Interior Ministry; *LKA* investigators and NRW Interior Minister Dr. Herbert Schnoor rush to the scene to be briefed on the situation. Then they are joined by members of the British Services Security Organisation *BSSO(G)*, the intelligence service of the British Armed Forces in Germany; for the man in the green military fatigues shot dead in the passenger seat of the car was a member of the British military, belonging to the

Royal Air Force and a member of the team working in the Communications Centre at RAF Wildenrath. On the base, the main gates have been closed by armed guards to prevent anyone exiting or entering; scores of airmen and their families are told that there had been an incident in the village and that no-one is being allowed to leave for their own protection. Everyone in the long snaking queue to leave the base knows just what the word "incident" means: not least by glancing at the large board next to the gate, on which white letters declare "KEENWIND STATE" on a black background and "RED" in black letters on a glaring red background. Most are hoping that maybe, just maybe, no one they know closely is involved but in the close-knit community of RAF Wildenrath, there are no strangers. The man shot dead by the gunmen, Corporal Mahesh Kumar Islania - originally from Tanzania and known to colleagues as "Mick"– was part of that community and indeed part of the wider Royal Air Force community since joining the service in 1974. Mick had been taking part in a training course on the base earlier in the day. Normally RAF personnel wear dark blue uniforms (so-called uniform "No. 2", "service working dress"; in the service colloquially called "blues"); on this particular Thursday, the training course had required Mick to wear "operational clothing" (uniform "No. 3" or "greens"), which is at first glance identical to the operational uniform of the British Army. After a long day training at the RAF base in Wildenrath, Mick and his wife Smita had driven to the NAAFI store "on camp", unstrapped their baby daughter Nivruti from her car seat and gone inside to stock up on groceries within the safe confines of the base. After finishing their shopping, it was too late to start cooking that evening, so the Islanias had opted to get a "schnelly" - a quick takeaway meal – on the way home, outside of the RAF base, at the snack bar next to the BP station. A series of innocuous, everyday decisions that led to brutal tragedy.

The team from Aachen – supported by the *LKA*, RAFP and *BSSO* - guard the bullet-ridden Jetta and investigate the crime scene, talking to witnesses and securing evidence; local Wildenrath residents keep the officers sustained with coffee and homemade sandwiches as they work through the misty night. Local police are joined in this unenviable nightshift by a number of Tatortgruppe (scene-of-crime) officers from the rapid-response team from the *Bundeskriminalamt* (*BKA*), the German Federal Bureau of Criminal Investigation. Amongst the items the Spurensicherung forensics team find on the forecourt is the pool of ten empty 7.62mm ammunition cartridges where the first gunman had opened fire, all marked with "ppu 762" in Cyrillic letters stamped on the bottom rim; a further, smaller calibre cartridge is found a few metres away towards the Jetta on the other side of the road. The cartridges are photographed, then sealed in transparent bags, labelled and taken away for analysis; to check for batch numbers, unique rifling marks, for corroboratory evidence possibly linking the bullets and weapon used in the attack to bullets and weapons used to kill other innocent people in other horrific incidents and thus provide clues to the identity of the perpetrators. On the base, the military police brief the waiting servicemen and their distressed families prior to the opening of the main gates: everyone is told to drive directly home, without stopping, to the RAF married quarter estates in the nearby towns of Wassenberg, Wildenrath, and Erkelenz, adding the instruction that they should under no circumstances even stop at red traffic lights - for fear that the gunmen are still in the area. Vehicles begin to leave the base with a sense of trepidation and urgency, with military men gripping the steering wheels in grim determination to get their family home to safety, ashen-faced wives in the passenger seats and terrified children cowering out of sight in the footwell between the front and back seats, not knowing if they will be the next targets.

However the Ford Granada and the gunmen are now quite a distance away from the scene and have no intention of returning. Yet. Confident they are not being followed, the car pulls over near a yellow telephone box and one of the men gets out of the Ford, whilst the other two wait in the vehicle. The man lifts the receiver, slides a coin into the slot and dials a telephone number. When the call is answered, the man in the telephone box utters a single sentence into the receiver:

"Patrick O'Neill is doing fine."

He replaces the handset into the cradle. The man returns to the car, which drives on into the night.

In Wildenrath village, a tow truck is summoned to remove the bullet-ridden car from the crime scene; once all the witnesses have been interviewed, the petrol station and snack bar closed for the night and the police and intelligence services leave, all that is left is a small pool of blood on the side of the road that remains tragically visible and indelibly ingrained on the minds of those who pass it in the coming days. Twenty-four hours later on the airbase, airmen, soldiers and their families stand in the draughty and cold hangar of the 60 Squadron of the Royal Air Force in Germany to solemnly pay their respects to Mick Islania and his baby daughter Nivruti Mahesh Islania. The white coffins of Mick and Nivruti – one large, one upsettingly tiny – lie on wooden stands, draped with the British flag, ready for their repatriation to the United Kingdom. At the ceremony, Wing Commander Will Roberts speaks:

"We are almost speechless in our sense of outrage. It is difficult to find the words but unfortunately it has to be said that we are gaining experience in finding the words in recent months."

A little over two hours later, at the Royal Air Force base in Northolt on the northern outskirts of London, the aircraft lands. Smita Islania, understandably still in shock, is helped down the steps to the tarmac to be embraced by disbelieving family members. As she does so, the two coffins are unloaded. Six servicemen carry the wooden box containing the body of Mick Islania away from the aircraft, flanked by another, lone serviceman, who stiffly, slowly and painfully marches alongside them, cradling in his hands the tiny white coffin of six-month old Nivruti Islania.

350 miles away - across the English Channel, across England, across the Irish Sea - in a non-descript run-down office, a short woman with an unkempt frizz of hair feeds a page of paper into a fax machine and keys in a number. Despite the number of times she herself has been involved in the murder and attempted murder of scores of innocent people, the paperwork of death remains an administrative banality to the woman – her mind is instead focussing on the flight to New York she has to take the following morning; The machine bleeps and connects. At the other end of the line, another fax machine chatters and spits out the same page of printed text.

The paper contains a short, terse statement.

"One of our active service units was responsible for the gun attack on a member of the British forces in Wildenrath, West Germany, which resulted in two deaths. We profoundly regret the death of the infant of the RAF officer and are certain that our volunteers were not aware of the child's presence when they opened fire."

The statement ends with a typed signature in capital letters at the bottom of the page.

"P. O'NEILL".

The *nom de guerre* of the Provisional IRA.

Note from the author

As the teenage dependent of a serviceman in the Royal Air Force stationed in Germany through the Eighties and early Nineties, I was in the vicinity of and personally affected by several of the incidents depicted in this book, as well as a Provisional IRA attack in mainland Britain. Most particularly the night of the IRA double murders in October 1989 in Wildenrath is burned indelibly into the memory. My father worked closely with Mick Islania in the Communications Centre at RAF Wildenrath, up until the night Mick was shot dead by the Provisional IRA at Willi Otten's petrol station in the village. A photograph captured at RAF Northolt two days after the murders puts the events of that Thursday night sharply into perspective; the white coffin containing Mick Islania's body, draped in the Union Jack, being carried by six men from the plane is enough of a shock on its own; but a lone RAF serviceman trails behind, walking in staccato rhythm, cradling the tiny white coffin of Nivruti Mahesh Islania in his arms. He carries the coffin lightly but the weight of the emotional impact is overwhelming. The picture encapsulates the simple horror of the situation and the effect the murders had on our small community far more effectively than a graphic photo of the crime scene can ever do. No one has ever been arrested or brought to justice for their murders. Neither has anyone ever been convicted for the murders of thirteen others - in the name of Irish Republicanism in Germany, the Netherlands and Belgium: between March 1979 and March 1980 Sir Richard Sykes, Karel Straub, André Michaux and Mark Coe; between May 1988 and June 1990 Ian Shinner, Miller Reid, John Baxter, Mike Heakin, Steven Smith, Heidi Hazell, Nick Spanos, Stephen Melrose, Michael Dillon-Lee. Fourteen families of fifteen victims denied closure. I myself spent the last thirty years permanently affected by the events of the night of October 26th 1989 - finally I decided to do something about it: I set out to find my own closure.

The research and interviews that form the backbone of this book has helped me on that road, as I hope the results of my work may help those even more directly affected. A considerable amount of literature and documents from the British, Dutch, Belgian, French and German intelligence services and police forces, eye-witness accounts, interviews with survivors, victims, members of the security services and law enforcement officers, as well as my own experiences and observations have been cross-referenced with information and recollections from former IRA volunteers, commanders and sympathisers. The results point very clearly to the names, modus operandi and whereabouts of those who pulled the trigger, pressed the button or flicked the switch; and those who ordered and expected them to do so.

The book describes in detail the personal backgrounds of the volunteers and commanders involved in European operations of the Provisional IRA, as well as those of their victims. It also deals not only with the detailed planning and execution of the operations, but is balanced by the efforts of counter-operations by law enforcement and intelligence service agencies into PIRA activities in Germany, the Netherlands, France, Belgium, Spain, Gibraltar, Northern Ireland, the Republic of Ireland and mainland Britain. The book also analyses the backdrop of the political situation of the time, describes what was going on away from the public gaze at governmental level and reveals hitherto secret deals made with the Provisional IRA in an attempt to bring the bloodshed to an end. Where information was missing or not available, logical inferences were made that have been checked many times for validity by myself and several external sources familiar with the events and the subject material. Nevertheless, the clandestine nature of IRA operations means that errors or false assumptions will be unavoidable - I invite those with whom I have not been in contact but who want to give their side of the story to get in touch to have any mistakes corrected - either on or off the record.

In the process of writing and researching this book, I have become more acutely aware of the upbringing, political convictions and backgrounds of the people who killed in the name of Republicanism and in part developed an understanding of "the other side." However much I still see these acts as brutal, evil and misguided, it is still important to understand the convictions and events that led to these acts being carried out in the first place; for far too long, it has been "us" and "them" and that is the blinkered thinking that contributed to the "Troubles" in the first place. Make no mistake; under no circumstances am I condoning these acts or adopting an overly-liberal stance; as the son of a serviceman, as a human being, I am still horrified at these brutal acts. Apologies have been feeble or non-existent; many things have been covered up (by both sides) and attempts to understand the reasons why certain acts were carried out will not bring back the dead, comfort those who have lost loved ones or those whose lives have been changed by the acts depicted in these pages. But now, more than at any time, as an armed minority continue to terrorise parts of the community of Northern Ireland, and Britain and Ireland face a politically and socially rocky road ahead in the face of Brexit, it is important to look back at the mistakes of the past, take responsibility for events, and find a way to prevent them happening again.

It goes without saying that such a body of work cannot be created alone. I would particularly like to thank a number of people who have contributed greatly with information and insights that have helped piece together the clandestine activities of the Provisional IRA in Continental Europe. Some contributors cannot for security reasons be thanked publicly and understandably must remain anonymous. There have been several others I feel I can and should thank by name.

A huge debt of gratitude is owed to Herr Joachim Rzeniecki, who between 1988 and 1990 headed the *SoKo PIRA* for the *Bundeskriminalamt* (*BKA*); the counter-terrorism unit of the German

Federal Bureau of Criminal Investigation which investigated the activities of the Provisional IRA Active Service Units in Germany during this time. Herr Rzeniecki provided a wealth of anecdotes, information and insights into the investigations, patiently answered many questions and gave up a significant amount of time to help fill in the blanks, rectify errors and give his valued opinions. Without him, this book would not have been possible. Former Northern Ireland Editor of the "Irish Times", expert and trusted voice on the "Troubles", former Director of the Boston College Oral History Project which documented secret admissions from both Republican and Loyalist paramilitaries on their role in the conflict, best-selling author and filmmaker Ed Moloney provided valuable insights into the political and strategic issues that drove the IRA's campaign in Europe via his book 'A Secret History of the IRA', which was a constant companion during the writing of this book: in my opinion one of the definitive works on the Provisional IRA and I urge you to read it. Heartfelt thanks also to Markus Schmitt, Federal State Prosecutor with the Generalbundesanwaltschaft (Office of the German Federal Prosecutor), as well as Jacqueline Heinzelmann and Franziska Klein at the German Embassy in London, Angela Vaupel, Consule for the Federal Republic of Germany in Northern Ireland and Lukas Herbeck, Karolin Wendt and Thomas Hermeling at the German Foreign Office in Berlin for help in finding reams of relevant information and explaining why certain documents remain classified to this day. Thank you also to Jerome aan de Wiel, Professor of History at University College Cork for unravelling some of the secrets of the Stasi's intelligence work on the Provisional IRA's operations in Germany.

Thank you also to Martin Dillon, Peter Taylor, Paul van Gageldonk and Toby Harnden. Without stumbling upon your valuable and powerful contributions to the documentation of "The Troubles", this book would have never been started in the first place.

Berlin, November 2020

THE OVERSEAS DEPARTEMENT

THE OVERSEAS DEPARTEMENT

Intro: 1969-1980

The Provisional IRA was born in December 1969.

For a long time, but more intensively since late 1968, the Catholic community, led by the Derry-based Civil Rights Association, had been protesting against institutional suppression of and discrimination against Catholics, as well as against sectarian violence from the Protestant community. This had led to civil unrest on the streets of Northern Irish cities, which in turn unleashed a violent backlash from Northern Irish authorities and an opportunity for certain parts of the Protestant community to demonstrate their hatred for those fellow countrymen born into Catholic families. In the summer of 1969, the traditional Protestant marching season – several weeks of events held annually in July to commemorate Loyalist victories over the Catholics in the Battles of The Boyne (1690) and Aughrim (1691) – became the flashpoint for a conflict that would come to span four decades. Orange marches led to counter demonstrations, which in turn led to brutal suppression of these protests by the Northern Irish authorities – the sectarian Ulster tinderbox ignited in Derry, Belfast and elsewhere in the province.

These clashes prompted the remnants of the first Irish Republican Army (the so-called "Old IRA") – formed to fight a guerrilla war against the British occupation of Ireland during the 1919-1921 Irish War of Independence – to position itself as the defender of the minority Catholic community. Partly against the authorities, partly against the majority Protestant community, which also included the mainly Protestant law enforcement services of the province, they struggled. Due to limited weaponry and other resources, as well as draconian measures by the Protestant-dominated authorities, the IRA was unable to prevent scores of Catholics being intimidated, detained, burned out of their homes, physically attacked and murdered by both Protestant civilians, paramilitary organisations such as the Ulster Volunteer Force (UVF) and rogue elements of the police force, the Royal Ulster Constabulary (RUC). Graffiti appeared on the gable ends of houses in the Catholic Falls Road area of West Belfast declaring "IRA = I Ran Away".

After three days of sustained rioting in the Catholic Bogside district of Derry in August and the death of a Belfast man, Herbert Roy, at the hands of an IRA gunman, British Army troops were sent to Northern Ireland as part of a "limited operation" to restore law and order. Their remit was essentially to help quell the disturbances and protect the Catholic community; they were greeted as saviours. As the Nationalist community welcomed the British Army, resentment grew within parts of the IRA, who were unhappy with seeing state forces on the streets of Ulster. A difference of opinion became apparent between two factions within the IRA as to how to address the situation. A group loyal to IRA Chief of Staff Cathal Goulding held the view that the overall situation could only be ended politically and to facilitate this, proposed to recognise that the Republic of Ireland and Northern Ireland were two separate states. The long held Republican core policy of "abstentionism" – refusing to recognise the Irish or British governments as legitimate, and therefore abstaining from taking up seats in either parliament via political campaigning – was to be dropped. A minority hard-line faction in the IRA around Belfast activists Joe Cahill and Billy McKee argued that there should be no compromise and that abstentionism should be adhered to; the only solution was armed struggle. Republicanism – the struggle for Irish independence in the north of Ireland – suddenly arrived at a crossroads in its history: the first ever IRA

General Army Convention was held in secret in the Republic of Ireland in December 1969, to give all members a vote on which direction the IRA should take. There was a roughly 50/50 split on votes and as a result, both factions decided to go their own ways: Goulding forming the majority Official IRA (also known as OIRA or the "Stickies"), Cahill and others forming a minority splinter group, the Provisional IRA; (PIRA or simply "The Provos") Both sides maintained both an armed paramilitary wing as well as a closely affiliated political party: whilst being completely separate entities, Sinn Fein (Irish for "We ourselves") represented the political aims of the Provisional IRA, without recourse to weapons. There was a certain overlap between members, particularly at executive level; Sinn Fein became an organisation generally for those too old to take up armed struggle or those who believed the pen was mightier than the sword. By no means was every Sinn Fein man (or woman) an IRA volunteer and not every IRA volunteer a member of Sinn Fein, but both shared a common goal: the withdrawal of the British occupying forces from the Six Counties and the restoration of a united Ireland.

As the Official IRA waged a somewhat limited campaign against the occupying British forces, pursuing a Marxist ideology with the intention of bringing about a "workers republic of Ireland", traditional Republicans were angered at the move towards Marxism and became more militant. The ranks of the Provos swelled in the summer of 1970 when the Catholic community turned against the British occupying forces; a house-search in the Falls Road area of West Belfast was escalated on the orders of a British Army officer, leading to riots and subsequently a curfew for Catholics in the area, effectively meaning they were not allowed to leave their houses. The Army shot dead four Catholic civilians who were found breaking the curfew – the outrage of the Catholic community propelled normal citizens into armed struggle and the Provisional IRA. The conflict ignited in a wave of sectarian attacks against Protestants, bomb and gun attacks against the British Army and the RUC, as well as the destruction of commercial targets. After the imposition of the controversial internment rule – imprisonment without trial – in August 1971, many IRA volunteers were arrested – as well as many innocent Catholics – and sent to Long Kesh prison outside of Belfast, amongst other institutions. Long Kesh, which was later renamed HMP Maze, housed several separate compounds or "cages" housing several hundred Republican, as well as Loyalist prisoners. Later, accommodation blocks formed in the shape of the letter H were built to replace the dilapidated Nissen huts. After the change of name, the prison was still generally referred to by Republicans and Loyalists alike as the "H Blocks" or Long Kesh.

In the early 1970s, the conflict was contained to Northern Ireland. However in the wake of "Bloody Sunday" in 1972, when the Parachute Regiment of the British Army opened fire on a mixture of innocent protestors and IRA volunteers in Derry/Londonderry, killing thirteen Catholics – the IRA leadership vowed to hit back and hard. In 1973, the Provos decided to extend their bombing campaign to England - the PIRA leadership realised that an attack on civilian targets on the mainland would garner many more column inches in the international press than an attack in Northern Ireland. In an attempt to bomb the British government into talks to defuse the situation, members of the Belfast Brigade were dispatched to London to wreak havoc. A concerted wave of deadly bomb attacks in Britain killed many people within the space of a few months but the responsible volunteers William Armstrong, Martin Brady, Hugh Feeney, Paul Holmes, Gerry Kelly, William McLarnon, Dolours and her sister Marian Price, as well as Robert Walsh were all arrested for the attacks and sentenced to long prison terms; Róisín McNearney was acquitted for providing information and a further IRA volunteer escaped back to Ireland. The campaign did however exert a certain amount of pressure on the British government, who entered into secret talks with the Provisional IRA in an attempt to end the conflict. When these talks produced little compromise on the part of the British, the IRA returned to bombing targets in Northern Ireland but in the meantime, had also set their sights on Germany, the home of the British Army on the Rhine.

After the Second World War, British military forces had remained stationed in Germany with a considerable amount of personnel based on the western side of the Iron Curtain, to counter the potential threat of invasion from Russian forces during the Cold War. By 1973, there were over 50,000 British servicemen stationed on German soil; The soldiers of the British Army of the Rhine (BAOR) were stationed at numerous Army barracks throughout the north and north-west of Germany, mainly in the states of North-Rhine Westphalia (NRW) and Lower Saxony: the airmen of the Royal Air Force – apart from an outpost at RAF Gatow in West Berlin - were spread across four main air bases, all in NRW; Gütersloh south-west of Bielefeld; Laarbruch, Brüggen and Wildenrath, all close to the border with the Netherlands. A joint base was situated in Rheindahlen, a suburb of Mönchengladbach. Rheindahlen not only housed Royal Air Force personnel but also British Army soldiers and officers, as well as those from fellow NATO partners the USA, Belgium, the Netherlands and Germany. British forces made up the bulk of the servicemen stationed there. The sprawling camp, surrounded by woods, was designated Joint Headquarters for the NATO Northern Army Group (NORTHAG), known simply as JHQ and was the central command post of the British military forces in Germany.

Despite the location close to the line drawn in the sand between Allied and Warsaw Pact forces after the Second World War and constant training and alertness for a potential flashpoint between the superpowers, being sent to Germany was for both Army and Air Force personnel a plum posting. A generous extra "overseas allowance" was paid to soldiers and airmen posted to Germany, made even more attractive by a beneficial exchange rate between the Deutschmark and British sterling; the extra money was spent on cars, Continental holidays, cheap and good German beer, tax-free cigarettes and tobacco, and an abundance of British food and drink available from the Navy, Army and Air Force Institute (NAAFI) store located on each base. Military life in Germany was good: servicemen and their families enjoyed a two to three year tour of duty in a country that felt faintly exotic but with all the luxuries of home and the financial means to take full advantage. However, the good times and feeling of security however made off-duty British forces in Germany let down their guard – a soft target for the IRA.

An IRA volunteer was sent to the Continent, James "Jim" McCann, who was on the run having escaped from Crumlin Road prison in Belfast in June 1971, where he was awaiting trial on weapons and explosives charges. McCann was a notorious figure within the IRA, using a huge personality to build up a large network of contacts used to not only procure weapons for the armed struggle, but also to engage in high-level drug smuggling. With the help of Irish immigrants in the Netherlands and Dutch sympathisers to the Republican cause, the IRA was keen to exploit lax security at British military installations in Germany. As Joint Headquarters, the prime target was to be Rheindahlen. On Saturday, September 15th 1973, the team planted two bombs on the base close to each other with each of the devices containing around one kilogramme of explosives packed into gas bottles. The first bomb was placed near to a workshop used by an Army school, the other a few yards away in the car park of the Globe cinema. McCann set the timers to explode at 11.15pm, when servicemen and their families would be pouring into the cinema car park after the end of the film. He miscalculated; the bombs exploded simultaneously but the film had long since ended; the explosions damaged the school workshop and a couple of parked cars but caused no injuries. Although a woman from Belfast and a Dutch man were later arrested for assisting McCann, they were soon released and McCann himself escaped back to the Netherlands. McCann would later be arrested in 1979 in the Republic of Ireland driving a van carrying twenty-one tea chests containing Thai marijuana and was convicted of drug smuggling. On his release from prison, he continued to smuggle arms for the IRA and dope with the legendary Howard Marks before finally being arrested in Germany in 1991, where he was again convicted for narcotics offences but not charged with carrying out the JHQ bomb attack.

1974 saw no let-up in the IRA's mainland offensive and indeed saw some of the worst atrocities in the thus-far short history of "The Troubles". A bomb exploded aboard a bus carrying British soldiers down the M62 in Yorkshire, killing nine; devices exploded at the Houses of Parliament and Tower of London; and worst of all were the now notorious bomb attacks on five different pubs – one in Woolwich, two in Guildford and two in Birmingham – which claimed 28 innocent lives, many of them young. On the Continent, Germany was already on high alert as the incarceration and hunger-strikes of the first generation members of anti-capitalist terrorist organisation the Red Army Faction stimulated a new wave of sympathisers, determined to hit back at the German state; the worries of the German authorities were compounded when they received intelligence that an IRA team were planning to carry out similar attacks to those in the UK against targets in the vicinity of army bases in

Germany. After concrete warnings that reconnaissance missions had been carried out at locations in Celle, Hannover and Bielefeld, the German authorities alerted the general public and security was stepped up: no further IRA attacks on the Continent took place and commanders concentrated their efforts instead on Northern Ireland and mainland Britain.

The bombing offensive of 1973 & 1974 also spawned a large number of hoax bomb threats that could not be attributed to the IRA. To distinguish real attacks from hoax threats, one of the IRA volunteers operating in London came up with the idea of using code words to signal when the attack or warning originated from the Provos. Derry-born Shane Paul O'Doherty began to plant smaller devices across the capital and telephoned the Press Association to indirectly forewarn authorities of devices and claim responsibility, using the self-devised codeword Double X. Once enough relatively small-scale attacks had been pre-confirmed in this way, the process of using codewords became established for the use of larger, deadlier devices. It took several months however before O'Doherty informed the IRA Army Council of the codeword process. Some in the Provos were opposed to giving warnings but eventually the idea was adopted for all IRA operations; individuals within certain units, including those in England were advised of the codewords to be used in their own operations. Eventually the devising and dissemination of codewords was controlled centrally, with the codewords being changed on a regular basis for security purposes. Although codewords were not publicly revealed by the press or law enforcement agencies, there was always a danger of a non-IRA organisation or individual getting hold of the current code word, so changing it sporadically avoided the IRA being blamed for incidents, injuries and deaths caused by operations not carried out by their own volunteers.

Engaged in the intelligence and law enforcement battle in Northern Ireland, the Republic and on mainland Britain with the Provisional IRA and their Loyalist paramilitary counterparts such as the Ulster Volunteer Force (UVF), Ulster Freedom Fighters (UFF) and Ulster Defence Association (UDA), were four main agencies. The Security Service (commonly known as *MI5*), the domestic intelligence agency of Great Britain worked closely with their sister organization the Secret Intelligence Service (*MI6*), the foreign intelligence agency of Great Britain, via a joint section that dealt with counter-terrorism. The activities of *MI5* and *MI6* (and communications agency GCHQ) were coordinated by a joint body – the Joint Intelligence Committee (JIC), responsible for setting priorities and co-ordinating the work of the separate intelligence services. On the island of Ireland, An Garda Síochána (known as the Garda or also in the plural form Gardai: "The Guards"), the police force of the Republic of Ireland was heavily involved, as was naturally the Royal Ulster Constabulary (RUC), the police force of Northern Ireland. As with police forces in mainland Britain, the RUC had a separate, special division that dealt with, amongst other things, counter-terrorism – RUC Special Branch liaised closely between the RUC, Special Branch (SO-13) of the Metropolitan Police Force in London and with *MI5*. Cross-agency cooperation became vital as the IRA widened their circle of operations from the Six Counties to England and on into Europe.

The command structure of the Provisional IRA from the 1970s onwards – unlike the loose, autonomous separate cell structure of ISIS and Al-Qaeda – was hierarchical and militaristic but to the naked eye democratic. Supreme power lay with the membership: The General Army Convention (GAC) met irregularly and in secret and consisted of delegates from all areas of the Provisionals, sent from all corners of Northern and Southern Ireland. The GAC voted twelve members from its ranks into the ruling IRA Executive, which in turn selected seven members to form the Provisional IRA's Army Council (PAC), the body responsible for day-to-day decision-making. The planning and implementation of Army Council decisions was carried out by staff of the IRA's General Headquarters (GHQ). GHQ was split into several sub-divisions: the Quartermaster General's department (responsible for acquiring, maintaining and distributing the IRA's arsenal of weapons), Engineering (development of new weapons, bomb-making), Intelligence, Finance, Training, Internal Security (counter-intelligence: the weeding out and execution of informers), Publicity, Political Education and – most importantly – Operations; the day-to-day planning and execution of attacks. These divisions oversaw two separate Commands: Northern Command covering the six counties of Ulster and Southern Command covering the Republic of Ireland. Under these Commands the various Brigades were organised: each Brigade corresponded to a geographical area such as Belfast, Derry, Dublin, South Armagh or County Down. Each Brigade consisted of separate Active Service Units or ASU's; the cells responsible for carrying out bombings and shootings on a daily basis. The Active Service Units replaced the older military "battalion/company" structure in 1977, after the IRA leadership perceived the larger, more conventional principle to be more susceptible from a security standpoint. The smaller, more agile ASU's were more tightly-knit, reducing the chances of being infiltrated and information on operations leaking out to security forces or Loyalists.

Also roughly attached to Northern Command - and personnel-wise closely linked to the dominant Belfast and South Armagh Brigades - was the "England Department"; responsible for the planning and execution of the campaign on the British mainland. As the tenth anniversary of the start of "The Troubles" - as they had come to be known - approached, the PIRA Army Council tasked a team to extend the scope of the armed campaign against British interests and take the conflict beyond Northern Ireland, and beyond mainland Britain and, for the first time, send Active Service Units rather than individual volunteers to carry out attacks in Continental Europe. This team, the "Overseas Department" – like the "England Department", for security reasons operated relatively autonomously to the rest of the PIRA, reporting only to the Chief of Staff and his right-hand man the Adjutant General, the top two military positions in the PIRA. In the summer of 1978, most sources concur that the Chief of Staff position was held by Martin McGuinness from Derry – according to Ed Moloney in his definite tome "A Secret History of the IRA", the post of Adjutant General was taken by Gerry Adams from Belfast. Together with the leadership, The Overseas Department set up a number of ASUs - containing a small number of volunteers – nominally based in the Netherlands and Belgium. The majority of volunteers were not permanently located on the Continent but travelled to and from Northern Ireland to carry out attacks on British military and political targets. Eight bombs exploded at British military installations in Düsseldorf, Mönchengladbach, Duisburg, Krefeld, Minden, Mannheim and Ratingen on the night of August 18th-19th but were ineffective, causing little damage and no casualties; several more devices were defused. The IRA were to learn from these failed attacks.

Two years previously, the IRA had scored a coup when they murdered the British Ambassador to the Republic of Ireland, Christopher Ewart-Biggs, using a powerful landmine which exploded next to his car near the ambassadorial residence in the Sandyford suburb of Dublin. Fellow passenger in the car, civil servant Judith Cooke, was also killed in the attack; driver Brian

O'Driscoll and another civil servant Brian Cubbon, were injured. Although the threat from the IRA was high, security precautions around British diplomats were at the time insufficient. Ewart-Biggs regularly varied his route to and from work for example, but this had not prevented the IRA from carrying out a successful attack. The British government realised in the face of the increased threat that measures had to be stepped up. British Prime Minster James Callaghan tasked Richard Sykes, Deputy Under-Secretary at the Foreign and Commonwealth Office, with the task of investigating the assassination of Ewart-Biggs and reviewing diplomatic security plans. Sykes was a very high-ranking diplomat in the FCO, with responsibility for defence, arms and security – and as such was already working closely with *MI5* and *MI6*. Together, the assassination was reviewed and weaknesses in security procedures identified. The plan Sykes finally drew up was highly confidential but tightened security around ambassadors and other diplomatic staff immensely, in the hope of preventing another such IRA attack from succeeding. Shortly after completing the plan, Sykes, who had previously been British Ambassador in Cuba, as well as Deputy Ambassador to the US in Washington, was posted to the Netherlands and took up his new position as British Ambassador in The Hague in June 1977. By early 1979, his tenure had seen some notable successes against the IRA in the Netherlands - popular with Provos and sympathisers alike - including the interception of a two-ton shipment of arms destined for Northern Ireland. The weapons were seized at Schiphol airport en route from Czechoslovakia and the interception may have been attributable to intensive monitoring efforts by the British Embassy in The Hague of IRA sympathisers based in the Netherlands. Ambassador Sykes was proving to be a thorn in the side of the Provisional IRA that the military command decided it needed to have extracted.

Sir Richard Sykes (having been knighted by The Queen in 1977), had developed a morning routine that he adhered to like clockwork. He left for work each day at the same time and from the same point in the open-ended courtyard adjacent to the Ambassador's Residence - completely disregarding the diplomatic security measures set out in the plan he himself had created for the FCO before taking up the post in The Hague. Nevertheless, this routine had gone unnoticed for two years – until March 1979. An IRA team had been sent from Belfast to Amsterdam – after staying in a safe house in the city, they travelled on to The Hague and took notes as the ambassadorial Rolls Royce came into view at the same time every morning onto Westeinde, the narrow road which snaked past the entrance to the Ambassador's residence. On the morning of Thursday March 22nd, shortly before 9am, two IRA gunmen dressed in dark suits and white shirts, watched from the other side of the road as driver Jack Wilson piloted the Rolls Royce off Westeinde and into the small courtyard between the official ambassadorial residence and the adjacent Church of St. Theresa. The door to the residence was opened by footman 19 year old local Karel Straub, and Sykes, together with visiting civil servant Alyson Bailes headed towards the car. As Ms. Bailes entered the left hand side rear passenger door, Straub held open the right hand side door for the Ambassador and allowed Sykes to make a step into the vehicle. At that moment, the IRA pounced. The gunmen ran into the courtyard brandishing handguns and got to around ten feet away from Straub and Sykes; one of the gunmen fired a small calibre pistol at Straub, who was hit and dropped to the floor. As he lay there, the shooter – unsure if the footman was armed - fired a second shot at Straub to make sure he stayed down - the second bullet hit him in the head. The other gunman aimed a long-barrelled revolver at the shocked Sykes and fired a number of shots at him, hitting Sykes four times in the head and upper torso. The gunmen ran back out onto Westeinde and escaped down one of the many alleyways leading off the street. As Straub lay bleeding on the street, realising that the Ambassador had been seriously wounded, Wilson drove the car at speed out of the courtyard and raced to the Westeinde Hospital just a few hundred yards away. Karel Straub had been mortally injured and died shortly afterwards. Doctors at the hospital were unable to save Sir Richard Sykes – he too died of his wounds just a couple of hours later. The IRA's thorn had been successfully removed.

The very same evening, the IRA struck again, this time 180 kilometres away in Brussels. The IRA team involved had targeted another diplomat, the UK's Ambassador to NATO Sir John Killick, but the plan had to be changed after reconnaissance showed that security measures around his home were too heavy and would make an attack too difficult to carry out. They turned their attention to his second-in-command instead. They observed Paul Holmer, Deputy Permanent Representative to NATO and noted when he usually returned to his home on Overhemlaan in the suburb of Uccle, an area where many diplomats lived. They waited until nightfall until a car matching the description of Holmer's pulled up on the street outside his residence. As the driver parked the vehicle, the gunmen ran up to the car and opened fire with handguns; they fired eight shots, hitting their victim in the head and killing him instantly. The gunmen escaped in a white Peugeot 404 at speed, driven by a third man – the car was later found abandoned by police, who recovered 9mm bullet cases from the vehicle. It was only later that it became apparent they had made a huge and tragic error. The murdered man was not Holmer, but Holmer's neighbour, 46 year old Belgian banking executive André Michaux, who drove the same make of car, and who the IRA team had mistaken for the British diplomat in the dark. It was not to be the last time that an IRA team in Continental Europe would make such a grave mistake.

The Belgian and Dutch police forces worked closely together to try and find the killers of Sykes, Straub and Michaux. Initially there was scepticism that the IRA was responsible for these killings, and indeed at one point the Belgian *Rijkswacht* police suspected left-wing extremists in the Michaux case. However, various pieces of information came to light that allowed the murders to be linked to each other. One witness identified Patrick Thornberry, a well-known IRA man from Armagh, from pictures supplied by Scotland Yard, as one of the gunmen. Thornberry had escaped from Portlaoise prison five years earlier with eighteen other Republican prisoners and was still at large – neither the Dutch nor the Belgians nor the RUC were subsequently able to track him down. A notorious left-wing activist and IRA sympathiser, Serge Cols, was however arrested in Brussels shortly after the murders and police found a case belonging to one of the gunmen in his apartment, containing submachine guns, pistols and 9mm ammunition. One of the other gunmen was also identified but never publicly named: he was spotted in Brussels four hours after the murder of Sykes and placed under surveillance by Belgian police at the request of their Dutch colleagues, in case he led them to further accomplices. But the IRA man managed to give the *Rijkswacht* the slip and returned to Ireland.

Later that summer, the bombing resumed. On July 10th 1979, two devices exploded at military installations in Dortmund; on August 28th, a device detonated under a stage at an open air concert taking place in Brussels Grand Place main square, wounding 15 members of the Duke of Edinburgh's Royal Regiment who were setting up their instruments in preparation for a performance. In October, an IRA cell planted a bomb at a NAAFI warehouse in Krefeld, which only caused damage to property. The attacks were coming thick and fast – the British authorities needed to act. After the bombings, Colonel Deller, the chief of British Army security and intelligence operations in Germany, devised a plan to infiltrate the large Irish ex-pat community in the Rhein-Ruhr region using agents, in an attempt to obtain forewarning of further PIRA attacks on BAOR targets. He was unaware that *MI6* already had a network of agents on the ground operating under the name Operation SCREAM, although the plan had not yet produced any results. He was told not to proceed but Deller ignored the command; by early 1980 five informants within the Irish community had been recruited and a small trickle of information began to flow. It was to prove useless. On the evening of February 16th 1980, a British Army officer stationed in Germany with the 1st Rhine Army Corps – 44 year old Colonel Mark Coe - was returning home to his house at Joseph-Hayden-Strasse in Bielefeld, West Germany at around 7.30pm after test-driving his daughter's Citroën 2CV. As his wife was putting the youngest of their six children to bed, Coe was moving the car from the street to the garage, when two IRA volunteers – a short man of about 30, dressed in dark clothes and with a strong, athletic figure and fair, slightly wavy hair combed to the front, and a blonde woman of around 25 in a heavy striped woollen coat - emerged from the darkness, ran up to the car and opened fire with revolvers through the driver's window. Coe was hit in the chest and stomach three times. As the two IRA volunteers escaped in a waiting red Opel, Coe managed to stagger to his house but despite an ambulance being called, a local doctor administering first aid and then Coe undergoing a lengthy operation in hospital, the Colonel died just after 11pm. The German authorities quickly moved to question a Dublin man and his German wife in their thirties who lived locally, but both were released without charge – the Germans offered a 60,000 Deutschmarks reward for information leading to the capture of the IRA unit responsible and Coe was posthumously awarded the OBE. It was later ascertained that the weapon used to kill Coe was the same gun used to kill Sir Richard Sykes in The Hague the previous March.

Exactly two weeks later, British military policeman Corporal Stewart Leach, aged 22, stopped his Ford Cortina patrol car at traffic lights at the corner of Bröderichweg and Kanalstrasse in the garrison town of Münster, on the way back from a routine patrol to Winterbourne Barracks in nearby Coerde. Two IRA gunmen stepped up to the car and fired a fusillade of gunshots from a 9mm pistol and an automatic rifle, hitting Leach. One bullet went through his body and the other lodged in his stomach. Leach underwent an emergency operation but survived, along with his passenger, colleague Corporal John Helly, 25, who was unhurt in the attack. German police later found 21 bullet cases at the scene. On March 10th, not far away in Osnabrück, Steven Sims, a 24-year-old British Army corporal with the Devon & Dorset Regiment, was jogging through the Heger Holz woods when he was hit five times by bullets from a 9mm pistol in the arm and hip. The gunman escaped in a green Vauxhall car. Despite being critically wounded, the athletically built Sims managed to run over a kilometre to the safety of a nearby German military hospital before collapsing; he survived.

The German civil police and British Military Police investigating the attacks made little headway. They followed a variety of leads including ones that led them to believe the IRA was being assisted by the latest wave of activists from the German terrorist group *Rote Armee Fraktion* (RAF or Red Army Faction) and various student "solidarity committees" across Germany – but the leads came to nothing. It was not until September that the first breakthrough happened, and not in Germany but in the Netherlands; a tip-off from an unknown source alerted the Dutch domestic intelligence service *BVD* (*Binnenlandse Veiligheidsdienst*) to the presence of a potential suspect in a small village in Noord-Brabant: the *BVD* commenced a two-week surveillance operation. The suspect - 29-year-old Patrick Magee from Belfast - was staying in a local family guesthouse in

Overloon and working in a local stone factory. The *BVD* and Dutch police pounced: Magee was arrested on suspicion of being part of the IRA unit responsible for the attacks in Germany and Belgium. The other members of the Active Service Unit escaped arrest.

Magee had help from one of the several solidarity groups for Irish Republicanism in Western Europe, the *Ierland Komitee Nederland*. Set up in 1972 in Breda by an anarchist collective and lead by Antoon Seelen and Ariane Kuil, the *IKN* with groupings in major conurbations - in particular in the city of Nijmegen on the border with Germany – supported the Irish Republican goal of a united Ireland, provided support to Irish immigrants and involved themselves in political activism on behalf of Republicanism, together with their West German sister organisation *Irland Solidaritätskomitee*. By 1975 they had started a regular publication Ierland Bulletin, which highlighted the issue of the repression of the Catholic minority in Northern Ireland and campaigned vigorously on behalf of the movement. Seleen, Kuil and other *IKN* members travelled regularly to Northern Ireland to meet members of the Republican movement, as well as taking part in international conferences with like-minded organisations. The organisation actively supported the IRA and other illegal groupings such as the Red Army Faction, helping prisoners, paying fines and expenses, and acting as both agitator and support group. The *IKN* put Magee in touch with a high profile young political lawyer from Amsterdam - Willem van Bennekom. Van Bennekom had made a name for himself early in his career, successfully preventing Vietnam War deserter Ralph Waver from being deported back to the USA in 1971 and henceforth specialised in political cases involving extradition proceedings – van Bennekom agreed to defend Magee in the resulting trial. Despite pleas from the British government, Dutch authorities acceded to van Bennekom's arguments and refused an extradition request in January 1981 on the grounds that Magee's action were politically motivated and he would not receive a fair trial in Britain; Magee was released and returned to Ireland. Aware that Magee had not been acting alone, the British Army turned to SIS, *BSSO* and German domestic intelligence agency *Bundesamt für Verfassungsschutz* (*BfV* - the Federal Office for the Protection of the Constitution) for support, and admitted they were working with informers. After several high-level briefings, Operation WARD was set up to run alongside SIS's Operation SCREAM and in summer 1981, German and British intelligence chiefs had given the plan their approval.

In the meantime, in October 1980, Republican prisoners in HM Prison The Maze, followed in December by inmates of Armagh Women's Gaol, had begun hunger strikes in an attempt to re-secure a special status as political prisoners, which had been withdrawn several years earlier. As some of the Republican prisoners were close to death, the British government agreed to concede to demands and the hunger strikes were called off. However as Magee was released in the Netherlands in January 1981, it became clear that the British government had conceded to none of the demands and Republican prisoners resumed their hunger strike on March 1st. The British government called the Republican bluff and waited with its arms folded to see when the hunger strike would be called off again. Support for the hunger strikers grew across Northern Ireland, Irish communities across the UK and in Continental Europe, as the British staunchly refused to give in to the Republican prisoners' demands. Shortly after the beginning of the strike, the incumbent Republican MP for Fermanagh and South Tyrone Frank Maguire died of a heart attack, precipitating a by-election. Bobby Sands was suggested as a candidate by Republican supporters and the other nationalist parties agreed not to field competition; on April 9th 1981, Bobby Sands was voted into British government from his prison cell: British Prime Minister Margaret Thatcher had grossly miscalculated the strength of Republican feeling. It was clear however that neither she nor the hunger strikers would step back from the brink. On May 5th, after sixty-six days of hunger strike, Bobby Sands died. Thatcher showed no sympathy for his death, telling the House of Commons

> *"Mr Sands was a convicted criminal. He chose to take his own life."*

This statement made her the ultimate target for the Provisional IRA and a hated figure in the Republican community. As a wave of further hunger strikers died, martyring themselves for the Republican cause, a wave of sympathy spilled over from Northern Ireland to socially liberal European countries such as the Netherlands. Concerned that adverse publicity would detract from the support that Bobby Sands and the hunger strikers had gained for the Republican cause, the IRA decided to halt their campaign on the European mainland.

This is the story of what happened next.

1 THE PADRE

Terence Gerard McGeough was born in 1958 in Carrycastle, in the Brantry, near Dungannon in County Tyrone, the eldest of four children. Like so many of his era, he experienced at an early age and at first hand the constant persecution of his fellow Catholics; firstly by the Protestant community, then the feared B-Specials, a division of the Ulster Special Constabulary the Northern Irish police force recruited predominantly from the more extreme and darker corners of the Protestant community, who wielded their power and batons indiscriminately against their Catholic countrymen. Then came the British Army, sent to Ulster to restore peace after the civil rights marches of the Catholic community expressing their dissatisfaction with the status quo threatened to turn into civil war. The British came as protectors, but before long were seen by the Catholic community as oppressors and the six northern counties of Ireland descended into the chaos and guerrilla warfare that was to become known as "The Troubles". Unlike many of his age who followed him into a paramilitary career, McGeough actually lived up to the stereotype of the devout, practising Catholic IRA man - but like so many of his less religious peers, McGeough saw no choice but to fight for his community and against the British Army. He joined Sinn Fein aged sixteen and as soon as he turned seventeen, he underwent the initiation procedure of being "green-booked" - being given the green-coloured pamphlet containing the rules and guidelines to being a volunteer in the Provisional IRA and then tested to see if everything had been understood - McGeough entered the world of the Provos. He joined the local East Tyrone Brigade and in early 1976 began active service, helping to carry out gun and bomb attacks against local RUC and Army patrols.

McGeough proved himself in operations and slowly rose through the ranks of PIRA. He began spending a lot of time at one of the centres of PIRA's activities, the Murphy farm complex in Ballybinaby, near Hackballscross in County Louth, known to security forces by the abbreviation HBX. The farm complex straddled the border between County Louth in the Republic and South Armagh in occupied Northern Ireland and fulfilled several functions in the PIRA structure. Firstly as the farm was both in the sovereign Republic of Ireland and British-held Northern Ireland, it was possible to take advantage of the differing subsidies and tariffs in the two countries by smuggling cattle and oil between the two countries, claiming subsidies and then smuggling the subsidised wares back across the border to repeat the process all over again with the same goods; all without leaving the farm. This steady stream of income from smuggling flowed indirectly towards the cause of Republicanism via committed Republican and later Chief of Staff of the Provisionals Thomas Murphy, who owned the farm and known by many simply as Slab. Not only did Slab become personally wealthy thanks to the activities, but the proceeds of smuggling also directly benefited the South Armagh brigade of the IRA, of which Murphy was Officer Commanding (OC), filling the war chest and paying for wages and weapons. The benefits to the IRA were not only financial but also operational; the farm complex provided a huge array of barns and outhouses in the South for holding meetings and preparing attacks and bombs in the North; in addition, it was the perfect bolthole for those returning from active service in the North to the relative safety of the Republic of Ireland. However, hiding at the Murphy farm was not a guarantee of evasion from justice and the southern end of the farm was regularly searched by Garda, the northern part by the British Army and RUC amongst others. McGeough was arrested by a joint SAS/RUC team at HBX in July 1977. He was taken back to County Tyrone to Cookstown Army Barracks, where interrogators beat him repeatedly and called him "a Provo bastard", but sticking to the rules of the Green Book, he refused to say a word and had to be released without charge - McGeough was able to continue active service with PIRA.

A year later in 1978, McGeough was arrested in London on a brief visit to England and deported back to Ireland, and forbidden from entering mainland UK ever again, or even serving in the British Army – not an idea McGeough was likely to entertain anyway. Undeterred, he continued to operate as a volunteer and was tasked with increasingly more dangerous missions. In June 1981, McGeough was on active service for the IRA in Aughnacloy, Co Tyrone. The target was Samuel Brush, a postman who was also a part-time member of the Ulster Defence Regiment, an infantry regiment of the British Army recruited largely from the Protestant community and who, as a UDR soldier, was armed with a personal weapon for self-defence, as UDR men had often been targeted by the IRA. At around 1.30pm on June 13th, as Brush posted a letter through the letterbox of a house, McGeough emerged from his hiding place in an adjacent shed and opened fire at close range on the postman. Not only was Brush armed, he was also wearing a bulletproof vest - although having been hit several times, Brush managed to fire off several rounds from his own weapon, one of which hit McGeough in the chest. McGeough nevertheless managed to escape from the scene of the attack and hid before being spirited away across the border to the Republic. Two hours later he admitted himself to the nearby Monaghan General Hospital, severely wounded. He was airlifted to Dublin where surgeons operated on his gunshot wound, leaving him with significant scarring on his chest. After a relatively short period of convalescence in Dublin, McGeough was returned to Monaghan on June 22nd to continue his recovery. As ballistic tests on the bullet removed from his torso in Dublin revealed he had been shot by Brush, he was placed under armed guard. A party of friends visited him in hospital, one of them wearing a wig. McGeough shaved off his moustache, pulled on the wig and exchanged places with his friend, leaving the hospital with the rest of his friends. The friend who was left in his place shortly afterwards shouted a goodbye to Gerry from the door, in the pretence that he was still in the hospital room, as he sauntered out of the hospital.

McGeough went into hiding in the Republic of Ireland, in Ballybinaby at the Murphy farm complex. By the autumn, Slab Murphy had entrusted him with a large amount of cash and a task: McGeough was sent to the USA to procure arms for the Provos. On the way there, transiting through Iceland, McGeough was troubled when, sitting at the airport in Reykjavik waiting for his onward flight to the US, a group of British soldiers entered the hall. Worrying that one or more of them may have recently served in Northern Ireland and recognise him from IRA mugshots, he kept a low profile until his flight to New York was ready for boarding. Initially eking out a meagre living in the Big Apple and staying under the radar of US and UK intelligence and law enforcement, he then flew to Florida. Here he spent the time driving around the state with a young American woman, buying weapons to be shipped back to Ireland. Using her driving licence and taking advantage of lax gun laws in the US, he purchased a huge amount of serious weaponry from gun stores and private collectors, including a number of Armalite AR15 assault rifles, as well as Heckler & Koch HK91 semi-automatic rifles. The weapons were sent to the docks at Newark in New Jersey, where pro-Republican dockworkers smuggled them via a camper van onto a ship bound for Ireland. On at least one occasion, McGeough carried himself back to New York on a Greyhound bus and had another heart-stopping moment when the bus was stopped and police boarded, obviously looking for someone. McGeough breathed a huge sigh of relief as it emerged the cops were not looking for him but a runaway teenage couple sitting further up the bus. The purchase and shipment process was repeated several times before McGeough returned to Ireland, with the final shipment containing 40-50 weapons, filling the armoury of the South Armagh brigade.

However, despite the modernisation of IRA weaponry in the South Armagh area there was a further problem. Due to the increasingly more successful gun (and bomb) attacks by the South Armagh brigade on British Army targets around the base at Bessbrook Mill (BBK), the Army had been forced to use helicopters to patrol

Armagh, which had become known as "Bandit Country" and also to fly troops in and out of BBK. Frustrated by the move, Murphy decided the PIRA needed to act in South Armagh. With the aim of continuing to keep the British Army at bay and the same time score a huge PR coup for the brigade and the organisation as a whole a plan was hatched to shoot down an Army helicopter. Although the brigade had a huge stack of weapons at their disposal, none of these had the appropriate firepower to seriously endanger a military helicopter. Murphy instructed McGeough to team up with one of the most senior IRA men based in the USA, Belfast-born Gabriel "Skinny Legs" Megahey, who was now living in New York City and working as a building labourer in Manhattan. In early 1982, McGeough flew back to the USA to join Megahey. They were tasked with buying weapons that could bring down an Army helicopter. The weapon of choice was the portable surface-to-air missile, such as a FIM-43 Red-Eye, or its newer updated and more expensive version, the FIM-92 Stinger. McGeough and Megahey were soon able to track down arms dealers who could procure Red-Eyes for the Provisional IRA. After a series of initial meetings, in early June in a warehouse in New Orleans, McGeough negotiated the purchase of five Redeye portable surface-to-air missile systems with the arms dealers.

> McGeough: "What we want is a weapon which will take down, at least take
>
> down, helicopters, choppers..."
>
> MAN A: "All right."
>
> McGeough: "Warships in the sky, right?"
>
> MAN A: "Yes"
>
> McGeough: "So we can take it from there?"
>
> MAN A: "Yes"

MAN A: *"Who are you representing? Here, let me ask you one thing?*

Who do you represent?"

McGeough: *"Did you ever hear tell of the Provisionals?"*

MAN A: *"Yeah, the Irish."*

McGeough: *"The Irish Republican Army."*

MAN A: *"Right."*

McGeough: *"That's who we represent."*

McGeough arranged a final meeting two weeks later in New York to finalise the purchase at a cost of $50,000. In New York on June 11th, Megahey met with the arms dealers at the St. Regis Hotel, located just south of Central Park, to confirm the deal. Megahey proposed a hostage situation to prevent either of the parties absconding with the weapons or cash. The arms dealers refused and pulled out of the deal.

However, unbeknown to Megahey, the arms dealers were actually members of the FBI's PIRA Squad carrying out a sting. Under the leadership of FBI Special Agent Louis "Lou" Stephens, the team had been set up in May 1980 to carry out "Operation Hit and Win" – the FBI's plan to curtail the Provos gunrunning activities from the US to Ireland. Stephens' team had borrowed a deactivated Redeye system from the US Marine Corp to use in the sting operation and had videotaped McGeough and Megahey's meetings with the FBI agents. But they were to wait another ten days before pouncing: on June 21st, 1982 the FBI arrested Gabriel Megahey as he arrived at work on a construction site. Despite the TV broadcast of the covert videotapes in an attempt to alert the general public, McGeough managed to evade arrest and fled to the unlikely location of Hawaii.

From summer 1982 to summer 1983, McGeough let the sun bleach his hair, began to dress like a local and occasionally slept on the beach. In August 1983, using a friends ID to gain a false US passport, he travelled to Sweden. McGeough arrived in Malmö on June 19th, 1983. Three days later, he filled out an application for political asylum in Sweden. Supporting the application was a lengthy statement explaining Irish history from the year 1200 to the present day, and an admission of IRA membership. He revealed in the application that he had joined the Provisional IRA in early 1976 and that thereafter he had been given increasing levels of responsibility. McGeough explained he had been tasked with taking part in the attempt to murder Samuel Brush in Northern Ireland and could not return for fear of being arrested, convicted or even killed. This he argued had been politically motivated and he longed "for the chance to live an ordinary life, free from the constant fear of death". The application was lodged with the police department in Malmö, from where it was sent to the Migration Board of Sweden. McGeough waited for his application to be processed and began making contact with various solidarity groups in Sweden, picketing official functions and helping to drum up support in left-wing circles for the Republican cause. In October McGeough went to a dance evening in the Kramer restaurant in the city and met shop assistant Pia Marita Håkansson. McGeough clicked with Håkansson and they became a couple. McGeough moved into her apartment.

Gerard Kelly was born in April 1953 as one of eleven children, brought up by his father and elder sister after the early death of his mother. He grew up in the Whiterock area of the city, not far from the epicentre of Catholic struggle the Lower Falls Road. Predictably, he joined the Provisional IRA in 1972 after the Bloody Sunday massacre in Londonderry, and was enlisted into the Ballymurphy battalion – according to many observers and contemporaries serving alongside the later Sinn Fein leader Gerry Adams. As a young volunteer, he was initially involved in criminal activities intended to bolster the coffers of the cash-strapped Provos: later that year, he was arrested for taking part in a bank robbery in Omeath, Co. Louth in the Republic of Ireland and held in St Patrick's Juvenile Detention centre in Dublin. However, he escaped from St Patrick's and went on the run, before being recruited by the IRA's Southern Command in Dublin to join a team of volunteers being sent to London on active service.

Armed with explosives and cash, the team identified potential targets in the British capital and on March 8th, 1973 planted four car bombs at various locations. Two of the car bombs exploded; one outside the central criminal court at the Old Bailey, one outside the offices of the British Forces Broadcasting Service. The blasts caused widespread devastation: 250 people were injured, some seriously. One of the victims injured in the Old Bailey blast suffered a heart attack and subsequently died. The two car bombs that failed to explode were analysed by forensic teams – the evidence left behind quickly led them to Kelly and the rest of the ASU. Kelly and others were arrested as he tried to board a flight back to Ireland at Heathrow Airport. For his part in the attack, Kelly was convicted and sentenced to two periods of life imprisonment, with another twenty years added on for good measure. Kelly and some of the others in the ASU commenced a hunger strike protest at their sentencing and treatment as criminals, rather than political prisoners. After 205 days of brutal force-feeding, the British authorities caved in - not yet hardened enough by "The Troubles" to risk the bad publicity of Irishmen dying on hunger strike in English jails - and transferred Kelly back to Northern Ireland to The Maze.

After nine years in The Maze, and surviving the 1981 hunger strike, Kelly was part of the group of 38 IRA prisoners who on September 25th, 1983 escaped from the maximum-security prison. Using six handguns and assorted other tools and weapons, the escapees overpowered guards on their way to freedom; one guard, James Ferris, was stabbed in the chest with a chisel and later died of a heart attack in hospital. Another was shot in the head twice but survived. Armed IRA units had been informed of the plan to break out of the Maze and crossed the border to await the escapees as they exited the prison. They waited an hour, but eventually gave up and left again when no one came out, leaving the escapees to make their way on foot when they finally emerged from the prison gates sometime later. Half of the 38 were rearrested almost immediately, but Kelly and others got away. They walked for days until they eventually reached the border counties and re-established contact with their IRA colleagues, who hid them in safe houses dotted around the border. From there, the escapers spread out across the Republic and in some cases even further afield: into Europe. Amongst the escapers alongside Gerry Kelly; prominent IRA members Dermot Finucane, Tony McAllister from Ballymurphy and the notorious Bik McFarlane from Ardoyne, North Belfast. Brendan "Bik" McFarlane had been serving a life sentence in HMP Maze, where his copious notetaking at IRA meetings with a ballpoint pen earned him his nickname and where he succeeded Bobby Sands as OC for the Provisional IRA prisoners after Sands' death. He had been sentenced for multiple murders, after being convicted in August 1975 of his involvement in the bombing of the Bayardo Bar in the Protestant Shankill Road area of West Belfast. Five men died in the attack, including three who Bik had allegedly shot dead with a machine-gun as they passed the bar. Bik was an extremely feared and high-ranking IRA man.

Meanwhile in England, IRA active service units sent over by the England Department continued to wreak havoc. The teams detonated bombs at a variety of locations in the capital, killing several people - most notably outside Chelsea Barracks in October 1981; inside a burger bar on Oxford Street two weeks later; in July 1982 bombs exploded in Hyde Park and Regent's Park, killing eleven soldiers and a number of horses. In the pre-Christmas shopping period of 1983, an IRA car bomb detonated outside the luxury department store Harrods in Knightsbridge, killing six. The most notorious attack was carried out by an ASU led by Patrick Magee, which had very nearly succeeded in decapitating the Conservative government, almost killing Prime Minister Margaret Thatcher; on October 12th 1984, a huge bomb destroyed the Grand Hotel in Brighton where the entire upper echelons of the Government were staying during the Conservative Party annual conference. Magee evaded capture but eight months later, he was spotted by officers tracking another IRA suspect and arrested at an IRA safe house in Langside Road in the South Side area of Glasgow, along with several others. However, one of those who managed to evade capture was the head of the England Department – Owen Coogan.

Coogan – known to some IRA volunteers as "Ownie" or to most others, due to his protruding ears, "Jug Heid" or "Jug Ears" - was only in his early thirties but already a veteran operator. Born in 1948 in Belfast, he was an integral part of the 2nd Battalion Belfast Brigade and was very much involved in IRA activities from the beginning of The Troubles. He was first arrested in 1973 but managed to escape by hiding in a dustcart. He was later recaptured in the summer and sent to The Maze where he was on close terms with interned members of the IRA leadership. On his release, Coogan returned to active service and was allegedly part of the team that detonated an incendiary bomb at the La Mon House restaurant just outside Belfast in February 1978. The device was intended to kill a team of RUC officers that IRA intelligence had targeted and who were supposed to be meeting in the restaurant at the time. The intelligence was however wrong and the meeting had actually taken place a week earlier; twelve innocent diners were killed in the blast and subsequent inferno. Despite the error, shortly afterwards Coogan was sent to England to coordinate the offensive on the mainland; linking up with his second-in-command Michael Hayes and intelligence officer Albert Flynn, Coogan and his team oversaw the bombing campaign in London until the arrest of Magee and the others after the Brighton bomb. Coogan returned to Ireland to oversee the overseas activities of the Provisional IRA from a safe distance.

The Glasgow arrests in 1985 severely disrupted the momentum of the England Department. The Provisional IRA Army Council decided instead to resume activities on the Continent. Owen Coogan contacted and briefed a team of Maze escapers from the Belfast Brigade, still on the run, first and foremost with a view to procuring weapons for the armed struggle but there was always also the possibility of targeting British forces in Germany and the Netherlands, as a way of ramping up the campaign and increasing support for the Republican cause back home. Alongside Gerry Kelly was Bik McFarlane. However, the key player to the whole strategy had been in place in Europe since well before the Maze escape: "the Padre".

Father Patrick Ryan, known in PIRA circles simply as "The Padre", was the Provisional IRA's quartermaster in Europe. He had been responsible for the procurement of arms for the cause since the early 1970s. He was an extremely senior figure within the organisation and had been involved in many arms deals alongside members of the Army Council, including many supplied by Libyan leader Colonel Gaddafi. Ryan was born in 1930 in Roscommon, Co. Tipperary as one of six children in a farming family. He was educated at the local Christian Brothers school and later joined the Society of the Catholic Apostolate, also known as the Pallottine Order: he was ordained as a Catholic Priest in 1954. He went to Tanzania and London and collected money for missionary work in Africa. As the Troubles broke out in 1969, his superiors began to notice that the amount of money collected and sent home for distribution was becoming less and less; when challenged, he openly admitted that he was using some of the cash to help support Catholic families in Northern Ireland. In actual fact, the money was going straight to the IRA. In 1970, he met Catholic spinster Catherine, who was taken in by Ryan's charms and they became a couple; Ryan spent long periods of time at Catherine's East London flat. By 1972, the elders of the Pallottine Order had had enough and suspended Ryan temporarily, giving him six months leave of absence. Father

Ryan used the leave of absence from church duties to follow his Catholic convictions in a different way; he flew to Dublin, met with senior IRA figures and offered his services. With a clean record and respectable clergy image, Ryan was perfect for the Provos. Ryan was tasked with a number of things; helping to organise supply lines to the IRA, organise logistics and find new sources of fundraising for the cause. He flew to Tripoli to meet with the intelligence service of Libya, that was keen on helping to destabilise the British government and possibly saw common ground with the IRA. Ryan held face-to-face discussions with the Libyans, who agreed to help finance the Catholic insurgence in the Six Counties and promised to transfer money to the IRA via Ryan. Ryan returned to Europe to set up bank accounts in Switzerland to receive the money, which came rolling in. He flew to Rome to meet with Italian priests and casually remarked that he hoped the IRA would bomb London to make them understand the situation in Northern Ireland; probably knowing that Gerry Kelly, Dolours Price and the rest of the IRA Active Service Unit caught in London that year were already briefed and ready to strike. The Catholic Church finally had enough and suspended Ryan indefinitely. By all accounts, Ryan transferred all the Libyan money sitting in Swiss bank accounts via Frankfurt to the IRA in Dublin.

In spring 1974, Ryan moved to France, setting up base in a tourist hostel in Le Havre, near the ferry port. From there he conducted IRA business and met with ferry stewards and lorry drivers sympathetic to the Republican cause, tasked with couriering money and information backwards and forwards from the Provos. He was unaware that his neighbour in the hostel, a Canadian man, had become suspicious of the long, international calls that Ryan could be heard making from his room. One day after Ryan had checked out of the hostel en route to an assignment, the Canadian gained access to Ryan's room, rooted through the bin and found reams of paper. The next day, the Canadian took a ferry to Southampton, contacted Hampshire Special Branch police and gave them everything. Special Branch analysed the papers and discovered a host of telephone numbers belonging to known IRA commanders; Special Branch contacted London's Metropolitan Police Anti-Terrorism Division, who set up a covert surveillance operation to watch Ryan's movements. They contacted their counterparts in the French police, as well as *MI6*, who between them tracked Ryan's every movement from then on. The surveillance teams in Le Havre were surprised when, in January 1975, one of the original founders of the Provisional IRA, Joe Cahill, and IRA Adjutant General Eamon O'Doherty appeared in Le Havre. *MI6* and French police watched on, making notes, as the trio flew to Paris to meet with an arms dealer and followed O'Doherty on to Switzerland, where he checked on the status of Ryan's IRA accounts. Not yet ready to pounce, the surveillance team noted the return of O'Doherty to Le Havre in early 1976, accompanied by IRA Chief of Staff Seamus Twomey and trailed them and Ryan to Tripoli for a week of meetings with the Libyan government, then back to Paris for a further week of discussions. The teams were also keeping tabs on Catherine, whose telephone number had been found in the waste paper basket in the hotel in Le Havre and followed her as she delivered a fake English driving licence and cash to Ryan in Le Havre.

After two years of shuttling between European capitals and organising weapons deals across the Continent, the 'The Padre's luck ran out. Catherine met with Ryan in Zürich on July 25th, 1976 and was subsequently arrested under the Prevention of Terrorism Act for her aiding and abetting of Ryan's IRA activities. Ryan himself was arrested in Partier Square in Geneva shortly afterwards. Catherine was questioned but it soon became apparent that she was innocent and unaware of the nefarious activities of Ryan, who himself later admitted that he was in fact the Quartermaster for the IRA in Europe. He threatened that further action against him would result in IRA attacks against targets in Dublin and London. Authorities were unable to pin any illegal activities or extraditable offenses on Ryan and he was subsequently released.

During the past few years accruing cash, weapons and contacts for the IRA, Ryan had stumbled on something unexpectedly small and useful that was to assist the IRA in their campaign more than actual weapons or money. The Memopark timer was a small clockwork device that was designed to be attached to a keyring but made to a high specification. Motorists could set the device to a certain time to remind them when they would have to return to their vehicle before their parking ticket became invalid. The appropriate time was selected by rotating a dial; when the selected time had been reached, a bell on the timer rang. Ryan found that by attaching a metal arm to the Memopark, instead of a bell being rung, an electrical circuit would be completed; and thus the mainstay of IRA explosive devices for the next twenty or so years was created. When used as part of a TPU (time-power-unit) of a bomb, all that the volunteer had to do was rotate the dial to start the countdown to the moment when the bomb was supposed to explode; no complicated electronic trickery was needed, just a simple cheap Swiss novelty gadget. Ryan located a store in Zürich that stocked the Memopark timer and bought all 400 devices that the store had in stock. Part of the stock was sent back to Northern Ireland, part was kept in Europe for use in devices planned for use on the Continent. Ryan's inventiveness cemented his position as a key player in the IRA's strategy, both at home and in Europe. The now-defrocked priest continued to move around, but was closely monitored by intelligence and police forces in Europe; Ryan was arrested in France in December 1976, in Italy two months later, and in Luxemburg in March 1977, and at the request of *MI6* was placed under surveillance by police in Spain but Ryan was always released. European authorities were never able to press charges or convict Ryan of anything specific, and he continued to live at large across a number of European countries, directing IRA supply lines and channelling weapons and cash for the cause back in Northern Ireland. He finally settled in the Belgian capital Brussels.

Following the daring escape from The Maze in 1983, Gerry Kelly and Bik McFarlane, along with many others of the escape team, had made their way to South Armagh. Kelly reached Lurgan and hid for days under the floorboards of a disused IRA weapons dump. McFarlane ended up in Camlough. After a period of lying low, IRA senior commanders ordered them to return to active service. A return to Belfast was however completely out of the question - instead Kelly and McFarlane were seconded to the South Armagh Brigade and returned to the armed struggle in late 1983, joining up with each other again. After a few months on active service in "Bandit Country", GHQ asked McFarlane to move to France to help with the IRA's activities in Continental Europe and thoughtfully supplied Bik with a Linguaphone course to help him learn basic French. In February 1984, Bik McFarlane left behind Gerry Kelly in South Armagh, as well as the Linguaphone book and cassettes and moved to Paris. Kelly took possession of the Linguaphone course and began to learn French as well. A few weeks later, on March 8th 1984, Kelly flew to Paris and joined McFarlane in the French capital. McFarlane and Kelly had been tasked with helping out with Patrick Ryan's European gunrunning operation and together they began to spend some of the nearly £1 million in IRA cash that Ryan had accrued for the cause; on weapons, timers and explosives, storing the materials in a Paris lockup. As the city was a handy staging post for other volunteers in Europe on IRA business – meeting ETA members in Spain and Portugal and contacts in northern Italy – McFarlane and Kelly were called upon to help give those IRA volunteers passing through France assistance. On one occasion in early summer 1984 for example, a senior female PIRA operative was returning to Ireland from meeting an ETA contact in Portugal and realised she was under close surveillance by the French domestic security service *DST*, who were following her at the request of British authorities. Kelly and McFarlane met the operative in central Paris on her arrival and helped to throw the hapless security services off her trail.

After an intruder broke into the Paris lockup, the team moved the material in case the criminal decided to inform the French authorities or plunder the materials himself. The team also moved into a different safe house in case the rental of the lockup was traced back to their address – the storage unit and safe house had been rented by clean French contacts so this was highly unlikely but the IRA team were taking no chances. Shortly afterwards, McFarlane left Paris and in November 1984, Gerry Kelly was also on the move again – this time to Amsterdam. In the Dutch capital, Kelly spent most of 1985 assisting Patrick Ryan with procuring and moving arms and explosives for the armed struggle back home. Kelly was reunited with his friend Bik when McFarlane also moved to Amsterdam and the pair found a flat in the southern suburb of Buitenveldert. A nearby lockup container was used to store materials and weapons. In order to assist the team to stay undercover whilst on the run and on IRA business in Europe, they had been supplied with a number of false Irish passports in different names; the passports were in fact part of a batch of around one hundred genuine Irish blank passports that had been stolen the previous year from the Department of Foreign Affairs in Dublin. Several of the stolen passports had already been recovered from Glasgow where Patrick Magee and others had been arrested in the aftermath of the Brighton bomb, along with detailed plans for a bombing campaign against British seaside resorts; more of the batch was to turn up the following year in the possession of IRA men on board the Eksund, a boat carrying an arms shipment organised by Ryan from Libya to the IRA that was intercepted off the coast of France. Using the false passports and the cash, they accrued hundreds of weapons for use against British forces. Kelly freely admits to once driving into Amsterdam in a hire car with McFarlane with over one hundred weapons in the boot.

In the dead days between Christmas 1985 and the start of 1986, Kelly and McFarlane were joined in Amsterdam by an old comrade from Belfast: William "Blue" Kelly. Fellow Belfast Brigade member and a former Battalion OC, "Blue" was a prominent IRA gunrunner who had been arrested together with another man, Denis Donaldson, on arrival in Orly airport in Paris in 1981 en route from Beirut, after returning from an IRA training camp in the Lebanon, but both were released without charge. He continued to operate on behalf of the IRA and joined the ASU in the Netherlands, to help Gerry and Bik acquire and hide weaponry. The arrival of "Blue" in the city - closely followed by a passing visit from an IRA courier a few days later in January – set alarm bells ringing back in London. Both men had been watched closely by the security services and, now aware that there were several IRA members in Amsterdam and fearing that some kind of attack on Dutch soil was being prepared, *MI5* alerted their counterparts in the Dutch intelligence service *BVD*. The *BVD* placed Gerry Kelly, Bik McFarlane and "Blue" under surveillance, watching them ferry material to and from the lockup. The decision was made to pounce: at 5am on January 16th 1986, Dutch police stormed the Buitenveldert flat. Shattering nearly every window, the police team took the IRA men unawares and half-asleep and met no resistance. The police arrested all three men and found a gun, the stolen passports and several hundred thousand dollars in different currencies. In the adjoining parking lot, investigators also discovered the IRA's haul of weaponry: seizing nearly 40 firearms, including 13 Belgian-made FN FAL automatic rifles, an AK-47 assault rifle, and assorted pistols, as well as two hand-grenades, nearly 70,000 rounds of ammunition and four drums of nitrobenzene – the carcinogenic chemical that had been used several times before in IRA bombs. The weapons, explosives and ammunition had been, according to police, ready for dispatch to Ireland.

„Blue" was deported two weeks after the arrests but Bik McFarlane and Gerry Kelly were detained in custody in the Netherlands. On February 3rd 1986, British authorities requested the extradition of Kelly and McFarlane back to Great Britain in order to be tried over the criminal offences committed during the Maze breakout, as well as to serve the remainder of their original sentences. As Patrick Magee had done in 1981, McFarlane and Kelly took on Willem van Bennekom as their defence lawyer; the IRA men stood before the Amsterdam Regional Court on the extradition requests. The court upheld the extradition request for McFarlane but refused to authorise Kelly's extradition; as Kelly had allegedly shot and seriously wounded a guard during the escape, it was feared that Kelly would subsequently be subject to abuse, inhuman conditions and maltreatment at the hands of prison guards back in Northern Ireland. On September 10th 1986, the Supreme Court (Hoge Raad) held a further hearing on the matter and declared that it was only prepared to extradite on the basis of crimes committed during the Maze escape. This presented British authorities with a headache; they could not get their hands on Kelly without quashing his original sentence. In the end, an unprecedented step was taken; using the little-used Royal Prerogative of Mercy, Kelly's sentence was quashed and on October 21st 1986, the Supreme Court agreed to the extradition of both McFarlane and Kelly. To allay fears of potential mishandling of the men upon return to the Maze, the Dutch authorities obtained official written assurances from the Deputy Director of HMP Maze that Kelly and McFarlane would be subject to the same rights and treatment as all other prisoners in the facility. The IRA men and their lawyer made one last ditch attempt to prevent Kelly and McFarlane being sent back to the Maze and on November 20th appealed to the European Court of Human Rights. Sitting on December 2nd 1986, the ECHR found no issue with the extradition and thus Kelly and McFarlane were extradited by helicopter back to Northern Ireland and imprisoned once more in The Maze.

***

In the meantime in Malmö, Pia Marita Håkansson had sold her apartment and moved back in with her family – Gerry McGeough moved into an asylum seekers centre. McGeough divided his time between Sweden and the Netherlands, for he had been charged with an important task: the Overseas Department wanted to recommence attacks on British military targets in Western Europe. With his European experience and an aptitude for foreign languages, McGeough was the prime candidate and already based on the Continent. He gladly accepted the challenge. In the first weeks of 1987, he made contact with other volunteers that had been sent to the Netherlands from Northern Ireland. The volunteers had been recruited predominantly from the Belfast Brigade, which at the time exerted a strong influence over the entire PIRA structure and from whose ranks Owen Coogan and other senior commanders running the Overseas Department came. One of the Belfast Brigade volunteers was Gerard Hanratty.

Gerard Thomas Hanratty was from Andersonstown in West Belfast. Roughly the same age as Gerry McGeough, Hanratty had started his Republican career at an even earlier age, joining PIRA's youth wing Na Fianna Éireann in 1971 aged just twelve after witnessing many violent incidents against Catholics in Andersonstown. By the time he turned sixteen he had joined the big boys of PIRA's Belfast Brigade. In 1975 he was arrested and convicted for the first time and sent to Crumlin Road prison, where he ended up in C-Wing, on the same landing as seasoned IRA activists like Jim Gibney. After nearly two years of mayhem and constant fights in Crumlin Road he was released in 1977 and returned to active service. He kept his freedom for nearly five years before being rearrested in 1982 and sentenced to four years. This time, instead of Crumlin Road, he had earned a stay in the H-Blocks of The Maze and moved to B-Wing H7 a few months before the Maze breakout in September 1983. He was not part of the escape team and served nearly two years before being released again in 1984. Once again, it was not long before he was back in trouble: in August he was arrested in Belfast by a joint RUC / Army patrol, suspected of having been the passenger in a car that had been involved in a high speed chase through the city, later to be found abandoned and containing weapons. He was held on remand before being released on bail in 1986 – he failed to appear at the resulting trial and went on the run.

Having earned his IRA credentials but a marked man in Belfast, Hanratty was chosen to team up in the Low Countries with McGeough and Ryan, to get plans for commencing attacks on British targets on the Continent back on track. To do this, they first needed to find suitable safe houses from which to operate. As the British Forces in Germany were largely stationed on the border to the Netherlands, it made sense to find somewhere in or close to Germany from which to carry out reconnaissance and launch attacks. The Netherlands had generally proved itself an ideal country to hide; few IRA men could speak any other language but English or Irish, so the Netherlands with a large proportion of English-speakers and a politically and socially more liberal outlook was far more suited for finding safe accommodation than in conservative, mainly German-speaking Germany. The pair scoured the border area for possibilities; in the narrow strip of Dutch territory a few kilometres southwest of Sittard and north of Maastricht, Hanratty found a suitable place to rent in the village of Lindenheuvel and set up base there. Whilst Hanratty worked by day, taking up a job at a local building contractor, McGeough secured student accommodation via the ASVA student union in Amsterdam, where he stayed when travelling to the city from Malmö. They met regularly to make plans and set up arms dumps to stash explosives, detonators and guns. Using a variety of rented vehicles, they spent their off-days and weekends driving across into Germany from Holland and touring the various military installations clustered along the border. During the reconnaissance trips, they also realised that for similar reasons to their own preference for the Netherlands, soldiers from army bases such as York Barracks in Münster to the north and RAF bases such as Laarbruch, Wildenrath and Brüggen to the south often crossed the border for nights out in towns such as Venlo, Nieuw Bergen and particularly Roermond. The lack of security procedures, the habits, activities, living quarters and location of military personnel and bases along a narrow strip of Western Germany were noted and plans made.

McGeough and Hanratty were joined briefly in early 1987 by a young but nevertheless seasoned operative also hailing from Andersonstown: Mairéad Farrell. Farrell was born on March 3rd 1957 into a middle-class Catholic but non-sectarian family. Her mother's side of the family had contained many that had even been part of the Royal Irish Constabulary (RIC) in the South and RUC in the North; the RUC in particular recruited generally from the Protestant community and the family, whilst being resolutely Republican in their views, had many Protestant friends. Farrell first experienced sectarian violence when she passed her 11+ examinations and continued her education at Rathmore, a local grammar school not far from the family home on Stewartstown Road. Her route to school on her bicycle took her through a Protestant estate and anti-Catholic catcalls soon turned into stones being aimed at her head, before she changed routes. As the conflict ignited in 1969, twelve-year-old Farrell soon experienced first-hand the brutality meted out to Catholics by the Protestants and the police, which was, in turn, to ignite her political convictions. When a neighbour was blinded by an RUC man who fired a rubber bullet at point-blank range through the window into her face, things reached a tipping point: Farrell resolved to join the fight back against the oppressors. She joined the Belfast Brigade of the Provisional IRA at the age of eighteen and became actively involved in operations around the city. Of the time she said:

> *"A lot of 17 to 19 year olds were involved, maybe looking back I was very young then but I was politically aware. I know that now because my views haven't changed if anything I have become stronger, more committed." One of the attractions was "being treated equal to the lads. I don't think sexism is rife in the Republican Movement, although that's not to say we*

> *were exempt from it either. I suppose I've always believed we had a legitimate right to take up arms and defend ourselves against the Brits' occupation. I wouldn't have got involved if I hadn't believed that."*

It was during this time, she met her first serious boyfriend Séan McDermott – also a member of the Belfast Brigade. In April 1976, together with McDermott and fellow volunteer Kieran Doherty, she was tasked with blowing up the Conway Hotel in Dunmurry as part of an IRA blitz on Belfast. Shortly after the three bombs exploded, she was arrested by RUC officers still within the grounds of the hotel; Doherty and McDermott escaped. McDermott broke into a nearby house and demanded that the owner hand over his car keys. Unbeknown to McDermott, the house owner was a reservist in the Royal Ulster Constabulary; the man, under the pretence of fetching his keys from upstairs, retrieved his service-issued weapon from his bedroom and attempted to overpower McDermott. In the ensuing melee the RUC man wrestled McDermott's gun from his grasp and with it, shot Farrell's boyfriend dead. The seeds of hatred within Mairéad Farrell began to germinate as she was sentenced to fourteen years imprisonment in Armagh Women's Gaol.

When Farrell entered Armagh, she was the first female Republican prisoner to be sentenced under new regulations and was refused special category status. She was isolated from the Republican organization in Armagh and only able to talk to the other thirty to forty Republican women for ten minutes after Mass on Sundays. She began a "no work protest" against the loss of special category status:

> *"I knew now the battle would begin - the real battle - that the struggle would be a long and lonely one for us all"*

As other newly sentenced women entered Armagh they joined Farrell in protests. Farrell first became OC (Officer Commanding) of the Republican prisoners on her wing, then became overall OC for the IRA prisoners in the whole prison.

> "There was no kudos in it, I had to take decisions that would affect all the prisoners. There were times I felt very alone, even though I knew I had the support of the others at all times."

Within Armagh Women's Goal, Friday February 7th 1980 became known as "Black Friday". At the time the Republican prisoners were able to wear their own clothes; the day before as was customary, the prisoners all dressed in black skirts and white blouses at a ceremony to mourn the death of fellow IRA volunteer Kevin Delaney, who had been killed by his own bomb when it detonated prematurely and who had three sisters serving sentences in Armagh at the time. The day after the ceremony, seemingly determined to crack down on this display of unity, a squad of 60 male and female warders donned riot gear and rushed into the canteen as the women were standing in line waiting for their lunch. The prison officers surrounded the women, and brutally punched and kicked the women. Their cells were searched and wrecked by the warders and after the women were returned to their cells,

> "Men in riot gear armed with batons appeared in the cells again. The girls were beaten and carried down the stairs to the guardroom to receive their punishment. The toilets were locked and they were confined to their cells for 24 hours. We were not allowed exercise nor out to the toilet or to get washed. We were locked up for 24 hours and allowed nothing to eat or drink. Male officers are still on the wing, they have not left and are running the wing got something to eat still not allowed use of toilet facilities. We have been forced into a position of "Dirt Strike' as our pots are overflowing with urine and excrement. We emptied them out of the spy holes into the wing. The male officers nailed them closed....Male officers are still running the wing...Lynn O'Connell was

> beaten twice, the second time was the worst. The officers jumped her as she was going out to the yard...her face is badly swollen and cut."

The "dirty protest" lasted 13 months. It was to Farrell the most frightening time of her imprisonment. On 1st December 1980, Farrell and her fellow inmates Mary Doyle and Mairéad Nugent went on hunger strike in support of the men in the Long Kesh 'H Blocks. Afterwards she recalled how important was the support received from outside but also how she hated the distress caused to her parents. She continued on hunger strike until 19th December when it seemed the Northern Ireland Office (NIO) – the British government ministry responsible for Northern Irish affairs - had agreed to the prisoners' demands. This agreement was then retracted. The "Dirt Strike" was called off in January 1981 in preparation for the second hunger strike in the H Blocks on 1st March 1981. However, the women prisoners made the difficult decision to refrain from participation in the men's hunger strike. It was the worst time for them as the women waited for news of the deaths. Farrell said:

> "I know it will be more difficult this time to win anything. It will take longer for the pressure to build up. I am a volunteer in the Irish Republican Army and a political prisoner in Armagh jail. I am prepared to fight to the death, if necessary, to win the recognition that I am a political prisoner and not a criminal."

In December 1982 strip-searching was introduced at Armagh. The female Republican prisoners refused to undergo these searches that were made before women were allowed out of the prison. The remand prisoners suffered most from strip-searching as they were searched before and after court hearings and were subject to regular beatings. The Republican prisoners ended their resistance to strip-searching because of the fear of increasingly serious assaults. In 1983, Farrell was joined in jail in Armagh by another female convicted PIRA operative, Siobhán O'Hanlon. Five years her junior, O'Hanlon came from a Republican family with far more pedigree in Republican circles than Farrell: her maternal uncle was feared hardliner, former Chief of Staff and one of the founders of the Provisional IRA Joe Cahill, with whom Father Patrick Ryan had negotiated Libyan weapons deliveries with Colonel Gaddafi. O'Hanlon had joined the Belfast Brigade at an early age but had been arrested in 1983, when the RUC raided a property in the Newington area of North Belfast and found an IRA bomb factory. O'Hanlon was held in custody before being convicted on explosives charges and sentenced to four years imprisonment. O'Hanlon and Farrell bonded quickly.

Mairéad Farrell was released on September 19th 1986. She enrolled in a course on political science at Queens University in Belfast and re-joined the IRA. She deferred the start of her course at Queens until October 1987 and told her mother she wanted to take a year-off to readjust to life outside prison before starting her degree. She travelled to Tenerife with friends but returned to Belfast at Christmas, being sighted at a Sinn Fein Christmas party in the city with a whole host of senior IRA figures in attendance. It was obvious to everyone but her family that she had returned to active service and indeed she admitted to her parents that she could be shot dead at any time, but that she was convinced her path was the right one to follow. Not long after, this path took her and her brother Niall to Germany. It is unclear whether this was official IRA business - either on active service or as a staging post for a trip further afield – and if she was placed under surveillance by the security services. It may merely have been a hugely coincidental holiday to the grey, bleak and wintry Germany, where Gerry McGeough and Gerry Hanratty, with the help of PIRA's long-standing quartermaster general in Europe, Father Patrick Ryan, were preparing the first of what was planned to be a wave of attacks against British military targets.

Not only were Mairéad Farrell, Gerry McGeough, Gerry Hanratty and

Patrick Ryan present on the Continent, there were other Provo visitors to Europe in late autumn and winter of 1986. Twenty-five kilometres from the border to Slovenia lay the small town of Ferlach in Kärnten, Austria; a town famed as much for its position in the global weapons industry as for its majestic Alpine mountain views. The town had developed a rich tradition of arms manufacture over the last hundred years and boasted at least a dozen master gunsmiths; little wonder that renowned Austrian engineer and gunmaker Gaston Glock chose Ferlach as the location for a major production centre for the production of weapons, from where Glock supplied police and military forces around the world with high-quality firearms. In this incongruous location, in October 1986, a visitor from Northern Ireland met with an Austrian gunsmith to conclude an arms deal intended to equip part of the Provisional IRA with modern weaponry. The exact identity of the person is a closely-guarded secret; not only within the IRA but also within the Austrian domestic intelligence agency the *Staatspolizei* (or *StaPo*), who observed the arrival of the woman from Northern Ireland, the Ministry of the Interior for Austria BMI, to whom the *StaPo* reported, and indeed within the files of the East German intelligence service the Stasi, who received the reports via a mole they had placed within the BMI. But a few details of the meeting have leaked out; the woman acting on behalf of the IRA was born in 1957, traveling on a British passport, entered Austria from the Federal Republic of Germany, and after the meeting travelled on to Bologna to meet an unnamed contact in northern Italy before returning home to Dublin. Trying to pinpoint exactly which IRA volunteer was the mysterious visitor to Kärnten is not easy but although the Provos rarely had a shortage of female volunteers, few had sufficient enough connections, skills or standing to be trusted with traveling to the Continent on important IRA business with a bag full of cash and a shopping list of weaponry. It is eminently possible that the recently released Mairéad Farrell was the one entrusted with the task, but suspicion also falls on another IRA volunteer more experienced as a courier: Eibhlin Glenholmes.

The same age as Farrell, Eibhlin Glenholmes was from the predominantly Catholic Short Strand area of Belfast. Her father Richard "Dickie" Glenholmes was a prominent member of the Provisional IRA and had been jailed for long stretches; in December 1979 he was arrested in London in a flat in Holland Park along with Gerard Tuite and Bobby Storey, who were in the midst of planning a daring mission to free Belfast IRA commander Brian Keenan from Brixton prison using a helicopter. Following in the footsteps of her father, Eibhlin began her IRA career as an arms courier before being asked by senior commanders to get involved in more "active" operations. And thus she came to the attention of the head of the IRA's England Department: Owen Coogan sent Glenholmes to mainland Britain in 1981 along with Tommy Quigley, Paul Kavanagh, Patrick McVeigh and John Downey. Together that autumn, the ASU planted a series of devices across London to devastating effect: a bomb exploded at Chelsea Barracks in southwest London in October, killing two and injuring 40; an IRA car bomb injured Royal Marines commander Lieutenant-General Steuart Pringle, when it detonated in Dulwich a week later; the same month, a device planted by the team in a Wimpy burger bar in Oxford Street killed the Metropolitan police explosives officer Kenneth Haworth who was trying to defuse it; in November a device detonated at the HQ of the Royal Artillery in Woolwich injuring two. In July 1982 things got worse: bombs exploded in Hyde Park and Regents Park, claiming the lives of eleven members of the Household Cavalry and the Royal Green Jackets, as well as a number of military horses. Eibhlin and the rest of the team returned to Ireland.

Police carefully investigated all the cases, sifting through masses of evidence and interviewing hundreds of witnesses: one lead in particular led them to Eibhlin Glenholmes. A witness reported that a few days before the blast, he had been asked by Glenholmes if she could borrow jump leads to help her start her white van - the same van that was later used to transport the Chelsea bomb. To make matters worse for Glenholmes and the IRA, in October 1983 police recovered the arms, ammunition and explosives dump used by the active service unit that had been hidden in a forest near Pangbourne in Berkshire – 118 pounds of explosives, 63 detonators, nearly 40 time-power-units, four handguns, two rifles and a sub-machine gun, as well as a mass of identity documents; birth certificates and driving licences. The police could link the material found to all the IRA attacks carried out by the ASU in London in 1981 and 1982 and furthermore, link those to Glenholmes and the rest of the team. Glenholmes was put on Britain's "most wanted" list. In September 1983 back home in Northern Ireland, Glenholmes appeared in court in Belfast charged with IRA membership but not relating to her activities in London; ex-Belfast Brigade adjutant turned supergrass Robert "Beano" Lean had informed the RUC that she was an active Provo. She spent a month in custody but was released when "Beano" later retracted his statements, saying that the RUC had forced him to make false confessions. Glenholmes fled to Dundalk in the Republic, although the British were aware of her whereabouts and prepared a comprehensive extradition request on the basis of involvement in the IRA's London offensive in autumn 1981. There was furore however, as in November 1984, not only did the Sunday Times reveal the details of the request in advance of it being handed to the Irish authorities but the initial request sent to Dublin had to be cancelled as the British had got Glenholmes' name and date of birth wrong. Finally, time ran out for Glenholmes in March 1986: she was arrested and appeared before Dublin District Court. But the judge dismissed the extradition warrants presented and Glenholmes left the building. There was chaos as she tried to get into a waiting car; the Garda fired up to nine shots, scattering passers-by, as the Irish police re-arrested Glenholmes a short distance away from the court. She was tried a second time but yet again freed. Despite pleas from the Irish Security Task Force for her to be held until new extradition papers arrived from London, Glenholmes and her lawyer were whisked away from the court - for debriefing by senior commanders and a subsequent return to active service for the Provisional IRA.

Glenholmes was very possibly the senior PIRA operative that Gerry Kelly and team had helped evade security services in Paris two years earlier – she was experienced, well connected and available for a mission to southern Austria.

Away from mysterious arms deals in the mountains of Austria and on active service on the ground in Germany, at the end of January 1987, McGeough and Hanratty began to undertake reconnaissance missions to British military installations in the west of the Bundesrepublik. On January 26th, they purchased a blue Opel Ascona car with the registration 35-UM-83 in the Netherlands and three days later used it to drive to Mönchengladbach, near to the Dutch border. There they took a look around the NATO base in Rheindahlen, the wooded suburb of Mönchengladbach where the Joint Headquarters of British Forces in Germany (JHQ) was located, on the lookout for a potential target and lax security measures. They found the perfect place: the E-Mess complex. Mess buildings were like private members clubs; at JHQ as with other bases, there were several different Mess facilities – each for lower-ranking servicemen, officers and civilian workers such as teachers and security personnel. Higher ranking airmen and soldiers alike often spent leisure time at their respective Mess; ate dinner with colleagues, played snooker, attended functions, received their mail and sometimes spent a few nights if they were in the process of being transferred to or from Germany. There would always be military personnel in the building, making it a good target and a concrete attack plan was drawn up. At the same time however, the British authorities became slowly aware that the IRA were planning an attack in Europe. There were many possible sources for this information: possibly from a mole within the IRA itself, possibly the arrival in Germany of known Belfast Brigade member Mairéad Farrell alerted the authorities. Possibly the warning was attributable to the arrival in Paris of a known member of the IRA's South Down Brigade who, at the request of *MI5*, was placed under close surveillance by French intelligence officers upon arrival in France.

The latter is the most likely reason that the authorities became jumpy, as on February 7th, British authorities in Paris issued a warning to its embassies and friendly European nations of a possible impending IRA attack in Western Europe within the following 48 to 72 hours; the *BSSO* raised the security threat level. The system of security threat level assessment as regards terrorism at British military installations in Germany was called "Keenwind", aligned with the more general alert state indicator "Bikini", which indicated the general threat level from Warsaw Pact forces, civil unrest or other non-terrorist sources. The alert state indicator was divided into colour-coded segments ranging from "White" to "Red" – with red denoting that an attack was imminent, had just happened or was in the middle of being carried out, for example if a suspected explosive device had been found. The current threat level was displayed on boards at the entrances to each Army and Royal Air Force base. The lowest level - "White" – meaning "situation stable" was never used. The next levels "Grey" and "Black" were more common – "Grey" signifying a general underlying threat but no concrete information on impending threatening activities, whilst "Black" meant an attack was possible. Most common of all was "Black Special": an increased likelihood of attack but with no defined target. The *BSSO* raised the level to the second highest alert state - "Keenwind Amber" signifying that „specific information has been received and it is assessed that there is a substantial threat to installations within a specified period of time." Patrols around British bases were significantly stepped up and security measures on entrance and exit to military bases were increased.

No attack was forthcoming, and the security level was dropped. McGeough and Hanratty were ready to carry out the plan but firstly needed another vehicle. The pair drove to The Hague on March 10th, where McGeough went to a second-hand car dealership and purchased a chestnut coloured Volvo 244 with the registration 38-UH-51 - using false ID in the name of "M. Heaney" claiming to have been born on May 6th 1956 and to live in J. van Geelstraat in

Rotterdam. Whilst Hanratty and the car remained in the Netherlands, McGeough returned to Malmö to receive some bad news: on March 19th, McGeough's application for political asylum was declined. Facing deportation back to the UK, which would mean certain arrest and conviction for the attempted murder of Samuel Brush, on April 5th 1987 he said goodbye to Pia; using a false passport, McGeough took a train from Malmö across the water to Copenhagen and then on to Bologna in Italy. The identity of the contact in Bologna who met both McGeough in April 1987 and the female volunteer involved in the Ferlach arms deal in October 1986 remains a mystery – it is known that the Provos had links to the Italian Red Brigades based in Bologna but it is possible that Father Patrick Ryan may also have been based in Bologna for a period of time. A few days later, McGeough returned from Bologna to the Netherlands to meet up with Hanratty, where the pair swapped the 38-UH-51 registration plates on the Volvo for fake British ones and prepared the vehicle with detonators and 135kg of Semtex.

On March 23rd, the plan was put into action; travelling in the Volvo and Ascona, which were sporting British registration plates, with McGeough and Hanratty dressed in British Army military fatigues so as not to arouse suspicion, they drove the few kilometres to Rheindahlen. They entered the complex via one of the main gates without being checked and headed towards E-Mess. Hanratty and McGeough had mistakenly chosen a Mess complex where very few British personnel spent time. The Mess they had chosen was usually used by visiting military personnel, often from the German, Dutch and Belgian armed forces. On this night in particular, German Bundeswehr officers were hosting a special "dining-out" night to say farewell to a colleague over beer, wine and filet of beef. The E-Mess and indeed E-Mess car park was full; McGeough and Hanratty were unable to park the Volvo as close to the building as they had planned and settled for leaving the car bomb around twenty metres from the main entrance. They fled in the Ascona and drove down the B230 in the direction of Roermond – as they passed by the town of Elmpt, they dumped the Army uniforms in a rubbish bin next to the road and crossed over the border back into the Netherlands. A call was placed back to Ireland by the ASU: the mission was on. At 10:05pm, the IRA unit called the DPA news agency in Düsseldorf and warned that they had planted a device. The DPA employee struggled to decipher the thick Irish accent at the end of the phone and missed vital information as to the location of the explosives.

At 10.28pm the car bomb detonated with tremendous force; ripping out doors in the Mess from their frames, smashing windows in the building and the surrounding buildings - such as Chatham House, one of the boarding school dormitories for Kent School on the base. Parked cars were destroyed, with the bomb tearing a hole in the road. The explosion was heard in the centre of Mönchengladbach, several kilometres away. In all, twenty-seven German military personnel, including a four-star NATO general, as well as three British and one Dutch mess staff member were injured in the blast, some of them seriously. The injured were taken to the RAF hospital in Wegberg, a few kilometres south of JHQ. The fact that heavy curtains had been hanging in the windows had prevented much of the shattered glass entering the room at high velocity and in addition, the car park had been so full that the terrorists had not been able to park the car bomb closer to the Mess: these two factors helped prevent loss of life, minimised the number of casualties and severity of injuries. It also prevented the attack being an unmitigated disaster for the IRA; had the bomb detonated closer, many more German lives would have been lost, and the start of the IRA campaign in continental Europe would have been a diplomatic catastrophe. Around two hours after the blast, a man purporting to belong to a group styling itself the "National Democratic Front for the Liberation of West Germany" called German police in Krefeld to claim responsibility for the blast and warned of further devices. The police were sceptical of the claim; especially as the man had attempted to claim responsibility two years earlier for terrorist incidents or threatened attacks that never came to fruition. When the information reached them from DPA that someone with an Irish accent had tried to phone through a warning 25 minutes before the detonation, the suspicions of the *BKA* fell on the IRA. The true identity of the organisation behind the attack was revealed later the same day, as IRA officially claimed responsibility in a statement issued via the Irish Republican Press Centre to the Associated Press in Dublin:

> *"British forces can count themselves extremely lucky. Our unit's brief was to inflict a devastating blow but was ordered to be careful to avoid civilian casualties."*

The statement contained a hidden hint of admonishment from "P. O'Neill" to Gerry Hanratty and Gerry McGeough: get it right next time. But the message to the outside world was clear: the Provisional IRA had signalled the start of a concerted offensive against British interests on the European mainland.

2 THE RATTLE OF HEAVY STUFF

The German Federal Prosecutor quickly instructed the German *Bundeskriminalamt* to oversee the investigations into the JHQ bombing under the file number 1BJs 61/87-4. The *BKA* set up a *SoKo* (Special Commission) unit in Mönchengladbach, based at JHQ in Rheindahlen, under the leadership of Karl-Heinz Pähler. As criminal investigators continued to pick through the mess outside E-Mess, the German authorities had to deal with further unsettling incidents. On April 5th and 6th, Angela Terzani, the wife of the Tokyo correspondent for the *Spiegel* news magazine received two phone calls from an anonymous caller. The man had a broad Irish accent and claimed to have been told by a drunken IRA man that the Provos were planning their next move: bombs were to be detonated at an unidentified location in Berlin, at the office of British Airways in Düsseldorf and at the British Embassy in Luxemburg. A day later, the man called back and reasserted what he had been told; Terzani then informed the German authorities, who passed on the information to their British counterparts at *BSSO* and *MI5* the same day. A day later, British military police alerted German authorities of a possible new car bomb under a vehicle in Hamelin, where units of the British Army were based. In the evening hours of April 8th, a suspected "under-vehicle-booby-trap" (UVBT) device was reported as having been discovered under a car belonging to a British serviceman – a metal box was apparently attached to the underside of the car, wires protruding from the box, and set to detonate at 9pm. British bomb disposal experts called for help from German colleagues from the *LKA*, who used a robot to investigate the device. After a tense few hours and clearance of the surrounding area, x-ray images revealed that the UVBT proved to consist of a twenty centimetre wide German-brand biscuit tin, sporting wires leading from the "device" to the interior, as well as a switch, but no explosives: no timer was discovered, instead the words "21:00 hours" had been carved into the lid of the tin. A crude hoax that - in the light of the events of March 23rd at JHQ and the suspicious calls to Tokyo - had the British and German authorities understandably on edge. However, the mystery of the call from the "National Democratic Front for the Liberation of West Germany" was quickly solved: on April 9th, a 27-year-old from Bremen was arrested in Daun, west of Koblenz, after he voluntarily checked into a hospital in Andernach for treatment. His parents recognised his voice from a recording of his telephoned claim of responsibility for the JHQ bombing to police in Krefeld and were able to advise police that their son was the mystery caller. After questioning, police ruled out a political motive for the calls and no threat from the non-existent group. But that was not the end of the hoaxes. The day after the arrest of the man, a German calling himself "Peters" placed calls to the daily newspapers Express and Bild Zeitung on behalf of a purported German IRA grouping calling itself "*Kommando Francis Hughes*", named after one of the Maze hunger strikers. In the calls, he claimed further attacks were shortly to take place. As police were assessing whether or not to take the call seriously, "Peters" telephoned the newspapers again and became more specific in the threats. He claimed that the German IRA group were placing two 100-kilogramme car bombs outside the British Embassy in Bonn, and the British Consulate in Düsseldorf, threatening further attacks on other targets in Düsseldorf, Mönchengladbach and Duisburg. The information was passed to the *BKA TE12* and *TE14* divisions, who checked with *BSSO* and concluded that whilst the calls were unsettling, the threats could not be treated as authentic and there was no indication that "*Kommando Francis Hughes*" or any other German IRA groupings were real.

Further north in Mönchengladbach, Pähler's *BKA* team followed up forensic and intelligence leads, working closely with Dutch colleagues, as they quickly discovered that the Volvo had Dutch number plates and had been purchased two weeks earlier in The Hague. The *BVD* uncovered the additional earlier purchase of the Ascona, and from the seller got a description of McGeough and details of the Heaney ID he had used in the transactions. *BKA* and *CRI* officers put out an urgent call for the Ascona to be found as McGeough, Hanratty and Ryan laid low in the Netherlands. It was a long painstaking search but finally the Ascona was located. McGeough had left it parked conspicuously on a street in The Hague. After residents called the police to have the vehicle on Adelheidstraat checked out, on June 19th, after clearing the area, Dutch EOD bomb disposal technicians investigated the car. In the vehicle they found no explosives or fingerprints but recovered a receipt from a supermarket in Mönchengladbach dated January 31st.

The ASU had an additional problem with which they had to contend: as the *BKA* were searching for them across Germany and the Netherlands and collecting evidence and information, a mole was passing information to the *Ministerium für Staatssicherheit* (*MfS* or *Stasi*), the security service of the German Democratic Republic, who had become very interested in the activities of the Provisional IRA. The identity of the mole has never been ascertained but suspicion falls on two individuals: one an unnamed *BKA* employee based in Wiesbaden, the other Dr. Gabriele Leinfelder of the West German domestic intelligence agency BND, who in actual fact was Gabriele Gast, who for twenty years acted as a double-agent for the Stasi, feeding intelligence back to her East German paymasters. In her high-ranking BND role, she was party to restricted documents from the *BKA* and other agencies regarding investigations into the Provisional IRA's activities in West Germany. In January the previous year, the Stasi had become alerted to Provo operations when a vehicle belonging to an East German soldier from the *Volksarmee* was blown up by a device in Berlin, killing one and wounding another: the Stasi attributed the attack to the IRA, although it is unknown on what basis this assessment was carried out. From then on it kept tabs on the Provisionals in a secret *Feindobjektakte* ("hostile target file") numbered XV5414/85. A 20 page Stasi document on the IRA, dated October 20th 1986, detailed a great deal about the Provos and their activities in Europe to date: included in the document was information on the Ferlach arms deal a few weeks before as well as a list of the weapons, complete with serial numbers, that had been recovered in January at the Buitenveldert apartment. The list had been supplied by a Stasi agent within the German Embassy in The Hague.

It was not to be long before the Stasi would have their first direct contact with the Provos. A matter of days after the writing of the report, an Irish man was temporarily detained and questioned at Berlin's Schönefeld airport, after being discovered carrying a huge amount of audio tapes, around 100 watches, Arabic typewriters and a range of blank false Iraqi and Lebanese passports, as well as two Irish passports in his own name but with two different serial numbers. Intelligence had discovered that the serial number of one of the Irish passports was in the J620701 to J620800 range of blank passports stolen by the Provisional IRA from the Department of Foreign Affairs in Dublin. The Stasi files do not reveal the identity of the arrested IRA member but do reveal that he flew to Berlin via Vienna and originated in Beirut; amongst the likely candidates is Denis Donaldson, the IRA man and later Sinn Fein politician who had been arrested with "Blue" Kelly at Orly Airport five years earlier on the way back from a Hezbollah training camp in the Lebanon, and who would later be revealed as one of the most high-ranking informers embedded within the IRA on behalf of the British security services. Also possible candidates are the few senior IRA men involved in Middle Eastern trips to conduct arms negotiations with Libyan leader Gaddafi a few years before - Joe Cahill, Mickey McKevitt and Patrick Ryan. The recovery of such material, in particular "watches" - not exactly defined in Stasi records but possibly some piece of timekeeping equipment other than wristwatches - lends weight to a theory that the man apprehended at Schönefeld was IRA quartermaster Ryan, one of the men responsible for the IRA's supply lines of bomb components in Europe and beyond. Interest in the IRA intensified after the JHQ bomb and the *BKA* mole provided the Stasi with regular reports detailing investigations into the Rheindahlen attack. Also leaked to the East Germans via the mole in the *BKA* was intelligence of possible impending attacks: on April 8th 1987, the information was communicated via the *BKA* to *MI5* and the authorities in Luxemburg about the strange warning call to Angela Terzani in Tokyo that the Provisional IRA were planning to carry out an attack on the British Embassy in Luxemburg on April 19th. Colonel Kempe from the Stasi's HA-X (International Relations) department used the information gleaned from the MfS source with access to *Bundeskriminalamt* reports to alert colleagues around the Eastern Bloc. The source of the information about the potential attack in Luxemburg would remain undisclosed and the planned attack was cancelled, but now not only were the authorities in West Germany watching every move, but also those in East Germany as well.

Unaware that the intelligence services of several countries were on the trail of the Active Service Unit, Gerry McGeough returned to Sweden. Mairéad and Niall Farrell had already returned to Northern Ireland before the Rheindahlen attack, where the IRA suffered their most serious blow in the history of the troubles. Early in May, the cutting edge of one of the staunchest and most effective PIRA brigades - East Tyrone - was almost completely wiped out in an ambush in the village of Loughgall, in the neighbouring County Armagh. A team of at least ten Provisional IRA men were involved in the planning of a plot to blow up the RUC station in the village – intelligence from a variety of sources alerted authorities to the plan and the house and telephone of IRA volunteer Colette O'Neill was bugged by RUC Special Branch. Via the bugging devices the intelligence services received the decisive information of when, where and how the attack was going to take place. The plan was to drive a bomb into the RUC station in the small Armagh village of Loughgall near Portadown to kill the RUC policemen as they were leaving for the evening. Accusations persist that the RUC were tipped off to the plan of the East Tyrone Brigade in the first place by high-ranking internal IRA sources; allegedly East Tyrone – under the leadership of Jim Lynagh – was unhappy with the direction the campaign was taking, and friction with the leadership led to the Brigade threatening to break away from the IRA altogether.

On May 8th 1987, two unidentified IRA volunteers drove in separate cars from Portadown into the village, passing by the RUC station. The intention was to wait some distance away from the station in order to take the rest of the IRA unit to a safe house once the attack had been carried out. One of the volunteers elaborates:

> "We were to sit there until the boys came back around again, until the bomb went off and they had shot (the station) up. The point of the operation was to get in before the RUC officers left, to take them out."

Other members of the IRA team stole both a mechanical digger from a farm just outside Dungannon as well as a blue Toyota Hi Ace van. One member of the unit, 21 year old Declan Arthurs from Galbally, was tasked with driving the digger, containing an old oil drum full of explosives in the front bucket, lighting the fuse and aiming the machine at the RUC station. The rest of the unit dressed in boiler suits and jumped into the Toyota van, parked outside the village: led by the Officer Commanding of the East Tyrone Brigade, Patrick Kelly, the team comprised some of the most senior, experienced and well-connected PIRA men in Northern Ireland: Padraig McKearney, Jim Lynagh, Gerry O'Callaghan and Eugene Kelly. Arthurs drove the digger and bomb into Loughgall. As they rode into the village, Arthurs spotted a local RUC police car and got cold feet; he drove through the village to where it was planned that the team would later be picked-up, in order to discuss with the other two volunteers how to proceed. After a few minutes discussion, one of the volunteers drove Arthurs back to meet up with the team in the Toyota. They talked to Kelly, who ordered them to proceed with the attack and sent them back into the village. The volunteer drove back into the village from the pick-up point to find Arthurs sitting outside the RUC station monitoring activity. It was decided that there was no time to lose; the two unidentified volunteers and Arthurs returned to the pickup point; Arthurs returned to the digger and drove back into the village. After sweeping past the RUC station one final time, Arthurs was joined by young volunteers Tony Gormley and Seamus Donnelly and the digger crew were joined by the team in the Toyota van. Arthurs aimed the digger at the heavy security doors of the station, produced a lighter and lit the 40-second fuse in the bucket. Putting the digger into first gear and letting it drive towards the station, the team jumped off the digger. At the same time the Toyota van followed the digger at a distance, before coming to a halt. The volunteers in the van jumped out; heavily armed with automatic weapons and pistols, they began to spray the front of the station with gunfire as the bomb detonated, blowing away a huge chunk of the façade. At the same time, the SAS team lying in wait opened fire: from at least three positions formulating a triangulated "kill-zone" that had been designed to kill everyone but reduce the chance of friendly-fire injuries. In a hail of gunfire, the entire IRA unit was massacred; the team from the van, including Donnelly and Gormley, as well as Arthurs who had attempted to escape down an alleyway but was hit by gunfire. Eight members of the unit lay dead on the road outside the smoking ruins of Loughgall RUC station; in a vehicle on the road outside lay the dead body of civilian Anthony Hughes next to his seriously wounded brother Oliver. Both were wearing blue boiler suits and had inadvertently and tragically driven past the station just as the SAS attack started. SAS soldiers assumed they were part of the IRA unit and riddled their vehicle with gunfire.

As the ambush played out, the two other volunteers were waiting nervously back at the pickup point. One describes what happened:

> *"We were at the pickup point and then there was a rip as the bomb went up. There was the rattle of stuff*

> *(gunshots) and then there was the rattle of heavy stuff (British Army GPMG machine guns). I turned to [the other volunteer] and said "they're giving her some rattle here". It went on and on and on, for what seemed like three or four minutes, it was fierce. Then out in the distance I saw a helicopter and I turned to [the other volunteer] and said "there's something badly wrong here". At this stage we were waiting on them (the rest of the team) to come down and get away."*

After no one turned up at the pickup point, the pair drove back into the village in separate cars and had just arrived at the scene when two SAS men jumped out and pointed their weapons at the two scouts. The volunteer continues:

> *"I sat frozen. At that stage there was still the odd, isolated shot. I could see the carnage down at the van...the boys (SAS men) who were with us were in control, but the boys around the van were in a frenzy, dancing...it was a shock to know everyone was away (dead)"*

He said that within minutes regular British Army soldiers jumped out of the helicopter he had seen earlier and made their way to where he was sitting in his vehicle.

> *"The SAS boys then just disappeared. We sat there frozen. There was an auld pair in the car behind and at this stage, there was five or six Brits around. I swore I was going to be dragged out."*

Instead, the soldiers told the two volunteers and the elderly couple to turn their cars around and vacate the area. Still fearing that the soldiers would open fire on him, the one volunteer drove away slowly in the opposite direction to the other, and turned off onto a country lane. There he briefly met another IRA volunteer Liam Ryan, who had been waiting and had maintained radio contact with the team in the Toyota until the shooting started. He explained the situation to Ryan and drove off, but only a few metres later ran into an RUC vehicle checkpoint; He was stopped and taken out of the car and questioned. Giving RUC officers false ID, he nervously waited to be arrested. He was surprised when five minutes later, checks completed, an RUC officer told him he could go on his way. The volunteer, like his partner and Ryan had miraculously escaped the massacre of the Provisional IRA East Tyrone Brigade; the IRA's single biggest loss of life in one incident in the whole of the conflict.

Four days after Loughgall, in an attempt to cash in on strong opinion polls, British Prime Minister Margaret Thatcher called the 1987 General Election, one year earlier than legally obliged. In Belfast, Mairéad Farrell took a break from PIRA operations and threw herself into Sinn Fein work and spent May and June working tirelessly to deliver leaflets and posters, as well as talking to Republican-leaning voters to try and persuade them to support local Sinn Fein candidates, instead of the more liberal SDLP. In the face of rising nationalist opposition, a new alliance between DUP, UUP and UPUP was formed and coupled with a strong showing from SDLP, Sinn Fein lost ground compared to their performance in the previous 1983 General Election. In Farrell's local constituency of West Belfast, Gerry Adams retained his (and Sinn Fein's only) seat in Westminster, although as in 1983, abstained from actually taking up his place in the House of Commons. Sinn Fein's (and the Provisional IRA's) Director of Publicity Danny Morrison had six years earlier made a famous speech about the Republican strategy of taking power in Ireland with a "ballot paper in one hand, an Armalite in the other"; Farrell's disappointment at the number of ballot papers with a cross next to Sinn Fein in her left hand hardened her resolve to concentrate of using the Armalite in her right.

Farrell re-joined her colleagues in the Belfast Brigade to find many familiar faces: Brendan "Ruby" Davison, Dan McCann, Sean Savage,

Siobhán O'Hanlon, Peter "Pepe" Rooney and Kevin Brady. O'Hanlon had been released from Armagh prison in February after serving her four year sentence and had gone straight back to active service. Peter Rooney, known as "Pepe ", was born in 1955 and brought up in Andersonstown, becoming an active member of the Belfast Brigade. His brother Daniel was shot dead in 1972 in dubious circumstances by the M.R.F., a controversial and shadowy unit of the British Army tasked with tracking down and eliminating known IRA volunteers, often trying to cover their tracks by making the murders look like Loyalist attacks. Rooney served a prison sentence for IRA activities, after forming part of the colour guard that fired the traditional three-volley-salute over the coffin of hunger striker Joe McDonnell as he was buried in the plot next to Bobby Sands in July 1981. He was arrested shortly afterwards, convicted and sentenced to imprisonment. On his release from HMP Maze, he had returned to active service for the IRA and had become a regular visitor to the Continent, bringing money and false passports to various members of the ASU.

Brendan "Ruby" Davison was OC of the Markets area and one of the most experienced men in the team. Sean Savage was young but had already proved himself on active service. Savage had been born into a Republican family and grew up in the Kashmir Road area of Belfast, not far from Clonard and, according to security service reports, was a quiet loner-type. Growing up, Savage had been an altar boy in the Clonard Monastery and although beginning to play a role in the local IRA at an early age - acting as a lookout for British Army patrols for more experienced operatives – he devoted a lot of time to his family, helping to care for his younger brother Robert, who was physically handicapped. As Savage reached his mid-teens, he became more active in the Provisional IRA and progressed to involvement in operations: in 1981, he was part of an IRA team that had fired an RPG-7 rocket at an RUC patrol on Glen Road in Andersonstown. RUC officer Michael Patterson was injured in the blast, driver Alex Beck was killed instantly. The unit escaped to a safe house but was arrested along with three others when RUC went through West Belfast with a fine-toothed comb looking for the rocket launcher used in the attack. Savage was later cleared of the murder charges, along with two other members of the unit: Davison and McCann.

30-year-old Daniel McCann grew up a few doors away from the Savage family in West Belfast and was an experienced volunteer; whilst not shying away from explosives and firearms he was mainly utilized as an intelligence officer. McCann's IRA career had begun in 1974, joining after he was released from prison, having served a six month prison sentence for taking part in a riot. After being cleared of the murder of Alex Beck, he returned to active service, only to be re-arrested in 1979 on explosives charges. He was convicted and spent two years back in prison, before being released in 1981. He returned to active service with the IRA and was a close friend of "Pepe" Rooney; McCann was an integral part of the Belfast Brigade for five years, before he took over the running of the family butchers shop just off the Falls Road in October 1986. However, as a known IRA man who the RUC knew to have murdered one of their colleagues, he was a target for Protestant policemen with a hatred for the Provos. He was naturally also a target for Loyalists. Over the next two months, the shop was daubed with anti-IRA and anti-McCann graffiti and McCann was goaded by visiting RUC officers telling him that they were going to kill him when the first opportunity presented itself. On one occasion a wooden cross was placed in front of the shop bearing McCann's name and the legend "R.I.P." Tired of the pressure, McCann took the unusual move of asking Davison that he be allowed to step down from PIRA active service to concentrate on making a success of the family business and move out of the limelight. Figuring that if the RUC and Loyalist gunmen heard of his retirement he would be less of a target, McCann publicly left the IRA. What he hadn't bargained for was that incompetence and tangled lines would make him just as much of a target as before.

Brian Nelson, from Shankill Road - the Protestant heartland of West Belfast - had served in the British Army's Black Watch Regiment before joining the Loyalist paramilitary Ulster Defence Association (UDA) in the early 1970's as an intelligence officer. In 1974, he was jailed for seven years for his part in the kidnap and torture of a Catholic, Gerald Higgins, and served three years of his sentence before release. In a similar attempt to McCann to make a fresh start, he left the UDA on leaving prison and after a brief stint as a construction worker in West Germany, he was recruited by the British Army and encouraged to re-seek UDA membership. His task was to infiltrate the organisation with the intent of passing information on Loyalist paramilitary activities back to the British government. Unbeknown to British intelligence, the flow of information went in both directions: intelligence on IRA activities collected by RUC Special Branch ended up in Nelson's hands and thus the UDA had access to information on their sworn enemy. Nelson passed this information to senior Loyalist paramilitary commanders, who used it to carry out the assassination of PIRA volunteers. It was such a piece of information that Nelson passed to the UDA's sister organisation the Ulster Freedom Fighters (UFF) regarding McCann's IRA activities, who decided to target McCann for assassination. The only problem was that the intelligence with which Nelson supplied the UFF had been compiled mid-1986 and therefore there was no mention that McCann had in fact left the IRA. Two UFF gunmen stormed the McCann family home on Cavendish Street with the intent of killing Daniel. One held McCann's mother whilst the other searched the house but McCann was not at home; the gunmen fired shots into the air in frustration and left empty handed and thirsting for blood. McCann realised that he would never be able to eliminate his IRA links in the eyes of others and was faced with a choice: fight or flight. He chose to fight and in April 1987 re-joined the IRA.

The Belfast Brigade which included Farrell, Savage, McCann, Davison, Brady, Rooney and O'Hanlon became prolifically deadly and at war with Loyalist paramilitaries in a tit-for-tat conflict: within the space of the four months from June to September they claimed several victims, often responding to Catholic deaths at the hands of Loyalist gunmen. They shot dead a British army soldier, Private Joseph Leach of the Queens Lancashire Regiment, on the Shaw's Road in Andersonstown on June 4th; Nathaniel Cush, an ex-UDR soldier was killed when a car bomb exploded under his car outside his workplace on Tomb Street on June 15th; RUC man Robert Guthrie was shot dead outside his RUC base a week later; Workers Party activist and alleged informer Thomas Wilson was shot dead just off the Falls Road the next day; Protestant John Tracey of the UDR was shot dead whilst renovating a house on Surrey Street on June 26th; two weeks later, UDA Loyalist William Reynolds was assassinated whilst playing pool with friends in a pool hall on Ligoniel Road; on July 12th civilian Alan McQuiston was killed during street disturbances in the Ardoyne area of the city. One of the most brutal attacks happened on August 26th, when the West Belfast hit squad around Savage, McCann and Farrell murdered Ernest Carson and Michael Malone, two undercover RUC detectives in the Liverpool Bar on Donegal Quay near Belfast Docks – cutting them down with automatic gunfire as they were drinking. Every time the IRA claimed another victim, Loyalist UDA / UFF paramilitaries killed a random Catholic in reprisal attacks and the vicious spiral continued into September: civilian Harry Sloan was shot dead by the IRA outside his home on Alliance Parade on September 7th; ten days later off-duty UDR soldier Steven Megrath was killed whilst visiting a relative on Hallidays Road in the Tiger's Bay district. Despite the carnage, eleven IRA victims killed by the same team in as many weeks garnered few column inches in the mainland British newspapers; the leadership of the Provisional IRA decided that they needed bigger headlines. Despite the risk of many of the team being known to the British security forces as active IRA volunteers ("players"), decided that, rather than using operatives who had not yet come onto the British radar ("clean-skins") the prolific Belfast Brigade were just the right team to make those headlines.

Back in Europe, German and Dutch investigators continued to look for the ASU. In the search for McGeough and Hanratty, a decisive piece of information came from Brussels. On September 21st, Belgian *Rijkswacht* police investigated reports of a suspicious vehicle in a car park in the city, which was sporting Dutch registration plates and had been sat there for some time. In the boot of the Mazda 626 were two sets of registration plates; one set were German, registered in Mainz with the number MA-XX858, and Dutch number plates bearing the registration 38-UH-51. Investigators now were able to link the Ascona to the Volvo, and both vehicles to "M. Heaney" and to the Rheindahlen bomb attack. They now had a clear description of one of the Provisional IRA team and the trail was getting warm.

Shortly afterwards in Belfast, the ears of the British security services pricked up on hearing of the Overseas Department's plans for certain members of the Belfast Brigade. Estate agent Joe Fenton was one of the men who helped provide the IRA with safe houses to help volunteers escape detection by the RUC and Army, interrogate suspected informers and hold secret planning meetings. One of Fenton's houses was used as a venue by senior IRA commanders to discuss the plan to create bigger headlines: Gibraltar, one of the last remaining outposts of the British Empire, was discussed as a possible target for an IRA attack. The British enclave housed a small British military presence, relaxed security and a quick escape route back over the border at La Linea to Spain. An incisive operation using some of the Belfast Brigade would create huge headlines and after the JHQ bomb, restart the IRA offensive on the Continent with a bang. Unbeknown to the men discussing Gibraltar, Fenton was not helping the IRA but was working as an informer for RUC Special Branch; the safe houses he offered the IRA to use were bugged. The details of the planning meeting were relayed by Special Branch to *MI5*, In turn, *MI5* alerted the Spanish Ministry for the Interior that an

IRA unit could be trying to operate on Spanish soil and give them a list of names, descriptions and possible aliases. Spanish security force agreed to track the movements of any IRA suspects arriving in Spain and keep the British informed of their movements. A covert surveillance operation was initiated by *MI5*: codenamed Operation FLAVIUS.

On November 5th, using false passports and under the guise of tourists, Sean Savage (using the alias "Brendan Coyne"), Daniel McCann ("Robert Wilfred Reilly") and Siobhán O'Hanlon ("Mary Parkin") travelled from Belfast via Madrid and Malaga to Torremolinos on the Spanish Costa del Sol. Whilst sifting through hotel records, Spanish intelligence flagged up the arrival of the team and informed British authorities. With agreement from the British side, Spanish police bugged the hotel room and eavesdropped on the IRA team's conversations. They realised that a bomb attack was being planned but were unsure where this would take place. Trailing the team firstly to Valencia and then on to La Linea, intelligence operatives watched as the trio had their passports stamped and crossed the border into Gibraltar. There they took in the sights, saw the monkeys who inhabit the southernmost European outpost of the former British Empire; and took copious notes of British military movements in the territory. Particular attention was paid to the changing of the guard at "The Convent", the residence of the British governor of Gibraltar since 1711. The regular ceremony involved members of the First Battalion of the Royal Anglian Regiment parading down Main Street, Gibraltar's main commercial and shopping district.

After consultation between Spanish authorities and London, the trio were not arrested but instead allowed to fly back to Dublin on November 15th. The intelligence services surmised that the likely intended target would be the changing of the guard ceremony at "The Convent" and on November 25th *MI5* sent a telex to Gibraltar authorities advising them of a potential IRA attack. The incumbent

British Home Secretary Douglas Hurd was also informed. On December 9th, Hurd took part in a meeting in Copenhagen with the Trevi Group, an intergovernmental workgroup set up in 1976 by twelve European Community states to coordinate counter-terrorism and policing measures in the EC; also taking part were a whole host of interior ministers from other EEC countries, whom he informed that the IRA were possibly preparing to attack British institutions in mainland Europe. He had good reason to warn his European counterparts; for unbeknown to many, the planned IRA attack in Gibraltar had already been thwarted the day before the Copenhagen meeting. The initial IRA plan had been to bomb the changing of the guard ceremony on December 8th, only three weeks after the reconnaissance team had returned home. The security services had just put a defence plan in place when they registered the arrival of a different IRA team in the area on December 6th; allegedly amongst them, IRA volunteer Eibhlin Glenholmes.

Codenamed "Miss F" by police during the surveillance operation, a female IRA volunteer checked into the Holiday Inn hotel in Gibraltar on December 6th 1987 – *MI5* watched her intently. When the following day Gerry Hanratty and Gerry McGeough also arrived in Gibraltar, the Security Service realised that the planned attack was imminent. In a hurry, the British authorities ordered the cancellation of the Changing of the Guard ceremony at the last minute, under the pretext of the guardroom needing to be repainted. Roadworks were spontaneously erected in the surrounding streets. Foiled, the IRA bombing team fled from Gibraltar before they could be arrested – it is likely that the explosives were transported back to Valencia to be hidden by Hanratty and McGeough, who then scurried back to the safety of the Netherlands. The IRA put the Gibraltar plan on the backburner. *MI5* however, continued to prepare for a potential attack and sent senior officials F5/0 (the head of counter-terrorism) and A4/0 (the head of the surveillance unit) to Gibraltar to discuss the potential deployment of a surveillance team on the Rock to monitor further IRA activity.

Whilst McCann, Savage and O'Hanlon had been on reconnaissance duties in Gibraltar, Provisional IRA comrades back home had committed an atrocity in the town of Enniskillen in County Fermanagh that would later have ramifications not only for the Gibraltar operations, but for the IRA in general: it was one of a few major turning points in the Troubles in terms of public opinion. Two separate units of PIRA volunteers from north and south of the border, moving in relay transported an 18kg bomb from Country Leitrim to Enniskillen, where on the night of November 7th, it was planted in the St. Michael Reading Rooms. Hidden in a sports holdall, the bomb rested against the inside wall of a room facing the square containing the town's war memorial, where the next day, Remembrance Sunday, hundreds of people were to gather to commemorate those from Enniskillen who had perished in the World Wars. Security was tight, yet incredibly the Reading Rooms were allegedly not checked, as security services assumed them to be secure. Questions remains today as to whether a member of the security services, under orders or acting alone, sought to discredit the IRA and help lose them support across Ireland, by deliberately allowing the bomb to be left undiscovered and explode discriminately. Whatever the case, one of Patrick Ryan's Memopark timers had been attached to the bomb and set to detonate at 10:43 on November 8th, just as the ceremony was about to get underway in the packed square. As many people stood in front of the Reading Rooms to watch the local UDR regiment march into the square, the bomb exploded and blew out the wall of the building. Chunks of masonry were catapulted with extreme force across the square, hitting many people fatally: eleven innocent civilians were killed in the blast but not a single intended target of the bomb: the UDR soldiers. A thirteenth victim went into a coma and died some thirteen years after the blast, having never regained consciousness. Over sixty people were injured, some of them children and all of them Protestants. The mistake cost the IRA dearly as support waned dramatically and IRA leaders were forced to take the unprecedented step of publicly apologising for the blast - the two units involved were subsequently disbanded.

Back on mainland Europe, the frustrated Hanratty and McGeough, with the help of Patrick Ryan turned their attention from the abandoned Gibraltar operation to a different plan. The IRA had learned that the British Foreign Secretary, Sir Geoffrey Howe, travelled regularly to Brussels for meetings and, crucially, there was a regular pattern to his movements. He was driven to his destination by the same route each time. A plan was devised to assassinate him by means of a remote-controlled bomb placed in a car parked at the side of the street. When Howe's car passed, the bomb would be detonated and one of Mrs. Thatcher's most senior ministers blown to pieces. The IRA leadership approved the operation, and the bomb was constructed using a red, Dutch-registered Renault 4. 110 kilogrammes of Semtex were rigged up to CIL detonators, which in turn were wired up to a Memopark timer and a radio unit that would be used to detonate the bomb remotely. The IRA team based in the Netherlands travelled to Brussels, but Howe's car, for the first time in months, failed to turn up. The IRA concluded that British intelligence had discovered the plan and changed Howe's itinerary. The bomb was deactivated and the vehicle hidden in a lock-up garage in Brussels in case they might be able to use it again. Again, Hanratty and McGeough fled back to the safety of the Netherlands.

Meanwhile back in Northern Ireland, Mairéad Farrell - in the middle of her first term of studies at Queens University - got engaged. Her fiancée Seamus Finucane was part of a staunchly Republican family and was an experienced IRA volunteer who had been arrested in 1977 together with hunger striker Bobby Sands and imprisoned for possession of illegal weapons. McCann and Savage were tasked by the IRA to eliminate a high-profile Loyalist paramilitary leader, "Big John". John McMichael was a charismatic and respected UDA commander from Lisburn, who at one time had ran the UDA South Belfast Brigade and been part of the team who attempted to kill Republican activist Bernadette McAliskey in Coalisland in 1981, an extremely high-profile target for Loyalist paramilitaries. She survived the attack and although three members of his team – Ray Smallwoods, Tom Graham and Andrew Watson – were later convicted for their part in the attempted murder, McMichael was later inexplicably cleared of all charges relating to the McAliskey attack. After being impressed by his Catholic counterpart Morrison's strategy of the ballot box and the Armalite, McMichael also attempted a foray into the political arena, standing as a candidate for the newly formed political wing of the UDA, the ULDP. He only gathered a little over 500 votes in the by-election and the disaster forced him back to expending his energies on less legal methods of trying to force change in Northern Ireland. He was respected by his mortal enemies in the IRA but also singled out as a top-level target whose assassination would be a huge blow to Loyalist paramilitaries. Controversially, he may also have been a target for the UDA as a non-conformer within their ranks, and it has been suggested that a prominent UDA member - later shot dead as an informer – may have passed information to the IRA that McMichael was to be at home on a particular day. McMichael was aware that he was a target and rarely visited his house in Hilden Court, Lisburn. But just before Christmas, he was due to return to Lisburn to take his wife to a medical appointment and then deliver turkeys to the families of local Loyalist paramilitary prisoners.

On December 22nd, members of the Belfast Brigade led by Séan Savage were sent to Lisburn. The team attached a bomb to the underside of McMichael's car parked outside his house in Hilden Court. Inside the house at the time were McMichael, his wife Shirley and his two-year-old son. At 8.20 p.m. John McMichael left the house and went to his vehicle. He turned on the ignition of his car and slowly reversed down the driveway; the mercury-tilt switch in the detonating mechanism of the five pound booby-trap bomb was activated and the device exploded. McMichael lost both legs in the blast and suffered grave internal injuries, although he retained consciousness. He was rushed to Lagan Valley Hospital. His 18-year-old son, Gary had been attending a Stiff Little Fingers concert at Belfast's Ulster Hall the time the bomb detonated. During the performance, a note was passed to the band's lead singer, Jake Burns, who then made an announcement from the stage that Gary McMichael was to phone home. By the time Gary had got to a phone box, his father had died in the ambulance on the way to hospital.

Savage, McCann, Farrell and O'Hanlon celebrated with other members of the Belfast Brigade at a Republican Christmas party in Andersonstown. The alleged Director of Publicity for the Provisional IRA, Danny Morrison, recalled:

> "I remember being at a big Christmas social in Andersonstown in 1987. It was like an ex-prisoners' reunion. Siobhan was there, again with a number of former prisoners, and introduced me to her sister, Éilis. Mairéad Farrell was having the time of her life, up on the dance floor. Kevin Brady was there with his girlfriend."

As McMichael was buried on Boxing Day, the leadership of the IRA weighed up its options for the next move on the Continent and decided to wait for the hubbub of the foiled Gibraltar attack to die down. The IRA realised the bombing team and plan had been compromised. To make matters worse, the car bomb in the lockup was discovered. On January 21st 1988, Belgian *Rijkswacht* police hunting for a gang of criminals involved in a series of armed robberies discovered the Renault left behind by McGeough and Hanratty. This piece of information was disseminated to the *SoKo PIRA* team in Wiesbaden, as well as other police forces across Western Europe. Dutch police were tasked with determining the ownership of the car. *MI5* worked in parallel to the Dutch and traced the bomb and explosives to the Hanratty / McGeough team, although unsure where the ASU was. British security services now knew that the same team was involved in the Rheindahlen bomb and Brussels and Gibraltar plots and bargained that it was only a matter of time before the team did actually manage to see an operation through to its conclusion once more. Registering the IRA's frustration at the foiled plots and the large amount of preparation that had gone into the planning of Gibraltar, *MI5* reasoned that before long, the team would make an attempt to detonate another device in Europe.

British authorities were keen to liaise more closely with their German counterparts to try to identify areas of cooperation. Anglo-German consultations on counter-terrorism were scheduled and a week after the discovery of the Brussels car bomb, a meeting took place in Bonn on January 28th, in advance of a planned meeting of the TREVI group. The British delegation included Under Secretaries of State from the Foreign and Commonwealth Office, the head of the FCO's Security Coordination Department SCD, a representative from the Police Division of the Home Office, counter-terrorism expert Eliza Manningham-Buller from K-Branch of the Security Service (*MI5*), members of the *BSSO* and British Embassy. On the German side, representatives from the German Foreign Office Auswärtiges Amt, the Interior, Justice and Transport Ministries, as well as high ranking members of *MI5* counterparts the Bundesamt für Verfassungsschutz (BfV), the foreign intelligence agency Bundesnachrichtendienst (BND). The high level round-table covered a range of terrorist threats from state actors such as Libya, Iran, Iraq but particular focus was given to the IRA. Previous IRA attacks on German soil were discussed and the head of the SCD explained the structure and operations of the IRA, as well as outlining the roles of the various law enforcement and intelligence agencies in fighting the Provos, including revealing the role of a hitherto unknown agency – the "External Intelligence Service – Counterterrorism Forces Overseas", whose existence was to remain a closely guarded secret. Possible joint areas of cooperation were discussed and plans made to widen efforts multi-laterally, including at TREVI level, at the Council of Europe and at the United Nations. The British did not apparently reveal they were sure the IRA was about to strike the European mainland in the near future.

The confirmation that the Gibraltar plan had been reactivated and that Dan McCann was going to be involved came two weeks later. Unbeknown to many in the IRA, the information came from relatively high up within their own ranks. Brendan "Ruby" Davison, in his function as the local commander of the area of Belfast city centre around the Markets area was a high profile and prolific Republican terrorist who was earmarked for promotion within IRA structures after the intense campaign of the summer and autumn of 1987. The position of OC of all of Belfast carried not only the cachet of being the leader of the most aggressive and high profile brigades within the IRA – one of those to which all brigades, except Slab Murphy's relatively self-contained South Armagh Brigade, looked up to – but was also potentially a route to a place on the seven man PIRA General Army Council, that dictated military strategy. Traditionally whilst the Army Council was voted for by all PIRA members and could include any of its senior local commanders, its makeup generally included people in a narrow range of positions: the Chief of Staff and his Adjutant General, Quartermaster General, the OCs of both Northern and Southern Command, as well as leading GHQ staff such the Director of Finance, the Director of Operations or the Director of Engineering. Occasionally, an OC of the Belfast Brigade with a strong reputation overseeing media-effective military operations was voted onto the Army Council, replacing one of the GHQ staff; in other cases, the OC of Belfast went on to become the OC of Northern Command, who was almost guaranteed a place on the Army Council. Davison was in pole position for a role in determining the future direction of the Provisional IRA.

Davison however, despite his successes as an IRA commander, was also on the payroll of the British government. The RUC's Special Branch had recruited Davison to inform on the activities of the IRA. Special Branch's previous top-level informant within the ranks of the IRA, Robert "Beano" Lean, had compromised himself in 1983. The RUC believed the evidence he supplied on IRA activities in Belfast would be enough to bring down the Provisionals completely.

He had revealed dozens of names – including Eibhlin Glenholmes - before he was moved into the maximum security Palace Barracks, near Belfast. But his former allegiances – or IRA threats – changed his mind - he claimed his statements had been made under duress and subsequently retracted them all. "Beano" confessed to his ex-associates. The IRA immediately ordered him to leave the city and he vanished without trace. Davison took his place. Operating under two codenames – to RUC Special Branch he was SEDATIVE, to *MI5* he was ASCOT - he regularly passed information on IRA volunteers and activities back to his handlers and was in a prime position to help prevent attacks on British military personnel. It is worth noting that, during the time Davison worked as an IRA informant, very few British military personnel were killed in Belfast in comparison to other areas of Ulster; the murder of innocent Protestants, known Loyalist terrorists and indeed Catholics who had incurred the wrath of the IRA were allowed to happen, whereas planned attacks against British soldiers were - with the exception of the murder of Private Leach - invariably nipped in the bud thanks to Davison's information.

In mid-February 1988, Daniel McCann bumped into Davison by chance in the Markets and the pair stopped to chat. Davison remarked on McCann's blonde, newly dyed hair. Before parting, Davison said he would give him a call soon – McCann responded that he would be going away for a while to Spain. When Davison asked when he would be back from his holiday, McCann told Davison "this is no holiday"; he was off to the Iberian Peninsula for "recce". Soon afterwards, SEDATIVE informed his Special Branch handlers of the conversation and that McCann was heading to Spain on an IRA reconnaissance mission. Immediately, RUC Special Branch passed on the information to *MI5*; after chancing on a La Linea stamp in McCann's passport during a regular "random" check in Belfast back in December, the information was the signal they were waiting for. Now it was time to fully roll out the critical phase of Operation FLAVIUS. On February 15th *MI5* officials Director FX, F5/0 and a representative for Cabinet Office department the Joint Intelligence Committee (JIC) flew to meet the Governor of Gibraltar, Peter Terry, to discuss the situation. On their return, the details of both the Brussels and Gibraltar plots were discussed with Douglas Hurd. It was decided that should IRA operatives be arrested in Spain or in the Netherlands, they would likely only be charged with minor, non-extraditable offences; they needed to be caught-red handed in Gibraltar. A plan was made: the IRA unit would be tracked, allowed to enter British territory and then apprehended. Hurd consulted Defence Secretary George Younger and in turn, Prime Minister Margaret Thatcher for approval –Thatcher told Hurd she wanted "to give the IRA a bloody nose in Gibraltar" and approved the plan on February 18th. The same day, the full *MI5* plan was set in motion: F5/0 and the Army commander responsible for the operation flew to Gibraltar; led by "Soldier F", a 22-man strong SAS "Pagoda" team from the Special Projects counter-terrorist division was dispatched a few hours later from their base in Hereford to join them, setting up base at Gibraltar's Rock Hotel. An advisory group was formed to advise and assist the Gibraltar Commissioner of Police, Joseph Canepa, in leading the operation to catch the IRA unit red-handed. The team consisted of "Soldier F", the senior military advisor and officer in the Special Air Service or SAS, "Soldier E" (an SAS commander known to comrades as "Gonzo"), "Soldier G" (bomb disposal expert), Mr Columbo (Acting Deputy Commissioner of Police), Detective Chief Inspector Ullger, attached to Special Branch, and Security Service Officers.

Unaware that the SAS and *MI5* were now in place, at the beginning of February, the IRA made their next move. Impatient for the long awaited high profile "spectacular", the Overseas Department decided to reactivate the Gibraltar plan. Assuming that as the initial planned attack had been foiled, and the actual bombing team identified, security services would think the Provisionals had abandoned the target and plan altogether, they engaged in a game of double bluff. Not knowing that the reconnaissance team had also been identified back in November, and that *MI5* had second-guessed their every move, the IRA decided to re-use the original reconnaissance team for the live operation: Séan Savage, Dan McCann and Siobhán O'Hanlon. O'Hanlon was to return to Gibraltar to check if the ceremonial parades had been recommenced. If they had, Savage and McCann were to follow and complete unfinished business.

As Prime Minister Thatcher gave her approval to the plan to apprehend the unit in situ, Siobhán O'Hanlon - using her "Mary Parkin" passport - flew to Spain and crossed over the border at La Linea into Gibraltar. As she did so, she was photographed reading a poster advertising the resumption of the changing of the guard ceremony. She checked into the Holiday Inn and began her reconnaissance duties; her every move watched, mapped and photographed by Spanish and British security services. On Saturday, February 20th, O'Hanlon was seen to walk around Gibraltar all day taking copious notes and concentrating in particular on the area around The Convent, returning repeatedly. When she returned to the hotel, she phoned McCann in Belfast with "good news". O'Hanlon told McCann she was going to stay for a few more days to more closely observe the parade. On Tuesday, February 23rd, security forces observed O'Hanlon amongst the throng of tourists at The Convent and saw her studying the parade in detail. O'Hanlon was tailed by the surveillance team to a Catholic church near The Convent and was observed praying and lighting candles.

The British authorities had, a couple of weeks earlier, got wind of the possible retrieval of Semtex explosives from the IRA arms cache in Valencia. Two IRA volunteers (to this day still not formally identified but possibly Hanratty, McGeough and/or Rooney) had been spotted in the city and British intelligence surmised that the IRA was in the latter stages of planning an attack. Fairly convinced that the target was to be Gibraltar but nevertheless worried that they were being wrong-footed by the IRA - or that Gibraltar was to be part of a concerted, coordinated attack on several targets across Europe - British authorities were unsettled enough to issue a communiqué to their embassies on February 24th, warning that the IRA were likely to attack British interests on the Continent in the near future; very specifically, the use of a car bomb similar to the one in JHQ was mentioned. The information was passed on by the embassies to friendly governments across Europe and several European countries, especially Germany – the home to thousands of British troops - went on high alert.

The following week, on March 1st in Gibraltar, the threat became more concrete; O'Hanlon was observed watching the changing of the guard and making notes once again. That evening, realising that the IRA was about to amount an attack, British and Spanish security services disseminated details of O'Hanlon's "Mary Parkin" passport, photos and other information on O'Hanlon, McCann and Savage to every airport and port in Spain. However, O'Hanlon was already on the way back to Northern Ireland. For she had called Belfast to tell the IRA leadership that the ceremony was running again as planned, but also told them that she had spotted what she thought was a security service surveillance team and had fled back across the border. The Overseas Department felt that the plan was too far-gone to abandon it once more and decided to continue with the operation. O'Hanlon had identified the best place to detonate the bomb; a small street on a square next to the ancient city wall a few yards from where the parade was due to end on Tuesday March 8th. The plan was deceptively simple: a "blocking car" would be driven into Gibraltar on Sunday March 6th and parked in the optimum position, being left there overnight. The following evening, the car containing the bomb would be driven into Gibraltar; the "blocking car" would be replaced by the bomb vehicle and the timing devices set to detonate the bomb as the parade ended around 11am the following morning. After leaving the bomb car in place, the IRA team would escape back over the border and would be mingling with the tourist crowds on the Costa del Sol as the bomb exploded on Tuesday morning March 8th 1988. The only difference to the plan was now that O'Hanlon would be replaced with another Belfast Brigade operative: the Overseas Department called Mairéad Farrell.

3 BUTTON JOB

On Wednesday March 2nd 1988, Mairéad Farrell headed off to university but returned a short time later, telling her parents she was off on a three-week break. Under the pretence of going away down to Dublin to visit school friends, she packed an overnight bag. Her mother asked her if she should expect her to be back by the weekend in time for Sunday lunch; Mairéad said she hoped so but not to save her any lunch if she did not make it back in time. The same morning, Séan Savage took a short flight from Dublin to Belfast and from there on to Barcelona. However, despite border police having his photograph and details of his false "Brendan Coyne" passport, he managed to enter the country unnoticed. He stayed overnight in Barcelona. Meanwhile, Daniel McCann – using a passport in the name of "Edward McArdle" and hair newly dyed - flew from Belfast to Paris and stayed in the French capital overnight.

On the morning of Thursday, March 3rd 1988, Farrell left home in Belfast, carrying her overnight bag and a large leather handbag; she drove straight to the airport and flew from Dublin to Brussels, staying overnight. Her colleagues were also on the move: Savage returned to Barcelona airport and flew on to Malaga, whilst McCann flew from Paris to Malaga. The pair met in the arrivals hall of Malaga airport and took a taxi to Fuengirola - some thirty kilometres away - where they were observed arriving at the Hotel Florida. The Spanish surveillance team unfortunately lost them at this point; they possibly assumed the two had checked in at the hotel, but instead the pair slipped out of the hotel into a waiting car parked outside the hotel. McCann and Savage drove back up the coast towards Malaga before stopping in Torremolinos where - via ETA contacts – a three-bed room had been booked at the Hotel Residencia Escandinavia. There they checked in at around midnight.

The next morning – Friday March 4th - Farrell took an early flight from Brussels to Madrid and then on to Malaga, travelling on a passport in the name of "Katharine Smith"; thus she slipped into Spain undetected, as the authorities were on the lookout for "Mary Parkin". However, security services at Dublin airport had noticed Farrell boarding a plane to Brussels the previous day and contacted Interpol in Vienna, who in turn passed on the information to Belgian police. Officers at Brussels Airport identified her and reported back to Interpol that she was boarding a flight to Spain. The information was passed back to the British security services and at noon, police in Malaga received an urgent message from London with a description of Farrell and details of her "Katharine Smith" passport. As Farrell arrived in Malaga around midday, she was spotted being picked up by McCann and Savage at the airport and together they drove to Hotel Residencia Escandinavia, where they spent the night.

Meanwhile in Gibraltar, the counter-terrorism team was briefed on the situation and issued with the official Rules of Engagement (RoE); guidelines drawn up according to the individual situation and handed out to every SAS unit before an operation. The RoE made several stipulations: the team was not to use force unless specifically requested to do so by senior police officers designated by the Commissioner or only in the event that immediate use of force was necessary to prevent loss of life. Furthermore, it was made clear that use of firearms was permitted when a verbal warning had been communicated and ignored by the target. Finally, the key rule to cover a worst-case scenario was stated:

> *"You and your men may fire without warning, if the giving of a warning or any delay in firing could lead to death or injury to you or them or any other person, or if the giving of a warning is clearly impractical."*

Early on Saturday morning in Gibraltar, a plan for evacuation of the area around The Convent was drawn up by Chief Inspector Lopez and the official order to engage was signed by the Commissioner. At the same time in Torremolinos, McCann and Farrell rented a white Renault 5 from the local Avis Car Rental franchise, and drove to Marbella, where they parked it in an underground car park beneath the Edificio Marbeland shopping centre. Savage – using a different fake passport in the name of "John Oakes" - rented a red Ford Fiesta with the registration MA-9317AF from a different car-hire company in Torremolinos. Savage drove to Marbella to pick up McCann and Farrell and together they drove nearly 650 kilometres along the coast to Valencia. There, they recovered some 64 kilogrammes of the Semtex plastic explosives that had been stored there after the previous attempt to carry out the attack. The Gibraltar ASU also recovered 2 kilogrammes of 7.62mm AK-47 ammunition for use as lethal shrapnel, four Canadian CIL detonators and two Memopark timers. McCann, Farrell and Savage drove back to Marbella, arriving late in the evening, parked their red Fiesta next to the white Renault 5 in the deserted car park and set about transferring the Semtex, ammunition, timers and detonators from one car to the other, stashing the explosives in the spare wheel compartment. The transfer complete, the team jumped back in the red Fiesta, leaving the white Renault 5 with its deadly cargo in the car park in Marbella, and drove back to their hotel.

As they arrived back at the Hotel Residencia Escandinavia in Torremolinos around midnight, in a joint operations room set up in Gibraltar, the Commissioner held a briefing, which was attended by officers from a variety of security services. These included seven members of the surveillance team, SAS personnel including Soldiers A, B, C, D, E ("Gonzo"), F and G as well as members of the Gibraltar police. The Commissioner briefed the separate teams on the intelligence situation, surveillance tasks, RoE, the collection of evidence in preparation for a trial after capture, as well as firearms procedures, should these become necessary. However, despite having second-guessed every move the IRA made up to this point, authorities had got one crucial element wrong; a miscalculation that would dramatically divert the course of events. The authorities surmised that Savage, McCann and Farrell formed the bombing team but reasoned that they would not use a "blocking car", as this would mean two trips across the border, increasing the possibility of detection. It was expected that the bombing team would enter Gibraltar with the bomb and park the car containing the explosives in the appropriate place. As to the mode of detonation, there were three possible options: either a car bomb would be attached to a command wire so that the terrorists could detonate the bomb from some distance away via a control unit; the second option was to use one of Ryan's Memopark timers so that the unit could flee across the border before the bomb detonated at a set time. Both of these options were discounted; it would be impractical to lay a command wire that could be discovered at any time during security checks; after Enniskillen, the authorities believed there had been a directive from the IRA leadership not to use timer bombs; in the event of the parade being called off at short notice due to rain or due to security concerns as in December, a timer bomb would detonate indiscriminately, killing scores of innocent civilians and possibly damaging the reputation of the IRA so badly that it would finish the conflict. Thus the authorities felt that the third – and only possible mode of detonation - would be via RCIED (Radio-controlled improvised explosive device) a small radio-controlled unit carried on the person that could detonate the bomb at the press of a button. Intelligence had revealed that radio operators in Gibraltar had picked up an unidentified, powerful radio pulse on a military frequency in early November 1987 – corresponding to the reconnaissance trip to the Rock by Savage, McCann and O'Hanlon – which had set alarm bells ringing. The teams present concurred that the device would be a "button job".

***

As the sun rose over the Rock of Gibraltar early on Sunday morning, March 6th, the joint operations room reopened in readiness for the impending operation. The Commissioner was on duty there from 10.30 to 12.30 hours. When he left, Deputy Commissioner Colombo took his place. Members of the surveillance teams were on duty in the streets of Gibraltar, as were Soldiers A, B, C and D and members of the police force involved in the operation. Soldiers A, B, C and D were in civilian clothing and were each armed with a 9mm Browning pistol which was carried in the rear waistband of their trousers. Each also carried a concealed radio. They were working in pairs. In each pair, one was in radio communication via the surveillance net – the radio network used for tracking the suspects – the other via the tactical net used to coordinate the interception of the IRA team. Three police officers were on duty to support the soldiers in any arrest, in plain clothes and also armed.

At 8.00 hours, Detective Constable Huart went to the frontier to keep observation for the three suspects from the computer room at the Spanish immigration post. He was aware of the real names of the three suspects and had been shown photographs. The Spanish officers had photographs. The computer room was at some distance from the frontier crossing point itself. The Spanish officers at the immigration post showed him passports by means of a visual aid unit. It appears that they only showed him the passports of those cars containing two men and one woman. Several pictures were flashed up for him during the course of the day but he did not recognise them, despite knowing the aliases of all three, as did the Spanish officers. On the Gibraltar side of the border, the customs officers and police normally on duty were not informed or involved in the surveillance on the basis that this would involve information being provided to an excessive number of people. No steps were taken to slow down the line of cars as they entered or to scrutinise all passports since it was felt that this might put the suspects on guard. There was, however, a separate surveillance team at the border and, in the area of the airfield nearby, an arrest group. A witness who led a surveillance team at the frontier later expressed disappointment at the apparent lack of co-operation between the various groups involved in Gibraltar but he understood that matters were arranged that way as a matter of security.

Chief Inspector Ullger was later to say, when pressed about the failure to take more scrupulous measures on the Gibraltar side, that

> "in this particular case, we are talking about dangerous terrorists. We were talking about a very, very major and delicate operation - an operation that had to succeed. I think the only way it could have succeeded is to allow the terrorists to come in and for the terrorists to have been dealt with in the way they were dealt with as far as the surveillance is concerned."

While Soldiers E and F made reference to the preferred military option as being to intercept and arrest the suspects in the frontier area, it appears not to have been pursued with any conviction, on the assumption that identification would not be possible in light of the brief time available for identification to be made (ten to fifteen seconds per car) and the lack of prior warning from the Spanish side.

The military option had been refined down to the preferred option of arresting the suspects when they were on foot in the assembly area, to disarm them and then to defuse the bomb. Four key indicators had been formulated by the Advisory Group with a view to guiding the Commissioner:

1. if a car was driven into Gibraltar and parked in the assembly area by an identified member of the active service unit;

2. if a car was driven into the assembly area by an ASU member without prior warning;

3. the presence in Gibraltar of the other members of the ASU;

4. if there was clear indication that terrorists having parked their car

bomb intended to leave Gibraltar, that is to say, they were heading for the border.

The plan was for an arrest to be carried out once all the members of the ASU were present and identified and they had parked a car that they intended to leave. Any earlier action was considered premature as likely to raise suspicion in any members of the ASU not yet apprehended, with possible risk resulting and as leaving no evidence for the police to use in court.

***

Back across the border in Torremolinos, the IRA unit rose early and drove back to Marbella, where Farrell got out. Savage and McCann returned to the hotel at 9am, and went for breakfast at a local bar; about an hour later, they returned to the Hotel Residencia Escandinavia, extended their hotel stay for an extra two nights, paying at the reception desk in cash, before driving off in their rented red Ford Fiesta, also in the direction of Marbella.

After being dropped off in Marbella, Farrell headed to a local car rental company. Using her "Katharine Smith" passport, she rented a white Ford Fiesta with the registration MA-2732AJ, and drove to the Edificio Marbeland car park, parking the car shortly afterwards in a space next to the white Renault 5. Shortly afterwards, Savage and McCann drove into the underground car park in the red Ford Fiesta. Parking between the white Renault and the white Fiesta together they transferred the deadly load - 64kgs of Semtex plastic explosives, 200 rounds of ammunition, the two Memopark timers and the four detonators - from the white Renault 5 to Farrell's white Fiesta, stashing everything in the spare wheel compartment; the bomb car was now loaded, and although the team had set the timers, the bomb was not yet primed or connected. Leaving the white Fiesta with its deadly payload in Marbella, at around 11:30am Savage set off alone in the now empty white Renault – the planned "blocking car"; Farrell and McCann followed in the red Fiesta. A 45-minute drive later, both cars arrived in La Linea, the small town next to the border between Spain and Gibraltar. McCann and Farrell parked the red Fiesta in a car park near the border crossing, leaving the key to the white Fiesta parked in Marbella inside. Savage continued towards the border in the Renault; Farrell and McCann proceeded on foot also towards the border.

***

Detective Constable Viagas was on surveillance duty in a bank, which had a view over the area in which the car driven in by the terrorists was expected to be parked. At about 12.30 hours, he heard a report over the surveillance net that a car had parked in a parking space in the assembly area under observation. A member of the Security Service commented that the driver had taken time to get out and fiddled with something between the seats. DC Viagas saw the man lock the car door and walk away towards the Southport Gate. One of the Security Service officers present consulted a colleague as to possible identification but neither was sure. A field officer was requested to confirm the identity, as DC Viagas could not himself identify the man from his position. At 12.45 hours, the surveillance team watched as a white Renault car drove up and parked; after two to three minutes, Savage got out of the car and walked away.

Savage was next spotted by the team at about 14.00 hours in the area. The member of the surveillance team sent to verify his identification saw the suspect at about that time and recognised Savage without difficulty. Another member of the team also saw Savage at the rear of John Mackintosh Hall and at 14.10 hours reported positive identification over the radio to the operations room, confirming that he was also the man who had earlier parked the car in the assembly area.

The Commissioner was not however notified of the identification of Savage until he arrived in the operations room at 15.00 hours.

Colombo did not hear anything about Savage either until it was reported that he had met up with two other suspects at about 14.50 hours. Soldiers E and F later recalled however that a possible sighting of Savage was reported at about 14.30 hours. Soldier G also later recalled the later sighting at 14.50 hours as the first identification of Savage. There appears to have been a certain time lag between information on the ground either being received in the operations room or being passed on. Soldiers E and F may have been more aware than the Commissioner of events since they were monitoring closely the information coming in over the nets, which apparently was not audible to the Commissioner where he sat at a table away from the control stations.

Savage was followed for approximately an hour by Witness H who recalled that the suspect was using anti-surveillance techniques such as employing devious routes through the side streets. Witness N was also following him, for an estimated 45 minutes, and considered that he was alert and taking precautions, for example stopping round the corner at the end of alleyways to see who followed.

Witness M who was leading the surveillance at the border stated that McCann and Farrell passed the frontier at about 14.30 hours, though apparently they were initially not clearly identified. They were on foot and taking counter-surveillance measures - Farrell looking back frequently. Although they didn't know it, their progress into Gibraltar was being closely monitored.

At 14.30 hours, "Gonzo" and Soldier F received a message that there was a possible sighting of McCann and Farrell entering on foot. The Commissioner was immediately informed. At about 14.50 hours, it was reported to the operations room that the suspects McCann and Farrell had met with a second man, identified as the suspect Savage, and that the three were looking at a white Renault car in the car park in the assembly area.

The three IRA volunteers spent some considerable time staring across to where a car had been parked, as if, they were studying it to make sure it was absolutely right for the effect of the bomb. DC Viagas also witnessed the three suspects meeting in the area of the car park at around 14:55 hours. At this moment, Security Services confirmed identification of all three suspects. The possibility of carrying out arrests was considered. Mr Colombo was asked whether he would hand over control to the military for the arrest, but that he asked whether the suspects had been positively identified; he was told that there was 80% identification. Almost immediately the three suspects moved away from the car through the Southport Gate. The movement of the three suspects towards the south gave rise to some discussion within the security service team as to whether this indicated that the three suspects were on reconnaissance and might return for the car. It was for this reason that the decision was taken not to arrest at this point.

At 15.00 hours, Mr Colombo rang the Commissioner to inform him that it was more and more likely to be McCann and Farrell. When the Commissioner arrived shortly afterwards, Mr Colombo informed him that the suspects McCann and Farrell had met up with a third person thought to be Savage and that an arrest had almost been made.

The Commissioner asked for positive identification of the three suspects. Identification was confirmed by 15.25 hours when it was reported to the operations room that the three suspects had returned to the assembly area and gone past looking at the car again. The three suspects continued north and away from the car. Control was passed to the military but immediately taken back as the Commissioner requested further verification of the identities of the suspects. The confirmation of identity that the Commissioner had requested was received almost immediately.

After the three suspects' identities had been confirmed and they had moved away from the assembly area, Soldier G examined the suspect car. He conducted an examination from the exterior without touching the vehicle. He described it as a newish-looking, white Renault. He detected nothing untoward inside the car or anything visibly out of place or concealed under the seats. He noted that the aerial of the car, which was rusty, was out of place with the age of the car. He was in the area for less than two minutes. He returned to the operations room and reported to the Commissioner that he regarded the car as a "suspect car bomb"; car parked in suspicious circumstances, where there was every reason to believe that it was a car bomb. Soldier G also reported the car was relatively new, yet the aerial on the car was relatively old, which added to the suspicion. He stated that as a result they treated it as a "possible car bomb". Soldier F also referred to the aerial as rendering the car suspicious and stated that this information was passed on to all the parties on the ground. Soldier E was more categorical and stated that as far as G could tell "from a cursory visual examination, he was able to confirm our suspicion that they were dealing with a car bomb".

Soldier A believed one hundred per cent that there was a bomb in the debussing area, that the suspects had remote-control devices and were probably armed. This was what he had been told over the radio. Soldier E confirmed to Soldiers C & D that there was a device in the vicinity of Inca's Hall, which could be detonated by one of three suspects - most likely to be Savage because he had been seen "fiddling" with something in the car earlier. Soldier C had also been told of the indication of an old aerial on a new car. No one told the soldiers that there was a possibility that the three suspects might not be carrying the remote-control devices with them on the Sunday, or that possibly they had not brought a bomb in.

Soldier G was the Ammunition Technical Officer or ATO, in effect the bomb-disposal adviser. He had experience of dealing with car bombs in Northern Ireland but was neither a radio-communications expert nor an explosives expert. He had not thought of de-activating the suspect bomb by unscrewing the aerial from the car, in any case attempting to unscrew the aerial would have been potentially dangerous.

After receiving the report from Soldier G and in view of the fact that the three suspects were continuing northwards leaving the car behind, the Commissioner decided that the three suspects should be arrested on suspicion of conspiracy to murder. At 15.40 hours, he made the decision - he signed a form requesting the military to intercept and apprehend the suspects. The form - which had been provided in advance by the military - stated:

> *"I, Joseph Luis Canepa, Commissioner of Police, having considered the terrorist situation in Gibraltar and having been fully briefed on the military plan with firearms, request that you proceed with the military option which may include the use of lethal force for the preservation of life."*

After the form was signed, Soldier F walked across to the tactical net and issued instructions that the military should intervene.

"Gonzo" ascertained the positions of the soldiers by radio. Soldiers C and D had been visually monitoring the movement of the three suspects in Line Wall Road and Smith Doreen Avenue. Soldiers A and B were making their way north through Casemates Square and into the Landport tunnel. The soldiers were informed that control had passed to them to make an arrest.

The soldiers had practised arrest procedures on several occasions with the police before March 6th, 1988. According to these rehearsals, the soldiers were to approach the suspects to within a close distance, cover the suspects with their pistols and shout "Stop. Police. Hands up." or words to that effect. They would then make the suspects lie on the ground, with their arms away from their bodies until the police moved in to carry out a formal arrest. Special efforts had been made to identify a suitable place in Gibraltar for the terrorists to be held in custody following their arrest.

***

On reaching the junction of Smith Dorrien Avenue with Winston Churchill Avenue, the three suspects crossed the road and stopped on the other side talking. Officer R, observing, saw them appear to exchange newspapers. At this point, Soldiers C and D were approaching the junction from Smith Dorrien Avenue. Soldiers A and B emerging from the Landport tunnel also saw the three suspects at the junction from their position where the pathway to the tunnel joined Corral Road. As the soldiers converged on the junction, however, Savage split away from suspects McCann and Farrell turning south towards the Landport tunnel. McCann and Farrell continued north up the right-hand pavement of Winston Churchill Avenue. Savage passed Soldiers A and B, brushing against the shoulder of B. Soldier B was about to turn to effect the arrest but A told him that they should continue towards suspects McCann and Farrell, knowing that C and D were in the area and that they would arrest Savage. Soldiers C and D, aware that A and B were following suspects McCann and Farrell, crossed over from Smith Dorrien Avenue and followed Savage. Soldiers A and B continued north up Winston Churchill Avenue after McCann and Farrell, walking at a brisk pace to close the distance. McCann was walking on the right of Farrell on the inside of the pavement. He was wearing white trousers and a white shirt, without any jacket. Farrell was dressed in a skirt and jacket and was carrying a large handbag.

In front of the Shell petrol station on Winston Churchill Avenue, as Soldier A was approximately ten metres behind McCann on the inside of the pavement, the sound of a police siren made McCann look back over his left shoulder. The arrival of the police car at the scene was an unintended occurrence. After the Commissioner had handed over control to the military at 15.40 hours, he instructed Mr Colombo to ensure that there was police transport available. Mr Colombo telephoned Chief Inspector Lopez at the Central Police Station, who in turn instructed the Controller Police Constable Goodman to recall the duty police car. The Controller recorded the call at 15.41 hours. He radioed the patrol car informing the officers that they were to return immediately. He did not know where the car was at the time or what the reason for the recall was. When the senior Gibraltar police officer in the car – Inspector Louis Revagliatte - asked if it was urgent, the Controller told him it was a priority message and further instructions would be given on arrival. At the time of the message, the police car was waiting in a queue of traffic in Smith Dorrien Avenue. Revagliatte told the driver to put on siren and beacons. The car pulled out into the opposite lane to overtake the queue of traffic. They cut back into the proper lane at the lights at the junction with Winston Churchill Avenue and continued north along Winston Churchill Avenue in the outer lane.

As he turned to register the unwelcome sound of the police car, McCann appeared to look directly at "A" and the smile left his face, as if he had a realisation of who "A" was and that he was a threat. "Soldier A" drew his pistol, intending to shout a warning to stop at the same time, though in retrospect the soldier was uncertain if the words actually came out. McCann's hand moved suddenly and aggressively across the front of his body. "Soldier A" thought that he was going for the button to detonate the bomb and opened fire. He shot one round into McCann's back from a distance of two to three metres (though it may have been closer). Out of the corner of his eye, "A" saw a movement by Farrell. Farrell had been walking on the left of McCann on the side of the pavement next to the road. "A" saw her make a half turn to the right towards McCann, grabbing for her handbag, which was under her left arm. The SAS man thought that she was also going for a button and shot one round into her back. Soldier A then turned back to McCann and shot him once more in the body and twice in the head from close range, around one to two metres away. "A" was not aware of B opening fire at the same time: "Soldier B" was approaching directly behind Farrell on the roadside of the pavement. He had been watching her. When they were three to four metres away and closing, he saw in his peripheral vision that McCann turned his head to look over his shoulder. He heard what he presumed was a shout from Soldier "A", which he thought was the start of the arrest process. At almost the same instant, there was firing to his right. Simultaneously, Farrell made a sharp movement to her right, drawing the bag that she had under her left arm across her body. He could not see her hands or the bag and feared that she was going for the button. The soldier opened fire with his Browning 9mm on Farrell. He deemed that McCann was in a threatening position and was unable to see his hands and switched fire to McCann. Then he turned back to Farrell and continued firing until he was certain that she was no longer a threat, namely, her hands away from her body.

Soldiers C & D had been following Savage, who was heading towards the Landport tunnel. Savage was wearing jeans, shirt and a jacket. Soldier C was briefly held up on the other side of the road by traffic on the busy road but was catching up as D closed in on Savage. D intended to arrest by getting slightly closer, drawing his pistol and shouting "Stop! Police! Hands up!" When D was about three metres away, he felt that he needed to get closer because there were too many people about and there was a woman - an innocent pedestrian - directly in line. Before "D" could get closer however, he heard the crackle of gunfire behind him as McCann and Farrell were gunned down. At the same time, "C" shouted "Stop!" in an attempt to initiate the arrest, and at the same time drew his weapon. Savage spun round aggressively and his arm went down towards his right hand jacket pocket. Both "C" and "D" believed that Savage was going for a detonator. At that moment, a woman on a bicycle brushed past and between "Soldier D" and Savage. "D" used one hand to push the woman out of line and opened fire from about two to three metres away. The SAS man fired nine rounds at rapid rate, initially aiming into the centre of Savage's body, with the last two at his head. "Soldier C" was around five to six feet from Savage and fired six times, as Savage spiralled down, aiming at the mass of his body. One shot went into his neck and another into his head as Savage hit the pavement. Both "C" & "D" kept firing until Savage was motionless on the ground, his hands were away from his body and both soldiers were sure that Savage was no longer in a position to be able to detonate a device. Daniel McCann, Séan Savage and Mairéad Farrell - three of the most experienced Belfast Brigade volunteers - and a major part of the European strategy of the Provisional IRA lay dead in the afternoon sun on a Gibraltar street.

***

Immediately after the shootings, the soldiers put on their beige SAS berets so they would be recognised by the police. They noticed the police car, with its siren blaring, coming south from the sundial roundabout down the far side of Winston Churchill Avenue. Three police officers jumped out of the car and leapt the central barrier. Inspector Revagliatte walked round the barrier before arriving at the bodies on the floor. "Soldier A" still had his warm Browning 9mm pistol in his hand. He put his hands up in the air and shouted "Police". The two other officers placed their jackets over the bodies. Whilst doing so, one of the officers dropped his gun and had to replace it in his holster. The other officer and Inspector Revagliatte carried out a search of the bodies. In Farrell's handbag, the officers found a keyring with two keys, and a tag marked with the registration MA-9317AF; also in the handbag was the false passport in the name of "Katharine Smith". Via radio, a message was relayed to the joint operations room to alert Spanish police to start looking for the red Fiesta with the registration number on the tag.

Several hours later, in the early hours of Monday, MA-9317AF was found in the car park at La Linea and opened. In the vehicle, the police discovered the key to the white Fiesta with the registration MA-2732AJ and put out a call to all units to search for it. It was not until Tuesday that police in Marbella found the vehicle in the car park where the IRA unit had left it earlier that morning and called the bomb disposal team. The officers searched the vehicle and opened the spare wheel compartment to discover the explosives, timers and detonators. One of the timers was set at 10 hours and 45 minutes; the other at 11 hours and 15 minutes; a double mechanism that would ensure if the first timer failed to detonate the bomb, the second timer would set off the explosion half an hour later. Had the plan succeeded and the bomb armed around midnight between March 6th and 7th as originally intended, the device would have exploded on a busy street at around 11am; just as the changing of the guard ceremony was taking place, or - in the case of the ceremony being cancelled at the last minute - simply in the middle of a crowd of innocent tourists wondering where to go for lunch. In the estimation of the security services, had the bomb exploded during the ceremony, the fatalities would have included all 50 troops and up to 250 civilians. The IRA would have been faced with another Enniskillen, but on an even wider scale.

At the Shell garage on Winston Churchill Avenue, the Gibraltar police commenced the gathering of forensic evidence – but shoddily. Shell cases and cartridges were picked up without their location being marked; the positions of the bodies of McCann and Farrell were also not marked. Where Savage had been shot dead, a few of the cartridge positions were marked in chalk and Inspector Revagliatte had made a chalk outline of the position of Savage's body, but incredibly, no forensic photographs were taken. Within the outline drawn around the body of Séan Savage, there were five strike marks; three clustered in the head area. Chief Inspector Lopez of the Gibraltar Police recalled all personnel and drove to the area where the Renault 5 was parked. The bomb disposal team opened the car suspected of containing a car bomb but it was naturally empty, the bomb still in the underground car park in Marbella; the police declared the area safe between 19:00 and 20:00 and removed the security cordon. In the meantime, the bodies of all three terrorists had been removed, stripped of all clothing and left in a secure morgue overnight. The following day, Monday, highly respected pathologist Professor Alan Watson from Glasgow University, who had been flown in from the UK, carried out the post mortems under difficult circumstances; in the facility there had been no X-ray facilities, no photographs of the bodies in situ were supplied, and as the clothing had already been removed, the task of determining entry and exit wounds was considerably hampered. Nevertheless the autopsy report was completed and handed over to Professor Derrick Pounder of Dundee University, acting on behalf of the families of Savage, McCann and Farrell. The next of kin were informed of the deaths and after consulting with Sinn Fein, Mairéad's brother Terence flew to Gibraltar with senior Sinn Fein figure Joe Austin on Wednesday, March 9th to identify the bodies. Despite the injuries caused by the gunfire, the pair had little trouble identifying McCann, Savage and Farrell.

What did prove more problematic was actually getting the bodies back to Belfast for burial in the Republican plot at Milltown Cemetery. Civilian airport staff at Gibraltar International Airport refused to handle the bodies of terrorists who had been killed whilst trying to kill their friends and family; Sinn Fein and the families struggled to find an airline that was willing to transport the bodies back home; and more tellingly, Irish Prime Minister Charles Haughey sent a secret communiqué to British authorities telling them that he was not happy to let the bodies return home via the Republic of Ireland and asked for them to be flown directly to Belfast instead. Staff at Aldergrove airport refused to handle the bodies if they landed in Belfast. The wrangling over the bodies took nearly a week before the families finally managed to charter an aeroplane that flew from Northern Ireland to Gibraltar. British military personnel, instead of civilian staff, loaded the coffins onto the plane and against the wishes of Haughey, returned not to Belfast directly, but to Dublin to reunite Savage, McCann and Farrell with their families in preparation for their funerals.

The Gibraltar plan had been foiled, Thatcher had given the IRA the "bloody nose" she intended, the IRA had incensed public opinion across Europe by attempting to kill innocent civilians unconnected with the conflict, IRA operations on the European mainland severely compromised with O'Hanlon, McGeough, Hanratty, Ryan and the rest of the IRA ASU's in place on the Continent on the run from the security services. The Provos called in the 'Nutting Squad'. The Internal Security Unit, better known within the IRA as the 'Nutting Squad' was led by ex-British Special Boat Squadron soldier John Joe Magee and his deputy Freddie Scappaticci (known as 'Scap'). The 'Nutting Squad' was responsible for investigations into botched operations and the interrogation, conviction and execution of informers within IRA ranks. As such the ISU played a central role in the organisation unrivalled to none: it had to know the fine detail of every single operation the IRA carried out in order to be able to work out why some operations worked and others didn't: in a sense the 'Nutting Squad' was at the heart of the IRA. At least one volunteer in each Brigade was responsible for internal security within their own ranks and thus reported back to Magee and Scap. The "Nutting Squad" lead an internal enquiry into how the British security services had gotten wind of the planned operation in Gibraltar. Possibly due to other British informers within the IRA – and the "Nutting Squad" in particular – the investigations were stalled in an attempt to prevent the unmasking of "Ruby" Davison as an informer – alongside dark rumours that "Ruby" was a paedophile, and that the IRA were keen to hide this fact, it is also worth noting that Ruby enjoyed a close friendship with "Scap" - the man tasked with carrying out the investigation into the Gibraltar disaster - and himself allegedly on the payroll of British security forces as *MI5*'s top spy within the IRA. Enough has been written however by others on the alleged role of Freddie Scappaticci as an informer within the IRA - and "Scap" is the subject of ongoing legal proceedings. This is not the controversial story of the man suspected to be the agent known as "Stakeknife".

There was to be another gruesome, footnote to the Gibraltar story: Brian Nelson, who had passed information on Dan McCann to Loyalist paramilitaries and prompted McCann to re-join the IRA, and put himself en route to his death on the streets of Gibraltar, turned his attention to Davison. Either unaware of Davison's role as British agent SEDATIVE / ASCOT, or indeed as part of a more complicated, double-crossing to protect the mole higher up within the Nutting Squad, Davison passed information on Davison once more to the UVF. On July 25th, alleged UVF gunmen wearing RUC uniforms stolen from the RUC base at Mountpottinger in Belfast were to drive the short distance across the Lagan to the Markets area, to call at Brendan "Ruby" Davison's house on Friendly Way and shoot him dead.

But back in March, months before the murder of the man who had alerted the British authorities of the Gibraltar plan in the first place, the IRA still had to give McCann, Farrell and Savage the full paramilitary funeral that death on active service traditionally earned. With emotions running high, the aftermath of the "Death On The Rock" incident was about to spiral completely out of control.

4 546, FALLS ROAD

The bodies of Séan Savage, Daniel McCann and Mairéad Farrell were driven the hundred or so miles from Dublin to Belfast to their respective family homes on Monday, March 14th, 1988, in preparation for their joint funeral. The trio were due to be buried in the Republican plot of Milltown Cemetery off the Falls Road on March 16th and tensions were running high in the Catholic community after the "Death on the Rock" killings. Security forces flooded Clonard and Andersonstown near the family homes to prevent any public displays to honour the dead. Local Republicans and the families were concerned that the British Army and RUC would adopt a heavy-handed approach to policing the funeral, which would invariably lead to reciprocal violence and mar the event. In an attempt to defuse the situation, the families asked a local priest, Father Alec Reid from Clonard Redemptorist Monastery - a short walk from the McCann family home - to liaise with the security services and ask them to keep their distance at Milltown. Reid was a well-known go-between for the Republican community in Belfast, the Provisional IRA and the British and Irish governments and was well respected on all sides. The security services relented on one condition: if the IRA guaranteed they would forgo the three-volley-salute traditional for the funerals of IRA volunteers killed on active service, the security services would watch from a distance and thus help in allowing the funeral to pass peacefully. Reid reported back to the IRA and to the families; as it was to be the most high-profile Republican funeral for several years and many of the IRA and Sinn Fein leadership would be in attendance, the IRA agreed to police the event themselves: led by the head of the IRA's Internal Security Unit former British Army paratrooper John Joe Magee and his deputy Freddie Scappaticci, a large number of IRA hard men were tasked with keeping order at the funeral. Agreement to the deal was passed back via Reid to the security services and the IRA promised no masked gunmen would appear over the coffins to fire three shots into the air in the usual mark of respect. This agreement was not made public but somehow the information of the deal filtered out of the Republican community via unknown informers, and thus the agreement was a massive contributing factor in what was about to happen on March 16th.

The Loyalist UDA had been itching for revenge on the Provos after the assassination of "Big" John McMichael in December. It was common knowledge in UDA circles that McCann and Savage were part of the ASU that planted the car bomb that killed him: when news came through to the UDA leadership regarding their funeral arrangements, they sensed a big opportunity to even the scores. The IRA and Sinn Fein leadership attending a public event with virtually no policing was a dream come true for the Loyalist paramilitary organisation; they would not only take revenge but also score a decisive direct hit on their sworn enemies that would cause huge damage to Republican moral. If an attack on the funeral was successful, the IRA leadership would be wiped out and by carrying out such an attack in full view of the Republican community whilst the IRA were supposed to be protecting their own, the UDA reasoned that the Catholic community of West Belfast would, in an instant, lose all faith in the ability of the Provos to protect "their" people; the IRA would be weakened to the point of collapse. The man chosen for the task of attacking the funeral was one of their top gunmen: Michael Stone.

Stone had worked directly under McMichael as a feared UDA gunman, and had carried out several murders for the Loyalists; he was the perfect man to exact revenge. Born to English parents in Birmingham, Stone's father enlisted in the Merchant Navy after his mother left him and Michael was sent to Northern Ireland to grow up with the family of his maternal aunt. Stone had originally joined the UDA in East Belfast but after several incidents, felt he was becoming too well known in the area and when he met John

McMichael – the Brigadier of the UDA's South Belfast Brigade - he jumped at the chance to join him. McMichael soon provided Stone with guns and placed him in a team whose ostensible purpose was to fulfil McMichael's hit list, a list of high-profile Irish Republican targets the Brigadier wanted killed. His first target was Owen Carron, who was Bobby Sands' election agent in the 1981 by-election and who subsequently became an MP himself. Stone trailed Carron for several weeks but on the day he was due to kill the Sinn Féin activist, Stone was tipped off that the RUC knew about the plan and were approaching, so the hit was abandoned. On 16th November 1984 Stone committed his first murder when he shot and killed Catholic milkman Patrick Brady, a man Stone claimed was a member of the Provisional IRA. Brady was a member of Sinn Féin, but he was not however in the IRA. This was followed in 1985 by an attempt to kill another Sinn Féin activist, Robert McAllister, but on this occasion Stone was unsuccessful. He subsequently killed Kevin McPolin in November 1985 and would also face charges for the murder of Dermot Hackett in 1987.

On the night before the Milltown funerals, as so often in "The Troubles", events went full-circle: senior UDA man and British informer Brian Nelson – the man whose out-of-date intelligence had nearly led to the killing of Dan McCann a year earlier – gave the go-ahead for the plan and Stone was given a Browning Hi-Power 9mm pistol, a Ruger .357 magnum revolver and seven RGD-5 grenades. He was told to take out as many Republicans as he could.

***

Wednesday, March 16th 1988. As British and Irish television cameras rolled and recorded the events of the day for broadcast on the evening news, the funeral service and requiem mass went ahead - and the cortege made its way to the entrance of Milltown Cemetery, 546, Falls Road, West Belfast. Present were thousands of mourners and top members of the IRA and Sinn Féin, including Sinn Féin leader Gerry Adams and Martin McGuinness. Two RUC helicopters hovered overhead. Stone mingled with the large crowd of mourners and entered the graveyard through the front gate. As the third coffin was about to be lowered into the ground, Stone threw two of his grenades - which had a seven-second delay - toward the Republican plot and began shooting. The first grenade exploded near the crowd and about twenty metres from the grave. There was panic and confusion, and people dived for cover behind gravestones. Stone began jogging toward the motorway, several hundred yards away, chased by dozens of men and youths. He periodically stopped to shoot and throw grenades at his pursuers. In the Irish Times, columnist Kevin Myers, an opponent of Republican paramilitary violence, wrote:

"Unarmed young men charged against the man hurling grenades and firing an automatic pistol [...] The young men stalking their quarry repeatedly came under fire; they were repeatedly bombed; they repeatedly advanced. Indeed this was not simply bravery; this was a heroism which in other circumstances, I have no doubt, would have won the highest military decorations".

Three people were killed while pursuing Stone through the gravestones: Catholic civilians Thomas McErlean (20) and John Murray (26), and IRA volunteer Caoimhín Mac Brádaigh (30): also known by his Anglicized name Kevin Brady – the Belfast Brigade comrade of Mairéad Farrell, Séan Savage, Siobhán O'Hanlon and Dan McCann. During the attack, about 60 people were wounded by bullets, grenade shrapnel and fragments of marble and stone from gravestones. Among those wounded was a pregnant mother of four, a 72-year-old grandmother and a ten-year-old boy. Some fellow Loyalists said that Stone made the mistake of throwing his grenades too soon after activation; the death toll would likely have been much higher had the grenades exploded in mid-air and rained lethal shrapnel over a wide area.

A white van that had been parked on the hard shoulder of the A1 motorway suddenly drove off as Stone fled from the angry crowd.

There was speculation that the van was part of the attack, but the RUC said it was part of a police patrol, and that the officers sped off because they feared for their lives. Stone said he had arranged for a getaway car, driven by a UDA member, to pick him up on the hard shoulder of the motorway, but the driver allegedly "panicked and left". By the time Stone reached the motorway, he had seemingly run out of ammunition. He ran out onto the road and tried to stop cars but was caught by the crowd. In the melee he was disarmed and the Ruger revolver taken off him – the weapon was now the property of the Provisional IRA. Stone was bundled into a hijacked vehicle. Armed RUC officers in Land Rovers quickly arrived and pulled him out of the vehicle, without a doubt saving his life. The RUC arrested him and took him to Musgrave Park Hospital for treatment of his injuries.

Immediately after the attack, the UDA denied any responsibility. The leader of the UDA West Belfast Brigade, Tommy Lyttle, said that Stone was a rogue Loyalist acting without orders from the UDA, although he did not condemn the attack. Lyttle told other UDA leaders to keep to this line. Former UDA member Sammy Duddy says now:

> "After [the funeral attack], two UDA brigadiers from two Belfast battalions telephoned the IRA to say they didn't know Michael Stone [...] But Michael was UDA, he was a travelling gunman who went after the IRA and Republicans and he needed no authority for that because that was his job. Those two brigadiers were scared in case the IRA would retaliate against them or their areas [...] so they disclaimed Michael, one of our best operators".

The UDA were disappointed that the attack had not claimed prominent IRA or Sinn Féin victims - their aim of decapitating the Republican movement thwarted. Relieved that none of the senior IRA and Sinn Féin leadership had been injured or killed, but nevertheless in shock, Republican sentiments boiled over into anger as violence broke out in West Belfast. Catholic youths rampaged through Republican areas in anger, hijacking cars and setting them alight and then attacking RUC policemen as they tried to quell the disturbances. As dawn broke, the violence subsided, but the Republican community was still seething as the IRA and the family of Kevin Brady began to make preparations for his burial; the second high-profile IRA funeral of the week in West Belfast.

***

Just three days after Stone's attack, the funeral of Kevin Brady took place amid an extremely tense atmosphere; those attending feared another Loyalist attack. As armed IRA volunteers acted as stewards for the day, the security services declared Republican West Belfast a no-go area for the armed forces; keeping instead to a minimum presence on the ground with an Army "helly-telly" Lynx helicopter fitted with surveillance cameras to following the funeral from the air. The funeral cortege passed along the Andersonstown Road towards Milltown Cemetery, headed by several black taxis acting as a guard of honour – Brady had worked as a 'black taxi man'. IRA members funnelled traffic away from the mourners and kept watch for anything suspicious. Just as the procession reached the gates, a silver VW Passat with two male occupants drove towards the procession; IRA stewards angrily signalled to the driver that he should turn round and leave the area; the occupants, clearly scared, turned the car sharply and, in an attempt to high-tail it out of danger, mounted the pavement, scattering mourners and turned into a small side road. When this road was blocked, it then reversed at speed, ending up within the funeral procession. The crowd, fearing that Loyalist paramilitaries were about to attempt to attack their second funeral in three days, surged forward and - led by Gerry Adams personal bodyguard Terence "Cleeky" Clarke - surrounded the car in rage; hell bent on revenge.

In the VW Passat were 24-year old Derek 'Del' Wood, from

Carshalton on the border where leafy Surrey meets South London, and David Howes from Northampton (23). The pair were not Loyalists but British soldiers; corporals in 14 Intelligence Company - a section of the British Army's Royal Corps of Signals known as 'The Det' or officially the Joint Communication Unit (JCU). As „prontos" or heads of the surveillance section, they were responsible for the overseeing of covert surveillance equipment on the ground, but on March 19th, they were off-duty and wearing civilian clothing. Wood had been in the British Army for about eight years having joined in 1980 and was about to finish his tour of duty of Northern Ireland; Howes had been based in Herford, Germany and had been sent to replace Wood as the JCU 'pronto' - he had arrived in Northern Ireland one week earlier. On the day of the funeral – despite warnings that West Belfast was on shutdown to military personnel – Wood, as with many other handovers from incoming to outgoing 'pronto' had decided to take Howes out to show him the Republican hotspots of West Belfast: to let him know what he was getting into. Leaving their base at Palace Barracks, Wood failed to look at the so-called „out of bounds" (OOB) board; a noticeboard that, had Wood have looked, would have shown that all of Belfast and a lot of the province of Ulster was classified 'code red' – all areas were declared off limits to military personnel for the day, due to the high-profile Republican funeral taking place at Milltown Cemetery.

As the "helly-telly" hovered overhead, delivering clear live surveillance video of what was happening back to headquarters, Corporal Wood attempted to drive the car out of the procession but his exit route was boxed in by black taxis – one in front and one at the rear. The angry crowd surrounded the car, smashed the windows and attempted to drag the soldiers out. Howes remained paralysed as Wood produced his Army-issue Browning Hi-Power 9mm handgun. Wood climbed partly out of a window and, showing remarkable restraint, fired a warning shot in the air instead of trying to shoot his attackers. The shot briefly scattered the crowd. The Republican mourners then surged back, with some of them attacking the car with a wheel-brace and a stepladder snatched from a photographer.

The corporals were eventually pulled from the car. According to 'Det' colleague Sean Hartnett, at that moment the situation could have played out very differently:

> "If you look closely...you can see that the magazine housing (of Wood's gun) is empty. Either he had been sitting on his pistol for quick access while driving around and accidentally sat on the magazine ejector switch, or it was ejected during the scuffle to get him out of the vehicle. Either way, when he went to fire a second shot, all he got was a 'dead man's click'"

The corporals were punched and kicked to the ground. IRA men disarmed Wood; the black Browning 9mm taken off him – as with the Sturm Ruger taken from Stone just a few days previously, the weapon was now the property of the Provisional IRA.

Journalist Mary Holland recalled seeing one of the men being dragged past a group of journalists:

> "He didn't cry out, just looked at us with terrified eyes, as though we were all enemies in a foreign country who wouldn't have understood what language he was speaking if he called out for help".

They were thrown over a stone wall into the nearby Casement Park sports ground, one of the corporals ripping his leg on a steel spike as he fell over the other side of the wall. The two soldiers were beaten, stripped to their underpants and socks, and searched by a small group of men. Digging into Howes' wallet, one of the IRA men realised that the pair were not Loyalists but British soldiers. In the wallet was a plastic SOXMIS card with which Howes had been issued. SOXMIS cards was issued to serving BAOR personnel and urged the holder to call a telephone number if they observed a vehicle with a special diplomatic registration plate, denoting the car as belonging to the Soviet Military Mission (SOXMIS), which had special rights to cross the border into Germany. SOXMIS, as with their British BRIXMIS counterparts, invariably abused those rights by driving into restricted areas, gathering intelligence on movements of troops and equipment of the enemy. The telephone number on the SOXMIS card read "HERFORD mil 2222". The IRA men misread "Herford" for "Hereford" – the British mainland headquarters of the SAS, the Special Forces unit responsible for the killing of the three Belfast Brigade members in Gibraltar just a few days before. The fate of Corporals Howes and Wood was sealed.

Father Alec Reid, intervened and attempted to save the soldiers. He shielded the corporals and asked for an ambulance to be called, but he was pulled away from them - in his own words, IRA gunman Alex Murphy at the scene told him: "Get up or I'll fucking well shoot you as well." The soldiers were bundled into a waiting black taxi. TV Camera crews filmed it driving off at speed, with one of its passengers triumphantly waving a fist in the air. The two men were driven less than 200 yards to a waste ground near Penny Lane, just off the main Andersonstown Road. In the back of the cab, the IRA gang carried out an even more frenzied attack than the soldiers had already received in Casement Park, beating both and stabbing Wood in the neck. The taxi stopped and Howes and Wood were thrown out into the gravel, surrounded by IRA men Alex Murphy, Harry Maguire, Pat Kane, Mickey Timmons and Séan O'Ceallaigh. The men took it in turns to vent their hatred: using both their own .22 weapons and the 9mm Browning taken from Corporal Wood, they passed the weapons from man to man, each taking turns to fire shots into the corporal's bodies from close range; Wood was shot six times, twice in the head and four times in the chest. He had also been stabbed four times in the back of the neck. Howes was shot five times: once in the head and four times in the body. Each also had multiple injuries to other parts of their bodies.

The Republican lynch mob quickly left the scene. Reid heard the shots and rushed to the waste ground. He believed one of the soldiers was still breathing and attempted to give him the kiss of life. Upon realizing that nothing could be done to save the soldiers, he gave them the last rites. According to photographer David Cairns, although photographers were having their films taken by IRA stewards, he was able to keep his by quickly leaving the area after taking a photograph of Reid kneeling beside the almost naked body of Howes, administering the last rites. 12 minutes from accidentally arriving on the scene of the Republican funeral, Wood and Howes lay dead.

The whole incident had been filmed by the British Army "helly-telly" hovering overhead. The Lynx helicopter had been frantically relaying information back to their operation room, having passed on the registration of the VW Passat in an attempt to identify the occupants. Tragically, the Army's own security procedures had helped to seal the fates of Wood and Howes, for JCU vehicles were not logged onto the normal vehicle registration system, but for security purposes were nevertheless assigned to civilian addresses and thus the vehicle was not flagged as belonging to the British military. The army held back, assuming this was another Loyalist attack, not realising that the car contained two of their own men. An unnamed soldier of the Royal Scots said his eight-man patrol was nearby and saw the attack on the corporals' car, but were told not to intervene. Soldiers and police arrived on the scene three minutes after the corporals had been shot, and established that the dead men were military personnel. A British Army spokesman said the Army did not respond immediately because they needed time to assess the situation – in retrospect they were scared of a full-scale gunfight breaking out between British Army soldiers and armed IRA volunteers in the middle of a high-profile Republican funeral: the potential scale of negative publicity and loss of life was immense.

The large funeral procession would have also prevented them getting to the scene quickly.

Shortly after the incident, the IRA released a statement:

> "The Belfast brigade, IRA, claims responsibility for the execution of two SAS members who launched an attack on the funeral cortege of our comrade volunteer Kevin Brady. The SAS unit was initially apprehended by the people lining the route in the belief that armed Loyalists were attacking them and they were removed from the immediate vicinity. Our volunteers forcibly removed the two men from the crowd and, after clearly ascertaining their identities from equipment and documentation, we executed them."

The bodies of Corporal Howes and Corporal Wood were repatriated to England. Prime Minister Margaret Thatcher was at RAF Northolt as the coffins were unloaded from the Hercules transport plane, calling the killings "an appalling act of savagery" and made her ever more resolute to stand her ground against the IRA. In the Republican community, there was a certain amount of revulsion for the mob lynching of Howes and Wood but at the same time, many falsely believed that the pair were actually SAS soldiers and that the killings had been justified in light of the Gibraltar murders; an eye for an eye. But the IRA felt that Howes and Wood were little more than collateral damage – they still wanted revenge for the deaths of McCann, Farrell and Savage. The Provos also now had two trophy weapons to assist them in that task: the Ruger revolver taken from Michael Stone and Corporal "Del" Wood's black Browning 9mm pistol: both guns would go on to play a powerful symbolic role in the IRA's quest to wreak revenge against the British for the Republican deaths in Gibraltar and Milltown.

5 THE POPE

The Overseas Department instructed the ASU based in the Netherlands and Belgium to hit back. To help them do this, Ryan, Hanratty and McGeough were supplied with more PIRA volunteers; some of them on the run from justice back in Ireland, some of them senior IRA figures. Owen Coogan turned to one of the most experienced and dangerous IRA volunteers of all: 'The Pope'.

Tall, strong with reddish hair, Patrick Murray was an ex-British Army paratrooper from County Mayo in the Republic of Ireland but was born in Dundee in 1943 and had subsequently spent much of his upbringing in Glasgow. Murray owed his nickname to the large tattoos on his forearms proclaiming 'God Save The Pope' and the large cross inked on his chest. Murray was an IRA volunteer feared by both the security services and his own side. According to former IRA comrade Sean O'Callaghan, Murray was a "classic sociopath":

> "Pat Murray really was a head case. He once headbutted a woman because she failed to step aside quickly enough for him."

Due to his many connections with mainland Britain, "The Pope" had been a key part of IRA operations in England since the early 1980's, working alongside Patrick Magee and being involved in, but never arrested for, a number of IRA atrocities. He was also involved in the planning of several more that were thwarted. On April 12th 1983, Murray travelled with Magee to Blackpool. The plan entrusted to them by Owen Coogan and the England Department was to carry out reconnaissance for an operation planned to be executed later in the year: a bomb was to be planted on a long-delay timer at the Imperial Hotel in the town in October, with the intention of killing and injuring Prime Minister Margaret Thatcher and other high ranking Conservatives staying there for the annual party conference. On arrival in the North West, they met up with IRA intelligence officer Thomas Maguire and his stepfather Raymond O'Connor, a locally living Irish Republican, who took them to the Eagle and Child pub near the Army base at Weeton, some ten miles or so outside Blackpool. Many military personnel drank in the pub, so an additional plan was hatched to park a Ford Cortina in the pub car park, as a holding car, then to be replaced by a hired van containing a bomb, with Magee driving off in the Cortina. Murray had previously lived in Preston and knew the town well – he used to sell IRA newspapers at the Irish Centre there. In addition, his brother James still lived there and their cousin Joseph Calvey lived in nearby Leyland.

Unbeknown to them, O'Connor was an informer for British intelligence services and tipped off authorities. Pictures were taken by a Lancashire police surveillance team and sent to Scotland Yard for identification. The team was tailed and photographed wherever they went. Patrick Magee was codenamed "the Mechanic", Murray "the Minder". On April 22nd, Magee and Murray travelled south using a hire car to an IRA arms dump in Pangbourne in Berkshire to retrieve explosives for the pub attack. The explosives were taken back to the North West and hidden in preparation for the attack. Four days later, on the afternoon of April 26th, Magee realised that they were being tailed by the security services and took flight, evading four cars in a high-speed car chase. Magee and Murray abandoned their hire car in the car park of Preston railway station with the doors still open and the keys still in the ignition but in fact did not take the railway. That evening, the pair arrived at Calvey's house in Farrington. Calvey had allegedly agreed to help because he was indebted to Patrick Murray for putting a new roof on his mother's house back in Rosturk. Murray's brother James turned up and together at around 10pm, the four of them set off in a car borrowed from Calvey's sister-in-law. They drove through the night to Newport in Wales, where early the next morning, Magee and Patrick Murray took the ferry from Fishguard back to Rosslare.

Murray remained on the run, on active service and a key member of the England Department. After the close call with security services in the North West, and the subsequent discovery at the end of October 1983 of the arms cache hidden in Pangbourne, the England Department abandoned the plan to attack the Conservative Party conference in Blackpool and reset their sights. The following year, the conference was due to be held in Brighton: in preparation Murray travelled with Magee to the south coast seaside resort. On the weekend of September 14th, the pair, along with IRA explosives expert Gerard McDonnell, checked into room 629 of Brighton's Grand Hotel – Magee under the alias of "Roy Walsh". Whilst Murray kept lookout, Magee prepared an explosive device, containing nearly ten kilogrammes of Frangex gelignite explosives taken from another Provisional IRA arms cache hidden in Salcey Forest near Northampton. He attached the explosives to a long-delay timer; only the second time such a long-delay timer had been used by the IRA, the first being an unsuccessful attack on the Sullem Voe Terminal in the Shetland Islands in May 1981, shortly before the Queen formally opened the new oil and gas facility. Magee then hid the primed device in a panel under the bath in the room. The pair returned to Ireland – the job done. Almost a month later, on October 12th 1984, as Prime Minister Margaret Thatcher worked through the night on a conference speech in a suite on the fifth floor directly below room 629, the timer stopped at 2:54am; the bomb detonated. The explosion tore a huge gash in the façade and the whole midsection of the hotel collapsed. Apart from damage to the Prime Minister's bathroom, Thatcher and her husband Denis however escaped unscathed. Thirty-nine others were not so lucky; 34 casualties were taken to hospital as the dead bodies of five conference attendees – including Conservative MP Sir Anthony Berry – were recovered from the rubble. Murray, Magee and the Provisional IRA had come within a whisker of wiping out the British government. Whilst Magee was arrested along with an IRA active service unit eight months later in Glasgow, Murray remained at large. He was involved in a shooting in Dublin in 1986 and arrested; after being given bail, he did not appear in court to face charges. Murray had already escaped to continental Europe and joined up with Ryan, McGeough and Hanratty to await further orders.

The ASU was complemented by two young volunteers who had been thrown together by the Overseas Department: Pauline Drumm and Donncha (Donagh) Mary O'Kane. O'Kane was born in England in Manchester but lived in Castlewellan in County Down – a small village on the east coast halfway between Belfast and Dundalk - and had been a promising Gaelic football player for the local GAA club. He grew up in a Republican family with sister Orlaith and brothers Eamonn and Fearghal – with whom he was later to play in the Castlewellan team – and drifted into active service with the IRA. He spent his early twenties as a volunteer in the South Down Brigade; a unit that, due to geographical and personnel reasons, occasionally worked together with the highly active South Armagh Brigade – and O'Kane soon came to the attention of the Overseas Department. He had never been arrested and was a "clean-skin" – the perfect profile for a member of an overseas Active Service Unit, as he was able to move around freely without attracting any heat from the security services. The IRA had learned from the experience of Gibraltar that it was extremely risky to send high profile activists that were known to the security services. Drumm was six years younger than O'Kane, born in Belfast but came from Kinawley in Co. Fermanagh. She had close links to the South Down Brigade – also sporting a clean record, she was selected by the Overseas Department to join O'Kane and travel to the continent to meet up with Ryan, Murray, McGeough and Hanratty: the team was complete.

Operating from a variety of locations; Amsterdam, Breda and Geleen in the Netherlands, the Uccle suburb of Brussels in Belgium as well as several other safe houses, in late March 1988, the team hatched a plan to strike British military targets. Soldiers and airmen and their families based in Western Germany were vulnerable to attack away from their heavily-protected military bases: whilst some accommodation was located actually on the bases themselves, many families lived in "married quarters" that were based in local towns - either on self-contained but nevertheless relatively open estates, or in rented properties within the German community. The team noted that military personnel, especially young soldiers and airmen were at their most vulnerable at weekends; drinking, sampling the delights of the Dutch coffee shops just across the border, dancing and trying to chat up local girls. Members of the team undertook reconnaissance in the border towns of Roermond and Venlo to ascertain where they were most likely to find potential targets. They noted three places in particular were popular with young servicemen: the King George pub opposite the train station in Roermond was the usual starting point for a night of hedonism in the town for airmen from the RAF bases at Wildenrath and Brüggen; after drinking gallons of Dutch beer and downing several shots of the local *genever* gin, the inebriated airmen invariably headed to a popular club, the Oranjerie - a short walk to the south of the town centre to drunkenly dance until it was time to go back home. The ASU also noted that servicemen from the RAF base at Laarbruch favoured a disco – "Bacchus" - in the town of Nieuw-Bergen, some 50 kilometres to the south of Roermond.

During the period of reconnaissance along the German-Dutch border, Gerry McGeough returned to Sweden for Easter to visit Pia and Sean. McGeough had been an infrequent visitor to Malmö recently –the previous year he had returned to on July 11th to celebrate Sean's birthday but during his stay, Pia had admitted to the Irishman that he was not Sean's father. Since that news he had only returned once before, at Christmas, arriving on December 17th but had stayed a week before returning to the Netherlands on New Year's Day. But the pair had stayed in touch via letter and phone. This time, Håkansson gave him the spare key to her apartment and once again he stayed for a week before heading back to Geleen. As the weather in the Netherlands became warmer and April gave way to a more balmy May, back in the UK, the smouldering fire surrounding the deaths of McCann, Farrell and Savage in Gibraltar flared up once more: Thames Television had sent a team to the Iberian peninsula to investigate and report on the incident, telling the story of what had happened, talking to some of those involved and more importantly interviewing several eye-witnesses who cast doubt over the official version of the events on March 6th. "Death On The Rock" was broadcast on ITV on Thursday night, April 28th and caused a considerable stir; not only with the British Government, who attempted - but failed - to block broadcast via a court injunction, but also within the Republican community and the IRA leadership, who felt themselves confirmed in their suspicion and anger at what they saw as three cold-blooded executions and proof of a purported British Army and RUC "shoot-to-kill" policy. Since the late 1970s and early 1980s, Republicans had accused both of the deliberate killings of suspected terrorists without any attempt being made to arrest the suspects first. In particular, three incidents that had taken place in 1982 came under particular scrutiny; one of those incidents involved the murder of INLA men Seamus Grew and Roddy Carroll by the RUC and an inquiry was set up under the leadership of Deputy Chief Constable John Stalker of Greater Manchester Police. Just before he was able to release his final report into the alleged policy, he was removed from the investigation due to allegations of association with criminals. He was cleared of all suspicion but did not resume leadership of the inquiry. The final inquiry report was inconclusive, leaving Republicans sure that the policy officially existed but was being hushed up by the British authorities. Stalker stoked tensions just a month before the killings in Gibraltar when he released his hotly disputed memoirs and referenced the inquiry, saying that he never found written evidence of such a policy, but that there was a clear understanding that such instructions were to be enforced by officers and military personnel. The killing of Savage, McCann and Farrell just weeks after the release of "Stalker" added fuel to the fire: against this backdrop, the Overseas Department gave the signal for plans to hit back to be carried out straight away.

On Friday April 29th, members of the ASU travelled to Roermond for the purposes of reconnaissance – witnesses recalled seeing men fitting the description of some of the IRA volunteers in Bakkerstraat, just two streets from the Oranjerie, as they entered, and then left a gambling arcade: they drove off in a blue car fitted with distinctive blue and white registration plates; a type of plate that had no longer been issued for ten years in the Netherlands, and likely false. After retrieving automatic weapons, Semtex explosives, Memopark timers, detonators, circuit boards and magnets from quartermaster Ryan's arms cache in Belgium, a number of car bombs ("under-vehicle-booby-traps" or UVBTs for short, also known in IRA slang as 'up-and-under' devices) were constructed on Friday, ready to be attached to the underside of an unsuspecting serviceman's vehicle. Saturday was a popular public holiday in the Netherlands, Queen's Day, this year marking the 50th birthday celebrations of reigning Dutch monarch Queen Beatrix - the town was packed with locals, tourists and servicemen alike enjoying the festive, relaxed atmosphere. The ASU sprang into action; armed with automatic weapons and divided into two teams, the volunteers drove to Roermond and Nieuw-Bergen; McGeough and Hanratty, parked outside the King George, whilst Pat Murray and the rest of the ASU drove to the Bacchus disco. As the ASU observed the variety of inebriated soldiers going into the club from their hire car, in Nieuw-Bergen the other volunteers pinpointed a red Ford Escort with tell-tale black British military registration plates parked outside the Bacchus club. The others remained in the car as one got out and walked over to the vehicle. He quickly crouched down and deftly attached the UVBT to the underside of the chassis with a magnet, before standing up and returning to the waiting car. The team drove off at speed, their job done.

Meanwhile back outside the King George, at around half-past midnight, McGeough and Hanratty watched a drunken group of airmen leave the pub and return to their vehicle. Senior Aircraftsman (SAC) Ian Shinner, SAC Jimmy Garth and SAC 'Taff'

Lewis from 16 Squadron of the RAF Regiment, clambered in with the intention of sleeping off their hangovers in the car, before returning the next morning to their accommodation at RAF Wildenrath, a short hop across the border in Germany. They turned off the light in the car, settling down for a few hours uncomfortable and drunken sleep. McGeough and Hanratty exited their vehicle and walked over to the driver's door. As they reached the car, McGeough knocked on the side window to get the occupants attention; as Shinner in the driving seat turned to look, the IRA men drew Kalashnikov AK-47 automatic weapons and fired a hail of bullets through the open passenger window. Shinner was hit multiple times in the face at close-range; Lewis received a number of bullet-wounds to the torso and arms; Garth was so deeply asleep that he didn't even hear the initial shooting but was shot in the shoulder; Police later counted 23 bullet holes in the car, over 60 shots were fired in all. Left strewn around the scene were ammunition cartridges from the AK-47, stamped with "ppu 762" on the base, which police would later identify as having emanated from Yugoslavia. McGeough and Hanratty rushed back to the getaway car and drove off at speed towards Breda, as door staff of the King George rushed to the car to help the airmen. They called for an ambulance, dragged Garth and Lewis out of the car to administer first aid to them straight away, which helped saved their lives; Ian Shinner's head wounds were too severe; according to a witness Shinner "had the whole left side of his face ripped off by the impact of the bullets." It was obvious nothing could be done for him; before the doormen had even reached the car, he was dead.

Around an hour later, as the four volunteers were already on their way back to the safe house, three young members of 1 Squadron RAF Regiment - Millar Reid, John Baxter and Andy Kelly - left the Bacchus nightclub in Nieuw-Bergen, ready for the ten kilometre or so drive back to their airbase at Laarbruch. All three were popular figures within the Regiment; in particular Reid and Baxter - known to all in the Regiment as JB - with their quick-fire Scottish wit, also worked together as barmen in the Squadron bar back at RAF Laarbruch. JB had been in the RAF for three years and at Laarbruch for two; Reid had joined the RAF in 1984 and after a spell in England, had been posted to Laarbruch in 1987. Reid and Baxter were avid football fans from different religious backgrounds: Reid a Protestant fan of Rangers, Baxter an ardent Celtic fan and Catholic. The trio were extremely close and were an integral part of the Regimental Cavalry team – they had been training hard for four months and the following day they were to travel to Wolfenbüttel on the border with East Germany to represent the Regiment at a horse-riding tournament. In high spirits, they walked to where Kelly had parked his red Ford Escort several hours before. Andy Kelly recalls:

> *We all arrived at the car at the same time and got in. Beforehand, we'd had a quick look under the car, just in case we saw something unexpected. I'm not sure why, but we just did! As the car park was really full because it was the Queen of the Netherlands' birthday (and therefore not safe, as we were told), I had parked on the pavement. So I had to manoeuvre the car off the kerb."*

To do this, Kelly had to keep the driver's door open, lean out of the car with his seatbelt off, to help him see where the kerb was. Kelly continues:

> *"As I rolled the car off the pavement, I suddenly felt a strong heat on my face and body and a dull thud in my ears, then a damp feeling on my clothes..."*

As Kelly rolled the car off the pavement, the mercury tilt switch in the bomb completed the electrical circuit of the bomb: a huge explosion ripped through the car, blowing the roof off, sending a large fireball, as well as metal and human debris, across the road in all directions. Club guests heard the explosion and ran out to the street; the scene of devastation that met their eyes was too much to bear; body parts lay strewn across the car park, many guests vomited or fainted. Those with stronger stomachs had the presence of mind to run back into the club and fetch fire extinguishers. But when they returned to a considerably sizeable crowd of onlookers they realized there was nothing they could do. Reid and Baxter had been killed instantly in the blast. However, thanks to the open driver's door and lack of seatbelt, Kelly had been catapulted sideways out of the car in the explosion and lay seriously-injured some distance away. An eyewitness described the scene:

> "I heard that bang and saw a very high ball of flame. Higher than the town hall. The car immediately caught fire...the roof was curled up all the way up. A moment later, I saw the boy who had been thrown out of the car. On one side he was covered in burns. He tried to get up, but he couldn't. When the light went on in the town hall, everyone saw for themselves how bad it was. I think it was a lot for people to take. I haven't slept too well myself."

Kelly was rushed to hospital in nearby Venray in a critical condition, where surgeons had to amputate one of his feet due to the severity of his injuries: but he survived.

The *Ierland Komitee Nederland (IKN)* waded in almost immediately with a statement of support for the IRA operation. IKN Representatives conducted an interview with daily newspaper *De Volkskrant* after the attacks in Roermond and Nieuw-Bergen:

> "The British themselves bear the blame for the murder of the three British soldiers (...) The committee has an understanding of the attack, although it believes that the fight between the IRA and the British Army should not be fought on Dutch territory, and regrets the deaths of the servicemen."

The statement blamed the "ruthless politics" of the British in the

Northern Ireland issue, echoing the official line taken by the Provisional IRA when they claimed responsibility for the attacks on Monday morning, May 2nd in a statement telephoned to the BBC's offices in Belfast.

> "We have a simple message for (Prime Minister Margaret) Thatcher. Disengage from Ireland and there will be peace. If not, there will be no haven for your military personnel and you will regularly be at airports awaiting your dead."

The last line of the IRA statement was not only a reference to the repatriation of the bodies of Reid, Baxter and Shinner back to the UK, but also a reference to Thatcher waiting at the airport when the bodies of Corporals Howes and Wood arrived back in England after being murdered in Andersonstown. This time Thatcher was not present, as, on May 4th, the coffins of the three slain RAF servicemen arrived back in the UK en route back to their families for burial. After a remembrance service in Nieuw-Bergen attended by all the men from the men's respective squadrons, the coffins were placed on board a military transport plane at RAF Wildenrath. The ceremony was accompanied by an RAF guard of honour and band, who played Chopin's funeral march, as an F4 Phantom bomber and two Harrier jump jets flew overheard in a mark of respect. The coffins were accompanied back to the UK, and in the case of JB and Reid all the way on to Glasgow by Squadron Leader DGE Evans, who, along with 38 members of the Regiment, attended the funerals of both his men on Saturday May 7th; one service Catholic, the other Protestant.

The statement issued by the IRA had made one thing clear: the murders of the RAF servicemen had evened the scores after Gibraltar in the eyes of the IRA but at the same time, the Provos also had no intention of stopping the carnage whilst British military personnel remained in Northern Ireland. As if to underscore the point, only three days after the Roermond and Nieuw-Bergen murders, the ASU undertook their next operation. Whilst the IRA leadership felt that the RAF murders were justified, the British Army, rather than the Royal Air Force, were the most important targets and instructed the ASU to move their focus to Army personnel. The team moved their attention to Germany; and to Catterick Barracks in the north-western town of Bielefeld, where several thousand troops were stationed at the heart of British Forces territory. Even before the bodies of Shinner, Reid and Baxter were repatriated to the UK, on May 3rd, the team was once again in action. A British Army captain had parked his British registered car outside Ripon Barracks in Bielefeld; on returning to his vehicle at around 4pm, he discovered that the IRA had placed an 'up-and-under' on the underside of the vehicle, set the timer on the device and made their escape. Back in the safe house, the team awaited news of the explosion and fatalities. But the soldier had alerted the Royal Military Police, who with the help of German bomb disposal experts, made the device safe. A plan that was designed to put more pressure on Prime Minister Thatcher backfired badly and instead created unnecessary pressure on the ASU: for the components of the unexploded device gave German investigators from the *Bundeskriminalamt* a lot of important information on the origins of the bomb. The device consisted of a wooden box, distinctive Dutch-made "Witte Kat" brand batteries, a mercury-tilt switch, a Memopark timer, circuit boards, a Canadian-made CIL detonator and 1.2 kilogrammes of Semtex explosive. The device had been attached to the underside of the vehicle via two powerful magnets. Although the Memopark timer had been set, as the clock had run down, it had somehow failed to complete the electrical circuit as planned, thus failing to activate the detonator. The whole device was completely intact and even the wooden safety pin that had been removed from the device to arm the detonation mechanism was found nearby.

The information was not only useful to the *BKA* but was also shared with *BSSO / MI5*, the Dutch secret service *BVD* and the *BKA's* equivalent agency in the Netherlands, *CRI*, as well as to other law enforcement agencies helping in the fight against Republican terrorism in Continental Europe. After the coordination of the information, Willem Kuppens, the head of the Dutch team in charge of the investigation in Limburg, travelled to Ulster to visit the Northern Ireland Forensic Science Laboratory on the outskirts of Belfast, to get more of an insight into the origins of the explosive devices. Quickly a picture of the modus operandi of the ASU became clearer. The device was virtually identical to the device used in Nieuw-Bergen on May 1st. The circuit board of the bomb was checked against known IRA designs to ascertain its origins: it matched quite exactly circuit boards seized five years earlier in the Republic of Ireland in the bomb-making factory of Donal Moyna, one of the IRA's most talented bomb makers. Moyna himself had been seen handing over a packet containing seventeen such circuit boards to convicted IRA bomber - and member of the England Department - Danny McNamee in the cafeteria of the Imperial Hotel in Dundalk the day before the raid. The circuit board found in Bielefeld also matched the circuit boards found in arms caches in Pangbourne in 1983 and Salcey Forest in 1985, which had been unearthed by police in the search for the IRA's England department. The device was covered in fingerprints that were sent to the RUC and British Army in Northern Ireland for analysis and checking against known IRA operatives. The timing device – one of Ryan's Swiss Memopark timers – was of particular interest, as it gave security services a trail to follow: where was the unscathed and pristine Memopark purchased? Most important was the recovery of the magnets. They were 'Sea-Searcher' magnets made by the Nautically company based in Shepperton, England. A high capacity magnet designed for marine use, the 'Sea Searcher' was able to bear loads of over 60 kgs; a rare, highly specific item sold in very few locations in Europe; in fact at that point in Europe only six retail outlets for the 'Sea Searcher' existed in the Netherlands, two in Belgium and one in the Federal Republic of Germany; the circle of people purchasing such equipment should be relatively small and investigators were sure the trail would lead to the European ASU.

With this new information, the security and law enforcement services of Great Britain and Western Europe investigated in all directions. Dutch police following up certain leads released a picture of IRA Maze escaper Tony McAllister, who was believed to have been spotted in Roermond in the days leading up to the attacks in Roermond and Nieuw-Bergen. McAllister had been on the run on the Continent since the escape and was one of the most senior IRA men at large. Several witnesses came forward in response to the photo, one claiming that he had had a conversation and a beer with a man closely resembling McAllister in a Roermond cafe. The man had told him he was travelling round Europe and was staying at a camp-site not too far from the town. Police collated all the witness statements and combed the campsites and hotels of Limburg for signs of McAllister, but to no avail. At the beginning of June, some more useful information began to filter back to the investigating *TRIO* team. *MI5* contacted their colleagues at the Dutch *CRI* to tell them an important piece of news: one of their intelligence sources in Northern Ireland had passed on the information that the ASU had been holed up in a small village near Breda in the Netherlands before the attack in Roermond; and that after the shooting, although not identified by the source, Drumm and O'Kane had not been stopped when they took the ferry back to Northern Ireland the following day. The *CRI* passed on this information to the rest of the *TRIO* participants. Furthermore, fingerprints on several components of the unexploded device in Bielefeld had been traced back to Patrick Ryan. Enquiries into the purchase of the Memopark timers and Sea Searcher magnets had also traced security services to Father Ryan. In light of the investigations in Germany and the Netherlands, the EU working group on counter-terrorism and coordination of policing, TREVI, met in a hotel in Horn, just outside Roermond from June 8th-10th to keep all interested parties abreast of the situation and improve ways of sharing information on the activities of the Provisional IRA. The conference was attended by technical, intelligence and tactical specialists from the Netherlands, Great Britain, Ireland, Spain, Denmark, Belgium, Germany and France, who discussed improved methods of cooperation across Europe to help track down and arrest the ASU, as well as unearthing as yet unknown cells.

Only two weeks were to pass before the improved cooperation lead to a massive coup in the fight against the Provisional IRA in Europe. Acting on information from a variety of sources including Scotland Yard, Belgian police stormed an apartment in the Brussels suburb of Uccle on June 30th. The occupants included two elderly women and a 58-year-old man who had been renting the apartment. The man was arrested on suspicion of using a false name and passport and taken away for questioning. His room, and another apartment rented by the man, was searched. Police found handbooks on the preparation of explosives, boxes of wires and batteries, as well as radio-control-units for the purpose of remote detonation, Canadian-made CIL detonators and a number of Swiss-made Memopark timers. Once the information of the passport had been disseminated and checked against records, Belgian police were able to confirm that the man sitting in detention in a cell in Brussels was none other than the elusive European quartermaster of the Provisional IRA, Father Patrick Ryan.

6 THE NEWRY CONNECTION

News of Ryan's arrest in Belgium reached the members of the ASU on the ground in Europe, who - whilst concerned - still had access to the weapons hides dotted across the Netherlands and Germany. With Ryan gone, new weaponry would have to be smuggled to the Continent eventually but for the moment, the ASU could remain functional. The IRA leadership did not seem overly concerned and continued to make preparations for a heightened offensive against British military targets in the Netherlands and Germany. Two volunteers from the South Down / North Louth Brigade played key roles in IRA planning: Leonard Hardy and Peter Keeley.

Leonard Hardy, known in Republican circles as 'Hardbap' or simply 'Bap', had a long history of IRA activity. Born in 1961 in Belfast, he had drifted from petty crime in his teenage years to joining the Provisional IRA's Belfast Brigade at the tail end of the 1970s and had a reputation for causing trouble, both for the security services as well as the IRA itself. A loud, brash character with a penchant for shooting his mouth off, Hardbap soon fell out with Belfast Brigade commanders for attracting too much attention to himself. In the autumn of 1981, whilst being known as a staunch Republican, he had also become a liability, a security concern, a so-called 'red light' – RUC Special Branch and *MI5* were keeping tabs on his movements. Along with other troublesome volunteers, the IRA leadership ordered Hardbap to leave Belfast and move to Dundalk, across the border in the Republic, seemingly out of harm's way. Due to the influx of exiled Belfast Brigade volunteers that spent their day drinking and fighting and bragging about their time in the IRA in the North, Dundalk soon became known as 'El Paso' – the similarity to the Mexican border town and its reputation for being a refuge for outlaws all too apparent.

In Dundalk however, Hardbap continued on active service but also continued to cause trouble. As part of the cross-border South Down / North Louth Brigade, he was involved in several IRA attacks that not only cemented his reputation as a hard man and dangerous operator, but also garnered him enemies within his own IRA unit. In February 1982, Hardbap was part of the ASU that blew up the Crown Hotel in Warrenpoint. After wheeling in the bombs placed in oil drums into the hotel lobby, Hardy disregarded orders from his commanding officer, robbed the hotel takings at gunpoint; with the money, he ordered and paid for a cab to take him back to an IRA safe house in Dundalk, instead of sticking to the getaway plan drawn up before the attack. A month later, his rash approach to operations claimed a child's life: after planting a bomb in Banbridge, he neglected to phone in a timely warning to authorities; only doing so 90 minutes later once back over the border in the Republic. By that time it was too late; the lack of an adequate warning had not given the RUC sufficient time to clear the area, the bomb had exploded and killed an eleven-year-old boy. His gung-ho style was further demonstrated in June when he was part of an ASU who raided and bombed a Customs & Excise bonded warehouse in Newry; as soon as it was clear that the IRA were launching an attack and meant the staff no harm, the employees calmly let the ASU go about planting the bombs, before Hardbap ran in waving an AK-47, threatening to kill everyone if they didn't comply. Some members of his own ASU despised him but were rightly wary of crossing him and his fiery temper.

For all his shortcomings, Hardy was nevertheless promoted by the IRA - when the previous incumbent had been exiled in disgrace, he was elevated to the rank of OC (Officer Commanding) in Newry but, as with many leading IRA men operating in the South Down and South Armagh areas, had to direct operations from Dundalk in the relative safety of the Republic as he was a wanted man in the North. He was also seconded to the Internal Security Unit or "Nutting Squad" on behalf of the South Down Brigade. It was a role that Hardy relished. In July 1984, he made his first ISU kill; shooting dead volunteer Brian McNally, who was suspected of having informed the RUC during questioning about IRA operations. It is questionable that McNally did anything of the sort, but Hardy was not really interested in the finer detail of ISU work and took great joy in executing McNally with a bullet to the back of the head. Despite his commitment to the "Nutting Squad", he did however make an enemy in Scap. Freddie Scappaticci was only too aware of Hardy's reputation as a bigmouth and hated him with a passion. Instead of bowing down to his superior, Hardy feuded openly with Scap, a disagreement that became more and more heated: things reached a head after a drinking session in Newry, Scap had had enough. He attempted to run Hardy over with his car in the street but only just missed; the incident was defused and senior IRA commanders in Belfast told the pair of them to kiss and make up; or least not try to kill each other. An uneasy truce fell over the relationship.

Hardy continued to make ill-advised decisions and disregard advice and orders. In September 1984, the South Armagh Brigade had a large unstable bomb that they no longer felt it was safe to use on active operations and Slab Murphy pulled rank, telling the South Down Brigade to dispose of it safely. Hardy drove to Hackballscross to pick up the bomb and promised Slab to dispose of it safely and discreetly. Instead, he drove on to Newry, planted the bomb in the centre of the city and detonated it; miraculously no one was killed but Slab Murphy was furious. Early the next year, when senior IRA man Patrick Joseph Blair – known to all as 'Mooch' – was released from prison after serving a long sentence for attempted murder, Murphy was instrumental in having Mooch moved to Dundalk and installed as the new OC of Newry, deposing Hardbap. Mooch was a far more efficient OC than Hardy and oversaw many "successful" operations; long gone was the slapdash approach to operations that had been the norm under the leadership of Hardy, instead replaced by brutally ruthless and effective tactics. Hardy was nevertheless still involved and for the first time, took orders from Mooch who he respected considerably. Mooch and Hardbap were involved in a series of devastating attacks on the RUC over the course of the next eighteen months; one of the most prominent being a joint operation in February 1985 with the South Armagh Brigade, involving the firing of nine Mark 10 mortars at the RUC police station on Corry Square in Newry, hitting a Portakabin housing the staff canteen and resulted in the death of nine officers and injuring 37. It was the largest loss of life in a single IRA attack on the RUC during the entire 'Troubles'. Further Mooch-led attacks by the Newry unit of the South Down / North Louth Brigade saw four other RUC officers, two civilians and an ex-UDR soldier killed in the town. Mooch was later arrested in Newry in April 1985 but moved to Dundalk in the Republic in January 1986 and continued active service for the IRA, involved in several notorious incidents, including the murder of three RUC officers in Newry in July the same year as they sat in their patrol car eating ice-cream.

Also part of the Newry unit was Peter Keeley. Born locally in 1961, Keeley's path to paramilitary violence was significantly different to many of his Provisional IRA comrades. At 16 he had joined the Merchant Navy but upon his return to land, left and joined the British Army, stationed at first in Ballymena in Co. Antrim, then in Berlin with the 1st Battalion Royal Irish Rangers. After finishing his overseas tour, he left the Army and returned to Newry but from 1982 starting spending a lot of time across the border in 'El Paso', hanging out in Republican watering holes in the company of Provos in Hogan Stand, the Dundalk Bar and Aidan's Bar; as well as round the offices of Erin Nua ('New Ireland' - a Republican support organisation.) After slowly easing himself into Republican circles, he began to let it be known that he would be interested in helping the cause: he was summoned to the offices of Erin Nua for an initial meeting with more senior IRA figures: instead of a casual interview regarding his potential suitability, members of the IRA South Down Brigade pinned him on the floor and a cold-eyed IRA volunteer put a gun to his head, screaming at him that they knew he was "a Brit agent" and that they were going to kill him. Keeley stood his ground and denied he was anything of the sort; the IRA men relented and laughed off the incident as a test. Nevertheless, the IRA ignored his interest in joining the armed struggle. During this time however he struck up a friendship with Mickey Collins, the cousin of high-ranking South Down IRA intelligence officer Eamon Collins – and himself a fearless IRA gunman who had killed several victims. Keeley got to know many of the South Down / North Louth volunteers through Collins and it wasn't long before he was unofficially being involved in IRA activities himself. One of his first engagements ended in disaster; a planned lorry hijacking that went wrong left him on the run from the RUC and in January 1985 he handed himself in to the RUC. Released on bail, he spent the rest of the year in Newry and Dundalk and by chance got to know 'Mooch', who had been released from prison early in 1985, with whom he got on well. Around the same time he was also introduced to another IRA man 'Conor', with whom he started to share a house. When the time came for Keeley to face charges in court, Mooch and Conor gave him advice and told him what to expect, how to act and with whom to get friendly if he was sent to prison. He was sentenced to two years imprisonment in Crumlin Road jail, where he got to know more IRA 'players' and was widely accepted as a card-carrying IRA man, although he had never actually officially joined the Provos. After his release in November 1986, that was to change.

Upon his release from Crumlin Road, he moved to Dundalk and in late 1987 and early 1988, spent a lot of time with Mooch, Collins and Conor. For the next fourteen months he was involved in a series of PIRA operations in Newry, Dundalk and the surrounding areas and was unofficially one of the gang. After the execution of Farrell, McCann and Savage in Gibraltar, there had been concern that certain people on the fringes of the IRA might have been involved in passing on information to the British security services and so the IRA leadership had declared that anyone involved in IRA operations had to go through the process of being officially inducted into the organisation. The process involved being given the IRA's code of conduct in a printed green booklet – learning the book off by heart and taking part in a six-week induction course held by a trusted IRA volunteer – and then being tested on its contents. None other than Mickey Collins held Keeley's induction course and in May 1988, Keeley was officially accepted into the Provisional IRA.

By May 1988, Mooch had been promoted to Officer Commanding for South Down, and Hardbap had once again taken over the reins of the Newry unit - Hardy called Keeley to a meeting a few weeks after the arrest of Patrick Ryan in Brussels to ask him about his time stationed in Germany with the British Army in the early 80s. He made it clear that he was trying to establish the feasibility of launching further IRA attacks in Germany. Hardy told Keeley about the ASU based in Europe and that the IRA leadership in Belfast felt that in the face of Gibraltar, it was time to ramp up the campaign in mainland Europe: was Keeley willing to discuss what he knew with two senior IRA men? Keeley was instructed to drive to a country house hotel outside Dublin and wait in the lobby. The two senior IRA men were not hard to spot: one dressed in a cream suit and sporting spectacles and smoking a pipe was accompanied by a squat and scruffy man in an old Parka coat, looking like a farm labourer. The older man immediately took charge and spoke with his light Belfast lilt, asking Keeley all about Berlin and the routine of the 'squaddies'. Keeley told him that the Brigadier in overall command of British forces in Berlin would be the most high-profile target, and ironically, the easiest target of all. The Brigadier lived in an unfortified home on the wide tree-lined Heerstrasse near the Olympic Stadium, guarded by one solitary unarmed police officer. Across the road stood the first trees lining the edge of Berlin's Grünewald Forest; the perfect cover for an IRA sniper. Nevertheless, Keeley told the men from Belfast that he had a plan of his own; the squaddies were actually at their most vulnerable and relaxed on so-called R&R trips – rest-and-recreation holidays in the mountains of Bavaria. The British Army regularly block-booked forty soldiers into a *Staatsbad* spa resort in Bad Reichenhall in the Alps. The two senior IRA men were impressed and told Keeley they would be in touch again. The most senior asked Keeley if he had discussed the plan with anyone else but them or Hardbap; Keeley had however also told his flatmate Conor about the idea, but lied to the senior IRA men. Keeley left the meeting and returned to Newry. A week later, Hardbap told Keeley he had been instructed by the leadership to "wrap him in cotton wool" until further notice. A month later, in late July, Keeley met the men again, who gave Keeley £2,000 in cash, telling him to carry out reconnaissance of the Brigadiers house in Berlin and the spa resort in Bad Reichenhall. Keeley was told which route to take and which modes of transport to use. Both men repeatedly told Keeley that he should abandon the mission if he thought he was being followed and ordered him not to discuss the plans with anyone else except his commanding officer Hardbap.

***

Meanwhile in Germany, Drumm and O'Kane had returned to the Continent and re-joined the ASU. They were joined on July 2nd by "Pepe" Rooney, who took the ferry from Cork to Roscoff carrying cash and instructions from Belfast to carry out reconnaissance and attacks on British targets in Germany. Particularly after Gibraltar, "Pepe" was very much on the radar of the security services in Northern Ireland and his sudden absence from the province stood out. *MI5* passed word to the intelligence agencies of several European countries that Rooney, a hardened operator with considerable experience in European travel had left Ireland and was likely on his way to the Continent. For example, after receiving the information that Rooney was heading to Europe, the Dutch *BVD* alerted their sister agency *CRI* as well as the BZC - a hybrid specialised intelligence and policing unit of the *CRI* tasked with the prevention and detection of terrorist crimes – who kept a close lookout for "Pepe". What happened in other countries is unclear - to what extent Rooney was tracked across Europe on his way to meet up with the ASU remains a secret. Nevertheless, despite being warned, European security forces missed the chance to apprehend the IRA Active Service Unit before they could strike.

Just before 3am on July 13th 1988, Drumm, O'Kane, Murray, McGeough and Hanratty cut their way through a steel perimeter fence surrounding an accommodation block of the Royal Corps of Transport at Glamorgan Barracks in the western city of Duisburg. They placed two bombs weighing around 20lbs each in light shafts five metres at the front of the accommodation block and rushed back to their getaway car, a gold coloured BMW Series 3 with false Dutch number plates (NY-93-FS). As they sped off, the bombs exploded simultaneously, blowing off the roof of the building and sending debris and broken glass across a wide area. Nine of the fifty soldiers sleeping in the block sustained minor injuries but were treated at the scene - thankfully there were no fatalities. The car raced through the streets of Duisburg, heading south. The ASU jumped a series of red lights – causing a nearby West German police patrol car to be alerted to the vehicle. The police intercepted the BMW not far from the block. The officers gave chase and, after around five kilometres, managed to get close to the getaway car. In a panic, one of the ASU leant out of the window and aimed an AK-47 automatic rifle at the police car. The IRA volunteer opened fire, spraying roadside buildings with bullets – but missing the car and officers. The policemen understandably broke off the chase and the ASU were able to escape. A close call for the military, police and IRA alike.

The German Federal Bureau of Criminal Investigation *BKA* quickly set up a *SoKo* unit (Special Commission) to investigate the attack. Under the leadership of Werner Reus, the *SoKo* gathered evidence from the scene: a number of spent 7.62mm cartridges were found. Several witnesses confirmed that one of the terrorists was female. But the police officers involved in the chase were not able to note the registration plate of the ASU's getaway vehicle and other evidence was scant. The IRA publicly claimed responsibility for the attack, and the spent cartridges were subjected to ballistics tests; the tests showed that the bullets had the same rifling marks as the empty AK-47 cartridges found at the scene of the murder of Ian Shinner in Roermond two months earlier. The *BKA* realised now that Duisburg was part of a campaign, and not a one-off; they knew that the Duisburg attack was linked to the murders in the Netherlands and surmised that more attacks were likely as the perpetrators had escaped, were armed and had a purpose; a local *SoKo* was not going to be sufficient. The counter-terrorism division of the *BKA* wisely decided that it would need a dedicated team to investigate Provisional IRA activities in Germany. The new team would firstly support the Duisburg *SoKo*, attempt to track down the ASU and then coordinate other local *SoKo* units if other attacks happened; liaise with British, Irish and Dutch police forces and intelligence services and build up a picture of what the *BKA* were dealing with. The dedicated unit was christened *SoKo PIRA*; chosen to head up the team was 37-year-old Joachim Rzeniecki.

Joachim Rzeniecki had been employed with the *BKA* for ten years. Prior to joining the service in 1978, the native of Mülheim-an-der-Ruhr had spent five years in the German Navy. Taking on an apprenticeship as a trainee naval officer, he spent the following years serving as a second, then first officer on the ship 'Düren', a minesweeper that formed part of the multinational fleet „Standing Naval Forces Channel". Under the command of a British captain known as 'Black Jack', one of the exercises Rzeniecki and his colleagues undertook was to take command of another vessel using a boarding team and search the boat; an unusual manoeuvre for the German Navy but commonplace for 'Black Jack' and the ships of the British Royal Navy patrolling the waters between England and Northern Ireland, on the hunt for smuggled goods and Provisional IRA arms shipments. Rzeniecki returned to shore with this newfound skill set and chose to join the *BKA*, going to work in their headquarters in Wiesbaden near Frankfurt-am-Main. After his initial apprenticeship, he went to work for the departments concerned with the illegal narcotics trade and organized crime, creating situation reports and analysis documents to combat international smuggling. In early 1988, he moved to the anti-terrorism unit and quickly proved himself in a short space of time, rising to Deputy Head of Division. With the wealth of skills Rzeniecki had accrued on land and sea in anti-terrorism, smuggling and organised crime and an ability to quickly adapt those skills to new situations, the head of the counter-terrorist unit TE14 had no hesitation in making Joachim Rzeniecki the head of the newly-formed team; Rzeniecki was to lead the *BKA*'s fight against the Provisional IRA.

Rzeniecki quickly put together his team, a mixture of seasoned officers and young, hungry talents. Many had had recent experience with investigating the spate of attacks carried out by the Red Army Faction (RAF) and Revolutionary Cells (RZ) and had considerable knowledge of how terrorist cells had to operate. In addition, some members of the team had been part of the units that had investigated the Provisional IRA murder of Colonel Mark Coe and the attacks on Steven Sims and Stewart Leach back in 1980 in the previous wave of Provo operations in Continental Europe. The team was assembled and a structure defined. The team was divided into two groups: ten officers would be on duty at all times, and had to be ready to go within 30 minutes of an attack taking place; the remaining officers would follow later as backup and to relieve the first group. All specialist roles were covered within the *SoKo*: from the Tatortgruppe (scene of crime officers), *Verbindungsbeamten* (VB) who acted as liaison officers between different services, technical officers, logistics and finance officers, *Lagedarstellung* (those officers responsible for situation reports) and data handlers; Rzeniecki had an experienced and well-trained team at his disposal. The unit began to liaise with a host of other police and intelligence services to try and build a picture of what and with whom they were dealing. The *SoKo* got in touch with a variety of sister agencies: the British *BSSO*, based at JHQ in Mönchengladbach, Colonel Ian Fulton and his team from the Special Investigations Branch (SIB), the detective branch of all three British military police arms; with the RUC in Belfast, the Irish police force An Garda Síochána in Dublin and their Dutch colleagues in the central criminal intelligence service *CRI* and the Dutch domestic intelligence service *BVD*, as well as the Belgian civil police service, the gendarmerie or *Rijkswacht*. Very soon, information was being exchanged across borders, and a multinational TRIO team was set up in the Netherlands involving officers from Holland, Belgium and Rzeniecki's *BKA* team to improve cooperation between services and work on the common goal of apprehending the Provisional IRA Active Service Unit.

The first step in moving along the investigations in Germany into the Duisburg attack was an unusual one. The police officers that had been following the ASU getaway car before coming under AK-47 fire had been unable to recall the number plate of the BMW; reasoning that the all-important number may however be buried in the subconscious, Rzeniecki called for the services of a hypnotist. The police officers involved were hypnotised in an attempt to get them to remember the registration number of the vehicle they had been chasing. Sadly, the unusual step did not bear fruit but it was a first sign that Rzeniecki and the *SoKo PIRA* were determined to use unconventional means to track down what was for the *BKA* an unconventional target. As the attack had taken place in the early hours of the morning, there had been few people on the streets; the few souls likely to have been out on the street between 3 to 4am would have been dog owners, newspaper delivery services or bakers; the *SoKo PIRA* team targeted these potential witnesses with flyers and posters in the vicinity and even with notices in the baking trade press, with a request to come forward with any information or sightings of suspicious activity that might be relevant. In connection with the investigations into the Duisburg attack, cross-border cooperation was increased: on the Dutch-German and Belgian borders, checks were stepped up and targeted Dutch registered vehicles with English-speaking occupants. Identity document checks were carried out and the results transmitted to the *BKA* team. The *SoKo PIRA* then crosschecked the documents with authorities in England and Ireland, amongst others, to check if the documents were valid or forged. The border was by no means impervious but the *BKA* were making it harder for the IRA to drive around Western Europe and carry out attacks at will.

Unaware of their formidable new opponent but frustrated by the apparent failure of the attack to do any serious damage, the ASU laid low and planned their next attempt. The border checks were unable to prevent the next attack. On July 29th, Hanratty and McGeough travelled to Mainz, where they rented a white Peugeot with the registration MZ-AP 762. After carrying out reconnaissance missions on several British military installations in the following days, they returned to Lindenheuvel. On August 5th, they crossed the border back into Germany in the white Peugeot, along with Murray, Drumm and O'Kane following in another German registered car. They drove to Ratingen near Düsseldorf where the ASU strapped a bomb - filled with numerous pieces of iron shrapnel made from building girders that Hanratty had likely taken from a building site where he was working, measuring four to five centimetres in length and one centimetre in diameter - to the underside of the seat of a purple touring bicycle stolen in Belgium, and propped up the bike against a two metre tall wire mesh perimeter fence of the British Army's Roy Barracks – home to the 91-man strong 14 Topographical Squadron, belonging to the Royal Engineers. Five yards beyond the fence lay several single-storey buildings used to store equipment and maps. The ASU pulled out the wooden safety pin from the detonation mechanism, arming the bomb and raced away from the scene in separate vehicles. As 58 soldiers and 25 civilian contractors were heading for lunch at around 12:10pm, the device exploded. The detonation destroyed a ten metre long section of the fence and sent debris across a wide area; the force of the blast sent roof tiles and bricks flying, and the local Roy First / Dalton Middle School buildings – thankfully closed and devoid of pupils due to the school holidays – were also damaged in the blast. Three British soldiers from the Royal Engineers and a German civilian employee – a female painter working for the Rhine Army - were injured in the blast but treated only for cuts & bruises. The cost of material damage to the fence and buildings were later estimated at around 75,000 Deutschmarks. Luckily and most importantly, there were no fatalities.

The *BKA* opened investigations into the attack under the file TE14 120 806/88 and instigated a local *SoKo Ratingen*, which set up base in nearby Düsseldorf, where they were soon joined by Joachim Rzeniecki and the *SoKo PIRA* team. The *BKA* began their investigations. Recovery of debris showed striking similarities to the unexploded 'up-and-under' in Bielefeld in May; again a wooden safety pin was found, as well as charred pieces of the Memopark timer used in the construction and fragments of the distinctive "Witte Kat" batteries. Rzeniecki's team was sure that the same ASU had been responsible for Roermond, Nieuw-Bergen, Bielefeld, Duisburg and Ratingen and the Dutch-made batteries added to the suspicion that the attacks were being prepared in the Netherlands. They concentrated their search efforts in the border area. On August 6th, the Provos issued the usual scornful claim of responsibility via the Associated Press, berating British Prime Minister Margaret Thatcher for recent statements made whilst on a recent tour of South East Asia and Australia, and claiming that the majority of the Irish population was in favour of a united Ireland. It was clear the response from the British government was unlikely to be favourable to the IRA, therefore it was extremely likely that the ASU would carry out more operations after Roermond, Nieuw-Bergen, Duisburg and Ratingen: on August 9th. In light of this assessment, *BSSO* raised the alert state level to "Keenwind Amber": another attack was on the way.

Keeping one step ahead of the German *BKA* and Dutch *CRI* investigators, the ASU suddenly changed their tactics. Carrying out an operation further afield – in Belgium – was an unexpected move that wrong-footed law enforcement and the security services. On the morning of August 12th, Regimental Sergeant Major (RSM) Richard Michael Heakin of the Royal Welsh Fusiliers left his married quarter at the Army base in Lemgo, near Bielefeld. The affable soldier known as 'Mike' to comrades in the RWF, Heakin was on the way back to Warminster in the UK to join his wife Irene, his nine-year-old son and seven-year-old daughter on holiday. Irene and the children had flown to Luton late the evening before and had been met by the regimental Families Officer, who had helped them check in to a hotel for the night. Mike Heakin was towing the family caravan behind his Vauxhall Cavalier – sporting a British number plate CSP 14 B. He drove the five hundred or so kilometres through Germany, into Holland and on through Belgium towards the port of Ostende to catch a ferry to Dover at 10.30pm. Shortly before 9pm, tired from the journey and looking forward to catching a couple of hours sleep on the overnight ferry journey across the English Channel, Heakin pulled up at a traffic light on Verenigde-Natieslaan not far from the port. Sitting on a bench next to the traffic lights were two figures. One around 1.80m tall, wearing jeans, a light-coloured shirt and a white hat – Gerry McGeough; the other smaller and dressed in a blue striped t-shirt - Gerry Hanratty: the pair quickly checked the number plate of Heakin's car – the B at the end of the registration indicated that the car was registered to British Army personnel – the volunteers pulled out Webley .38 revolvers, stepped towards the driver's door and fired a volley of shots through the open window. Heakin was hit by six bullets and died instantly in the gunfire. McGeough and Hanratty escaped back over the grass verge and ran back towards the nearby Maria Hendrika Park. Belgian police arrived quickly on the scene and interviewed witnesses, who were then taken to the port and made to scrutinise every passenger on the Prins Albert ferry on both the 10.30pm and 2am crossings to Dover, in the hope that one would recognise the gunmen but McGeough and Hanratty had already fled Belgium in another direction; back to the Netherlands.

Peter Rooney had left the Continent three weeks before the Ostende murder to return to Ireland. "Pepe" had been a regular visitor to the Continent in recent months, liaising between Belfast and the overseas IRA units, bringing money, false passports and orders. On July 20th, Rooney travelled to Roscoff in France to get the ferry back to Ireland; the security services were waiting for him. When he alighted in Cork, he was arrested by the Garda for producing a false Irish passport and driving license and on suspicion of membership of a proscribed organisation. He was taken to Portlaoise prison and on August 15th appeared before the High Court in Dublin: he was however released on £10,000 bail – four days later he appeared in Cork district court to answer charges and denied that he had any connection to the IRA or to Farrell, McCann and Savage. Once again he was released on bail but the ASU on the Continent became nervous that Rooney or investigations into his activities might give away their whereabouts: Hanratty went into hiding in the Netherlands whilst McGeough took the opportunity to travel to Sweden to see Sean and Pia.

Back in the UK, the Families Officer of the Royal Welsh Fusiliers had driven back to Warminster to be given the terrible news of the murder of Heakin:

> "I was met immediately upon my arrival and informed of Richard's murder. Because he was my friend, I volunteered to drive back to Luton and pass on the awful news to his family. I had to wake them at 5am and tell a distraught woman that her husband and the kiddie's dad had been murdered by the IRA. That was the most horrible moment of my life."

In Germany, news of the murder was met with dismay that the ASU had struck again. But that was not all. Just a few hours later, the German police were on high alert once more. At around 12:20pm, a British soldier at Quebec Barracks discovered a suspicious package attached to a wall outside a shop. Taped to a gutter pipe at about waist height, the box had two wires leading out which were affixed to the adjacent lightening conductor rod. The soldier alerted British explosives experts who sealed off the area around the shop and examined the package. With the blood of a colleague not yet cold after the latest IRA outrage, the team took no chances. At 3pm, they carried out a controlled explosion on the device, which however on closer examination did not contain explosives. It was unclear whether the device had been planted by members of the ASU as a dry run for a potential attack or a hoax perpetrated by school children, drunken squaddies or a local either sympathetic to the aims of the IRA or just simply disturbed. The British intelligences suspected it hadn't been the IRA but nevertheless, the dummy bomb had the British military community and the German police on high alert just a matter of hours after the murder of Mike Heakin.

That weekend, the fatal shooting in Ostende was publicly celebrated in Republican circles in Belfast. Vice-President of Sinn Fein, and the man who was now the head of the IRA's Northern Command, had sanctioned the attack in Belgium, Martin McGuinness, made no bones about rejoicing in the murder of a British soldier. Addressing a Republican rally in Belfast to commemorate the 17th anniversary of the introduction of internment, jubilantly telling the crowd:

> "It shows the ability of the IRA to bring about a final victory in Ireland. We saw the IRA battalions at work in Belgium, as well as Holland and Germany. They speak for us. They speak with one voice...we see the Continental battalions in Holland, Germany, in Belgium and London as freedom fighters."

Buoyed up by the plaudits from the IRA's military command and the fact that they had wrong-footed the authorities, the ASU decided to continue the random pattern of attacks and keep law enforcement and security services guessing their next move. They decided to strike again near the border between the Netherlands and Germany, far away from the Heakin murder, a couple of weeks later at the beginning of September. McGeough returned from his two-week sojourn in Malmö, arriving back in Germany late on August 27th. He met up with Hanratty and travelled once again to Mainz, where on August 29th he rented the same white Peugeot 205, registration MZ-AP 762, from the car hire company in Mainz as they had used in the attack on Roy Barracks. Once again the car was hired using the false passport in the name of 'Michael John Tite', born April 5th 1957. Driving back up the Rhine, they spent the following day on reconnaissance around the RAF base at Wildenrath, before returning back over the border to the Netherlands, where they visited an arms and logistics cache in preparation for the launch of a planned attack. There they unearthed several weapons, including the Webley revolver used to murder Mike Heakin two weeks before, two AK-47s - one of which had been used to kill SAC Shinner in Roermond in May and used in the attack in Duisburg. They also had with them the false Dutch NY-93-FS number plates they had previously used on the BMW in Duisburg. On the reverse of the plates – made of wood - written faintly in pencil were the words 'front' and 'back'. Completing the equipment needed for an attack were two handheld ICOM IC4 radio transceivers. ICOMs were a favoured tool of the IRA whilst on live operations; a set had been found in the Buitenveldert flat in Amsterdam after the arrest of Bik McFarlane and Gerry and William Kelly in January 1986. The ICOM handsets could be used either as simple radio communications devices for teams to keep in touch with each other on operations. Occasionally though, the handsets were fitted with DIY encoders and decoders and used to send a clean audio signal via a UHF frequency from one handset to another. A particular frequency could be dialled into the transmitting handset, both handset and encoder turned on and the transmit button pressed. A second ICOM handset set to the same frequency – in this case a channel usually used by Amsterdam police – and fitted with a decoder, could be set up to form part of an appropriate electrical circuit. Upon receipt of the transmitted encoded signal, the decoder on the second handset would unscramble the signal and complete the circuit; thus remotely detonating an explosive device – the so-called "button job".

Allegedly the plan was to drive across the border, where other members of the ASU would be waiting to receive the weaponry for carrying out the operation. McGeough and Hanratty would then return back to Geleen. They put the plates, the handsets and some of the weapons in the boot, and put the rest in a bucket, which McGeough stashed in the footwell on the passenger side. They drove back towards the border. The road lead pretty much straight to Germany, straddled on the German side by the hamlet of Waldfeucht, on the Dutch side by the village of Echterbosch. The border was usually unguarded and Hanratty and McGeough had travelled across many times without being stopped – no big deal. They drove through Echterbosch and slowly approached the border to Germany. Waiting on the other side, in a white VW Golf with number plates registered in Bergisch-Gladbach near Cologne, were other members of the Active Service Unit.

At the same time, three customs officers were patrolling the border area in their van as usual: drug smugglers often used the border crossing at Waldfeucht / Echterbosch to transport narcotics legally purchased in the Netherlands over to Germany, where they were prohibited. The van pulled over to the side and the lead officer got out to take up position, as the other two drove to park a little further down the road, maintaining radio contact with their colleague. As the customs officer waited, he noticed the white Peugeot 205 slowly crossing the border. The customs officer was wary: once before already he had been shot at by smugglers, and this time drew his gun as he stepped out into the road holding aloft a stop "paddle". Hanratty and McGeough pulled to a halt and nervously got out of their vehicle waiting for the inevitable; the customs officer asked the pair to get out of the car and put their hands on the roof. As they did so, the customs officer saw the barrel of an AK-47 in the back of the vehicle. He aimed his weapon at Hanratty and McGeough, whilst radioing for backup from his other two colleagues. Before they arrived at the scene, the customs officer had already carried out a cursory body search; when his colleagues arrived, they opened the boot to discover Hanratty's building tools, the rest of the weapons and the false Dutch plates. Searching the car thoroughly they found – amongst other things – the ICOM handheld radio units, both set to channel 556, a frequency used by local police in Amsterdam. There were also eight keys on a key ring; six of which were not immediately identifiable, but one that could be attributed to the Duisburg area and one made in Sweden. Also recovered was McGeough's address book, which contained a whole host of contact addresses in Amsterdam, as well as Pia's address in Malmö. In the car was also a Swedish transport ticket indicating that McGeough had used public transport in Sweden on August 27th, three days before. On the other side of the border, the ASU members in the white VW Golf realised that Hanratty and McGeough were being arrested – or had been warned via the ICOM unit – the rest of the ASU quickly drove off before they could be challenged or chased by police. Hanratty and McGeough were put into handcuffs, driven back to the main police station in Heinsberg. The contents of the vehicle were documented and photographed: two AK-47 automatic rifles, neither of which was loaded, but also seven full ammunition magazines for the weapons. A number of individual bullets were also found. Three Webley Mark IV revolvers had been recovered; one was fully loaded with six bullets in the chamber. One of the others contained four bullets, the other two. In the revolvers were two and four empty cartridges respectively: the six rounds that had caused the six fatal wounds sustained by Heakin in Ostende a few weeks before.

In Heinsberg Hanratty and McGeough were photographed and their identification checked. In charge at Heinsberg police station was criminal police inspector Bodo Strickstrock:

> "The colleagues from the uniformed division had acted very prudently. Both persons had to undress completely,

> *were given blankets and put into cells that were far apart from each other. The vehicle was cordoned off quickly and guarded by colleagues. I immediately informed the Central Criminal Police Office, the state president of NRW, the state Landeskriminalamt (LKA), and the federal BKA. As expected, the BKA took over investigations together with the Federal State Prosecutors Office in in Karlsruhe. Colleagues from the BKA were given office space at the police station from which to work."*

Pretty quickly, the true identity of the pair was ascertained. Rzeniecki and a team from German elite special forces GSG9 flew to the west of Germany the next morning to pick up Hanratty and McGeough - the pair were flown in handcuffs and under armed guard by two separate helicopters the following lunchtime back to Karlsruhe for interrogation; purely by luck and the suspicious eye of a German customs officer, two important members of the Provisional IRA on active service in Europe found themselves in *BKA* custody.

7 DESSIE

After the arrests of Hanratty and McGeough, there was some interesting information from the United States of America. The FBI's PIRA Squad had received a tip-off that guns destined to replenish the IRA's weapons stocks in Europe were on their way to Germany – a whole container-load. The FBI informed the *BKA* of the possible delivery and the information landed on the desk of Joachim Rzeniecki in the *SoKo PIRA*. Both the FBI and Rzeniecki knew of McGeough's gunrunning activities in the States a few years previously, and that the IRA had tried to purchase Red-Eye missiles. The container ship was due to dock and unload the container in either Bremen or Hamburg; Rzeniecki wasted no time. Driving to Hamburg and Bremen, he petitioned the relevant Staatsanwälte (Public Prosecutors) for permission to carry out a so-called CD (Controlled Delivery) and search the containers. The request was granted and teams were sent to Hamburg and Bremerhaven. The excitement of possibly heading off a major IRA weapons smuggling delivery was dashed on arrival at the container handling companies: the FBI had not provided a container number and there were 1,000 containers due to be offloaded in Hamburg, 1,500 in Bremerhaven. Rzeniecki did some sobering mental arithmetic; it would cost at least 500 DM per container to conduct a search, even before personnel costs and compensation claims. A worst-case scenario of the weapons being in the last container to be searched – or not at all – would cost northwards of a million Deutschmarks. The searches were aborted and it remains unknown if the weapons delivery did actually go ahead without being detected, or whether the IRA had cancelled the delivery in light of the Waldfeucht arrests. Either way, Rzeniecki and his team were frustrated.

The Provisional IRA was also frustrated. With the identification by the security services of O'Hanlon, the deaths of Farrell, McCann and Savage and the arrests of Ryan, Rooney, McGeough and Hanratty in the space of five short months in 1988, IRA operations in mainland Europe had virtually ground to a halt. A variety of ASU members still remained at large: amongst others Patrick Murray, Pauline Drumm, and Donagh O'Kane. But ASU operations were paused for fear of further compromising the team. Back in Northern Ireland however, preparations were being made to relaunch the Continental offensive with different actors.

Desmond 'Dessie' Grew was a second-hand car dealer in his mid-thirties, living on Main Street in Charlemont – a few hundred metres from The Moy near to Dungannon in East Tyrone. Grew was the second eldest in a family of seven girls and four boys born to Kathleen and Patrick Grew. He was educated at primary level at Knockaconey Primary in Armagh, before moving to the local Christian Brothers secondary school, where he excelled in both O- and A-Levels. Grew spoke fluent Irish and represented his school and local parish at Gaelic football. The Grew family lived in a predominantly Loyalist area and as Catholics were targeted by sectarian hatred. Their family home was attacked on a number of occasions. After the house was burned down by Loyalists in 1972, the family moved to Charlemont, where once again they were targeted by loyalist paramilitaries. These attacks were not however randomly sectarian in nature – by that time, Dessie Grew had become a highly active paramilitary operator himself. He enjoyed a fearsome reputation within Republican paramilitaries, although he spent more time in prison than as a free man. Dessie originally joined the IRA at the end of the 1960s and was active in Armagh at an early age. After the split in the IRA ranks, he joined the INLA and had his first taste of prison in 1972, after being sentenced in the Republic to nine months imprisonment for membership of a proscribed organisation. By 1974, he had risen to the rank of OC in his native Armagh, but was arrested in a bomb factory at Threemilehouse in County Monaghan in the Republic and sentenced once again. He joined other INLA colleagues in Cage 14 of The Maze, and in May 1976 was involved in the plan to escape from Long Kesh; many of his comrades actually escaped but Grew was apparently unable to scale the wall – it is likely that Grew opted to remain in the Maze and not risk escape and subsequent recapture, as there was not much time left to serve of his sentence. However after his release, he was subsequently rearrested and sentenced in Belfast to six years imprisonment for kidnapping Councillor William Johnston – a member of the police authority of Northern Ireland. Johnston was later to be found murdered near the border. Released from the Maze after only two years in July 1978, he was immediately extradited to the Republic for his part in an armed robbery on the Northern Bank in Kells in County Meath - this time on behalf of the Provisionals, whom he joined after leaving the INLA – found guilty of resisting arrest and possession of a multitude of weapons – and in October 1980 was sentenced to ten years imprisonment. Whilst in prison in Portlaoise in the Republic, his brother Seamus had taken over as OC of the INLA in Armagh. Seamus was part of the INLA team that was ambushed and shot dead in December 1982 by the RUC's E4A unit. Dessie applied for compassionate leave to attend his brother's funeral a few days later, but Portlaoise governors declined the request on account of the severity of his conviction, as well as the likelihood of absconding whilst on leave. Grew served eight years of his sentence and was released on June 2nd 1988. He moved to East Tyrone and went straight back on active service for the Provos. It wasn't long before representatives of The Overseas Department got in touch with Dessie and asked him to help in the European campaign. He learned of the compromise of the ASU and the arrest of Ryan – that Murray was still on the run on the Continent but that despite the seizure of several of the weapons used by the ASU, the bulk of the IRA's weaponry remained in place and ready to use. The weaponry was hidden in an underground depot in woods between the towns of Rhynern and Werl, not far from Dortmund in Germany – rifles, handguns, ammunition, explosives and detonators lay a foot or so deep, wrapped in plastic refuse sacks, in a leaf-covered hide.

Grew agreed to use his formidable connections to put together a new team to reassume the offensive. Firstly he looked close to home: the East Tyrone Brigade had several men who had – despite involvement in many successful PIRA operations – relatively clean records and who might be willing to travel to Continental Europe. A year earlier, Tyrone volunteers East Tyrone volunteers Patrick ("Paddy") Fox and Dermot Quinn had escaped the carnage of the Loughgall massacre; Quinn had just been cleared of involvement in an IRA shooting in Dungannon and wanted to get away from Tyrone for a while; Fox was not only related to Dessie Grew (and another well-known Armagh Republican family, the McKearney's) through marriage, but was an explosives expert, whose experience with handling Semtex, mortars and other explosives made him a possible candidate as a replacement for Ryan as the IRA's Quartermaster in Europe, at least until someone more experienced could be put in place. Grew looked further afield for additional recruits; notably to Newry and Dundalk.

Bap Hardy's girlfriend was an intense 19-year old, middle-class, convent-educated girl from the Derrybeg estate in Newry, Donna Maguire. The daughter of Newry businessman Malachy Maguire, Donna was already an integral part of Republican circles and had struck up friendships with several members of the Belfast Brigade. Maguire had been at the Sinn Fein Christmas Party in Andersonstown just three months before the Death on the Rock incident, together with Mairéad Farrell; Farrell's boyfriend Seamus Finucane and her brother Niall, Siobhán O'Hanlon, Dan McCann, Kevin Brady, Peter Rooney and many more members of the IRA's Belfast Brigade. But whilst she had been closely mingling with high profile Brigade members, she was yet to be involved in operations, having recently moved to England and was working in a pub - she had not yet appeared on the radars of Special Branch or *MI5*. With a clean record, an outgoing personality, good looks, strong convictions and the added bonus of being romantically involved with the OC of the South Down Brigade – who had also been involved in discussions on PIRA activities abroad with Owen Coogan – Maguire was almost the perfect addition to the growing ASU. Maguire had however no operational experience and no formal weapons training. Nevertheless Grew was impressed by Maguire's drive and took her personally under his wing - in the autumn of 1988, Grew met Maguire at a remote IRA hideaway in the Republic for firearms training, where she proved herself adept handing a range of weaponry – from AK-47 automatic rifles to smaller handguns like the preferred weapon of both the IRA and the RUC, the medium calibre Ruger .357. Grew's protégé became an integral part of the plans. Despite reservations about Hardy, Grew knew that he would be able to utilise him together with Maguire for certain operations – the fact that they were actually a couple in real-life would remove the need for at least part of the cover-story they would have to use whilst on active service. The Overseas Department also made suggestions of their own as to further potential volunteers; having been promoted to Director of Operations, Slab Murphy had made recommendations from his own South Armagh Brigade that, due to his standing within the organisation, were difficult to ignore. Twenty-five-year-old Paul Hughes - an electrician by trade and the younger brother of Murphy's right-hand-man in Armagh, Sean Hughes – was on the list. Another promising volunteer earmarked for overseas action was Martin "Golfball" Conlon from Armagh City and part of the IRA's North Armagh Brigade, who despite being only seventeen years old, was an excellent sniper, but more importantly, had a disarmingly charming and gregarious personality which helped him get along with a wide variety of people. In addition, he was good-looking and could potentially be used to help with logistics whilst the ASU was on active service –being utilised by the IRA as a "honey-trap", he could enlist help from unwitting but willing local young women. Grew accepted the suggestions: the team was complete.

The Overseas Department had earmarked the team for the execution of a plan based on Keeley's idea of carrying out attacks in Berlin and Bad Reichenhall. Before the plan could be put into action, Keeley had to do a reconnaissance mission to Germany to finalise the plans for attack. According to Keeley's version of events, in September 1988 - with £2,000 and a rail ticket from Paris to Berlin in his pocket - he took a ferry from Rosslare to Le Havre. Alighting in France, he was perturbed to notice several irregularities, which began to make him suspicious. He successfully negotiated a hastily constructed temporary passport checkpoint at Le Havre station before realising that he was being watched by several men – both on the bus from the port to the station, then on the train from Le Havre to the Gare du Nord station in Paris. Walking from *Gare du nord* to *Gare de l'est* to catch the train to Berlin, he spotted two men trailing him and turned round to face them. The men looked shocked and turned hastily away to look in a shop window. Unsure as to whether French secret service had been tipped off of his presence, if the men belonged to *MI6* or whether he was being tailed by the IRA's own internal intelligence officers, charged with the task of finding out if he met or talked to anyone outside of the organisation, Keeley aborted the mission.

> *"I had been advised to abandon the entire mission if I spotted anything suspicious. In my book, being pursued by half a dozen men in trench coats and fedoras qualified as suspicious. I stopped at a stationery store and bought an envelope and some postage stamps. I placed my train tickets to Berlin in the envelope, sealed it, scrawled my mother-in-law's address on the front, stuck on the stamps and plopped it into a letterbox. I then hailed a taxi and jumped in. "Take me to an airport with flights to the Irish Republic", I said. "Pardon?" the driver said with more than a hint of disdain. "Take me to the fucking airport, now!" I spat the words out and he knew I was in no mood for*

games."

At Charles De Gaulle Airport, the next Aer Lingus flight to Dublin was due to leave the following morning, so Keeley checked into a hotel near the airport. As he left the hotel in the morning to catch the flight, the men were sitting in the hotel lobby watching him and followed him all the way to the departure gate.

Exactly whether or not the trip to Paris was undertaken alone, or whether events there unfolded exactly as Keeley says is however subject to doubt. For Keeley had good reason to cloud the exact truth. At their meeting back in the summer, the senior IRA men had told Keeley that their discussion was not to be revealed to anyone except Bap Hardy, who had set up the meeting in the first place and who was Keeley's commanding officer. Keeley however, at his own admission, had told three other people of the meeting: his housemate "Conor", who Keeley trusted implicitly as a dyed-in-the-wool Republican and long-time confidante; the other two were "Bob" and "Andy", Keeley's handlers with the Force Research Unit (FRU), a covert military intelligence unit of the British Army tasked with recruiting IRA informers.

Keeley, over several years, had been slowly working his way into the ranks of the Provos to become a valuable British intelligence asset, now embedded in the heart of the South Down Brigade and involved in the IRA's European offensive. Also operating under the alias Kevin Fulton, Peter Keeley had first been recruited as an informer for British intelligence in 1981 on his return to his hometown of Newry from his posting to Berlin with the British Army. At first he was merely asked for information on local people suspected of membership of the IRA and pointed out to him on photographs; whether he knew them, where they lived, what job they did. Before long, "Bob" and "Andy" were asking Keeley to integrate himself further into Republican circles and get to know more senior IRA men, with the task of getting actively involved and reporting back. As time went on, Keeley became an important player in the IRA in South Down working alongside Mooch, Hardy, Collins and others – he was perfectly placed to feed useful information back to the FRU. Keeley's information led to a wide range of operations being compromised, but despite investigations by Magee and Scap in the Nutting Squad, the finger was never pointed at Keeley directly and he was allowed to continue on active service whilst slipping his handlers important intelligence on IRA operations. With Keeley now involved in the Provisional IRA's European activities and in close, trusted contact with the major players, the British intelligence community had an insight into the Provos attack strategy on mainland Europe like never before. But they had to play a careful balancing act; whilst they needed Keeley to give them the information they required to prevent loss of life and eventually arrest the ASU, they needed to keep Keeley deep undercover and help maintain his credibility within the IRA, which meant that not every operation could be compromised – after too many botched jobs, Magee, Scap and the Nutting Squad would invite Keeley to a nondescript house somewhere in North or West Belfast for an explanation, before forcing a confession out of him and putting a bullet in the back of his head. *BSSO*, SIS and *MI5* would be left empty-handed and the IRA would score important points in the propaganda war. The existence of Keeley as an informer was to remain a closely guarded secret, kept in particular from the *BKA* and other European authorities for fear of the information leaking back to the IRA leadership and signing Keeley's death warrant.

The alleged trip to Paris however throws up several pertinent questions that remain unanswered to this day. It is unusual for an IRA reconnaissance trip to be carried out by a single person, for this leaves the organisation heavily reliant on the information from one single source – if this source is compromised it leaves the IRA completely exposed to misinformation. Keeley was (officially at least) a relatively new recruit to the organisation, a potential warning signal that the IRA leadership would and should have noticed. If Keeley had been accompanied on the trip by someone else, it would have been another, more senior volunteer such as Hardy - Keeley is however at pains to point out that he told Hardy about the abortion of the mission when he returned and that Hardy was genuinely perplexed. Keeley also omits to mention the reaction of the Overseas Department on hearing of events in Paris; a compromised mission of this nature would likely have involved questions at high levels and quite possibly a call from the Nutting Squad: both worthy of mention. Keeley later refers to "hi jinks" in Germany in a period shortly before 1989, which leaves open the option that he is unwilling to disclose that he – with others – actually made it to Germany during this visit, or earlier in the summer of 1988 and was an integral part of the ASU. Admitting to his presence in Germany as a member of the IRA during this period would make him potentially liable for arrest relating to some or all of the attacks, and to potential extradition to Germany for prosecution. This regardless of the fact that he was at the time working as a double agent for British intelligence to stop further IRA attacks happening. What can very much be assumed is that Peter Keeley was present in Germany for some period of time between March 1987 and August 1988 (and possibly also during a period in 1989) on IRA active service and was involved in several of the operations, including some that were compromised. During this period the ASU had hatched a plan: to shoot down a Harrier jet from 3 Squadron of the Royal Air Force as it came in to land at RAF Gütersloh. Much mystery surrounds the actual type of weapon intended to be used in the attack: either an infrared "MANPAD" (Man-Portable-Air-Defence-System) surface-to-air missile such as a Stinger or Red-Eye or a less-sophisticated, but equally deadly rocket propelled grenade launcher such as the RPG-7, which the IRA had used many times in Belfast and Lurgan, Co. Armagh against British military targets during the "Troubles". Whatever the weapon, it is likely - if the consignment ever reached Germany - that the weapon was part of the weapons delivery sent to Bremerhaven or Hamburg, that evaded detection by the *SoKo PIRA* due to the sheer cost of carrying out a search without a container number. Information relating to the operation was communicated from the British to the German authorities – both the source of the intelligence and the counter measures taken remain a secret. Former Federal State Prosecutor Peter Morré states that the German authorities – on the basis of the intelligence passed from the UK - were able to prevent the plan being executed: it is possible that the police presence near to the base was visibly stepped up to hinder the operation, but that nevertheless would have given the ASU a second opportunity to carry out the attack once the police operation was scaled back. A collaborative operation with the British military in temporarily grounding 3 Squadron for a time would have had the same effect. Another possible scenario was that the weapon was "jarked" (tampered with) to prevent the missile or grenade being fired, which would point to an active hindrance of an operation by an informant within the IRA Active Service Unit, or someone from the German authorities having access to the weapon. Certainly no preventative arrests of PIRA suspects took place and no suitable weapon was ever recovered in Germany or elsewhere on the Continent. Tellingly, *BKA* reports from around the time – unlike all other similar documents relating to IRA activity in Germany – remain classified to this day: possibly an indication of the time-frame of the planned attack, as well as the extremely sensitive nature and source of the intelligence that led to the scuppering of the IRA's plan. No information on the incident ever reached the public domain at the time, which clearly points to an "inside job" within the IRA to protect an embedded informer - evidence points to Peter Keeley being the source of the intelligence from within the Provisional IRA Active Service Unit itself.

The intelligence war was a complicated affair. In late 1983 and early 1984, senior *BSSO* officers overseeing Operation WARD had prepared a series of documents in readiness for meetings with British diplomats, members of *MI6* and *MI5* and the German domestic intelligence agency, the Office For the Protection of the

Constitution Bundesamt für Verfassungsschutz (BfV) in Bonn. The documents from file S/16173/4 were stored at *BSSO* headquarters at JHQ, Rheindahlen as paper copies stamped 'UK SECRET' – copies of the documents were presumably disseminated to *BSSO*, *MI6* and *MI5* officers. These copies would have been numbered differently to ensure traceability. Contained within the documents were the full details of all sixteen agents passing information covertly from within the Irish community of Republican sympathisers in West Germany, including analysis of their reliability and credibility, code names and more importantly, their real names. Named in the documents, amongst others, were former IRA South Down Brigade members Aidan Jordan, Larry O'Rourke and Brendan 'Bo' Crossey, who had been relocated to Germany by the British government after providing the authorities with information on IRA activities. It is clear from the documents that the information supplied to by Operation WARD was not only of minimal use to British intelligence, but the agents themselves were rated as completely unreliable. The only information of any value was the names of the informants. This information however was worth its weight in gold to the Provos: somehow the files were stolen from *BSSO* HQ in Rheindahlen and passed back to the IRA – a counter-intelligence coup. The IRA used the documents to contact the agents and confront them with their activities. The agents themselves were unable to deny their involvement but as the IRA knew, the information the agents had passed on bore little threat to IRA activities. Some agents were instructed to return to Ireland, but some were turned into double agents – feeding misinformation back to the British, whilst at the same time helping to strengthen the Republican support networks in Germany and serve as communications channels between the IRA and the various 'Irish solidarity committees' across North-western Germany. The Operation WARD double agents seem to have provided some assistance in providing a smokescreen to cover IRA operations on the Continent. It was a dangerous game no matter where the loyalties of the former IRA men lay: the informants had been relocated to Germany but nevertheless remained under the watchful eye of British security services. Aware of the possibility of double agents, *BSSO* and members of the Intelligence and Security Group of BAOR constantly monitored the activities of the relocated informants, watching for signs of contact with any members of the European ASU. Those who were acting as double agents needed to avoid putting the ASU in danger, those who had transferred their loyalties to the British side needed to keep their location secret for fear of a considerably more unwelcome visit from former IRA comrades that would likely end with a bullet in the back of the head.

8 FIREBALL

In the autumn of 1988, British authorities in Germany significantly stepped up measures to protect the military community from Provisional IRA attacks. Since the first major wave of IRA attacks at the end of the 1970s and early 1980s, it had long been standard procedure for any vehicles entering British military bases in Germany to be thoroughly checked before being allowed to enter. The procedure included not only identity checks on drivers and passengers, but also visual checks of the outside and underside of every vehicle. To check to see if an IRA team might have attached an "up-and-under" explosive device to the chassis, sentry guards used mirrors on long poles to visually scan the underside of a vehicle. After it had become apparent that the IRA had not only put bases under surveillance but also military housing estates away from the base, it was decided that each family should also take responsibility for precautionary security measures themselves whilst not on base; to this end each serviceman was issued with a under-vehicle mirror, similar to the ones used at entry gates, and servicemen were instructed to check under their vehicle for explosive devices before getting into their car. For families, it became standard procedure on leaving the house or returning to a parked car whilst out shopping to send the father - armed with a security mirror – ahead to check under the car, as wife and children stood on nervously at a safe distance in case he discovered a device. Every serviceman and family was also issued with a twenty-page pamphlet called the "Personal Security Guide – Don't Be Next". The guide gave valuable advice on security measures and behaviour: how to maintain anonymity and not immediately identify oneself as a member of the military community, security measures at home, precautions to take whilst away from home, vehicle security and procedures for reporting suspicious individuals, vehicles and incidents. A further measure designed to protect against a potential IRA attack against military dependents was to introduce irregular patterns to transport services; school buses and those connecting housing estates with the bases varied their routes and times from day to day, so as to avoid establishing a routine that could help any IRA team carrying out surveillance to plan an attack.

The British worked closely with the German authorities on further, more wide-reaching security measures. One of the most obvious ways of identifying British servicemen was via their vehicle registration plates. Vehicles were issued with British registration plates, which distinguished them at first glance from German, Dutch or Belgian cars. But there were naturally many tourists from the UK travelling across the Continent on holiday in their own vehicles – what made vehicles belong to the military stand out was a combination of white lettering on a black background, instead of the standard black on white. Additionally, the final letter of the registration plate was a dead giveaway; a "B" denoted that the vehicle belonged to a member of BAOR personnel. As was seen in the murder of Mike Heakin, it was therefore extremely easy for an IRA ASU to differentiate between a British tourist and a "legitimate" target; all the ASU had to do was wait for a vehicle with black number plates with a "B" at the end of the registration number and open fire. To discuss ways to tackle the issue, a meeting was held in the British Embassy in Bonn; hosted by the British Ambassador Sir Christopher Mallaby, the meeting was attended by Joachim Rzeniecki on behalf of the *BKA*, as well as British military officers, including Lieutenant-Colonel Russell Wright. A solution to the problem was suggested: that British officers should be issued with specially created German license plates (so-called *Tarnkennzeichen*) to prevent them from being readily identified as British servicemen. Rzeniecki however saw several flaws in the plan: a British serviceman could readily be identified as such if wearing British Army or Royal Air Force uniform, regardless of the number plate. In addition, servicemen generally drove right-hand-drive cars, rather than left-hand drive vehicles; even without an occupant, a right-hand-drive car with German license plates would be easily identifiable as British military-owned at a glance. In residential districts and near or on bases, vehicles using parking spaces reserved for British servicemen and their families would again give themselves away. There would have to be a complete ban on any kind of British or military connected stickers on British vehicles with German registration plates. Rzeniecki made the assertion that going through the complicated process of issuing and tracking special German license plates would be of no benefit and that the idea was impractical. The other participants at the meeting concurred and the plan was abandoned. Instead it was decided that right hand drive vehicles registered to British servicemen would in future carry standard British black on white licence plates. Lieutenant-Colonel Wright was put in charge of the operation: Project ALBRIC was announced on August 24th and envisaged the exchange of registration numbers of 60,000 vehicles by December 31st of the same year. The project, in light of the recent IRA attacks, was given top priority and completed within only fourteen weeks. It was to take another eighteen months before the second part of the plan was rolled out – codenamed Project HAGEN. Left-hand-drive vehicles belonging to British servicemen were issued with standard German registration plates in 1990.

In East Germany, there was also much activity. The Stasi had continued to gather intelligence on the IRA, both via documents channelled to them via moles in West German intelligence and also via the interception of communications. The Stasi had intercepted faxes from US press agency Associated Press to the German DPA (*Deutsche Presseagentur*), communicating the Waldfeucht arrests; the information was fleshed out by details gleaned from *BKA* files. The Stasi had every reason to keep a close eye on the activities of the IRA: they were beginning to pose an indirect threat. As the PIRA ASU had been carrying out reconnaissance missions and attacks on British military installations in West Germany, East German agents had been hampered in their spying missions on BAOR bases; both the Stasi and the Russian KGB had a network of agents based across West Germany whose task it was to provide intelligence on British military capabilities. The heightened security and the presence of police and alert locals caused by the IRA attacks meant that Eastern bloc surveillance had been endangered and had to be scaled down for fear of agents being discovered and apprehended. The HA-XXII department of the Stasi prepared a report for the foreign intelligence division HVA detailing the activities of the Provisional IRA in Germany, providing analysis of their operations and the resulting effect on East German intelligence gathering in the West. The HVA decided to keep even closer tabs on IRA active service units operating in Europe; a detailed document was produced on what measures needed to be taken to keep the IRA under surveillance, where they were likely to find sympathisers for logistical support in Germany – on the basis of this report, a decision was taken to attempt to infiltrate the organisation. By all accounts, the Stasi were successful in acquiring an informer *("inoffizielle Mitarbeiter"* or IM for short) from within the ranks of the IRA. He was codenamed "IM Harfe" (the German word for "harp", the national symbol of Ireland).

There was movement at a political level behind the scenes as well, conducted at the instigation of an unlikely source. The move threatened to potentially negate the IRA's raison d'être. The subject of a possible political solution to "The Troubles" was to be discussed in secret - away from the glare of Ulster, Westminster and Dublin - in Germany. The instigator was German lawyer and ecumenical leader Dr. Eberhard Spiecker. Born in Duisburg in 1931, Spiecker took over the local presbytery from his mother in 1968 and quickly built up a reputation as a facilitator for cross-faith communication, widely respected in the community on all sides. The Northern Irish conflict caught his attention:

> *"It really peeved me, that since 1968, they'd been saying 'it's Catholics against Protestants'. I thought: oh boy, you*

can't be serious. And then Prior Grünberger put me in touch with a Premonstratensian canon from Northern Ireland who was studying in Münster."

He was soon invited to Northern Ireland, where he made contact with representatives of both the Protestant and Catholic communities.

His heartfelt desire and goal was to bring the two communities closer together, not just in Duisburg, not just in Germany but also beyond borders. He set up the Hamborner *Ökumenische Gesprächskreis*, a regular series of round table discussions bringing together local, national and international representatives of all faiths and built up a huge network of useful contacts, including members of the Catholic and Protestant churches in Northern Ireland and nudged the two opposing sides gently into contact with each other. In 1985 and 1987, he set up exploratory meetings in Germany – in Boppard and Essen respectively - and led discussions between interested parties in an attempt to find common ground and open up channels of communication that could potentially lead to a mutually beneficial understanding and willingness to negotiate a peaceful settlement to the conflict. By the autumn of 1988, it was clear that the discussions could move to the next and possibly decisive stage: getting the political parties of Northern Ireland around a table to work out a future plan for working together. However, there was one stumbling block: the four mainstream political parties of Northern Ireland – the Democratic Unionist Party (DUP) and Ulster Unionist Party (UUP) on the Protestant / Unionist side; in the centre the liberal Alliance Party; on the Catholic / Nationalist side the Social Democratic and Labour Party (SDLP), would not be able to negotiate any meaningful progress without hearing and taking into the account the position of Sinn Fein. None of the mainstream parties could be seen to be sitting around a table with the party that most saw as the mouthpiece of the IRA. But at the table they needed to be. To circumvent the problem, Eberhard Spiecker invited representatives of the Alliance, DUP, UUP and SDLP to a secret meeting in Duisburg in the middle of October 1988 but via ecumenical channels invited a contact who knew the views of Sinn Fein and the IRA, was acceptable to both Unionists and Nationalists and had acted as a trusted go-between on many other occasions. Authorised to speak at the meeting on behalf of the Republican movement, but who could under no circumstances be revealed as a participant, was the familiar figure of Father Alec Reid.

On Friday 14th October, Father Reid met MP Austin Currie from the SDLP, Gordon Mawhinney from the Alliance Party, the DUP's Peter Robinson and the UUP's Jack Allen in the departures lounge at Heathrow and flew to Düsseldorf. They were picked up at the airport by Spiecker and his assistants Mr. and Mrs. Becker and driven to Duisburg. They arrived in mid-afternoon at the Hotel Angerhof, just a short distance drive up the Düsseldorfer Landstraße from Glamorgan Barracks, where just thirteen weeks earlier McGeough, Hanratty and the rest of the European team had detonated an IRA bomb and fired a fusillade of shots from an AK-47 at a German police car trying to capture them. The politicians were not asked to check in to the hotel and their presence there was not recorded.

Over the next twenty-four hours, the representatives of the four constitutional parties of Northern Ireland, as well as Father Reid on behalf of Sinn Fein, gave their community and party standpoints on the current political situation. Whilst it was clear that there were deep-rooted political differences between the major players, such as the Unionists election promise to only enter talks if the Anglo-Irish Agreement of 1985 were put on ice, and the Nationalist sticking point of policing, there was also - possibly for the first time - a growing understanding of each other's positions and an honest approach to finding common ground. Any solution would need to have the backing of each respective community, the feeling that no-one had a secret agenda, an equal sharing of power in any future devolved Northern Irish government, and the explicit agreement of the British and Irish governments. The key aim of the meeting was achieved: agreement as to the final destination, if not actually the route to be taken. Father Reid, whilst reiterating Republican strategy and opinion on political violence and that the issue of the Provisional IRA would need to be dealt with, agreed along with the others that delaying the next meeting of the Anglo-Irish Conference to give the politicians present time to discuss the issues raised at the Duisburg meeting with their own party leaders would be reasonable or acceptable. A draft declaration was drawn up stating that the next Anglo-Irish Conference meeting should be convened at a date in the future to facilitate discussions between the four constitutional parties of Northern Ireland. Secretary of State for Northern Ireland Tom King would then invite the party leaders for talks. The meeting broke up with the representatives of the DUP, UUP, Alliance, SDLP and Father Reid on behalf of Sinn Fein agreeing that they wished to see a devolved administration for Northern Ireland and were prepared for a power-sharing agreement to be put into place. It was a promising move by all that threatened to remove the thin rug of claimed legitimacy from under the feet of the Provisional IRA; it remained to be seen if the wording of the declaration could be agreed upon by the party leaders and made public.

Away from the dark corners of undercover espionage and secret political discussions, out in the glare of public politics, events in other places in the autumn of 1988 preoccupied both the IRA and the news media. Father Ryan, who had been arrested in Brussels at the end of June, was the centre of a protracted wrangle between the British, Irish and Belgian authorities over the issue of what to do next with him. Much of the wrangling was conducted via the media. The starting shot was fired by Dublin via The Sunday Tribune. Referencing investigations carried out by the Flemish *De Standaard*, the paper claimed that the Belgian authorities had been alerted to the presence of Ryan on Belgian soil and in light of his classification as a dangerous man, had recommended close surveillance. Nervous about an impending visit to the Low Countries by Margaret Thatcher, the Belgian authorities had decided to make the arrest. After his detention, the Belgian police, like their counterparts in the UK and France, subsequently were not able to pin any IRA activity in their country on him but nevertheless kept him on remand. In September 1988, two and a half months after his arrest, Britain officially requested extradition, predominantly on the basis of explosives charges. Also included in the paperwork of the extradition request were charges of conspiracy with persons unknown to kill persons unknown in the territory of the United Kingdom. This presented the Belgian authorities with a problem, as these charges were not covered by extradition rules in the European Convention on the Prevention of Terrorism, which had been ratified two years earlier. Ryan himself wanted to be extradited to Ireland, where he knew he would be given an easier ride than in the UK.

As the legal struggle continued, Ryan remained in detention in Belgium. Finally on November 3rd, three Belgian judges examined the extradition request; under Belgian law the judges were only able to advise the government on a course of action rather than approve the request themselves. In protest at an impending extradition to the UK, Ryan commenced a hunger strike. On November 17th the judges recommended that the extradition request be granted. Not wanting to invite IRA attacks on Belgian targets or have Ryan die in custody, the Belgian authorities caved in and approved extradition to Ireland. After 22 days of hunger strike, on the evening of November 25th, Ryan flew from Brussels to Dublin; the British government was incensed by the decision, feeling that the Belgians had given in too easily. To make matters worse, on Ryan's return to Dublin, the Irish authorities stated that they had no reason to arrest Ryan. An emaciated Ryan was met by his lawyer Elio Malocco and admitted to a clinic in Blackrock to recover from his hunger strike – after which Ryan was free to return home to Rossmore in Co.

Tipperary. Britain immediately formally requested the extradition of Ryan from Ireland to the UK under the terms of the mutual extradition treaty drawn up between the two countries in 1965. The Irish government pondered the request. On November 29th, Conservative MP Michael Mates called at Prime Minister's Questions for the immediate extradition of this "terrorist". Mrs. Thatcher responded:

> "The failure to secure Ryan's arrest is a matter of very grave concern to the Government. It is no use governments [of Belgium and Ireland] adopting great declarations and commitments about fighting terrorism if they then lack the resolve to put them into practice."

The next day in parliament Tony Benn MP raised with the Speaker the following point of order:

> "Father Ryan is wanted on a serious charge. It could hardly be more serious. It is in accordance with the practice of British courts that anyone charged is presumed innocent until convicted. Therefore, when a senior Member of the House says, and it is confirmed by the Prime Minister, that that person is a terrorist, it is impossible from that moment on for that man to have a fair trial. The BBC broadcast those remarks and every newspaper has highlighted them. Yesterday, the House of Commons became a lynch mob, headed by the Prime Minister, whose remarks are bound to prejudice any jury or judge if Father Ryan is brought to this country."

Michael Mates MP was the next to speak:

> "Further to that point of order, Mr. Speaker, I am grateful to the Rt Hon. Member for Chesterfield (Mr. Benn) for the courtesy of telling me that he was going

> *to raise this matter. I used the phrase yesterday solely in the context of my outrage at the fact that that person was not being brought here to face trial. It was not intended to be an intimation of guilt. Strictly, I should have said, 'Ryan is the man the security forces most want in connection with serious offences.' I am happy to make that plain."*

On December 1st 1988, the Attorney General, Sir Patrick Mayhew, asserted that the extradition paperwork sent to Ireland was in order and the government's claim to have Ryan extradited should be acceded to. However, Father Ryan said that he would rather die than face a British tribunal, as he believed Irish people could never receive justice through the British legal system.

The Ryan affair led to a heated exchange between Thatcher and the Irish Taoiseach Charles Haughey at the end of a meeting of the European Council in Rhodes on December 3rd. She described Father Ryan to Haughey as a "really bad egg".

> "I and my soldiers — we are at the receiving end. Ryan is a very dangerous man. Both the Belgians and our services know this. He is at liberty still. People like Ryan with contacts with Libya, with expert knowledge of bombing — they can skip — I feel so strongly on this and feel so badly let down."

Haughey defended the decision, saying that when Father Ryan arrived in Dublin, officials had no knowledge as to why he should be extradited.

Mrs. Thatcher said the extradition process here was not working.

> "There is hostility all the time. No matter what we send, your people object".

Mr. Haughey told Mrs. Thatcher that he had never heard of Father

Ryan until he appeared in Belgium. Thatcher replied:

> "You amaze me. From 1973 to 1984, he was the main channel of contact with the Libyans."

Mr. Haughey replied:

> "Ryan is an extraordinary case. You have a mad priest careering around Europe, arrested in Belgium, and then flown to us in a military plane, avoiding British airspace."

As documents have since shown, both Thatcher and Haughey knew the truth about Ryan and the case came up in their correspondence many times over the next months, both leaders sticking to their standpoints. Haughey maintained the position advised by his Attorney General John L Murray had advised: that Ryan would not get a fair trial in the UK and delivering Ryan to Mrs. Thatcher would be portrayed as giving in to the former colonial power.

The extradition controversy was heightened by the publication of a letter in The Guardian of 7 December 1988 from Patrick Haseldine, a British Foreign Office official, accusing Mrs. Thatcher of "double standards on terrorism". Haseldine referred to a 1984 decision to allow four South Africans charged with arms embargo offences to leave the country after a South African embassy official agreed to waive diplomatic immunity and stand surety for them. The embassy gave assurances they would return to Coventry Magistrates Court for their next hearing. They did not do so.

A week later, in an interview with The Tipperary Star, Father Ryan made his own statement on the issue. He said that he had raised money both inside and outside Europe for victims on the nationalist side in "The Troubles" of Northern Ireland, but insisted he had never bought explosives for the IRA or anybody else, and had never been requested by the paramilitary group to do so. The British government was exasperated and furious – on December 13th 1988,

Charles Haughey, announced in the Dáil Éireann that the serious charges levelled against Ryan should be investigated by a court in Ireland and, because of prejudicial remarks made in the House of Commons, Father Ryan could not expect to receive a fair trial in Britain. Ryan remained in Ireland, temporarily a free man, and a trial date was set for early autumn 1989.

After their arrest, the two other arrested members of the IRA's Continental Europe ASU - McGeough and Hanratty - had been sent to Frankenthal prison, situated on the outskirts of Mannheim. They remained in detention, in virtual isolation but with the occasional chance to meet and chat with each other – as McGeough puts it "it was like a concentration camp". At the same time, the German and Dutch authorities were gathering evidence. As professional building tools had been found in the Peugeot at Waldfeucht and Hanratty had 'worn-down' hands, the *BKA* surmised correctly that Hanratty worked on a building site; in addition, the iron shrapnel found in the debris caused by the bomb in Ratingen had been analysed and found to be made from construction girders. In an attempt to find the safe house the ASU had been using, Rzeniecki ordered teams to comb every single building site – some 14,000 locations, from large commercial sites to single-property privately contracted renovations – in the large conurbations Dortmund, Cologne and Düsseldorf. Informing their colleagues in the Netherlands of the search, the TRIO team also searched locations on the Dutch side of the border; in November they located the safe house used by Hanratty and McGeough in Lindenheuvel. The Dutch police were also busy gathering witness statements in an attempt to accrue enough evidence to press charges for the Roermond and Nieuw Bergen murders; several witnesses had seen McGeough running away from the scene, other witnesses had seen Hanratty on a train to Amsterdam between Sittard and Roermond a few days after the murders and several people recognised the pair from around Lindenheuvel and Landgraaf – it gave the TRIO team an insight into the modus operandi of the ASU but not enough hard evidence. The fact that they had been caught transporting the murder weapon used in Roermond was also not sufficient evidence to press charges – the fingerprints on the weapons could have been transferred there during transport and no witnesses saw McGeough or Hanratty pull the trigger. The Dutch police instead shared all the information they had with the German *BKA*, who were working on charges relating to Duisburg, Ratingen and the 1987 car bomb at JHQ in Rheindahlen. On September 8th, Swedish police had raided the Malmö address of McGeough's girlfriend that had been found in his address book when he had been arrested on the German / Dutch border. There they found a variety of false identification papers: a British passport in the name of John Benedict Virgilino Donnely, a US passport in the name of Jerry McLaughley, US birth certificates and driving licences in the names of Sean Fahey and George Mark Dreiser, as well as a US press ID card bearing the name Peter McCann. They also recovered folders containing copies of McGeough's asylum application and correspondence relating to it. On the asylum application McGeough had of course admitted he was a member of the IRA and the material was sent back to Germany to be used in evidence against him. Forensics examination of the weapons found in the car when McGeough and Hanratty were arrested were conclusive: the AK-47 was the same weapon used to killed SAC Shinner in Roermond, and was also the same weapon fired at the police car in Duisburg. The Webley revolver was the same weapon used to kill RSM Heakin in Ostende. With paperwork proving - by his own admission - that McGeough was an IRA volunteer, the pair having been caught red-handed with weapons that had been used in IRA attacks on the Continent, and witness statements placing at least one of them at the scene of an IRA attack, by the end of 1988 the case against McGeough and Hanratty was starting to take shape.

As the case against McGeough and Hanratty took shape, so did the plans for an end to the political impasse that had propagated "The Troubles" for nearly two decades. There were intense discussions within the Unionist and Nationalist leaderships around the issues that had been discussed – under the moderation of Dr. Eberhard Spiecker - by Jack Allen, Peter Robinson, Gordon Mawhinney, Austin Currie and Father Alec Reid in the Hotel Angerhof in Duisburg in October 1988. The top-ranking members of the DUP, UUP, Alliance and SDLP continued discussions when back in Northern Ireland, trying to clarify points and finalise how any agreement might actually work. The Secretary of State for Northern Ireland Tom King was kept abreast of developments, whilst not being told the exact details of the plan, and despite the staunch and public refusal of DUP leader Dr. Ian Paisley to meet with the SDLP, all participants were feverishly working towards the next stage of negotiations, laying the groundwork for a possible historical breakthrough. Aside from the content of the ongoing discussions, there was another important prerequisite to the success of the endeavour: the discussions should remain a closely guarded secret. In particular, the SDLP, in the form of leader John Hume and Duisburg participant Austin Currie were keen to keep the existence of the Duisburg meeting completely under wraps. A variety of journalists did become gradually aware of the negotiations and a select few managed to piece everything together and trace the negotiation process back to Duisburg. They did however promise to keep the story to themselves for the time being to avoid jeopardising the talks. The discussions ran through November and December 1988 and into January 1989.

Meanwhile diplomatic attempts to secure the extradition of Gerry Hanratty and Gerry McGeough from Germany to the UK continued apace. On January 27th the UK's Foreign Minister Geoffrey Howe delivered a paper to his counterpart at the German Foreign Ministry (Auswärtiges Amt) outlining the government's position. In return the Auswärtiges Amt requested evidence or documentation that could be used in court to support any extradition request – documentation was collated that detailed the paramilitary activities of the two Gerrys and a little over a week later, on February 8th, the

British Ambassador to Germany, Christopher Mallaby, handed over the papers to the German Foreign Office in Bonn, who forwarded everything to the German Ministry for Justice, the BMJ. Secretary of State for Northern Ireland Tom King wrote to Howe five days later, advising him of his intention to formally seek extradition but advising them of some concerns in light of a deadline for the Germans to extend custody of the two IRA volunteers.

> "The RUC have no grounds on which to seek the extradition of Gerry McGeough (although the FBI may be interested in him...there is a strong case for the extradition of Hanratty...so as to ensure that Hanratty remains in custody...it would be necessary to have an extradition request with German authorities before the review takes place."

Having learned of the pitfalls encountered by other British administrations during previous IRA extradition proceedings, King acknowledged that it was a delicate tightrope act - failure to request extradition would cause a storm, but equally if the request were to be turned down, after the Ryan affair it would be the second such rejection in the space of a few short months and would leave the government open to heavy criticism. He also foresaw that gaining extradition would be no easy task; King had concerns that Hanratty would be likely to raise the question of future treatment at the hands of Northern Irish police and prison authorities, as Gerry Kelly and Bik McFarlane had done to try and hinder their extradition from the Netherlands. The Secretary of State for Northern Ireland was also aware that concerns might be raised by the Germans over Britain's handling of the case, referring to areas such as possible infractions of the Criminal Evidence (Northern Ireland) Order 1988 and derogation from the European Convention on Human Rights. He explained he had been advised there was a strong case for securing a conviction for Hanratty but admitted he could not foresee the German courts would see the case.

Howe replied a couple of days later, acknowledging the risks and called on Home Secretary Douglas Hurd to give his assessment. Hurd agreed with King's analysis and advised that the British government should await the outcome of German proceedings against McGeough and Hanratty before submitting any formal extradition request, so as not to exert any outside pressure on the German process and later have both the Germans and the British accused of trying to politically influence criminal proceedings. Nevertheless Christopher Mallaby met with German Federal Justice Minister Klaus Kinkel to unofficially raise the possibility of a future extradition of Hanratty and Kinkel told him that the IRA pair were only to be held on illegal possession of weapons charges, which the Germans were not inclined to see as any political act in itself – a clear indication that any extradition request would be looked at favourably.

As tentative German-British diplomatic efforts to resolve the situation as regards McGeough and Hanratty continued, the Duisburg bombshell hit. On February 2nd, 1989 the British Broadcasting Corporation – unable to ignore the scoop any longer – chose to run with the story and on their BBC Spotlight current affairs programme, revealed to the world details of the secret negotiations, as well as their origin; not only the fact that the four constitutional parties of Northern Ireland put aside their differences to meet in secret in Duisburg, but also that there was a mysterious fifth participant, without revealing that Father Reid had been present on behalf of the Provisional IRA. Many reading between the lines correctly deduced however that the fifth place at the table had to be someone speaking on behalf of Sinn Fein, which was a political bombshell. In the words of Dr. Spiecker, the revelation was a "fireball" which engulfed the nascent Duisburg Agreement and the plans to move towards a long-lasting solution to "The Troubles", leaving in its wake the smouldering remains of the Northern Irish peace process.

9 FERMDOWN

At the beginning of 1989 in Belfast, the Director of Publicity for Sinn Fein – and allegedly also the Provisional IRA - Danny Morrison asked one of the surviving members of the Gibraltar ASU to come and work for him. As *MI5* had long been aware of her membership of the Belfast Brigade and her close links to Farrell, McCann and Savage, O'Hanlon was a "red light" and no longer usable as a front-line volunteer; Morrison came up with the idea of employing her at the Republican Press Centre; O'Hanlon would henceforth be involved in claiming or denying IRA involvement in attacks. For the first few months though, she had very little to do, at least in terms of European operations: on the Continent, the IRA team on the ground was wondering what to do next. The new ASU recruited by Grew were not yet in place, the existing volunteers lying low in the Low Countries had resumed reconnaissance missions in February and March, hiring a number of vehicles to visit a variety of potential targets, but had not yet made any concrete attack plans. In addition, the Provisional IRA was struggling to find suitable volunteers to send to Europe to replace Hanratty and McGeough. Joachim Rzeniecki of the *BKA* explains why it was difficult for the IRA to get the right personnel:

> "Any volunteer (sent to Europe) had to have a good enough command of German to at the very least be able to read road signs...and had to master driving on the right. There were not many people who fitted the bill."

There may have been other factors: Owen Coogan had been named in the press as one of the masterminds behind the Gibraltar operation and possibly there was some restructuring going on behind the scenes. Secondly, the leadership had likely been a little rattled by the disturbance of the Paris / Berlin mission and were hesitant to make the next move. Reconnaissance missions to targets in the Rhineland still continued, and although the IRA operatives on the Continent had been briefed on tactics, the teams had been very much left to their own devices as regards choice of targets and how they went about carrying out attacks. Intelligence gathering and the study of security measures to circumvent continued but there were no definite plans made to recommence attacks. As regards the new recruits, Grew, Hardy, Fox and Maguire were busy with frequent active service operations in East Tyrone and South Down; in the case of Dermot Quinn, waiting for the heat to die down from previous operations. In the previous year, Quinn had nearly been taken out of the game but had managed to evade conviction: on April 13th, 1988 he was being driven by his employer Mary McCartan to his girlfriend's house in Dungannon, having an hour earlier participated in a nearby ambush where the IRA had attempted to murder two RUC officers. Upon being stopped at a roadblock, Quinn explained that he had been at work picking mushrooms at McCartan's farms and told officers where he was going. His employer – the driver – confirmed Quinn's statement. Nevertheless, both McCartan and Quinn were arrested under the Prevention of Terrorism Act (NI) and taken to Gough Barracks for questioning. In line with guidelines set out in the IRA's 'Green Book', Quinn exercised his right to remain silent during interrogation but the RUC maintained they had enough evidence to convict him anyway, and on April 21st after the mandatory seven-day limit had been reached, Quinn was charged with two counts of attempted murder and possession of firearms. Five months passed in preparation for the court case, but when the when the case came to court, witnesses refused to testify for fear of IRA reprisals; in September, all charges against Quinn were dropped. Breathing a sigh of relief, Quinn likely realised he had had a close call and probably decided not to chance his luck too soon. Above all, there was concern that even though a case could not be made to stick against Quinn, the intelligence and police services had realised he was an active Provo and were likely to be following his every move. His absence from Ulster might set alarm bells ringing; rather than travel to the Continent and potentially compromise the rest of the ASU, Quinn laid low.

There were enough operations going on in Northern Ireland however to keep several of the European team busy. One operation in particular involved not only several ASU members, but also half the South Armagh and South Down / North Louth brigades and caused huge repercussions for everyone involved: the IRA, the RUC, An Garda Síochána in the Republic of Ireland and British intelligence. In the aftermath of the Loughgall ambush, RUC Chief Superintendent Harry Breen had held a press conference on television, explaining about the operation against the IRA and showing the arsenal of Provo weaponry that had been recovered at the scene. Breen had long been a target for the IRA going back as far as June 1978 – then a plan had been made to abduct and kill the RUC officer. The South Armagh Brigade stopped a vehicle at Sturgan Brae, close to Camlough Lake, shooting dead the occupants RUC Constables Billy Turbitt and Hughie McConnell. Turbitt bore a close similarity to Harry Breen and an IRA informer later admitted to security services that they mistook Turbitt for Breen. Breen's involvement in the Loughgall press conference reignited the IRA's interest in him and put the now high-ranking RUC officer under close surveillance, hoping to get the chance for revenge. They monitored his activities, travel plans, vehicles and security arrangements and took up residence at a vacant house at 12, The Crescent, overlooking the Garda station in Dundalk. They regularly watched Breen visit the station for meetings, always using his personal car – a red Vauxhall Cavalier - with the registration plate KIB-1204. The IRA surveillance team noted every visit.

Breen and his colleague Superintendent Bob Buchanan had received instructions from UK Secretary of State for Northern Ireland Tom King to do something about the blatant cross-border smuggling activities of Slab Murphy - and indirectly about the Provisional IRA South Armagh Brigade - a thorn in the side of the British security services that had thus far proved tricky to remove. Breen and

Buchanan were drawing up plans for a coordinated effort between the RUC and Garda to smash Slab's smuggling empire. Murphy on the other hand had no desire to be limited in his various activities, declared Breen "Public Enemy Number One" and gave the order to his second-in-command Sean Hughes (also known as 'The Surgeon') for something to be done about the situation. Hughes coordinated with the South Down Brigade to pull together a big team of volunteers in preparation for an ambush.

According to IRA sources, there were three initial attempts to stage an ambush: in November and December 1988, and January 1989. On each occasion, two Active Service Units took up position in quiet, discreet locations and waited for the vehicle to arrive. In November and December, the car failed to appear and the ASU's packed up and went home. In January, there were too many British troops on the ground, making it impossible to carry out the operation without capture. Finally, on March 20th 1989, Buchanan called a meeting at the customary short notice such sensitive operations demanded with senior Garda officers to draw up the plans for Operation AMAIZING – a coordinated strike against the smuggling activities of Slab Murphy - and scheduled an informal conference with the Gardai to be held at Dundalk police station in the Republic later that afternoon. Although never conclusively proved, a PIRA informant within the Garda station allegedly passed word to Hughes, who quickly assembled a team of thirty to forty volunteers from South Armagh and South Down – including Hardy, Mooch and Hughes' younger brother Paul, ready to strike. Breen and Buchanan travelled from the North to Dundalk in plain clothes and without escort in Buchanan's personal unmarked car: the red Vauxhall Cavalier that was not armoured-plated and did not have bulletproof glass. Buchanan had used this same car on all of his previous visits to Dundalk and other locations in the Republic of Ireland and always used the same route. Both officers were unarmed, as it was illegal to transport weapons into the Republic of Ireland; another detail that did not go unnoticed by the IRA. Arriving in Dundalk, Buchanan and

Breen met with senior Garda officers – starting at about 2.10pm inside the office of Garda Chief Superintendent John Nolan. Breen was also due to meet with Customs & Excise officials the following morning. Buchanan drove away from the Dundalk Garda station after the meeting had ended at about 3.15 p.m. and turned off the main Dublin-Belfast road onto the Edenappa Road, which passes through the South Armagh village of Jonesborough.

Under the command of 'The Surgeon', the IRA had set up four checkpoints on each of the four roads leading out of Dundalk: Dundalk-Omeath, Dundalk-Carrickmacross, Dundalk-Newry, and Dundalk-Jonesborough. At around 3.40 p.m., Buchanan's Cavalier crossed the Northern Ireland border at Border Check Point 10 on the Edenappa Road. Yards up ahead, at the top of a hill on a tree-lined section of the road just south of Jonesborough, the heavily armed IRA waited to carry out the ambush. The site the IRA chose was in "dead ground", meaning that they could not be seen by the nearby British Army observation post. The secluded back road was considered to be one of the most dangerous in south Armagh and as such, a "no-go area" for the security forces as it was regularly patrolled by the South Armagh Brigade. As Buchanan reached the hilltop he was flagged down by an armed IRA man standing in the middle of the road wearing Army battle fatigues and camouflage paint on his face. Another armed man, dressed in a similar fashion, stood in a ditch by the roadside by four cars he ordered to stop and their drivers to position so only one car could pass the road at a time and even then only slowly. Buchanan, assuming it was a British Army checkpoint, slowed down and stopped. At that moment, a stolen cream-coloured HiAce van, which had been following behind his car – as it had done so on three previous occasions over the past few weeks - overtook and pulled into the laneway of an empty house opposite. Four more armed IRA men wearing battle fatigues and balaclavas leapt out of the van. They approached the Cavalier. According to the IRA,

> "when the vehicle was intercepted, the two male occupants were challenged to step out of the car with their hands up. The car was put into reverse and attempted to escape. Instructions had been to intercept the vehicle and arrest the occupants but if this was not possible then they were to ensure that neither occupant escaped."

In fact it seems no such challenge was issued; IRA gunmen immediately began shooting, mainly at the driver's side, hitting the two officers. Buchanan made two frantic attempts to reverse and escape but his car stalled on each attempt and he was already dead before his car came to a standstill. Examination of the car the following day found it still to be in reverse gear with Buchanan's foot fully pressed against the accelerator. Breen, despite his gunshot wounds, managed to stumble out of the car, waving a white handkerchief at the gunmen in a gesture of surrender. One of the gunmen walked over to him, told him to lie on the ground. When he did so, the gunman fired a shot into the back of his head, killing him instantly. Another gunman then approached Buchanan's already dead body in the car and shot him again in the side of the head at point-blank range. After removing security documents relevant to the meeting with Garda from the Cavalier and personal belongings of the two officers, including notes for a history of his church Buchanan had been writing and a diary from Breen containing the contact details of informers, as well as those of an RUC assistant Chief Constable whose house was later bombed, the gunmen drove away from the scene of the killings at high speed. Not only had the Provos scored a major coup in gaining important intelligence documents from the enemy but the IRA had - once more - taken revenge for the massacre in Loughgall.

The shock of the Jonesborough ambush reverberated around Northern Ireland: it was a massive coup for the IRA and Breen and

Buchanan were to be the most highly-ranking RUC officers to be killed in the Troubles - the ambush was one of the most audacious the IRA had carried out in South Armagh. Within the IRA itself, there was unease; the documents removed from Buchanan's Cavalier were written in code but using the documents, the IRA leadership claimed to have identified a number of RUC informers within their own ranks and informed all IRA volunteers that they were announcing an amnesty; anyone admitting to collaboration with the security services could come forward without harm. It is still unclear whether the amnesty was a double bluff to flush out informers or whether the leadership really had worked out the names; in any case, unsurprisingly no one took up the offer.

In an attempt to track down the IRA team responsible for the Jonesborough ambush, the RUC started to carry out intensive questioning of known IRA volunteers and searched their houses for clues. Hardy, Mooch and the others all produced alibis; most of these were not watertight and the heat was on. For some, it was sure to only be a matter of time before the RUC would be beating down the door or attempting to snatch suspected IRA volunteers from the streets of South Armagh and South Down. Nevertheless, the South Down Brigade, and Bap Hardy in particular, felt that the IRA needed to keep up the pressure on the RUC and step up the campaign. South Down chose to bomb the RUC station in Warrenpoint, a small town on the banks of Carlingford Lough, a few minutes' drive from both Newry and Jonesborough. On April 12th, Bap Hardy led an Active Service Unit to Warrenpoint's Charlotte Street where the RUC station was located, armed with a large explosive device fitted with two timing mechanisms. The plan was to have the main bomb detonate one hour after priming, then set off a smoke grenade fifteen minutes after the main device in order to hamper recovery efforts once rescuers had arrived at the scene. Beforehand, Hardy would phone through a coded warning so that the main bomb would cause extensive damage but avoid casualties; however, the blast would attract RUC and emergency services, which would then be caught up in the secondary detonation. The van containing the bomb parked outside the RUC station, one of the ASU set about priming the detonators and timing devices. In doing so he accidentally triggered a microswitch on the device. The bomb detonated with no warning, blowing a huge hole in the RUC station and the hardware store next door, where 20-year-old Catholic Joanne Reilly was working behind the counter. The blast ripped her apart, the next innocent victim of the bungling Hardy's Newry team. The predominantly Republican population of Warrenpoint was incensed at the IRA killing one of their own: it was the perfect time for some of the volunteers involved to spend some time away from Northern Ireland until the heat died down – in Continental Europe.

Over on the Continent, Gerry McGeough and Gerry Hanratty remained on remand in Germany and continued to be questioned separately by the *SoKo PIRA*. Adhering strictly to the rules laid down in the IRA 'bible', the 'Green Book', the prisoners divulged little to no information to *BKA* investigators. The two Gerrys were much more forthcoming with information on the circumstances of their arrest and conditions in prison when asked by Republican sympathiser group *Irland Solidarität Gießen* to pen some notes for their irregularly published Irland Solidarität Info pamphlet, circulated in left-wing circles. On April 8th – the anniversary of Bobby Sands being elected as an MP whilst being on hunger strike in the Maze – Gerry McGeough wrote a description of life in JVA Frankenthal from his prison cell:

> „During the first five months of my imprisonment I was kept in virtual isolation. In the first six weeks – until I got a radio – I had no idea of what was going on outside my cell; world events during this time remain a secret to me! Every day I was allowed one hour of yard exercise, watched as now by an armed guard and a camera. It was of course solitary yard exercise and for 116 days, until Christmas when they stopped this

disgusting practice, my arms were bound behind my back. (this created interesting problems when I wanted to scratch my head or indeed, other parts of my anatomy...) Apart from yard exercise and showering three times a week – both of which activities have been accompanied by strict security procedures including clearing the entire cell block whilst this „evil terrorist" has a wash – I have spent the entire time in my cell. The cell itself by the way is also completely secure, e.g. with a perforated screen in front of the window made of glass and concrete struts. Since the end of January I have been allowed to take yard exercise with a handful of other prisoners, and I am now permitted to watch one hour of TV per night. In addition, since March it has been possible to take part in mass – the previous restriction I see as an unnecessary infringement of my religious rights. Opportunities for further education or recreational activities have been denied."

As one ASU sat in prison awaiting trial, another was embarking on active service in Europe. On April 14th 1989, Leonard 'Bap' Hardy took a ferry from Rosslare to Le Havre in France with girlfriend Donna Maguire. But far from lying low in Europe until the aftermath of Jonesborough and Warrenpoint had died down: Maguire and Hardy had people to meet and plans to be made. Together they drove through France and Belgium, into Germany and headed to the picturesque Eifel region. In the hilly Reichshof area between Gummersbach and Olpe around 65 kilometres west of Cologne, sat the village of Eckenhagen. There in a small house lived Pauline Drumm and Donagh O'Kane. The couple preserved a veneer of normality and anonymity; they occasionally met neighbours for coffee and the couple was also often seen jogging in the woods around Eckenhagen. Hardy and Maguire joined up with Patrick Murray and then with Drumm and O'Kane: from March 28th onwards, the Active Service Unit rented a series of holiday apartments in Eckenhagen, Wolfseifen and Mühlenschlade, posing as Canadian and Australian tourists. The area was perfect for covert IRA operations; about an hour's drive from the Royal Air Force bases dotted along the border between Germany, Netherlands and Belgium; a two hour drive from British Army barracks scattered across the northern Rhineland and East Westphalia; the support networks of Republican sympathisers further south in the Rhein-Main area also only around 150km away. The Eifel region attracted enough tourists not to stand out too much, as well as offering ample, secluded holiday accommodation. In addition, the countryside between the hundred or so villages making up the Reichshof area provided the optimum location for hiding arms caches, and the seldom frequented, protective woodlands were the perfect place for testing weapons undetected. As soon as Hardy and Maguire arrived however, there was concern; on the night of April 16th, the owner of a medical supplies store in sleepy Eckenhagen, where the ASU was based, was gunned down as he tackled a burglar who had broken into his store, the latest in a series of break-ins. The car the man used was stolen and fitted with false number plates; the intruder did not utter a word when tackled, prompting suspicions that he was not German, and the description of the man closely matched Hardy. Police were put on high alert in the area. The ASU were initially forced to lie very low to avoid inadvertently being caught in a police dragnet intended for someone else - only months later was the culprit - a small time criminal - apprehended.

In May, the team rented a spacious holiday cottage in north-eastern France, La Vignette. It was perfect for the ASU's needs: next to the main road, offered space to hide vehicles and materials, on the edge of a dense forest and adjacent to the main autoroute de l'est running from Paris to Germany. O'Kane and Drumm took over the property on June 4th and were soon joined by the others. The cottage in Clermont-en-Argonne, around 100 kilometres from the Belgian border and 150 kilometres from Saarbrücken in Germany, acted as an IRA safe house and gave the team another location from which to plan and launch attacks. Whilst making reconnaissance trips to RAF bases dotted along the border, as well as trips to the Netherlands – Maguire and Drumm were seen by witnesses several times in Bergen op Zoom, some 40 kilometres west of Breda - Belgium and France, the ASU concentrated on the cluster of Army barracks around the Northern Rhine and East Westphalia. The reconnaissance missions were extensive and detailed: the unit researched and scouted Ripon Barracks in Bielefeld, Birkenfeld, Celle, Lothian Barracks in Detmold, Roy Barracks in Düsseldorf-Ratingen, Glamorgan Barracks in Duisburg, Fallingbostel, Mansergh Barracks in Gütersloh, Gordon Barracks in Hameln, Cromwell Barracks in Hamm, various NAAFI facilities in Hannover, Hammersmith Barracks in Herford, Tofrek Barracks in Hildesheim, a NAAFI facility in the Rodenkirchen suburb of Cologne, Bradbury Barracks in Krefeld, Lemgo, Tunis Barracks in Lübbecke, Clifton Barracks in Minden, JHQ in Rheindahlen, Wrexham Barracks in Mülheim an der Rühr, Oxford, Waterloo and York Barracks in Münster, Nienburg, Osnabrück, Paderborn, Soest, Caithness Barracks in Verden, Viersen, RAF Wildenrath and Northampton Barracks in Wolfenbüttel. Not only were barracks and airfields themselves observed, analysed for potential targeting and assessed for which methods of attack would be best suited, but also areas away from barracks where families and German civilians lived. The British Army garrisons in the northern towns of Celle, Münster and Osnabrück were singled out for extensive observation. Trenchard Barracks in the north of Celle was watched, as well as the small village of Adelheidsdorf to the south of the town. There the unit eyed-up a culvert running under the B3 motorway and toyed with the idea of placing explosives under the bridge to be detonated by remote control when a suitable British Army target went past. Osnabrück housed the largest unit of the British Army outside of the British Isles: the eight individual barracks were spread out over a wide area of Osnabrück and the huge amount of military personnel dominated the town, especially after nightfall. The soldiers stationed in Osnabrück and nearby Münster were always to be found drinking in pubs and clubs around the town: previous PIRA operations including Roermond and Nieuw-Bergen had proved that inebriated soldiers were off-guard and easy targets. Indeed, this had already been realised within the British Army itself and the Intelligence & Security Group, charged with designing measures to combat IRA attacks on personnel and locations in Germany, carried out extensive work in this area themselves. The team searched barracks by daylight and at night-time, trying to ascertain weak spots where the IRA might be able to penetrate defences. In the evenings the team covertly spoke to soldiers returning from a night-out, the squaddies often the worse for wear, and only too keen to let slip information that, in the wrong hands, could be used by the IRA for intelligence purposes. Covert threat reports compiled by the Intelligence & Security teams were passed over to the Commanding Officers and Regimental Sergeant-Majors of each barracks, highlighting the lax security. But the advice and warnings fell on deaf ears; the general response to security advice from senior personnel was "nothing will happen on my watch" – the reports were either ignored completely or not taken seriously. Concerned at the security situation in Osnabrück in particular, the Intelligence & Security Group, together with liaison officers from the *BKA*'s *SoKo PIRA* team, undertook a CTA (Covert Threat Assessment) of Quebec Barracks, detailing exactly how easy it would be for the IRA to mount an attack and how they would do it. The report was submitted – and ignored.

The ASU were one step ahead and in a position to exploit the gaping hole in security measures. They may have also have had access to 'insider info' from an unlikely source: a British Army soldier nicknamed "Dixie". Michael Robert Dickson came from Scottish Catholic background. Born into a military family, his father had also been stationed with the British Army in Germany and Dickson was born in the military hospital in Hanover in 1964. After spending his childhood in Port Glasgow in Scotland, Dixie chose to follow in his father's footsteps and applied to join the British Army, opting for the

Royal Engineers. Shortly after finishing his basic training in England, where - amongst other things – he learned to handle explosives, his regiment was sent to the South Atlantic to the Falkland Islands and Dixie spent a six-month tour of duty helping to build, demolish and rebuild bridges. On his return to Europe, 23 Engineer Regiment to which Dickson belonged, was deployed to Germany and sent to Osnabrück to support the 12th Armoured Infantry Brigade. The unit was based at Quebec Barracks, located in Atter – a western suburb of Osnabrück, right on the state border between Lower Saxony and North-Rhine Westphalia. An avid football fan – a supporter of Celtic in particular – Dixie spent a lot of his free weekends traveling to Hamburg to watch Bundesliga games at HSV and their local rivals, the left-leaning FC St. Pauli. Dixie preferred the atmosphere at St. Pauli's ground situated at the heart to the Reeperbahn district; and their politics. Whilst the hardcore HSV fans had a reputation of being right-wing, St. Pauli fans were most definitely at the left-wing end of the political spectrum, and sympathetic to the plight of Catholics back in Northern Ireland; Dickson was a little surprised to see the Irish tricolours bearing the legend 'I.R.A' being held aloft in the home supporters end. Republican literature and magazines were also sold at the ground; Dixie was intrigued enough to buy a copy of 'Republican News'. From then on, he regularly devoured the magazine as he began to develop a picture of life as part of the downtrodden Catholic minority and the purported injustices and brutality meted out by the British Army in Ulster. As a British soldier – a sworn enemy of the Provisional IRA – Dixie knew that he had to keep his Republican reading material secret from his comrades back at Quebec Barracks, pretend to laugh at anti-Catholic jokes, pretend to be angry whenever the IRA pulled off a successful attack, whilst at the same time sympathising more and more with the Republican cause. In June 1988 he travelled to Stuttgart to watch the UEFA European Championship game between England and the Republic of Ireland and was arrested by police for fighting with England fans on the side of the Irish. Released without charge, Dixie realised he could not continue to pretend anymore and decided to leave the British

Army and Osnabrück, demobbed and returning to Scotland at the end of 1988. Dixie soon made contact with local Republicans in Scotland, drinking in Catholic bars and telling drinking companions stories of his life as a Republican in the British Army. Over time, word filtered back to Belfast and the IRA's Overseas Department about the ex-soldier: Dixie could be a source of useful information that could help with IRA plans to hit British military targets in Europe. Dixie's detailed information on British Army installations, personnel, movements and habits may have helped form an integral part of the IRA attack plan.

The ASU rented an apartment in the town as a base and got to work. Under the guidance of Patrick Murray, the most senior IRA man in the team, the ASU retrieved firearms, Memopark timers, mercury-tilt switches, detonators and 150 kilogrammes of Semtex from the arms cache in Werl, bought five – three twenty-litre, two ten-litre - oil canisters from a DIY store and returned to the apartment in Osnabrück, to set about preparing the explosive devices. The two ten-litre canisters were taped together to form an improvised twenty-litre device – to each of the four devices, Murray attached a small wooden cigar-box sized construction; the time-power-units or TPUs. Inside the boxes there was contained a microswitch connected to one of Patrick Ryan's Memopark timers and wires to connect the detonating mechanism to the canister. Each box was secured against premature detonation via a wooden pin attached to a length of cord, which acted as a circuit breaker. When in place, the timer would be set to anywhere up to 60 minutes and the pin removed, activating the bomb. When the timer ran down, a metal arm attached to the Memopark would connect to a wire soldered to the base of box; the electrical current would travel down the wire into the canister and detonate the 30 kilogrammes of Semtex-H plastic explosives packed into each one.

On June 16th, two of the team – it is unclear who exactly, but likely including Maguire as intelligence officer - visited the barracks for a final reconnaissance check and made notes of how to get into the base, identifying the ideal location to cut through the wire fence without being disturbed. Two days later, on June 18th 1989, Maguire, Hardy, Drumm, O'Kane and Murray loaded the assembled canister bombs into a rented black Saab 9000 and - armed with AK-47 automatic weapons - drove under cover of nightfall to Quebec Barracks. Cutting through the wire perimeter fence next to an accommodation block – part of the Sergeants Mess, where six soldiers were sleeping – Hardy and O'Kane carefully unloaded the bombs and placed them up against the outer wall of the accommodation block, right underneath a window. Shortly after 1am, 62-year-old German civilian Gunter Kittelmann was making his nightly rounds. The German civil engineering firm that was in the process of constructing storm-water tanks on the base had employed Kittelmann as a night watchman, whose duty it was to check the pumps that ran 24/7, pumping off the excess water caused by the high ground-water level. As Kittelmann swung his torch, he saw the devices propped up against the wall – then he saw in the beam the figure of a man dressed in a dark boiler suit and carrying an AK-47. Startled, the IRA volunteer aimed the AK-47 at Kittelmann and pulled the trigger: the rifle was set to semi-automatic and the single shot missed the German night watchman by inches. Kittelmann grabbed the barrel of the gun and pushed it away; the IRA man hit Kittelmann in the face with the rifle butt and knocked him out. The gunfire and shouts awoke the sleeping soldiers and one went out to investigate - the ASU ran back through the fence to the waiting getaway car to avoid capture, racing away from the scene with tyres screeching in the dirt. As more soldiers arrived on the scene, Kittelmann slowly regained consciousness, and crawled into one of the two nearby building site huts. Noticing the bombs, and realising they were under attack, the soldiers raised the alarm and all 800 people housed in the rest of the barracks were evacuated - just in time, as one of the bombs exploded, a huge detonation pushing the outer wall into the building, demolishing furniture, the roof of the accommodation block, the other building site hut to the one Kittelmann was in. Had Kittelmann taken refuge in the other hut and the soldiers in the accommodation block still have been asleep, the night watchman and the majority of the soldiers would have been killed in the blast.

A few hours after the foiled attack, in Karlsruhe the Federal State Prosecution Office GBA opened case file 1Bjs 186/89-4 and instructed the *BKA* and Joachim Rzeniecki's *SoKo PIRA* to carry out the investigation. Together with the state police of the Landeskriminalamt Niedersachsen (*LKA*) and the local *KPI* (*Kriminalpolizeinspektion* or criminal investigation police), a local *SoKo* unit was set up using the abbreviation *SoKo* Osnabrück and investigators got to work. Examining the crime scene, they found not only the Semtex-filled canisters but also the AK-47 cartridge ejected from the assault rifle after the IRA fired on Gunther Kittelmann.

Later that day, the spokesman for the Federal State Prosecution Office BGA Hans-Jürgen Förster issued a statement.

> *"The four unexploded bombs were not set to detonate, presumably because the perpetrators were disturbed by an employee."*

British Forces spokesman Nigel Ginnis added that the 62 year old night watchman

> *"was going about his business and discovered two men outside the building...a shot was fired...and he was hit in the face with a gun belt or something of that nature."*

Kittelmann, although shocked, had however only been superficially injured and was treated for cuts and bruises. Thanks to his intervention however, the ASU had not been able to set the detonators on the other four bombs and thus greater devastation and casualty numbers were averted. Kittelmann would later be awarded a medal for his bravery by the State of Niedersachsen. In

1991, he was due to receive the Queens Gallantry Medal at the British Embassy in Bonn, when he sadly suffered a massive heart attack en route and died two months later.

As dawn broke on June 19th, Reuters in London received a telephone call from a man speaking English with a heavy foreign accent, claiming responsibility for the attack on behalf of an undefined "*allgemeines Kommando*". Unconvinced by the use of a German phrase, Joachim Rzeniecki and his team knew that the attack bore all the hallmarks of the Provisional IRA. Sure enough, later that day the suspicions were confirmed as the Provos placed a telephone call from the Republican Press Centre to the BBC in Northern Ireland, publicly claiming responsibility for the blast and promising further attacks.

The next attack in the campaign would soon follow but using a different strategy. Amongst other targets, the ASU focused their attention on the city of Hanover – where Dixie had been born and where his father had been stationed in the Army. There was still a considerable military presence in the city, with single soldiers living in barracks, married soldiers living with their families in houses in residential districts. Once again, they made for soft targets; apart from a rather lax security regime, despite changes implemented as part of Lieutenant-Colonel Wrights Project ALBRIC, the private cars of British personnel were left-hand-drive vehicles, fitted with British number plates and parked in areas that British tourists were unlikely to be; it was simple for the IRA to identify a vehicle as belonging to a serviceman. On June 26th, Pauline Drumm rented an Audi 80 car with the registration HG-CA 599 from the Avis car rental branch in Cologne in the name of Elisabeth Forbes, and the team drove north to Hannover. A short drive through the city was all it took to identify a whole host of potential IRA targets. One such area was in Oststadt, a few streets away from Hanover Zoo, where around 25 British Army personnel and their families lived – a quiet, unpatrolled civilian area. The ASU drew up an attack plan. The devices were prepared; around 1.25 kilogrammes of Semtex-H explosive were placed into an empty wooden box, rigged up to wires and attached to one of Patrick Ryan's Swiss-made Memopark timers. The ASU cut down a Sea Searcher magnet into two parts and affixed them to the device. On the afternoon of Sunday July 2nd, led by Patrick Murray, the ASU drove to Hannover in two rented cars – a BMW 316i and the Audi 80 - and targeted two British-registered vehicles parked a few metres apart on the sedate, tree-lined Kaiserallee. Surreptitiously the IRA attached the car bombs to the underside of each vehicle and parked a short distance away to watch events unfold.

31 year old British Army Corporal Steven Smith - known to all as "Smudge" – was from Cleckheaton in West Yorkshire and a rations officer with the 1 Royal Tank Regiment, based at Tofrek Barracks. He lived on Kaiserallee with his wife Tina and four young children Louisa (aged 11), Lee (9), Leanna (7) and Jade (2). He had joined the Army in 1975 as an eighteen-year-old, following in the footsteps of his father, who had served as a gunner during the Korean War. Enjoying the relaxed life of a posting to Germany, on that Sunday, Steve and the family were looking forward to visiting the local *Kirmes*, the annual summer festival held at a fairground not too far from the Smith's apartment. At around 6:15pm, the family left their married quarter apartment block to head to the fairground. Going ahead, Corporal Smith crossed the road to open their red Daimler Benz 230 parked opposite Kaiserallee 3 and next to a fenced-off communal park. But fatefully - like so many Forces personnel and despite repeated advice about personal security from the Army - Steve Smith forgot to check the underside of the vehicle. He climbed into the car and sat down in the driver's seat, as the ASU drove off at speed in two cars.

As Corporal Smith turned the ignition key, the car vibrated as the engine started. On the outside of the cigar-box device clamped to the underside of the vehicle, the mercury bubble in the tilt switch shifted slightly and made contact with a wire attached to a microswitch; this in turn was connected to a small metal rod attached to the Memopark timer. Having run down, the timer had turned to a position where the metal rod attached to the Memopark had made a connection with the microswitch connected by wire to the mercury-tilt switch on the outside of the box and the Canadian-made CIL detonator embedded in Semtex-H explosive inside it– the circuit between mercury-tilt switch, microswitch, timer, detonator and explosives completed, an electrical pulse flowed in a fraction of a fraction of a second to the detonating mechanism, into the Semtex-H. The car bomb detonated with a deafening bang, shaking the windows of the nearby apartments. The vehicle exploded and caught fire - debris was hurled over one hundred metres; Smith's young family stood only a few feet away.

Minutes later, ambulances, the Royal Military Police and local German police arrived at the scene on Kaiserallee. Sometime later, Lower Saxony *LKA* officers, followed by Rzeniecki's *SoKo PIRA* team appeared to a scene of devastation. Joachim Rzeniecki remembers the traumatic view that faced investigators on their arrival:

> *"Corporal Smith had been torn to pieces by the force of the blast, before the very eyes of his wife and children – it was horrific."*

Steven Smith had been killed instantly in the explosion; his wife Tina had been seriously injured, and besides shrapnel wounds, had to be treated for burns to 30% of her body. The children were wounded by shrapnel from the bomb, but escaped with relatively minor injuries, being treated for shock, bruising and lacerations. Ammunition Technical Officers (ATOs) from the bomb disposal squad were in place and sealed off the area as they checked for secondary devices. The second UVBT had been attached to the underside of a Datsun Bluebird hatchback belonging to Sergeant-

Major Raymond Clark: the device under the chassis on the passenger side of the vehicle was quickly located. The UVBT was made safe by explosive experts using a high-powered water jet, before the PIRA could claim another innocent victim on the streets of Germany.

Once again the PIRA claimed responsibility for Corporal Smith's murder and issued a statement the following day:

> "We are forced to take our struggle beyond Ireland because the British public are restricted by their government from learning of its failure in Ireland and the resistance to its rule."

Nevertheless, the interception of the device under Sergeant-Major Clarks vehicle was a blow to the IRA; not only did it mean a loss of 'material' without the planned bloodshed for which it was intended, it also provided German civil and British military investigators with valuable evidence that might help to track down the ASU. The Northern Ireland Forensic Science Laboratory (NIFSL) would once again have the chance to pull apart an IRA device to check the source of the components and possibly recover fingerprints, which could be checked against existing databases. This information would likely link back to previous attacks and help the investigating teams build up a picture of who they were looking for. By now, the *BKA* and the other members of the cross-border TRIO team had been in extensive contact with their British and Irish police and security service colleagues and the openness of information exchange had given them a clear list of suspects to track down. The Dutch *BVD* and *CRI* gave the ASU the codename FERMDOWN, a reference to Co. FERManagh and Co. DOWN, the counties from where the individual members hailed. Initially, the teams had only been able to act in a reactive fashion after an attack, now they were able to proactively conduct a dragnet investigation in an attempt to find the ASU. On July 10th, *BKA* investigators met with their Dutch *CRI* counterparts to discuss the IRA situation. At the meeting the *CRI* handed over the sketch of border crossings near Bad Bentheim which had been found when Dutch police had stormed the Buitenveldert flat and arrested Bik McFarlane, Gerry and William Kelly. The *BKA* began to carry out checks at usually unmanned border crossing points between Oeding and Gronau, at weekends and during the hours of darkness. The measures were subsequently extended to border checkpoints on the Belgian and French borders as well.

Joachim Rzeniecki and the *SoKo PIRA* team of the *Bundeskriminalamt* had also been able to gain further deeper insights into the modus operandi of the Provisional IRA units in Europe as regards movement and logistics using computer data. During the offensive of the mid-1980s, it had been commonplace to purchase or steal vehicles for use in reconnaissance and attacks. As the purchased vehicles had been relatively easily traced, the IRA moved to eliminate or at least reduce the risk of detection when procuring transport by increasingly using car rental companies. Hanratty and McGeough had rented a number of vehicles in 1988 before their arrest; the FERMDOWN unit was relying heavily on rental cars. Rzeniecki and his team decided that this was an area of IRA logistics that could prove to be a weak link. Using data going back to January 1st 1989 from Avis and Hertz, obtained via court injunctions, the team analysed the behaviour of foreigners when renting cars in Germany and made some logical deductions: in stark contrast to German citizens, who generally used current account debit cards for payment, foreign businessmen or women renting a vehicle from a car hire firm would generally use a credit card. In addition, a valid reference or home address would be given on the rental form and at time of rental, there would usually be the opportunity for the person renting the car to make small talk; they would often say why they needed the vehicle and to where they were planning to drive, whom they were planning to meet. When the rental car was returned, the distances covered during the rental period would generally be low, the car having been used to transfer from airport to city or drive to meetings a few kilometres away and back. However, analysis of the rentals involved in known Provisional

IRA activities demonstrated completely different characteristics: the rental price would be paid in cash to minimise traceability, often a hotel address – or a completely fake address – would be given on the rental form. The IRA volunteer renting the vehicle would not be forthcoming with information, bar the occasional brief cover story when pressed, about the purpose of the rental. The distances covered during the period of rental would often be huge; several thousand kilometres would be clocked up within the space of a few days as the ASU carried out reconnaissance of targets in many different places in a short space of time or ferried weapons and explosives between delivery points, arms caches or target locations. In addition, the papers provided to prove identification would either be stolen and doctored, or completely fake – the validity of identification papers could easily be checked by local police and *BKA* via databases or calls to issuing authorities, including those in other countries. With this matrix of criteria, the technical team of the *SoKo PIRA* was able to programme a piece of computer software called CARS. The CARS software allowed a systematic searching of all rental contracts with the car hire firms taking these criteria into account, as well as the use of Anglo-Saxon sounding names. This cross-referencing of data to pinpoint possible suspect rentals helped narrow down the search for the IRA: rental agreements identified by CARS were followed up and the vehicles involved searched by forensic teams. In many cases, the forensic analysis produced results: traces of Semtex and gun oil were found in several vehicles, including the BMW and Audi cars used in the operation in Hannover. The rental periods of these identified vehicles were finally cross-referenced with CCTV video seized from the relevant car hire firm; thus not only were the *BKA* team able to build up a picture of the movements of the ASUs, they would also be able to capture video pictures of the suspects, which could be sent to Northern Ireland for identification. In addition, once a potential IRA car rental had been identified, Rzeniecki and his team were able to retrospectively check recordings of all police radio calls in the states of Lower Saxony and North Rhein Westphalia to determine whether or not the vehicle and its occupants had been the subject of any vehicle check whilst in use by the ASU. In this way, the *SoKo PIRA* team was to trace 29 rentals by Drumm, O'Kane, Murray, Maguire and Hardy in the period from April to July and to a large degree piece together the movements of the ASU. Positive identification of the ASU members involved meant Rzeniecki and his team now knew exactly who they were looking for and how they were operating. The net was starting to close in on the Provisional IRA but for now, the Provos were still just one step ahead.

Unaware and undeterred, Murray, Drumm, O'Kane, Hardy and Maguire planned the next attack. This time the target was not to be military but political. After the bomb Murray and Patrick Magee had detonated in Brighton in 1984 had failed to kill their main target, "The Pope" and the IRA had a long-standing score to settle with British Prime Minister Margaret Thatcher. They had a new opportunity to do so. Thatcher was due to visit Paris shortly after the murder of Corporal Smith for the G7 economic summit. The IRA saw a chance for a 'spectacular': kill the British Prime Minister, score a huge propaganda hit against the British government and rid the IRA of their nemesis. The ASU drove to Clermont-en-Argonne, and from there began to carry out surveillance on the summit locations and Thatcher's hotel in Paris. However, it soon became clear that security at the summit was too tight for an attack to be mounted and that they might be being followed by intelligence services: the ASU decided to go separate ways and regroup later back in Germany or the Low Countries. Whilst Murray, Drumm and O'Kane stayed in France, Hardy and Maguire packed rucksacks and cases and took with them reconnaissance and other photos, maps of the Northern Rhine region, a telescopic sight for a Belgian-made FN rifle, a small amount of sodium chlorate wrapped in black plastic and a handful of the mercury tilt switches used in the 'up-and-under' UVBT devices they had been using. They had also written a shopping list detailing the stocks from the arms cache that needed to be replenished after being plundered for the attacks in Osnabrück and

Hanover and took with them notes they had made during reconnaissance missions. The pair headed for Le Havre and boarded the ferry St. Patrick heading for Rosslare in the Republic of Ireland. What they did not know at the time was that the *French Direction de la surveillance du territoire* (*DST*) – the directorate of the French Police Force, which acts as a domestic intelligence agency dealing with counterespionage and anti-terrorism – had been watching the ASU. The *DST* tipped off the Irish Garda via Interpol that two IRA suspects were travelling back to Ireland from France: on arrival at Rosslare on July 12th, gardai searched the luggage of Hardy and Maguire, found the bomb components, forged passports in the names of Pentony, Williams and Jacobsen and the other paraphernalia, and arrested them on explosives charges and on suspicion of being members of a proscribed organisation. Also found in the bag searches was a notebook containing addresses and telephone numbers in Germany – one in Mühltal, just south of Darmstadt, and one in France: the address of the restaurant adjacent to the safe house in Clermont-en-Argonne. But there was more: pages of handwritten notes detailing all the reconnaissance operations the ASU had carried out across Germany in the past few months on the Continent that Hardy and Maguire intended to hand over to their superior officers in the PIRA's Overseas Department. The notes were comprehensive, the reconnaissance thorough: military installations in twenty-nine different towns and cities had been surveyed. Alongside locations in Düsseldorf, Bielefeld and Duisburg that had already been targeted by the Geleen ASU the previous year, barracks in garrison towns such as Celle, Detmold, Herford, Hamelin, Mülheim and Minden had been observed and assessed, as well as locations in other towns across north-western Germany where British servicemen might be targeted, such as telephone boxes in Bielefeld, bus stops in Fallingbostel, from where a service back to the UK ran, and a hotel in Paderborn that had been noted as a place where (British Army) "majors meet". Not only were the British Army a potential target: the team had also scouted the vicinity of the Royal Air Force base in Wildenrath, not far from the city of Mönchengladbach, noting its close proximity to the border and the lax security of personnel away from the base. The notes also contained ideas for methods of attack, ranging from "mortars", to the ominous "half-tonner" – larger bombs used by the IRA with dramatic effect back in Northern Ireland and in mainland Britain and which contained 500kg of explosives. Crucially for investigators seeking to tie the pair to the Osnabrück bombing, Quebec Barracks appeared in the notes, the date of the attack scrawled next to it. Chillingly, completing the damning haul of evidence were notes on targets in Münster: Oxford, Waterloo and York Barracks were accompanied by the words "job planned" and colour reconnaissance photographs of Waterloo, Swinton and Buller Barracks, likely taken two years earlier by the Geleen ASU during reconnaissance operations. Hardy and Maguire were hauled before a court and, in view of the recovered material and documentation, the Irish judiciary had no option but to remand the pair in custody.

News of the arrests of Hardy and Maguire travelled fast. The security services passed on the information on the arrests to European neighbours, and warned that an attack on Margaret Thatcher on her visit to Paris might be imminent, owing to the mention of the La Vignette guesthouse. At the same time, Murray, Drumm and O'Kane realised that the arrests would likely lead French intelligence and law enforcement services straight to La Vignette. On July 14th the team quickly packed their things, jumped into their hire car and sped towards the border on the autoroute de l'est. It proved to be too late; the *DST* were watching: a French security service surveillance team trailed them along the motorway until the ASU got just beyond Metz; near the toll station at Saint-Avold, some thirty kilometres before the border to Germany, the *DST* pounced. Patrick Murray, Pauline Drumm and Donagh O'Kane were arrested at gunpoint.

Recovered from the Audi 80 were Memopark timers, a variety of detonators, a black balaclava, two blue boiler suits (on which forensics analysts would later find traces of PETN and RDX, the constituent elements of Semtex explosives), documents containing two handwritten telephone numbers in Germany, handwritten notes that the ASU had written whilst carrying out reconnaissance at Quebec Barracks in Osnabrück, York Barracks in Münster, as well as targets in Hannover and other places. The notes on Osnabrück contained a route description that exactly matched how the team had penetrated the base to plant the bombs and how the Security & Intelligence Group had predicted. Importantly for Joachim Rzeniecki and his *BKA* team, glue residue found on the Memopark timers later proved to exactly match glue residue on the Memopark timers that had been attached to the oil drum bombs in the operation at Quebec Barracks, creating a direct link between the captured volunteers and the Osnabrück attack. The IRA members were in possession of a number of hire car agreements documenting the cars they had used over the last few weeks, and notes on border crossing points between the Netherlands, France and Germany. Rounding off the incriminating haul were nineteen different false identity documents – Patrick Murray claimed to be 'Graham Livings', O'Kane 'James Fitzpatrick'; Drumm had a multitude of false passports and driving licenses in the names of Irene Balomedas, Kathleen Teresa Prior, Helena Patricia Feed and Elisabeth Forbes.

The trio were taken to Paris in handcuffs. The TRIO team was jubilant at the arrest of the core members of an Active Service Unit. A week later, the German Federal Prosecutor had been able to formally launch proceedings against the five captured IRA volunteers in France and Ireland and instructed the *BKA* to take all necessary steps to bring them to justice. The *BKA* had done sterling groundwork in gathering the basis of information for the extradition and had been able to retrospectively and accurately track the movements of the FERMDOWN ASU. Car rental agreements had been analysed and linked to the ASU; a systematic search of telephone lines where a line had been rented but no calls made had led them to the Reichshof area, where O'Kane and Drumm had been based. The couple had also been seen by locals jogging in the woods around Reichshof, and on one occasion observed clearing the car boot of leaves and twigs, leading the *SoKo PIRA* team to suspect that an arms cache was hidden in the woods. Rzeniecki called in the German air force Luftwaffe, who took thermal photographs of the woods in the hunt for weapons – an analysis of the pictures by the military did not lead them to weapons but nevertheless the evidence pointed to Murray, Drumm and O'Kane being a central part of one of the Provisional IRA Active Service Units based on the Continent, who were now under lock and key in France.

Once again, a combination of sloppiness, bad luck, excellent police work and streamlined international cooperation had dealt a severe blow to the operational capabilities of the Provisional IRA in Continental Europe.

10 THE GERMAN

On June 2nd 1989, Old Bailey bomber and one-time Maze escaper Gerry Kelly was released from Long Kesh. His release precipitated a flurry of secret dispatches between security services across Europe; all sat up and took notice. In particular, the Dutch *BVD* paid close attention – communiqués were circulated upon his release owing to his links with the Netherlands, his original arrest in Amsterdam in January 1986 and subsequent deportation to Northern Ireland twelve months later. As a high profile IRA man and a known operator on the Continent, Kelly was however unlikely to return in person to mainland Europe. He soon had enough to keep him busy back in Belfast. He went to work for Sinn Fein's POW department for a short spell, liaising with families and Republican inmates, before moving to the Republican Press Office to work alongside Siobhán O'Hanlon. He was approached by Northern Commander Martin McGuinness and Chief Of Staff Kevin McKenna to take over the vacant position of Adjutant General (AG) of the Provisional IRA. The role of the AG was essentially to ensure that the military strategy agreed by the Army Council – after being turned into an operational plan by the Chief of Staff - was communicated to Northern and Southern Command and effectively executed. In addition, the AG worked closely with the department heads at GHQ, and took part in Army Council meetings, albeit without voting rights. Kelly was impeccably connected within the upper echelons of the IRA, having close ties to McGuinness, Slab Murphy (due in part to Kelly's brief secondment to South Armagh in late 1983), and others, as well as having operational experience with many IRA leaders, including Owen Coogan, who in the light of the breakdown of European operations had moved to a slightly different role within the organisation - in the wake of the Gibraltar fiasco he was also too high-profile, having been named by several newspapers as having been involved in the planning of the foiled attack. The military leadership of the Provos saw in Gerry Kelly a man who commanded respect with grassroots volunteers, an impressive operational track record and a man to be trusted to get things done. All of these talents he was to need straight away – due to his European active service experience, he was the perfect candidate to join the Overseas Department. One of his first tasks was to help coordinate activities to get the European campaign back on track.

By this point at the end of the 1980's, operations in Continental Europe were overseen by a small band of senior IRA figures. Kelly's direct superior Kevin McKenna had the final say as the Chief of Staff, but the day-to-day planning of activities in mainland Europe was handled by a select team of senior IRA commanders and GHQ staff. Working alongside Gerry Kelly was the OC of Southern Command. Due to an ongoing court case, the man cannot be named here for legal reasons but originally from Belfast and then in his mid-thirties, he had served time with Bobby Sands and other senior figures in Long Kesh and was now based in Tallaght in Dublin. As well as Belfast Brigade veteran Owen Coogan, Director of Operations Slab Murphy and OC of Northern Command Martin McGuinness were also heavily involved in the organisation of the European offensive. Michael McKevitt as Quartermaster General bore ultimate responsibility for ensuring the Active Service Units were appropriately armed.

European activities had however by July 1989 – once again – temporarily and briefly been made more complicated. Murray, Drumm and O'Kane were incarcerated just outside Paris, awaiting an initial hearing and possible extradition to either Germany (the Generalbundesanwalt in Karlsruhe had formally requested extradition from France to Germany for the 1988 attacks in Duisburg and Ratingen, and the 1989 bombing of Quebec Barracks, as well as the murder of Corporal Smith in Hanover) or the Netherlands (for their involvement in the attacks in Roermond and Nieuw Bergen of the same year.), Hardy and Maguire were sent to

Mountjoy and Portlaoise prisons in the Republic of Ireland to await hearings. In Paris, Murray, Drumm and O'Kane were presented in court in front of judge Mr. Gilles Riviére on July 18th, where they admitted to membership of the Provisional IRA, hoping that their case would be seen as political, and hence hinder extradition proceedings. Hardy and Maguire were remanded in custody in the Republic, with a trial date set for October. With the 20th anniversary of the Troubles in August 1989 fast approaching, the IRA leadership needed to act fast to continue momentum.

Kelly and the Overseas Department looked to Dessie Grew. Grew had likely already been sent to the Continent shortly before the arrests in Rosslare and France; it was also likely he took with him two trusted comrades from the East Tyrone Brigade, Paddy Fox and Dermot Quinn. Setting up base in the Netherlands near to the German border in the region between Enschede, Oldenzaal and Hengelo, Grew began to plan how to recommence operations. On July 30th, the first shots were fired in anger. Gunfire was reported outside Barker Barracks in Paderborn in the northwest of Germany, home to 5 Royal Inniskilling Dragoon Guards. Not only was the unit the first Irish regiment to be deployed in Northern Ireland during the "Troubles", but that tour took them to the province at the height of the 1981 Maze hunger strikes. The targeting was likely not random, but well researched, deliberate and significant. The execution was however less so - the shots reportedly fired from a white van near to the barracks injured no one. Nevertheless, Danny Morrison's Republican Press Centre issued an ominous statement on behalf of the IRA on August 2nd, warning dependents and civilians in Continental Europe to steer clear of military personnel and their vehicles; a thinly veiled threat of further attacks. Further operations were jeopardised shortly afterwards: whilst in the Netherlands, the team returned to Northern Ireland to take part in an IRA operation back home: in August, dressed in British Army fatigues they headed to the port in Rotterdam to get the ferry back to Ireland. Dutch customs officials did not believe that the three men with broad

Northern Irish accents were members of the British Army. They checked their passports and arrested the trio on suspicion of travelling with false documentation. After checks were carried out and their passports – if not their story – standing up to scrutiny, they were allowed to board the ferry and returned to Ulster. Disaster had been averted – for now.

Dessie's plans for a European offensive had already been pieced together on paper but were to some extent already compromised. Paddy Fox and Dermot Quinn were young but already on the radars of British, Irish and European security services – indeed the British and Dutch intelligence services were already aware of their presence in Enschede. Paul Hughes and Martin Conlon, who had been part of the Armagh team behind the Jonesboro ambush were also young yet experienced volunteers but came with considerable baggage; both of whom having been put forward as candidates by Slab Murphy, and Hughes being the brother of Sean 'The Surgeon' Hughes, the formidable commander of the 'bomb-alley' area of South Armagh and second in command in the Brigade behind Slab. Bap Hardy and Donna Maguire were now unavailable due to their arrests in Rosslare. Grew however had two other important and capable acquaintances in mind: Gerard Harte and Sean Hick.

Twenty-five-year-old Gerard Majella Harte grew up on the Kilwilke estate in Lurgan, Co. Armagh and was from a staunchly Republican family – his grandfather Thomas had been a member of the 'Old IRA', who was executed in September 1940. His grandson followed in his footsteps; Gerard's career as a Republican activist started at an early age, and he was trained in firearms and explosives by the IRA's Fianna Éireann youth wing. Born in 1963, by the time he had reached the age of sixteen, he was already in trouble and on the run: in 1979, he was accused of petrol-bombing an Orange Order hall in his home town, which caused £75,000 of damage, as well as possession of firearms. He had been caught and remanded in custody at St. Patrick's Training College, but he absconded before the case even came to trial and went into hiding in the Republic. This did not however curtail his IRA activities, for like so many on the run, he ended up in 'El Paso'. In Dundalk he got to know a whole host of Provos, including Bap Hardy and Mickey Collins and before long had built up a fearsome reputation as a fearless gunman. Harte was involved in a number of murders in the North and revelled in the bloodshed: "Stare down the dark black hole" he would utter menacingly at his victims before pulling the trigger, according to Peter Keeley. Harte had been the cold-eyed IRA man who had screamed at Keeley in the Erin Nua office, whilst pointing a gun against his head. Later Keeley and Harte became closely acquainted, and Harte would laugh off the incident in sarcastic tones. Harte was not only involved in a series of operations from across the border but also within the Republic. One of these operations was an armed robbery on the offices of the Electricity Supply Board in Dundalk in July 1982, where his luck ran out: he was arrested by gardai and sentenced to five years imprisonment in Portlaoise for possession of firearms. His reputation preceded him amongst the other PIRA inmates of the prison; fellow inmate Dessie Grew in particular was impressed and the two became close, discussing potentially working together in IRA operations upon their release.

In 1986, Harte had served his sentence in full and was released. However, he was not a free man: he was served with an extradition warrant from the Republic to Northern Ireland relating to the firearms and petrol-bombing charges back in Lurgan. The District Court ordered his extradition but Harte appealed to the Supreme Court and he was inexplicably released on bail. Naturally, Harte jumped bail and went back on the run and back to IRA operations. The Garda finally re-arrested him in August 1988, where his extradition was the first to be confirmed under the terms of a new treaty between the UK and the Republic of Ireland; on August 23rd he was driven back over the border under armed guard to appear before Craigavon Court on charges of malicious damage, stealing a shotgun and throwing petrol bombs. The case was referred to

Belfast Crown Court and after four months on custodial remand, in December 1988, Harte was sentenced to twelve months imprisonment. After the four months remand had been taken into account, Harte was released in August 1989. One of the first to contact him after his return to Lurgan was Dessie Grew, with an offer of a few weeks 'holiday' in continental Europe.

Sean Edward Hick was from the prosperous Dublin suburb of Glenageary. Seven years younger than Grew and the son of a butcher, he had joined the IRA in his early twenties in 1981 whilst studying for a degree in Business at University College Dublin. On active service, he was arrested in 1984 for his part in the kidnap of Martin Foley – an infamous Dublin drug dealer – on behalf of the IRA, and had shot a garda in the process of trying to evade capture. He was sentenced to seven years imprisonment. He was very different to the hard working-class Northerners; combining a middle-class upbringing with a university degree and an aptitude for language: in particular, Hick spoke fluent German. His talents did not go unnoticed by fellow Portlaoise inmate Dessie Grew – together with Gerard Harte, it was not long before the three had formed a close bond and began making plans for joint operations after their release.

At the end of August 1989, Grew, Harte and Hick had all been released from Portlaoise. Grew had his team together but the arrest of Hardy and Maguire complicated things. As it looked like Bap Hardy was going to be convicted and sentenced to several years in Portlaoise, Grew reckoned with Donna Maguire likely being released on remand pending a trial later in the year. Under this assumption, the plan was hatched to team up Harte and Maguire to travel over to Germany as a couple to form the nucleus of a new ASU. Harte was horrified at the prospect; newly married with two young kids, he thought it was hard to explain to the neighbours in Lurgan that barely a few weeks after release from prison, he was off to Europe with an unmarried woman, pretending to be part of a couple with

Donna Maguire, even if most people knew he was travelling on IRA business. As it turned out, at the next court hearing in Dublin, Maguire was remanded in custody along with Hardy on explosives charges, pending a trial early in the New Year - thus the "couples plan" was rejected. So Grew rethought the plan: Hick 'The German', Harte, Paul Hughes and Conlon were called to the Continent to join Grew (and possibly Fox and Quinn) and spread themselves across several different locations in the Netherlands and the Lower Saxony region of Germany.

Driving to the Continent, they stashed weapons in the side panelling of their vehicles and drove through ports and border posts undetected. Amongst the guns smuggled into Europe by the ASU were two of the 'trophy weapons' most prized by the IRA: the Ruger .357 taken from Michael Stone during the Milltown Cemetery attack on March 16th 1988 and the Browning 9mm taken from Corporal Derek Wood three days later. Both weapons had been used since March 1988: the Browning was used in a fatal gun attack on UDR Lance-Corporal Roy Butler in Belfast in August the same year. The Ruger had been used to shoot dead Colin Abernethy as he commuted to work from Lisburn to Belfast by train in September. The Ruger and the Browning were apparently used in the murderous attack on off-duty RUC officer John Larmour as he worked in his brother George's ice-cream parlour on the Lisburn Road in Belfast in October 1988, as later detailed by George in his book 'They Killed the Ice Cream Man'. Both weapons were of extremely high value to the Provos, having been confiscated from the possession of the UDA and the British Army, two of the sworn enemies of the IRA; the fact that Dessie Grew and the ASU were entrusted with these weapons underlined the importance to the IRA offensive of the mission they were undertaking.

Nevertheless indications are that the ASU did not have all the material it needed in place in Germany to be able to commence the offensive. One incident in particular, which may be linked to Dessie

Grew and his team, took place in the garrison town of Detmold in late August. At 2.15am on August 22nd, two masked men scaled the perimeter fence of a British Army weapons dump and disabled the security alarms in what the *BKA* assessed as an attempt to steal ammunition and explosives stored there. The two intruders were discovered within the compound by a passing guard – the guard drew his weapon and threatened to open fire at the men, who nevertheless escaped into the night.

The team spread out as briefed. Martin Conlon went to The Hague to set up an IRA logistics base in the Netherlands and moved into an apartment in Hendrik Zwaardecroonstraat in the north-eastern suburb of Bezuidenhout, a short tram ride from the Central Station. He quickly secured a job at the *Haagse Tram Maatschappij* (HTM), the public transport company in the city and appeared by day to the outside world like many of the numerous Irish immigrants living and working in the city. At night and at weekends however, Conlon was on operational duty for the Provisional IRA, acting as an intelligence officer with responsibility for – amongst other things – the reconnaissance of potential targets and locations. Meeting up with different combinations of the other ASU members, they drove around northern Germany making notes, watching the movements and habits of off-duty military personnel, carrying out surveillance exercises on military married quarter estates and finding possible locations to mount an attack. A number of potential target areas were identified: the married quarter areas in the northern city of Hanover, where the IRA had killed Corporal Smith a few weeks before; Münster – home to York Barracks, where there was a large Army presence; the married quarter estates in Dortmund and Unna-Massen where British Army personnel and their families were housed; and the RAF bases at Brüggen and Wildenrath.

Details of the movements and activities in the last week of August 1989 are sketchy in places, but in others very clear. On August 28th, the ASU planted an 'up-and-under' under a red Rover 216 saloon car parked on Scheffelfeld, a street in Hanover's Bothfeld district. The car had British registration plates – F225 ORY – and belonged to a British Army staff sergeant based at nearby Chatham Barracks with 24 Transport Regiment, who had parked it on Scheffelfeld the day before. Later that afternoon, the soldier returned to his Rover to retrieve something he had left behind in the vehicle – as usual, before opening the car door, he carried out a cursory security check, looking under the chassis, He immediately saw the wooden, cigar-box sized device with microswitches on the side and containing 1.5 kilogrammes of Semtex-H explosives. German bomb disposal experts were called, who made the device safe and took the UVBT away for examination. The *BKA*'s *SoKo* Scheffelfeld recognised the device straight away, for it was nearly identical to the car bombs used in Bielefeld in May 1988 and the device that killed Steven Smith in July, just a few weeks earlier.

An intriguing incident took place just 36 hours after the discovery of the Scheffelfeld device, which could possibly be attributable to the ASU. Just before 1am on August 30th, in the commune of Betzdorf on the outskirts of Bonn, a police patrol car noticed a suspicious vehicle – a green Ford Fiesta. A check on the registration plate revealed that MK-AV795 had been stolen in early July in Iserlohn and the police approached the vehicle with the intent of questioning the driver. The vehicle first braked as if the driver was stopping to talk to the police, but as they drew up behind the car, the driver suddenly sped off, the police quickly following in hot pursuit. The police officers relayed over the outside loudspeakers for the driver to give himself up but he did not comply, instead swerving the car off the road and across an open field. The police car caught him up but when at a distance of 10-15 metres from the suspicious vehicle, the driver drew a weapon and opened fire on the police officers: firing firstly five shots, then after a pause – possibly for a magazine change – a further three to four shots. One of the officers was hit in the thigh by a projectile; the other was luckier as one of the bullets merely hit the heel of his boot. The driver grabbed a bag from inside the vehicle and ran off, managing to evade capture. On investigation of the vehicle, the officers discovered a number of stolen number plates from Gummersbach, near to where the "Fermdown" team had been staying in Reichshof, as well as plates registered in Detmold and Paderborn, both towns with a sizeable British Army presence. The clock of the car, which was brand new and had been stolen in Paderborn on July 2nd, showed that the vehicle had driven more than 15,000 kilometres by the end of August – a considerable mileage and an indicator that, if the car had been appropriated by the IRA, that the ASU may have been using the stolen car to carry out reconnaissance missions and ferry material around.

Whatever the truth behind the events in Betzdorf, the interception of the explosive device in Hannover frustrated Dessie and the team; the ASU struck back quickly. Although the notes had been confiscated on her arrest at Rosslare the previous month, Grew's team had been briefed on the reconnaissance missions carried out by Donna Maguire – next to the entry on York Barracks in Münster, Maguire had written 'job planned' – it was now time to carry out the plan. Two nights later on Friday, September 1st, three members of the ASU, dressed in British Army uniforms and armed with a mean-looking Kalaschnikow AK-47 with the serial number NK-8441 engraved on the side, and a Webley revolver with the number 58311, travelled to Münster in a rented Audi 80 and at around 22:45 hours drove slowly through Albersloher Weg, the main road running through in the Gremmendorf district, Two young off-duty soldiers from Greater Manchester, Lance-Corporals (name redacted) and (name redacted), aged 18 and 19, and stationed at the nearby York Barracks with the 14th / 20th Kings Hussars, were sitting at the bus stop 300 metres from the entrance to the base. The car drove over to the pair with the windows wound down. To test if they were dealing with German civilians or English servicemen, the driver told the soldiers in English they were lost. Could the pair give them directions to Dortmund? With many fellow servicemen hailing from Ulster, the Northern Irish accents of the IRA volunteers apparently did not raise any suspicions with the two soldiers, but the broad Northern Irish accent was difficult to decipher; one of the soldiers asked the driver to repeat the question. As he did so, a passenger in the back seat pointed the barrel of the AK-47 through the open window, aimed it at one of the soldiers and squeezed the trigger. The driver also opened fire with the Webley at the other soldier: both Lance-Corporals were hit multiple-times at close-range. As the Audi raced off at high speed, German civilians from a nearby pizzeria rushed out to help the injured soldiers - one of the servicemen was seriously injured, the other critically wounded. An ambulance was called and the two soldiers were taken to nearby hospitals for treatment. Despite being shot at such close quarters many times in the stomach, arms and legs, both miraculously survived. During the operation on one of the soldiers, surgeons managed to remove a nearly intact .380 Webley bullet, which was handed over to the *BKA* as evidence. The forensics team of their *SoKo* Münster unit set up to investigate the shootings also recovered spent 7.62mm ammunition cartridges at the scene stamped with 'ppu 762' on the bottom rim in Cyrillic letters; the projectiles had been fired from the AK-47.

The following day, the IRA claimed responsibility for the attack in a statement telephoned from the Republican Press Centre to a news agency in Dublin. The Provos explained:

> "While the undemocratic partition of Ireland is maintained by British military might, the I.R.A. reserves the right to strike at the British Government and British Army wherever they seek respite from their war against the Irish people"

The *SoKo PIRA* team got to work. One of the wounded soldiers was fit enough to be able to give an account of what had happened and a description of the men in the vehicle – in their mid-twenties with Northern Irish accents. In addition, the soldier was able to identify the make of car the IRA volunteers had been using; the police searched feverishly for the Audi 80 in which the team had escaped.

Rzeniecki called in helicopters that photographed large swathes of the wider area over a period of days – at different times of the day. The photographs were then analysed and compared; any vehicle that had remained stationary over a period of days that could be an Audi 80 was investigated. Tapes from traffic cameras were also seized in an attempt to find the vehicle and the ASU, but with no success – the *BKA* had a description of the volunteers but were unable to locate them.

Another incident perplexed *BKA* investigators that weekend. On the evening of Sunday, September 3rd, two young Irish women were discovered and questioned at Napier Barracks in Dortmund, home of several Regiments, including 36 Regiment of the Royal Artillery who had been deployed at Long Kesh at the end of 1976 and early 1977. Examining the passports of the two Irish women, the police noted the addresses of the pair as well as the emergency contact details noted in the back of the identity documents. The Germans let the women go without charge but passed all the details to the British authorities, who reported back some interesting information to the *BKA*. The addresses given by the girls had proved to be false but more tellingly, the emergency contact details for one of the girls matched those of convicted IRA man John McNally. McNally had been arrested in February 1975 aged nineteen at a farmhouse where a car full of explosives had been discovered, as well as a rifle hidden in a shed, and had subsequently been sentenced to 12 years imprisonment. He had been imprisoned in HMP Maze / Long Kesh in Cage 9 - together with many fellow Co. Tyrone Provisional IRA prisoners such as hunger striker Martin Hurson and Ivor Bell, one-time OC of the cage, who would later go on to become PIRA's Chief of Staff. McNally was released in February 1981. Using McNally as an emergency contact throws up a couple of intriguing possibilities; either the woman was close to McNally, either in a family capacity, or that McNally was acting in some way as an "official" contact point within the Republican movement should anything happen to the woman. McNally had excellent contacts within the ranks of the PIRA and considering that the women were using false addresses - possibly even false passports - it is not too far-fetched to assume that the women had been present at Napier Barracks on IRA business – the question remains: who were the women and were they part of Dessie Grew's Active Service Unit?

The attempted murders in Münster showed that the European ASU had yet again carried out an attack, but again one that had failed to kill and achieve its primary objective: the death of a British serviceman to show the Republican community back home that it meant business and shoot and bomb the British government to the negotiation table. The ASU and Dessie Grew wanted to carry out the next operation as soon as possible and make amends, but they needed help; someone at home in military surroundings who would be able to help identify targets and patterns correctly and avoid making any mistakes. Two possible candidates for this role were Peter Keeley and Michael "Dixie" Dickson, both ex-members of the British Army.

The city of Dortmund housed - amongst other military bases – Napier, West Riding, Moore and Ubique Barracks - and was home to a sizeable part of the Army's Artillery Regiment and also to a small deployment of women belonging to the Women's Royal Army Corps (WRAC), a regiment with a history of being caught up in the "Troubles". The WRAC had been deployed to Northern Ireland in 1969 to assist the RUC maintain order and in 1974 lost two members who died in the bombing of the Horse & Groom public house in Guildford. The majority of servicemen and their families lived, as at most BAOR locations, in residential accommodation, either in individual houses or apartments, or in married quarter estates dotted around the city and the neighbouring towns. One such estate was located just west of Unna, a town around 25 kilometres away from Dortmund, in the suburb of Massen. As with many military estates around the Northern Rhine region, the task of reconnoitring the location fell to ASU intelligence officer Martin

Conlon. It is still unclear who helped him carry out this task: Peter Keeley – or "Dixie", freshly demobbed from the Royal Engineers? Or both men? At any rate, on September 6th, using a hire car with false British number plates, Conlon and his accomplice – whoever that may have been - drove slowly through the estate, made notes and observed the serviceman and their families. Around the same time, witnesses have reported that two supposed door-to-door salesmen for a TV listings magazine were present in the area at the time, interviewing military dependents with a pushy line of questioning. It is possible that these two men were part of the IRA unit carrying out reconnaissance, although having direct contact with potential targets and talking to them with Northern Irish accents would be too risky a tactic. Nevertheless, Conlon was good at affecting English or Scottish accents and Dickson's Glaswegian lilt would not have seemed out of place in the environment. Keeley and Dickson would have been at home in a military living area, having both served in the BAOR region and would have both been able to give a reasonable backstory when challenged. In addition, Conlon's role as an intelligence officer - rather than as an active shooter - would reduce the chances of being recognised in any operation carried out on the back of his intelligence work. In any case, the ASU surmised once more there was lack of a heightened state of security to be exploited, especially surprising considering that the IRA attack in Münster had taken place only five days previously - they passed on the intelligence they had gathered back to the rest of the team and the decision was taken to carry out the operation the following evening.

The apparent lack of heightened security was deceptive: at least one resident was unnerved enough by the door-to-door salesmen to call the Royal Military Police. They gave the RMP a detailed account of what had happened and a description of the men - they were reassured that the matter would be looked into. The RMP passed the information and the descriptions to *BSSO*, who in turn liaised with their colleagues at their sister organisation *MI5*. *MI5* were likely unsurprised; they probably already knew about the reconnaissance mission from another source; Peter Keeley himself. Whether he was there or not, Keeley had likely passed word back to his FRU handlers and warned that an attack in Unna-Massen was imminent. Somewhere down the line of communications, a decision may have been made to allow what is termed a 'firebreak': to prevent the spread of fire in a wooded area, a 'firebreak' is created by removing closely grouped trees and clearing a space, thus impeding the rapid progress of the fire. In intelligence terms, a 'firebreak' could be created by allowing an IRA operation to go ahead, for the sole purpose of protecting an important intelligence source higher up the chain, thus potentially helping to prevent more catastrophic incidents elsewhere and allow a more high-ranking IRA "player" to be taken out of circulation. Someone, somewhere – possibly a combination of *BSSO* and *MI5* officers – either made a huge mistake or made the decision to quietly ignore witness statements and clear descriptions of the IRA men, and to neglect to inform the *BKA* of an impending IRA operation on German soil. In order to protect Keeley, one of British intelligences most valuable assets within the Provisional IRA, a 'firebreak' created by British intelligence may have condemned an unwitting innocent victim to death.

11 FIREBREAK

On September 7th, the ASU – likely consisting of Desmond Grew, Sean Hick, Gerard Harte and a further volunteer – possibly either Peter Keeley or Michael Dickson - dressed in British Army camouflage jackets and military berets, and under cover of darkness drove in separate vehicles to Unna-Massen. The suburb lays just off the main A2 autobahn, which runs from Berlin in the east, via Hannover to Oberhausen in the Ruhr valley. The team arrived in the estate in a Ford Capri and a VW Golf and drove onto Otto-Holzapfel-Strasse at around 21:00, parking outside house number 27, opposite the Evangelical Friedenskirche Church. Grew and Harte got out; Grew armed with an AK-47 automatic rifle, Harte with the Ruger revolver, the men pulled balaclavas over their faces and hid in the shadows of the entrance gate. Hick remained in the Ford Capri parked across the street, the other volunteer drove the VW Golf along Otto-Holzapfel-Strasse and turned into Stefan-Zweig-Strasse around 150 metres away from the scene before parking – the other volunteer remained in contact with Hick via ICOM radio unit. A witness reports seeing the other volunteer on Stefan-Zweig-Strasse, wearing Army camouflage but no beret, and the witness was later able to give a good enough description for police to issue a photofit of the suspect – the picture bears a stunning likeness to Michael Dickson.

At around 21:50, they watched intently as 26-year-old Heidi Hazell arrived at Otto-Holzapfel-Strasse 27 in her dark blue Saab 9000i with the British registration F-260-KFO. A German citizen originally from the Bremen area, Heidi had met and married British Army Staff-Sergeant Clive Hazell three years earlier – they lived on Otto-Holzapfel-Strasse in Unna-Massen, around 13 kilometres from nearby Dortmund. On the evening of September 7th, Heidi was returning from her usual Thursday night slimming class at the

Officers Mess in Ubique Barracks in Dortmund. Heidi was alone in the vehicle: her husband Clive Hazell was away on an Army training course in the south of Germany for several days and Heidi had already dropped off a friend from her class in Dortmund twenty minutes earlier. As Heidi drove up to the entrance to the communal parking spaces outside the married quarters, Grew and Harte sprang into action: as Harte neared the entrance with revolver drawn, Grew ran straight up to the car from the left side, aimed the AK-47 at Heidi and fired fourteen shots through the window of the Saab at close range, shattering the glass.

An off-duty British soldier was nearby:

> "I heard the sound of the magazine of an automatic rifle being emptied, and I recognised it instantly. It was followed by the roar of a car engine and a loud impact noise as the car hit something."

Heidi pressed her foot on the gas pedal and tried to reverse away as the shooting started but she did not stand a chance; the car crashed into a tree next to the wall of the vicarage on the other side of the road. The soldier who witnessed the attack describes:

> "I saw a black Capri car, a pretty old model, racing down the hill with its tyres screaming. There were two men in the front seats and the headlights were full on."

Hick in the waiting Ford Capri drove up to the scene, Grew jumped in and they sped away, leaving the dead body of Heidi slumped behind the wheel. The driver of the VW Golf had sped up to the scene, picked up Harte and raced away in the other direction. Two other soldiers in the vicinity of the Saab ran to the vehicle and pulled Heidi out, laying her on the pavement with the intent of administering first aid; but it was clear from the multitude of bullet holes in her back and side that Heidi was beyond help. Ten minutes later, the emergency services arrived but could do nothing; the doctor who attempted to treat Heidi knocked on the door of the vicarage – the local pastor Reverend Wilfried Scholzen opened the door to find the doctor covered in blood and extremely distressed. The clergyman described what he faced as he arrived at the scene:

> "When I got there, two poor soldiers were looking down at the girl but she was gone and there was nothing anyone could do. A doctor from the town came to help but when he saw her he just walked away into the church, shaking his head. I think we all knew what had been happening elsewhere in Germany, and if I had thought we might attract the terrorists, but in my heart of hearts I never really believed it. One of our girls is dead and now we have joined the war. She was too young to die and too innocent."

As one half of the team headed west back towards the Dutch border and the other getaway car in the direction of Hannover, a police investigation team - *SoKo* Unna - was rapidly formed and secured the crime scene. Members of the centralised *BKA SoKo PIRA* unit arrived shortly afterwards to coordinate investigations. They found fourteen empty 7.62mm ammunition cartridges inscribed with "ppu 762" stamped on the bottom rim in Cyrillic. It was quickly ascertained that the ammunition recovered in Münster-Gremmendorf and in Unna-Massen was identical: it was little surprise when at 4pm the following day, the Provisional IRA released the usual statement from Dublin:

> "An IRA Active Service Unit carried out last night's shooting in West Germany. The woman killed was believed to have been a member of the British Crown Forces garrisoned in Dortmund. It has now emerged that she was the German wife of a British Army staff sergeant. As we intend continuing our campaign until the British Army withdraws from Ireland, the outcome of last night's attack reinforces a warning we gave on

Aug. 2, 1988, for civilians to stay well clear of British military personnel. This warning applies to the use of vehicles personally belonging to British soldiers and all modes of military transport."

In the second week of September, an IRA spokesman with alleged responsibility for European operations contacted Warner Poelchau, a journalist for German weekly news magazine Stern. Stern printed a transcript of the conversation on September 14th using the name 'Sean' to preserve the anonymity of the IRA man. The identity of the spokesman remains a mystery, despite Poelchau subsequently being taken to court in an unsuccessful attempt to make him reveal the name of the spokesman. 'Sean' could have been any one of those with responsibility within the Overseas Department, or even the IRA's alleged Director of Publicity Danny Morrison, but suspicion falls strongly on the spokesman being Gerry Kelly, who also worked in Sinn Fein's press office and likely used to dealing with the media. Whatever the identity of 'Sean', he responded to Poelchau's questions with answers that were at turns apologetic, revealing, defiant and obstinate.

> POELCHAU: The IRA shot dead the German wife of a British soldier in Unna. What has that got to do with the liberation of Northern Ireland?
>
> 'SEAN': The murder of a German national is clearly damaging to our image. It was not our intention to kill the wife of a soldier. Our active service unit presumed she was a member of the „Women's Royal Army Corps" which is stationed in Dortmund. It does not serve our cause to enter into conflict with the German, Dutch or Belgians. But we have no other choice. To make it clear what is happening in the occupied part of Ireland, we have decided to attack the Brits wherever they might

be.

POELCHAU: *Again and again, IRA operations have claimed civilian victims. And again and again, it is claimed that a mistake was made, that in future civilian casualties are to be avoided. Until the next time.*

'SEAN': *I can only repeat, we express our regret. But that's the way it goes, every war has civilian casualties.*

POELCHAU: *That sounds pretty cold.*

'SEAN': *It's the tragedy of war. The Brits calculate civilian casualties into the whole war plan intentionally. With us it's an accident. We pay for it with our reputation.*

POELCHAU: *You always emphasise that you are fighting for a just cause. But where is the difference between your means and those of your enemy?*

'SEAN': *We certainly do not use the same means. Last year in Germany, we aborted 20 missions because they would have had to be carried out in close proximity to civilians. Instead, volunteers risked their lives to break into British barracks to lay bombs there.*

POELCHAU: *In the face of the unification of Europe, the merciless Northern Ireland conflict is becoming less and less understandable. Are you not clinging onto an antiquated notion of nationalism?*

'SEAN': *No, we are fighting for peace and equality. We want to achieve national democracy in the whole of Ireland. The British government has already said that 1993 will not see the end of partition. The fact is that the Brits only last Thursday once again blew up an* important transit road to the South. I am sure that the people of West Germany, if suppressed as we are, would fight in the exact same way.

POELCHAU: Are there – as so often claimed – connections to other terrorist organisations such as the RAF (Red Army Faction)?

'SEAN': No, the RAF does not represent the people and is not a movement. The IRA on the other hand is the product of a long tradition. We are supported the strongest by the suppressed nationalists in Northern Ireland where the most battles take place.

POELCHAU: Nevertheless, the Northern Irish population does not decide on whether the armed struggle is continued. That is decided by the IRA Army Council.

'SEAN': First of all, there is unity amongst our supporters, that armed struggle is necessary. And the IRA has no difficulty attracting new recruits. We have been fighting for twenty years and are still fresh.

POELCHAU: Worldwide there is a tendency towards negotiation instead of fighting. When are you going to start?

'SEAN': We've tried. The British government negotiated with us but they abused the ceasefire twice. We want to talk now. We have asked the British government to explain why they deny the Irish people the right to decide on their own future.

POELCHAU: According to a report in the „Sunday Times", even within your organisation the strategy of armed struggle is divisive.

'SEAN': Rubbish. The „Sunday Times" is the mouthpiece of the British government. The owner Rupert Murdoch is a personal friend of Maggie Thatcher. That alone explains why they write that kind of rubbish.

POELCHAU: Under what conditions and when can the conflict be ended?

'SEAN': It could end today. We could recall our volunteers from England, the continent and the Federal Republic of Germany if the British government declare that it will withdraw its troops from Ireland within the foreseeable future. We want a national democracy which naturally also confers the Protestant unionists the same rights. Equality for everybody.

POELCHAU: It is hardly to be expected that Mrs. Thatcher is going to agree to that – so are there going to be further IRA attacks in the Federal Republic of Germany?

'SEAN': Yes, I'm sorry. The British soldiers think they can come to us in Belfast and Derry and kill and torture us and then go back to Germany for a rest. They are going to hear from us wherever they are."

Despite the warnings in both the interview with Poelchau and the IRA statement issued after the murder of Heidi Hazell, the IRA leadership were unhappy with Grew for messing up yet another operation; bringing the organisation a whole host of negative publicity, damaging support for the Republican cause in Europe and USA and causing even the staunchest of IRA supporters back in Northern Ireland to call the campaign into question. The ASU were chastened, dismayed at yet another mistake and vowed to get things right next time.

Once more, the team appeared to change tactics - two days after the mistaken assassination of Heidi Hazell, the ASU was apparently once again on active service. At around 11am on September 9th, four shots were fired from a handgun from a passing car at Kingsley Barracks in Minden, the home of 211 (11 Armoured Brigade) HQ & Signal Squadron. No bullet holes were found in the building that had been targeted but a 9mm ammunition case was found at the scene. Early that evening, Mülheim an der Ruhr was the next town to see an attack – this time two shots were fired at the entry to Wrexham Barracks, home of 38 Squadron of the Royal Corps of Transport on Oxforder Strasse from a gold-coloured Daimler Benz 8 series. The ASU had already once a few weeks earlier been disturbed trying to breach the perimeter fence at the rear of the barracks and escaped. Two hours later, there was another firearms incident, this time 75 kilometres away. Shots were fired at off-duty British soldiers in the garrison town of Hemer, near to Barossa Barracks and Pensinsula Barracks; the bullets missed their target. They were fired from a white Renault fitted with false number plates - the plates, as with the registrations found in the green Ford Fiesta that had been intercepted by chance 10 days earlier in Betzdorf, had been stolen in Iserlohn in July. Whilst the execution of the attacks had been a little speculative, the targeting may not have been coincidental: 38 Squadron had been deployed to Northern Ireland in the late 70s and early 80s, completing tours of duty in 1979 and 1980 from their base in Mülheim. 211 Signal Squadron had also carried out tours of duty in Ulster. The attack in Hemer had taken place near to Barossa and Peninsula Barracks, homes of the 3rd Bn Royal Regiment of Fusiliers and 3rd Royal Tank Regiment respectively, units that had both been deployed in Northern Ireland on many occasions during the Troubles, including around Long Kesh / The Maze, Dungannon and Armagh.

The attacks of September 9th did not cause any injuries or even generate any press headlines for they were kept under wraps by the

British military and German authorities for security reasons – frustrated at not having carried out a successful operation, the ASU went back to the drawing board and reconsidered their plans. At the heart of the new strategy was IRA intelligence officer Martin Conlon. At 19 years old, Conlon was very young but had already gathered considerable experience in IRA operations. Back in Northern Ireland he had been utilised as a sniper and gunman. Grew however had needed an intelligence officer for the European ASU and with enough trigger experience in the team already had a specific task earmarked for the young man from Armagh City. Gregarious and good humoured, good looking and young, Conlon perfectly fitted the bill as a honey-trap. Grew tasked Conlon with setting up logistics in The Hague and recruiting unwitting local women to assist him by using his charms. After a few abortive attempts, on October 18th, Conlon found the perfect target. Late in the evening, on the way home from a night out and alighting at The Hague Central Station, he walked off the station concourse to get the tram for the one stop to his flat in Hendrik Zwaardecroonstraat. Waiting at the tram stop was a young, vaguely pretty, heavy-set blonde woman about the same age as Conlon. He engaged her in casual conversation whilst they were waiting and they hit it off instantly. Ingrid Hijman was a 19-year-old social geography student from Amsterdam, living in student campus residence Uilenstede in the Amsterdam suburb of Amstelveen and fascinated with all things Irish – very quickly she became fascinated by Martin Conlon. After sharing a bar of chocolate, they exchanged telephone numbers and parted, making plans to meet the following week.

The following day Conlon met up with Grew in The Hague and told him he had met someone who was going to be able to help them. Acting on a tipoff from contacts, Conlon and Grew visited Café Nato in The Hague to potentially purchase a car on sale at a knock-down price by one of the bar staff. The barman was surprised that used-car dealer Grew only asked one question: whether the car was fast. Handing over a false passport in the name of Daniel Martin Caldwell adorned with his own passport photo, Grew purchased the vehicle from the barman and drove with Conlon to Germany in the gold coloured Ford Granada station wagon with a brown vinyl roof. The IRA team later surreptitiously exchanged the real plates with false ones bearing the registration number 'DT-CV-764'. The vehicle would therefore appear to be registered in Germany, in Detmold, a small town with a sizeable British Army presence; the car could therefore be used in the area without standing out as much as a vehicle registered with Dutch number plates. Wearing British Army fatigues so as not to arouse suspicion, Grew and Conlon picked up another volunteer en route: this may have been Gerard Harte or Sean Hick, but questions remain whether it may have even been either Michael Dickson or Peter Keeley, who as former soldiers would have been able to give their insights on the habits of British Forces personnel and help identify potential targets. The trio drove to Nijmegen and onto Venlo, where they observed military families shopping at the Trefcenter, a large shopping mall just over the border from Germany that was popular with the families of servicemen based at the RAF bases Wildenrath, Laarbruch and Brüggen. From there, they drove to Reuver on the Dutch side of the border to fill up with fuel at a local petrol station. There they also purchased five rolls of coloured isolation tape - the cashier observed as Grew opened the car to stash the tape and noticed three identical, brand new rucksacks stored in the luggage compartment. The trio left the petrol station and skipped across the border – they drove to the British Forces married quarter estates at Elmpt and Geilenkirchen, near to Brüggen to carry out surveillance on the soldiers, airmen and their families living there. By early evening, they had reached Wildenrath. On Heinsberger Strasse, the main thoroughfare from which residential streets housing both locals and military families fanned out to form the small village roughly a kilometre away from the main gate of the Royal Air Force base, the IRA team paid particular attention to two locations. Directly across the road from the local Catholic St. Johannes Kirche church was the local pub/restaurant Zur Post, a favourite haunt of not only RAF servicemen but also their dependants, in particular sons and daughters in their mid- to late teens. The British patrons were welcome and frequent guests but their clothing and language made it very easy to identify them as belonging to the military. The second location in the village with a steady and visible flow of British military visitors sat half a kilometre further up the main road: a petrol station. Although the Second World War had ended over forty years earlier, each British serviceman based in Germany still carried and used a ration card. Rationing had been introduced to prevent over-purchasing of high-demand, low-supply goods such as flour, meat, coffee, tobacco and petrol but in the decades after the war, supply became less of an issue; taxes did. These products were tax-exempt to NATO servicemen based on the Rhine and thus much cheaper than in the local German community. In order to prevent servicemen reselling duty-free products to German friends and neighbours, the use of ration cards continued and servicemen were limited in the amount of meat, alcohol and coffee they could purchase tax-free. The same applied to fuel: as part of the wide-ranging SOFA (Status of Forces Agreement) struck between occupying NATO allies and the Federal Republic of Germany, servicemen could purchase petrol and diesel – both normally highly-taxed commodities at local German filling stations tax-free, saving them a small fortune. To facilitate this, agreements were made with fuel providers and fuel cards issued, which on presentation would allow servicemen to buy tax-free fuel. The cards however could only be used at certain filling stations: by far one of the most popular in the vicinity was Willi Otten's BP garage on Heinsberger Strasse in Wildenrath. Many of the cars driving onto the forecourt to fill up were the personal vehicles of RAF and Army personnel, which were immediately identifiable both by their British registration plates and their uniformed occupants. It was early evening and several of the military visitors were at Willi Otten's not only to fill up their vehicles but also their stomachs. The BP garage forecourt also offered an adjacent snack bar selling takeaway food to those returning home from the base to their living quarters - Willi Otten's was a popular destination. Grew, Conlon and the other volunteer parked a short distance away in the Ford station wagon and - unnoticed by passers-by – observed and noted the steady stream of British military personnel buying petrol and bratwurst.

After a while they left Wildenrath, driving back past the Royal Air Force base and on to the nearby town of Wassenberg to take a brief tour around the narrow streets of the married quarter estate housing RAF personnel and their families. Finally, they drove the twelve or so kilometres through the villages of Myhl and Gerderath to their final destination, the small area of military-occupied apartment blocks on the Bauxhof road in the town of Erkelenz. There they parked in a dark corner of one of the parking bays and for a while observed servicemen, families and children arriving home from work or school, or leaving the estate for shopping trips, football training or other social reasons. On the drive back to the Hague, the ASU exchanged views and notes: carrying out an attack directly within the narrow street layout of married quarter estates - with many bends and turns to negotiate and close-knit military communities who were likely to notice and report any vehicle that looked like it did not belong there - was unlikely to be an optimum location for an operation. Due to the steady stream of military personnel in an open German civilian area, the close proximity to several border crossings to the Netherlands, the open main road in front of the BP garage and a conveniently dark corner next to the snack bar, the best place to carry out an attack was going to be Willi Otten's in Wildenrath. Whoever was unlucky enough to enter the crosshairs of the IRA unit on Heinsberger Strasse would be a sitting duck.

As the Provisional IRA planned their next move, so did the *BKA*'s *SoKo PIRA* team. The case against the "FERMDOWN" ASU members Pauline Drumm, Donncha O'Kane and Patrick Murray was being prepared, as well as for the extradition of Donna Maguire and Leonard Hardy, and investigations into the movements of the IRA unit continued. Apart from pictures of British military installations, there had been further photographs recovered during the arrests in France and Ireland – one of which showed an unknown man who *BKA* investigators were keen to trace. The most obvious place to look was at the German address that had been found along with that of the holiday home in Clermont-en-Argonne. Proceeding were opened under file 1 BJs 218/89-4, in connection with which the *SoKo PIRA* applied for a search warrant for the German address which was granted on October 17th. Three days later on October 20th, investigators arrived at the apartment in Mühltal / Nieder-Ramstadt, a few kilometres south of Darmstadt and arrested the mysterious Irishman in the "FERMDOWN" photo. The *BKA* searched the apartment, vehicle and workplace of the suspect and the man was questioned but released the next day without charge. In the meantime, *SoKo PIRA* chief Joachim Rzeniecki prepared a 26-page report on the activities of the Provos in Europe, and Germany in particular since 1987. The report listed details of every incident from the JHQ bombing to the shooting of Heidi Hazell and detailed the investigations and evidence gathered, listing names, fake passports, car registrations, known movements of IRA volunteers, prevented attacks, recovered vehicles and weapons as well as arrests made. The final paragraph gave a grave prognosis and quoting from the Stern interview of September 14th, assumed correctly that the negative headlines from the botched operation in Unna were in no way going to stop the IRA. The next attack was already in the final stages of planning.

Unaware, the British security services had other IRA-related issues to contend with. On October 20th, investigative journalist Duncan Campbell dropped an intelligence bombshell in an article published in The New Statesman. The article made public the theft of the Operation WARD documents and shone a light on the running of informants within the Irish community in Germany by the British security services. To make matters worse, Campbell chose to name some of the ex-Provos involved – Bo Crossey, Larry O'Rourke and

Aidan Jordan - putting them in considerable danger from retaliation from the IRA. A member of the covert British intelligence team involved in Operation WARD and security measures to combat the IRA offensive in Germany recounts the reaction of the security services to the threat to Crossey, Jordan and O'Rourke:

> *"After the article was published, we realised that we had to warn them off that they may not be as safe as we hoped. So, with my boss, another operator and I drove to their location and the streets where they were. My colleague and I staked out the ends of each street, whilst the boss went forward and briefed the unfortunate individuals. Once the task was done, we all got back into the car to head home, but in the days before satnav, we got hopelessly lost in a one-way-system! All my boss said afterwards was that we had displayed excellent anti-surveillance skills and that it showed the benefit of local knowledge...we couldn't tell him that we had never been there before!"*

Back in the Netherlands, confident that the plan for an attack at the petrol station in Wildenrath was going to be a success, Conlon met up with Ingrid Hijman for a date in the café-restaurant 'De zwarte ruiter' in the Grote Markt pedestrian precinct of The Hague on Wednesday October 25th. During the conversation, Conlon told Hijman about his upbringing and about the situation in Northern Ireland and probed her on her views. He explained that the Catholic minority was downtrodden and abused and told her he sympathised with the Republican cause; stopping short of revealing that he was a member of the Provisional IRA. Hijman was interested but wondered if there was not a political solution, instead of armed struggle. Conlon told her that everything had been tried; the only language the British understood was violence. They agreed to meet up again on Friday evening to talk more; Conlon walked Hijman to the Central Station so she could get a train back to Amstelveen and return home. He met with Dessie Grew, who had just returned from a trip to Germany; Grew had been to the IRA arms cache in the woods near Dortmund. From the weapons dump he unearthed the AK-47 automatic rifle that had been stashed away after the disastrous operation in Unna-Massen, the Ruger .357 revolver and ammunition, as well as a quantity of Semtex, before replacing the plastic bags back in the ground, covering them with a thick layer of soil and leaves and returning to the Netherlands via an unmanned border crossing with the weapons stashed hidden in the side-panelling of the Ford station wagon.

Once again, Peter Keeley – the British security services embedded agent within the IRA's European Active Service Unit – may have informed his FRU handlers that an attack on British Forces in Germany was about to take place. Once again, the security services may have chosen to allow a firebreak: if the operation were to be compromised, fingers would be pointed at Conlon and Keeley. Conlon was just an expendable Provo; Keeley was however too valuable a source to lose in the wider war against the IRA - the security services were prepared to lose this battle and accept collateral damage in order to protect him. The next day, Conlon and Grew left The Hague with another passenger in the back seat. Grew needed a proven gunman to pull the trigger: Gerard Harte. Together, Grew, Conlon and Harte drove through the Netherlands. By early evening they had reached their regular stop-off point, the petrol station in Reuver, where they filled up the Ford with fuel. Together they continued on their way, drove around the outskirts of Roermond and across the border between Maalbroek and Elmpt.

By 6.30pm it had grown dark, as Conlon dropped Harte and Grew off - armed respectively with a black AK-47 automatic rifle and the Ruger .357 revolver confiscated from Loyalist gunman Michael Stone after the Milltown Cemetery attack in March 1988 - inconspicuously at Willi Otten's BP garage in Wildenrath and parked a short distance away.

There Martin Conlon sat, hands gripping the wheel of the Ford station wagon, and waited for the operation to begin.

12 AFTERMATH

After the murders at Willi Otten's petrol station in Wildenrath, Conlon, Grew and Harte had fled the scene in the Ford station wagon. At the scene, civilian and military police were busy coordinating the next steps. The Federal State Prosecutors Office the GBA had opened case file 1 BJs 222/89-4 and instructed Joachim Rzeniecki's *SoKo PIRA* team to carry out the investigation. Working alongside the *SoKo* Wildenrath team sent from Wiesbaden, in charge for Heinsberg police - as on the night of the arrests of Gerry McGeough and Gerry Hanratty in nearby Waldfeucht in August 1988 - was Chief Inspector Bodo Strickstrock:

> "Of course the press arrived at the scene pretty quickly too. As I feared that radio frequencies were being monitored – regional journalists always seemed to arrive at the scene of traffic accidents and the like far too quickly – and as the radio communication thus far could have led to information filtering out that should not have been in the public domain, I used the mobile communications unit offered by the RAF Police to communicate from Wildenrath to the police station in Heinsberg. The British colleagues always had such a unit in their vehicle. As we did not have such equipment at the time, with the help of the British we were able to coordinate measures and information on when the colleagues from the BKA would arrive to take over."

The Wildenrath murders were another public relations disaster for the IRA. The reaction in mainland Britain and Germany was understandably and obviously incensed, but at home in Northern Ireland, the Republican community was also shocked and to some extent outraged; a host of Nationalist politicians took the relatively unprecedented step of concurring publicly with the British government, asking Republicans to disown the IRA. Seamus Mallon, deputy leader of the SDLP, said the murders would revolt anyone who had a concept of justice, adding

> "Those who have carried it out have disgraced everything that they espouse."

Former Irish Foreign Minister, Peter Barry said that Irish people must let the IRA know that they were not acting for them. Peter Brooks, the Northern Ireland Secretary in the British government said he hoped the supporters of the IRA were asking themselves if any of their aims could ever justify the slaughter of a baby, saying

> "they must know that the whole of the rest of the world is asking this question."

The Irish Taoiseach, Charles Haughey, also condemned the murders unreservedly:

> "All reasonable people must be appalled by this callous act. I offer my deepest condolences and those of the Government to their bereaved family and friends."

As a serviceman, Mick Islania was seen by the Provos as a legitimate target; the murder of his baby daughter Nivruti however was different. The IRA had long been able to claim the moral high ground in the war against the British. They purported to target only military personnel, the RUC and the occasional Loyalist paramilitary, taking care to avoid civilian casualties, especially children, but at the same time accused the British Army of doing the opposite. Whilst the murder of Nivruti had not been intended, the ASU had not taken enough care to ensure avoidance of 'collateral damage'. The murder of a baby would not only be detrimental to support in Northern Ireland, but more importantly across the Atlantic. The scorched earth left behind by the barbaric murder of a baby might threaten the flow of liquid assets from the USA and the financial support of the Irish-American community partly responsible for bankrolling the IRA and Sinn Fein.

It was against this backdrop that Siobhán O'Hanlon – now working for Danny Morrison in the Republican Press Centre - arrived in New York on the weekend immediately following the Wildenrath murders. On arrival, she filled out a visa waiver card and, together with senior Sinn Fein press officer Martha McClelland, travelled on to Philadelphia to the sixth annual Irish American Unity Conference, held at the Sheraton University City Hotel, where both women were booked as speakers. Following the conference, O'Hanlon travelled around the US, to cover speaking engagements on behalf of the Republican movement in San Diego and San Francisco. As she did so, eagle-eyed US immigration officials were busy carrying out background checks on O'Hanlon and two other Republican figures on tour in the US – they discovered that she had been convicted and sentenced for the 1983 explosives charges arising from her arrest in a Belfast bomb factory but had neglected to note the conviction in the appropriate place on the immigration paperwork. The FBI was alerted and on November 9th, as O'Hanlon was about give a speech to NORAID members at the Sprinkler Fitters Union Hall in Whittier, Los Angeles County in California, they arrested her and took the former European ASU volunteer into custody. At an initial hearing four days later, and after various American sympathisers had vouched for her, federal US magistrate Charles F. Eick granted her bail on a $25k bond, saying the nature of the charges "militates heavily against detaining the defendant". The magistrate said that much of his decision to grant bail was due to commitments from members of the local Irish-American community to offer their homes as collateral for the bond; according to immigration attorney Peter Schey at least ten couples had done so. Judge Eick however set a further hearing for November 16th for a decision on whether to move the impending trial to New York, where O'Hanlon had entered the USA. At the hearing three days later, it was decided to deport

O'Hanlon back to Belfast, which incensed the Irish-American community and denied O'Hanlon and Sinn Fein further opportunity to raise some much needed positive profile – and cash - in the States.

Back in Continental Europe, Wildenrath was recovering from the shock of the cold-blooded murders as *BKA*, *LKA* and Heinsberg police continued their investigations. Bodo Strickstrock details what happened:

> *"The crime was reconstructed at the beginning of November, under similar circumstances to the evening of the attack, by specialists from the BKA. There were extensive roadblocks cordoning off the B221 which ran through Wildenrath village, and back at the station in Heinsberg, we had a lot of officers from all over the place running round the building...the level of concern and sympathy from the local population was remarkable. The people who lived in the direct vicinity of the attack not only kept the colleagues from Aachen supplied with coffee and sandwiches as they worked through the night but also took part in huge numbers in a multi-faith service held a week later in the Pfarrkirche in Wildenrath. The service had been organised by both Catholic and Protestant communities, in conjunction with the British military chaplains. Members of the Anglican church and the Hindu faith also took part – after the service the participants left the church and filed past the crime scene in a silent march. The church bells rang. Locals had put out candles and lights on their window sills and had laid wreaths at the scene."*

As the local community continued to unite in sorrow and shock, the *SoKo* Wildenrath team left Heinsberg in the second week of November and returned to their base in Wiesbaden. Those who had carried out or assisted in the cold-blooded murders scattered and awaited the inevitable reprimand over the disastrous operation from the Overseas Department. Keeley returned to Newry, Harte and Hughes to County Armagh. Hick sought shelter with Republican sympathisers affiliated to the Irland Solidarität group based in Göttingen. Grew, Fox and Quinn either lay low or were back in Northern Ireland. Only Conlon in The Hague remained active, but downcast that his reconnaissance intelligence had gone to waste and that the operation had gone so spectacularly wrong. Keen to continue momentum, he decided to see how far he could go with recruiting Hijman for the cause. He called Hijman the day after the attack in Wildenrath and arranged to meet in Amsterdam. That evening, Hijman noted that he was very down and slowly began to become aware that Conlon might have had something to do with the operation. Nevertheless she agreed to meet him again two weeks later; again in Amsterdam. At their meeting on November 12th, she confronted Conlon with her suspicions, who – whilst not completely admitting to his exact role – gave a detailed account of why the operation went wrong. On the back of a beer mat from the bar in which they were sitting, he drew a plan of the BP station forecourt, drew two boxes and a series of crosses and arrows to indicate the vehicles, gunman and victims, explaining how the gunmen had made mistakes; he would have carried out the operation differently. Hijman was more inquisitive than shocked, which Conlon took to be an encouraging sign; he asked her to spend the following weekend with him in the south of the Netherlands and she readily agreed.

On November 18th, Conlon and Hijman travelled first to Venlo, then on to Roermond, where they visited the King George pub next to the train station; as every weekend, the pub was heaving with British military personnel and dependents; Conlon and Hijman sat in the corner and talked in hushed tones below the loud music and rowdy chatter. After they left the pub, Conlon made a bold move and told her that several of the servicemen had been looking her up and down and surely found her attractive. He asked if she could imagine asking one of them to go outside with her to the alleyway next to the pub, with her under the pretext of getting them alone; Conlon said that he could arrange for an IRA gunman to be waiting to have the soldier killed and a getaway car waiting for her. Shocked at the prospect, Hijman declined. Reasoning that Hijman might not want to be so directly and personally involved in a murder, he took another tack: could she imagine taking a bag full of explosives into the bar, leaving it under a chair, making her escape unnoticed before the bomb detonated? Hijman declined again. The following day the pair travelled back to Amsterdam, the blossoming 'relationship' having cooled dramatically over the weekend. Conlon returned to work in The Hague, Hijman returned to her studies in Amsterdam and the pair broke off contact.

Investigations into the series of attacks carried out by the ASU from July to October meanwhile continued apace. The Dutch TRIO team and the *BKA*, as well as members of the *BSSO* cooperated and shared information and met on a regular basis. Information, eyewitness reports and forensic evidence was pooled; cartridge cases found at the scenes of the shootings in Münster, Unna-Massen and Wildenrath were collected. The head of the *SoKo PIRA* team Joachim Rzeniecki took a bag of the recovered AK-47 ammunition cartridges, flew from Frankfurt to Northern Ireland without being searched once and handed over the bag of ammunition to astounded RUC colleagues who met him on his arrival at Belfast airport. The cartridges were passed on to the Northern Ireland Forensic Science Laboratory NIFSL; unsurprisingly the results confirmed that the same AK-47 automatic rifle had been used in all three attacks, the weapon leaving the same rifling marks on the cases. In addition the "ppu 762" stamp on the base of each ammunition case found at the scenes was identical; - it was clear that the same weapon had been used in each incident; this was an indication but by no means confirmation that the same person had fired the weapon that had critically injured two off-duty soldiers in Münster, killed Heidi Hazell in Unna, as well as Mick and baby Nivruti Islania in Wildenrath. Aware of how the IRA operated and in particular how arms caches were used, Rzeniecki and his team reasoned it was perfectly possible that not only one ASU was operating on the Continent but several – all availing themselves of the weapons cache - and eye-witness reports varied as to descriptions of the possible perpetrators. The *BKA* appealed successfully to the Federal Supreme Court Bundesgerichtshof for powers to set up roadblock checkpoints in certain locations across Germany to attempt to ensnare the ASU. On the basis of evidence gleaned from the arrests of the "FERMDOWN" ASU – those of Maguire and Hardy in particular – permission was granted for police to set up time-limited control points in North Rhine Westphalia – in the administrative districts of Cologne, Düsseldorf and Münster, as well as Dortmund, the neighbouring districts of Lüdenscheid and Soest – and in Lower Saxony around Lüneburg, Hanover, Osnabrück and the East German border regions around Wolfenbüttel and Helmstedt. These were carried out in the period between November 8th and November 30th, but with the majority of the ASU lying low and the remaining members being aware of the roadblocks, the checks were futile and failed to deliver any tangible results.

Provisional IRA operations in Germany in late 1989 and the resulting *BKA* investigations took place against the backdrop of a socially and politically hugely significant period in German history. Twenty years after the civil rights movement had marched through Northern Ireland in 1969, with demonstrations against social injustices, religious oppression and unjustified violence against citizens spilling over into violence against the state, the citizens of East Germany were fighting against the draconian Communist rule – but without recourse to armed struggle. The peaceful revolution gathered pace as East Germans fled to West Germany via neighbouring countries who enjoyed a more porous border to the West, putting pressure on the East German government to act. Finally, on November 9th, the government announced the relaxing of travel restrictions and – albeit inadvertently – announced the opening of the Berlin Wall, the Iron Curtain being swept aside after it had divided Western and Eastern Europe for two generations. It was the beginning of the end for the East German Communist rulers – and for the hated Stasi secret police, which had gathered millions of pieces of information on their fellow citizens over the previous decades. Only a few months later, as the state machinery of the GDR began to fall apart under pressure from its citizens, East German people stormed the Stasi headquarters and ransacked the files, reading what information had been collected about them and either stealing the documents or ripping to pieces in anger and joy. Amongst the millions of documents sat Feindobjektakte XV5414/85; the Stasi's file on the activities of the Provisional IRA, to which a copy of Joachim Rzeniecki's report from September 1989 – acquired via the same mole responsible for previous leaks on the activities of the *SOKO PIRA* - was one of the most recent additions. As the authorities stepped in to prevent the destruction of important evidence of the long-term misdoings of the Ministerium für Staatssicherheit, file XV5414/85 and the important information contained in it, including the real identity of "IM Harfe" - the Stasi's contact person within the Provisional IRA – was saved from shredding and a little over a year later, on August 31st 1990, handed over to the West German ZKA (*Zollkriminalamt*) for further scrutiny as the country prepared for the long-awaiting reunification of the Eastern and Western halves of Germany.

Back over the border in still West Germany, by November 1989 one thing had become clear to police and security forces; Dessie Grew was the man directing the IRA teams on the ground in Continental Europe. Intelligence information had highlighted that he was conspicuously absent from East Tyrone and South Armagh - and this information had been circulated across Europe; Peter Keeley had also confirmed to his FRU handlers (who in turn passed on the information to *MI5*) that Grew was on active service in Europe. The information trail had also led back to Café Nato in The Hague where the barman remembered the English-speaking man who had only asked one question: "is the car fast?" Video from the BP station at

Wildenrath had shown a man with a striking likeness to Dessie Grew on the night of the Islania murders. Rzeniecki's *SoKo PIRA* team had been searching for the gold-coloured Ford Granada with the brown vinyl roof for a long time, when it was finally located at Frankfurt Airport. *BKA* forensics officers swabbed every surface for prints and pulled the vehicle apart in the search for evidence: they struck gold. Clear fingerprints of Dessie Grew were all over the vehicle. When the side panelling of the Granada was removed and the insides swabbed, traces of gun oil, as well as traces of RDX and PETN - the chemical constituents of Semtex - were discovered. The *BKA* used the CARS software to cross-reference rental agreements and found rental agreements in the name of Daniel Martin Caldwell, which matched the name given to them by the barman at Café Nato who had sold a gold-coloured Ford station wagon to a second-hand car dealer from Northern Ireland. Staring back at *BKA* investigators from the photo on the driving licence and passport in the name of Daniel Martin Caldwell was the face of Desmond Gerard Grew. With all the strands of evidence weaved together, in early November the *BKA* issued a *Merkblatt* advisory notice to all units in the search for Grew, detailing Grew's movements and the numbers of the Daniel Caldwell passport and driving licenses that Grew was using. Officers were asked to retrospectively check with the landlords of holiday accommodation who might have rented property to "Daniel Caldwell" since July 1st and show them the picture of Dessie Grew. At the same time, the Generalbundesanwalt put out a Europe-wide arrest warrant; Grew was placed on Interpol's watch list. Like the warrant issued for the arrest of Donna Maguire in the case of the Osnabrück bombing, the document was sent to Northern Ireland - with the request that Desmond Grew, should he be apprehended in the Six Counties or in mainland Britain, be extradited to Germany to stand trial for the murder of Mick and Nivruti Islania. The Northern Irish authorities earmarked the document for translation from German in English but seemed in no particular hurry to do so.

The Europe-wide arrest warrant did at least serve to alert those law enforcement agencies of neighbouring countries, who could either understand German or were minded to translate arrest warrants as a matter of priority, to the possible presence of IRA activists within their borders – and they acted accordingly. In Belgium and the Netherlands, police presence was stepped up with checkpoints being set up at major ports such as Rotterdam, in an attempt to apprehend members of the ASU before their own citizens were caught in crossfire. Already caught in the crossfire though, were other Republican terrorist groups operating on the Continent and whose links to certain members of the ASU caused a major distraction in the hunt to find Grew, Maguire and the rest of the PIRA European team. 42-year-old Peter McNally and 30 year old Anthony Kerr were from West Belfast and present in Europe; McNally in particular had links to Dessie Grew, having served together in the INLA in the 1970s. Whereas Grew had left the INLA and transferred his loyalties to the Provisional IRA, McNally had joined the Irish Peoples Liberation Organisation (IPLO) in the mid-1980s and together with Kerr, travelled to the Low Countries with the intent of purchasing weapons for the organisation. Basing themselves in Amsterdam and using a variety of addresses in the city, McNally and Kerr set about procuring arms to take back to Belfast, under the radar of the security services. Their luck ran out when, on December 9th, they ran into a roadblock checkpoint in Antwerp set up to catch the PIRA Active Service Unit. As driver McNally slowed down at the checkpoint near the port and the vehicle was approached by a Belgian *Rijkswacht* officer, Kerr panicked and fired several rounds at the policeman, wounding him in the arm. The pair sped away from the scene but abandoned the car nearby and escaped on foot, one of them hijacking a truck to Amsterdam. When police found the abandoned vehicle, they discovered several of the IPLO purchases that had been left behind: amongst them four handguns and around 500 rounds of ammunition. Assuming that they were close to apprehending part of the PIRA ASU, Belgian and Dutch police combed Antwerp and Amsterdam: two days later on December 11th, they arrested Kerr, at an apartment on Herengracht in Amsterdam. Initially Kerr provided a false name to police. A large number of firearms were also found at the apartment, along with some ammunition, and including the firearm used to shoot the Belgian police officer. The Dutch police also seized two passports; one Irish and one British in the name of Peter McNally, as well as McNally's Northern Irish driving licence. Kerr had in his possession a false passport in the name of Terence Anthony McDonagh. Dutch police also found a shopping list of firearms and a diary with English writing on it, including the words 'FAT PAT' beside the word 'shop'. In addition, police also recovered a birth certificate in the name of Desmond Black, as well as some Bank of Ireland materials marked with Black's name and what appeared to be the bank sorting code of a branch in the Andersonstown area of West Belfast. Dutch police passed on the information to colleagues in Northern Ireland and continued their enquiries as to whether the man they were holding in custody would lead them to Dessie Grew and the elusive ASU. Their enquiries would eventually lead to the capture of McNally some eight months later, prison sentences for McNally (two years) and Kerr (four years) for firearms offences in December 1990, as well as the identification, capture and conviction of Patrick Guiness ('Fat Pat') - who owned a fish and chip shop on the Ormeau Road in Belfast - the following year, and who had supplied the IPLO with a host of false identification papers. But, despite the IPLO and INLA being old acquaintances, and the obvious links between the INLA and the Provos, the IPLO were operating completely independently of both other organisations and thus police investigations in December 1989 into the IPLO case did not help the law enforcement agencies get a single step closer to catching the Provisional IRA European ASU. In light of the stepped-up security measures and police investigations, Martin Conlon took the opportunity to leave The Hague temporarily and return to Armagh City to visit his family over the Christmas break. Higher up the command chain, the Army Council called the traditional general temporary halt to hostilities over the Christmas holidays, so that volunteers could spend some time with their families. But as ever it was to prove a brief moment of calm before violent winds once more began to whip across Northern Ireland, mainland Britain and Continental Europe.

January 1990 arrived in West Belfast: Siobhán O'Hanlon returned to work for Director of Publicity of Sinn Fein (and the Provisional IRA) Danny Morrison at the Republican Press Centre. Morrison was not to remain her boss for very long: on January 4th, the Provisional IRA's Internal Security Unit the "Nutting Squad" lured suspected IRA informer Sandy Lynch to a house in Carrigart Avenue, West Belfast to be interrogated about his part in a police raid in the New Lodge area of the city two months earlier. After Lynch was tortured for three days but refused to admit to passing information to the FRU or Special Branch, Danny Morrison visited the house on Sunday night, January 7th. The RUC had been keeping track of his movements and stormed the house, arresting Morrison and four other men, freeing the extremely lucky Lynch. Morrison claimed he was there to hold a press conference outing Lynch as an informer - but the IRA did not hold press conferences in such matters, they merely waited until security services found the executed informer with two bullets in the back of their skull by the side of a country road and issued a statement: unimpressed, the RUC held Morrison in custody. With Morrison out of the picture, there were two key changes in the Republican movement. After once succeeding Danny Morrison as editor of An Phoblacht, Rita O'Hare once again followed in his footsteps and took over the vacant post of Director of Publicity for the Provisional IRA and Sinn Fein. Sinn Fein president and alleged IRA Army Council member Gerry Adams saw an opportunity to poach Siobhán O'Hanlon and asked her to become his personal assistant; an offer that O'Hanlon readily accepted.

Returning to The Hague, Conlon re-established contact with Hijman. On February 4th they met up, with plans to travel to southern Holland – at Conlon's apartment before they left the phone rang: Hijman's mother asked if Ingrid was there. Ingrid had told her mother she was visiting a cousin. On the train on the way to Venlo, Conlon asked her where her mother had got his number; Hijman told her she had written it down in her diary, which she had left at her parent's house. Her worried mother had wondered where she was and looked through her things. Conlon told her to scratch out any information relating to him out of her personal effects. They carried on to Venlo. There they checked under false names in the Hotel Grolsch Quelle; in the room Conlon looked out of the window at the street junction below, asking Hijman "which of these roads leads to Germany?". Conlon also asked Hijman for her help: he needed to rent a new apartment in The Hague but alleged he could not afford a security deposit on a new apartment, which was likely to amount to around a thousand Dutch guilders; Hijman, although by this time aware of Conlon's IRA activities, agreed to help him find an apartment and to loan him three hundred Dutch guilders towards a deposit.

The Federal State Prosecutors Office Generalbundesanwaltschaft in Karlsruhe and the leader of the *BKA SoKo PIRA* unit leading the investigations into the activities of the Provisional IRA in Germany, Joachim Rzeniecki, finally received a response from British authorities on the request for the extradition of Dessie Grew that had been submitted to the Crown three months previously. The Northern Ireland Office had received detailed information on the evidence to support the request - a video of Grew at the murder scene; documentation showing that he was in possession of the vehicle seen racing away from the scene and carrying the two gunmen; Grew's corroborated fingerprints on the vehicle, traces of gun oil as well as residual traces of PETN and RDX, the constituents of Semtex explosives. But there was one fatal problem; it had taken some time to locate the Ford Granada and the car had been rented over 165 times in all by the time it was found in Frankfurt. Under German law, the body of evidence was strong enough for both extradition and likely a conviction. As the German authorities were about to discover however, British law stipulates that the so-called 'continuity of evidence' must be upheld. Had the car been located and analysed before someone else had rented the vehicle, the chain of evidence would have been unbroken. This was however not the case; despite the overwhelming evidence to place him at the scene and his playing an active role in the murders, the German authorities were dismayed to receive news that British Crown had refused to extradite Desmond Grew from Northern Ireland to Germany on the basis of a interrupted chain of evidence. However, the *BKA* remained resolute and vigilant: Rzeniecki was convinced that Dessie Grew, as the experienced and battle-hardened leader of one of the Provisional IRA's European Active Service Units, was likely to rear his head on the Continent once more.

In the Republic of Ireland, the trial of Bap Hardy and Donna Maguire finally got underway. The West German authorities had filed an informal request to have Maguire and Hardy extradited to Germany, having on September 13th the previous year already issued arrest warrants pertaining to file 1Bjs 186/89-4 (the Osnabrück bombing in June) and 1BJs 197/89-4 (the murder of Steven Smith in Hannover in July). But the German Federal Prosecutors Office received word from Irish authorities that proceedings in the Republic would take priority and declined the request. On February 15th at the Special Criminal Court in Dublin, the pair answered charges of "knowingly having in their possession explosive substances under such circumstances as to give rise to a reasonable suspicion that they did not have them in their possession for a lawful object, contrary to Section 4 (1) of the Explosives Substances Act 1883." Hardy and Maguire both pleaded "not guilty". Maguire said before Judge Liam Hamilton that she barely knew the defendant and had no idea that Hardy had sodium chlorate in his luggage. The possession of mercury tilt switches, telescopic rifle sights, shopping lists of weapons and photographs of British military installations was not technically illegal; however the possession of false passports and the possession of explosives substances was, particularly considering that the rest of the luggage contents indicated that the sodium chlorate was not, as Hardy maintained, to be used as weed killer; on February 22nd after three trial hearings, Hardy was found guilty and sentenced to five years imprisonment in Portlaoise prison. But at the second day of trial on February 16th, Hamilton had listened to Donna Maguire's explanation of the circumstances and her protestations of innocence; he stated in court

> *"It may well be that they were engaged in some kind of joint enterprise and the circumstances are, to say the least, extremely suspicious. But the court is not satisfied beyond reasonable doubt that they were engaged in an enterprise to import these articles."*

Judge Hamilton found no legal grounds on which to convict Maguire and dismissed the case against her. Maguire was whisked out of the court by friends and family, jubilant and relieved at her unjust acquittal. The Generalbundesanwaltschaft in Karlsruhe quickly sent another request asking for the possibility of extradition of Maguire to Germany, but the Gardai were unable to rearrest her due to the lack of formal extradition papers. What neither An Garda Síochána nor the German *BKA* both didn't know was that she was no longer in Ireland. Telling friends and neighbours that she was backpacking to Italy with the intention of watching the Irish football team play in the 1990 World Cup, Donna Maguire had slipped back into Germany to re-join her mentor Dessie Grew on active service for the IRA in Europe.

13 SAFE HOUSES

In the search for an apartment for Conlon, Hijman had scanned through the local newspapers and found a small flat on the corner of Gouwestraat and Pletterijstraat, a quiet residential street in the Rivierenbuurt area of The Hague, immediately adjacent to the city centre. Hijman arranged for them to view the apartment and on March 7th, the pair met and took a look around Pletterijstraat 23. It was perfect for the needs of Conlon and the IRA: Hijman told the landlord that she and her boyfriend wanted to rent the apartment; she paid the thousand guilders security deposit and signed the rental agreement on the property herself, without Conlon having to provide any details. The Provisional IRA now had the keys to a brand new safe house in the Netherlands.

On the very same afternoon, 500 kilometres away in Paris, a trio of French appeal court judges sat in session to assess what to do with the three members of the FERMDOWN ASU that had been captured on the *autoroute de l'est* in July 1989. In the intervening eight months, Pauline Drumm, Donncha O'Kane and Patrick Murray had been held in custody and the Federal Republic of Germany had applied for their extradition from France on the basis of arrest warrant 1BJs 197/89, issued on September 13th 1989 by the German Federal Prosecutors Office indicting Murray, Drumm and O'Kane (and also Donna Maguire), pertaining to the murder of Corporal Steven Smith in Hannover and the foiled oil drum bomb attack on Quebec Barracks in Osnabrück. The trio of judges deliberated the case, tasked with making a recommendation to the state as to whether the extradition request should be granted. They reviewed the material sent to them and the charges presented by the Germans – assassination, destruction by explosives, criminal association and arms violations. Defence lawyer Antoine Comte fought the extradition request on the grounds that once in West

Germany, the three IRA members were likely to be re-extradited to Great Britain, claiming that as Northern Ireland was in a state of civil war, it would be impossible for Irish subjects to be judged fairly in a British court. The judges disagreed with this and instead agreed that all extradition conditions had been met - they recommended that the request be acceded to. They recommended that Murray, Drumm and O'Kane should be the first suspects ever to be extradited from France under the terms of the European Convention on Terrorism of 1977 (the agreement having only been ratified in France the previous year) and should thus stand trial for their offences in Germany. As per French law, the extradition had to be ratified and a subsequent approval hearing was thus set for July 24th - in the meantime, the judges held that the trio must first stand trial in France on the charges for which they were being held: namely criminal association and forging documents. Murray, O'Kane and Drumm were not going to Germany just yet.

Sean Hick - thanks to a variety of false identification papers and his language skills - had remained undercover and undetected in Germany. After staying at several different locations, including Göttingen, he was joined by Donna Maguire. More volunteers planned to join soon. The Dutch ASU comprising Grew, Fox, Quinn and Conlon was to operate from the Hague and be based in Pletterijstraat; the German ASU needed an additional safe house somewhere in the north-western area of Germany where the British military was based, at the northernmost tip of the state of Hesse and the border to Lower Saxony. A search lead them to Döhren, a southern suburb of Hanover, where the ASU would have direct and quick access to the A2 and A7 autobahn routes, connecting them with the Netherlands, as well as Dortmund, Duisburg and many of the British military bases in North Rhine Westphalia via the A2 and one of the main north-south routes, the A7, which also ran through Göttingen. Only a stone's throw from the road leading to the motorway junction they found a suitable apartment in Cäcilienstrasse. Using a false US passport in the name of Robert

Spade, Hick viewed the apartment at Cäcilienstrasse 14 and signed a rental contract on March 27th, allowing him to assume tenancy at the end of April. The Provisional IRA now had at least two safe houses (police suspected that another unidentified apartment in Hannover had also been rented by Hick.) The two locations could be used interchangeably and allow both the Netherlands and German-based ASUs to prepare attacks and accommodate additional personnel. In addition, having a choice of two safe houses allowed for an alternative location should one of the safe houses become compromised and in the light of stepped-up border security, it was advisable for volunteers returning from active service operations on British personnel in Germany would no longer invariably have to make a risky border crossing to the safety of the Netherlands.

Although there had not been an IRA attack since the Wildenrath murders in October 1989, the BKA was still on the trail of the Active Service Units. As the effective investigation of attacks and the neutralisation of the IRA threat to military personnel in Germany and the Low Countries was reliant on close cross-border cooperation, there was a deepening of cooperation between the police forces of the United Kingdom and Germany. One of the measures taken was the posting of a dedicated BKA Detective Inspector to London. With the aim of improving cooperation and accelerating the flow of information between the Special Branch of the Metropolitan Police and the Bundeskriminalamt, the DI took up his post in the European Liaison Section at New Scotland Yard on April 17th. From then on, pertinent information on Provisional IRA activities in mainland Britain and Northern Ireland had begun to flow even more freely between London and Wiesbaden. The week after the installation of the BKA officer within Special Branch, the head of the SoKo PIRA unit himself visited the UK. Three days before Hick signed the rental contract on the apartment in Cäcilienstrasse 14, Joachim Rzeniecki flew to London at the invitation of British counterpart - and close colleague in the police work into the IRA offensive - Colonel Ian Fulton of the SIB, the detective branch of the

British military police. Extensive Investigations into the murders in Unna and Wildenrath, and the attempted murders in Münster were still to be carried out, despite the apparent period of IRA inactivity, but Rzeniecki had an important appointment to keep: with Elizabeth Windsor. The Queen was due to visit the Royal Military Police Training Academy in Chichester to get a first-hand glimpse of how recruits were being trained in the fight against the IRA. As an integral part of the ongoing investigations and working closely with the RMP, Rzeniecki had been invited to be involved in the event. The head of the *SOKO PIRA* spent a week in the UK: on March 24th, Rzeniecki and Fulton - and various members of the Royal Military Police staged a reconstruction of the Unna attack in front of the British monarch. The Queen watched as RMP officers posed as the IRA active service unit, and a female RMP officer played the part of Heidi Hazell; the murder of Heidi was re-enacted as a prelude to a speech from Rzeniecki detailing *BKA* investigations into the attack and the cooperation with the RMP based in Germany. Every last detail of the night was included in the reconstruction, right down to Heidi's blue handbag on the seat of the Saab 9000. The Queen watched intently as the scene played out, seemingly unmoved; it was only as the officers from the *BKA* Tatortgruppe appeared on the scene to secure evidence, that the Queen was visibly moved as the officers removed the blood-splattered bag from the passenger seat. After Rzeniecki had explained in detail about how the *BKA* were on the trail of the ASU, the development of the CARS software, the tale of how Rzeniecki had flown from Frankfurt to Belfast with a bag full of AK-47 ammunition to personally hand over the recovered evidence to the RUC and how the *BKA* were cooperating with the RMP, as well as the RUC Special Branch, SIB and *MI5*, Rzeniecki met the Queen in person, who told them how moved she had been to see Heidi's handbag covered in blood. She asked them further details about investigations and thanked them for their ongoing efforts. Rzeniecki flew back to Frankfurt the same evening and returned to the *BKA* in Wiesbaden to continue to lead the *SoKo PIRA* in the hunt for the IRA. A short time later, Rzeniecki would return to London to follow another invitation; this time from *MI5*. Together with *BKA* President Hans-Jürgen Zachert, Rzeniecki visited *MI5*'s Millbank headquarters to meet with Security Service counterparts; in the evening *MI5* boss Stella Rimmington hosted a lavish dinner in a London hotel in honour of the important guests from Wiesbaden. The next morning was an eye-opener for both the British and the Germans. Accompanied by an *MI5* officer, Zachert and Rzeniecki flew to Belfast to meet RUC colleagues; the RUC were surprised that such high-ranking law enforcement officers were prepared to see for themselves the Northern Irish conflict zone without a whole entourage in tow; the *BKA* men were equally impressed to be taken on a tour of the city in an unmarked car through "no-go areas" and to be able to see first-hand districts firmly under the control of the Provisional IRA. Mutual respect and even closer cooperation between the RUC and *BKA* were thus solidified on the streets of West Belfast.

Back in the extended conflict zone of Continental Europe, in The Hague, Conlon had entrusted Hijman with a bulging holdall when they had met four days after signing the rental agreement for the apartment in Pletterijstraat. He had forbidden her from looking in the bag, told her that it needed to be hidden somewhere but that he would need access to it from time to time: Hijman told him she knew the perfect place and would hide the bag in the cellar of her parents' house in the Rijswijk suburb of The Hague; Conlon agreed but warned her to be careful with the holdall, and threatened to kill her if she opened it. She did as she was told and stowed the holdall in her parent's cellar. On March 29th, Conlon called Hijman and told her he needed something out of the holdall; they agreed to meet the following night in Rijswijk, Hijman retrieved the holdall from the cellar and transported the holdall on the back of her bike to meet Conlon. Looking slightly worried, Conlon carefully unzipped the holdall and removed something the size of a sandwich but wrapped in plastic, stashing it in his jacket pocket and quickly zipping the holdall shut again. Hijman took the holdall back to her parents' cellar.

Although the contents of the plastic-wrapped package officially remain a mystery, there were several similarly wrapped packages in an underground hide dug into the soil in a secluded wooded area between Rhynern and Werl, around 40 kilometres west of Dortmund. Small, orangey-brown plasticine-like bricks, wrapped individually in plastic, lay in rubbish sacks under the earth, each covered with a paper wrapper marked 'Semtex-H'. It is therefore logical to assume that if the package in Conlon's holdall was actually the Czech-made plastic explosive, that he removed it for the purpose of it being used in the near future rather than being added to the existing stockpile in Werl. Equally unlikely than being added to the weapons cache was the intention for it to be used in an attack in Germany. Likely, but not conclusively provable, was that the Semtex was being moved to a new, safer location: for by the end of April, Conlon – and his possessions - were on the move. With the safe house set up in The Hague, Conlon had no real need to have direct contact with Hijman himself – and could be utilised elsewhere. The logistics for the Dutch ASU were in the process of being finalised and the ASUs decided that an arms dump needed to be set up somewhere in the Netherlands or Belgium to facilitate attacks in the Low Countries, instead of volunteers being reliant on ferrying weapons across the border from Germany to carry out these attacks. Crossing borders with explosives or firearms shortly before or after operations was inherently riskier than doing so in a so-called quiet period – it had been over six months since the last IRA attack on mainland Europe and the initially tight security measures across the Netherlands, Germany, Belgium and France were starting to wane – the perfect opportunity to do some housekeeping and prepare for the next wave of attacks.

Charged with acquiring vehicles for the next attack, dividing up the Werl arms cache and establishing a second dump in the Low Countries was the IRA's logistics man in Germany: Sean Hick. Firstly on April 11th, a VW Golf with the registration H-TS 359 was stolen from outside a car dealers in Falkenstrasse in the centre of the city. Travelling from Göttingen to the southern town of Koblenz the next day, Hick walked into a hire car firm armed with cash and a New Zealand passport bearing his photograph in the name of "Stephen Paul Marshall". Hick signed the rental contract on another VW Golf with the registration N-XM 219 and drove back north. With the help of tools and a new roll of plastic rubbish bags, he oversaw the unearthing of the Werl cache, the removal of packages of Semtex-H and several weapons and undertook the risky business of crossing into the Netherlands. Donna Maguire, Gerard Harte and Martin Conlon had been busy scouting for potentially suitable locations along the border. Close to the border with Belgium, south of Breda, in a wooded area between the village of Heerle and the small town of Meerle, the ASU found a secluded area not far from a manor house that seemed to be uninhabited. They had purchased large swing-top Click-It rubbish bins; two large holes were dug not far from each other and there the ASU stashed the explosives and weapons in the relatively waterproof Click-Its, covering them with a layer of soil and leaves. Conlon returned to The Hague; Hick and the rest of the German ASU crossed back over the border and returned to Göttingen. They spent the next few days drinking and dancing. Back in County Tyrone, Dessie Grew began to become concerned at plenty of reports of his ASU spending their time and IRA cash at Wilfi's Disco in Göttingen and no reports of IRA attacks on British military targets. Grew travelled over from Northern Ireland to read them the riot act. Suitably chastened, the ASU began to sober up and plan their next move. In the meantime however there appeared a solid reason to go drinking and dancing: in The Hague at Martin Conlon's leaving party.

To extract himself from the Hijman situation, Conlon had told her to retrieve his holdall from her parents on April 13th and revealed to Hijman that he was going to leave the Netherlands at the end of the month and travel round the USA. Conlon said that she shouldn't worry about the Pletterijstraat apartment; he had some friends that could move in and pay her the rent, just as he had done. He would introduce them to her at his leaving party the following weekend; their relationship pretty much over anyway, Hijman left the following day to visit Lourdes in south-western France for a week, but agreed she would come to his farewell party. Conlon threw the party on April 22nd at Café Spoor, near to the Holland Spoor rail station, a short walk away from Pletterijstraat 23. He was keen to introduce Ingrid Hijman to the two Irish friends who would be taking over the apartment, who had just moved from Germany to The Hague: Desmond Grew and Sean Hick. Hijman was particularly taken with Sean Hick, who Conlon had introduced as his friend 'Jim' and it would not be long before Hick and Hijman became an item.

The week after Conlon's leaving party, on Friday 27th April, Hick – as Robert Spade – took possession of the keys to Cäcilienstrasse 14 in Hanover - he now had the keys to two IRA safe houses. The Dutch and German ASUs had two bases from which to operate, were suitably armed to carry out attacks and the teams in place. Dessie Grew and his East Tyrone brigade colleagues Dermot Quinn and Paddy Fox, Martin Conlon and Gerard Harte from Armagh, Sean Hick from Co. Dublin, and Donna Maguire from Newry were joined by Paul Hughes, newly arrived on the Continent, and brother of South Armagh Adjutant General Sean Hughes, would work in fluid combination with each other on active service, operations being prepared from their bases in The Hague and Hannover in a variety of personnel combinations.

The first target to be identified was close to one of the safe houses but required a lot of travel to logistically organise an attack. Langenhagen Barracks was a British Army complex situated just north of Hanover and home to, amongst others, part of the Royal

Logistics Corps. After several reconnaissance runs to the base and the subsequent formation of a plan, the ASU needed to prepare the devices. Hick and Hughes drove the 200 or so kilometres to the weapons cache in Werl, unearthing the plastic refuse bags before filling two olive-green rucksacks with orange, putty-like Semtex-H, timers and other components as well as retrieving an AK-47 automatic rifle and ammunition. The plastic bags were once more covered with earth. They drove on to Saarbrücken, where on May 2nd they handed back the rental car and took the rucksacks and the disassembled AK-47 back to Hanover – presumably by train. During Thursday, May 3rd, in Cäcilienstrasse 14, they prepared the explosive device. Packing nine 2.5 kilogramme blocks of Semtex-H into one of the rucksacks and ten into the other, they joined two detonators together with wires and pushed one into each rucksack. The wires were connected to a block of six 1.5 volt batteries that they taped together. A Memopark timer was prepared and secured with a screw that prevented the metal arm attached to the Memopark from completing the electrical circuit and thus avoiding the device exploding prematurely during transport. The whole detonating mechanism was placed in a plastic canister – the bomb was ready.

In the dead of night, Hick, Hughes and Harte set out in two vehicles – the stolen and the rented VW Golf cars – and headed for Langenhagen armed with tools, the explosive rucksacks and the reassembled and loaded AK-47. Arriving at the barracks just before 2am, they proceeded to cut a hole in the perimeter fence surrounding the barracks. The IRA team placed the rucksacks up against the wall of an accommodation block, which was only twenty metres inside the perimeter and housed 70 sleeping soldiers from the 1st Postal and Courier Regiment. As they did so, a civilian guard accompanied by a German shepherd dog named "Pebbles" was making routine checks of the perimeter and discovered the hole;

before the volunteers had the chance to arm the explosive device, the guard spotted the three IRA volunteers and shouted in challenge. Disturbed by the unexpected visitor, one of the ASU fired four shots with the AK-47 at the guard – all of which missed him – and ran off – they fled in the stolen Golf. They abandoned the vehicle around 5 kilometres away in Verdener Strasse in the northern district of Ledeburg and proceeded back to Cäcilienstrasse in the rental car. The guard raised the alarm and whilst the three IRA volunteers escaped, the sleeping soldiers were woken by the gunfire and were immediately ordered out of the building. A full search of the accommodation block was carried out and the rucksacks found. Bomb disposal experts were called to the scene and the devices made safe; as Colonel Henry Day, Chief of Public Information for British Forces Germany stated the next day, it was lucky the devices were found, as their detonation would have 'caused a hell of a lot of damage", with probable loss of life and substantial injuries. As it was, the unexploded devices, the abandoned stolen VW Golf and the four spent AK-47 cartridges gave the BKA and security services more important forensic evidence in the hunt for the IRA team; for the Provisional IRA, the resumption of attacks by those volunteers on the ground in Europe had yet again proved to be a misfire.

Working on the premise that yet again a rental vehicle had been used in the attack but realizing that the use of the CARS software only permitted movements to be checked retrospectively, Joachim Rzeniecki and his *SoKo PIRA* team at the *Bundeskriminalamt* decided to become more proactive. Rzeniecki requested backup from the *Bundesgrenzschutz* (Federal Border Guards), the police agency responsible for border, railway and air security. The agency was tasked with dealing with small-scale threats to the security of West German borders, both international and inner-German, and were armed with sub machine-guns. Rzeniecki's request was approved: a twenty-man team was detailed to help the *BKA* hunt down the IRA whilst their volunteers were on a live operation. The CARS software checked for suspicious car hires matching the criteria expected to identify potential vehicle rentals by the IRA, but critically added one further criterion; the rental period had not yet expired and the vehicle was still in use. The BGS officers went from one rental firm to another, working in pairs. Whilst there, they checked the physical paperwork and talked to staff - if the rental looked suspicious enough, an armed *MEK* was dispatched to await the return of the car – and its occupants. The *SoKo PIRA* were hot on the trail on the Provisional IRA and it was surely only a matter of time the *BKA* would catch up with them.

In light of the failure of the Langenhagen explosives attack, the IRA were forced to change strategy once again: the British military's "Keenwind" security status remained at "Black Special" after the use of UVBT devices in July and August in Hanover, and commanders had begun to press home to servicemen and dependents the personal safety message; they issued under-car mirrors to each family, so that the chassis of family vehicles could be checked more easily before each journey. A series of "Personal Safety Booklets" were also issued to all personnel and their families detailing the modus operandi of the IRA on the Continent, which heightened security awareness on and off the military bases. The foiled bomb attacks at Osnabrück and Langenhagen deterred the ASU from filling rucksacks or canisters full of Semtex and letting them be discovered by security forces before they had the chance to be detonated. The only strategy that had so far worked, in an operation sense at least, were so-called CRA's - close range assassinations. Picking out a definable target, getting close to the targeted person and then opening fire had so far been much more effective than planting bombs, even if the previous two attacks had resulted in the deaths of a German civilian, an RAF airman rather than an Army soldier and an innocent six month old baby girl. The decision was made to return to using firearms and to stick to locations where the IRA had been successful in the past, and at a time where military personnel were most likely to be caught off-guard: the CRA specialists in the ASUs were Dessie Grew and Gerard Harte; Roermond in the Netherlands chosen as the perfect location to strike at close quarters. The best time to strike would be on a Sunday evening, when servicemen and their families would be enjoying the end of the weekend before returning to work on Monday morning, relaxed and unaware that they were in the crosshairs of the IRA.

The logistics of planning an attack were complex: firstly weapons needed to be retrieved once more from the arms depot on the Belgian border. Grew and Harte were in Hanover and needed to travel to the Netherlands to prepare and carry out the attack on Dutch soil; more importantly the question of transport needed to be addressed. An instantly traceable hire car that would be identified at the scene could not be used. Hick was in any case not keen on using hire cars for everything; hiring cars meant leaving a paper trail and the more often a member of the ASU used one of their false passports the higher the risk that the identification papers would one time not stand up to scrutiny. Furthermore an expendable vehicle would need to be acquired for travelling to and from the operation; one which could be sacrificed to destroy fingerprints and other evidence. Once the vehicle had been destroyed, the teams would need transport back to both safe houses in The Hague and Hanover, so two further vehicles would be required, making three. To acquire the relevant vehicles and minimise the risks, a plan was hatched. Instead of using up valuable and limited IRA cash to purchase a new car, the ASU would steal one of the required vehicles back in the UK; stealing a car in the Netherlands or Germany and retaining it for use over a longer period would increase the risk of apprehension. Northern Ireland made the most sense as a location to steal the vehicle. To get back to Northern Ireland and to get close enough to Roermond without actually having the vehicle present at the scene, they would need a hire car. Once a third vehicle had been stolen for use in the live operation – the one that would later need to be destroyed – the hire car could be driven to a separate location, to where the ASU would later return, destroy the stolen car and any evidence – and return to the safe house using the hire car, which would then be innocently returned, hopefully devoid of evidence. The risks would be thus minimised.

On May 21st 1990, the plan was put into action. Hick visited the Europcar concession in The Hague and handed over his "Stephen Paul Marshall" passport to rent a red Opel Kadett with the registration YF-08-UN. He drove the 400 kilometres to Hanover to the safe house at Cäcilienstrasse 14. There he picked up Paul Hughes, and also the man who in April had waved goodbye to his Dutch girlfriend and supposedly left the Netherlands for the USA. Martin Conlon had indeed left the Netherlands, but instead of travelling back to the UK and on to America, he had joined the German ASU in Hanover. Hughes had with him a pair of false British registration plates with the registration number D 204 YMY that he had created using a mould. The trio drove back to The Hague to drop off Hick, who had to oversee preparations in the Netherlands; Conlon and Hughes drove across the Low Countries, took the ferry to Ireland and the next day arrived in Conlon's hometown of Armagh, which he knew like the back of his hand. On that evening – May 22nd – the chairman of the local Gaelic Football club, Brian McKinley, was driving his red Ford Sierra away from the GAA ground when he came across an improvised IRA vehicle checkpoint. Dressed in camouflage and balaclavas, Conlon and Hughes ordered him out of the vehicle at gunpoint and sped off. Exchanging the vehicle licence plates for the false D 204 YMY ones to hide the fact that the car was stolen, the pair drove back to the ferry – Hughes in the Sierra, Conlon in the Opel Kadett. Arriving in France, the pair drove first to Paris.

From Paris, Conlon and Hughes continued on to The Hague, where Sean Hick had been busy addressing accommodation issues. Gerard Harte and Donna Maguire had left Hanover and met Hick in

Enschede on May 18th before travelling back to The Hague. On May 20th Hick called Hijman to arrange to pick up the keys to Pletterijstraat 23; all four met at the central railway station in The Hague with Hick introducing the other ASU members as 'Mary' and 'John'. They walked the short distance to the apartment together. On May 22nd, Hick and Maguire once again met up with Hijman at Central Station, and returned to Pletterijstraat 23 to find Harte there. Harte and Maguire had earlier met up for a drink in Jim & Joe's Place, a bar in the centre of The Hague. With the ASU largely assembled in the Hague, the next step was to carry out a dry run without weapons - the Opel Kadett was used to drive to Venlo and Roermond and back for reconnaissance purposes – in Roermond, Dessie Grew made discreet enquiries in a handful of restaurants situated around the market square on *Marktplein*. In the Cafe de beurs, he casually asked the owner Paul Reijngoud why there were so many cars with British number plates parked on the square; the owner told him it was a favoured location for British servicemen and their families to enjoy a leisurely meal on a Sunday evening. The ideal location for an attack had been found. In the meantime, Hughes used the Sierra to drive through the Netherlands to Belgium and found a suitably secluded location near Hechtel-Eksel, off the main road between the small towns of Valkenswaard and Leopoldsburg that would serve as the perfect place to swap vehicles after the attack. The final piece of the jigsaw was to retrieve weaponry for the operation. Again the Opel Kadett was used to drive to the Dutch weapons depot; once again, the Click-Its were unearthed and opened. The AK-47 with the serial number NK-8441 engraved on the side, used in the murder of Mick Islania, the Münster and Langenhagen operations, as well as the Ruger .357 revolver used at the BP petrol station in Wildenrath to kill baby Nivruti Islania were removed, along with ammunition for both weapons, and the Click-Its reburied. Reconvening in The Hague, the ASU were happy that the complicated preparation had gone well and the operation had been planned to precision. This time the Active Service Unit was convinced that this time nothing could go wrong.

THE OVERSEAS DEPARTEMENT

14 SITTING DUCKS

On the morning of Sunday, May 27th, four young Australian tourists awoke in a hotel in Arnhem in the Netherlands, twenty kilometres from the border with Germany. Stephen Melrose, 24, from Brisbane, his wife of nine months Lyndal, 25, Stephen's friend and colleague Nick Spanos, 28, from Sydney, and Nick's girlfriend Vicky Coss, 24, were eager to make the most of the last day of an extended weekend vacation on the Continent, and after breakfast the foursome left the hotel to take in the national park *De Hoge Veluwe*. They had left London on Friday, visited the beach at Scheveningen, the Van Gogh exhibition in Amsterdam and taken a boat ride of the famous canals of the city. Stephen as an avid amateur photographer was keen to document the city and their weekend away, taking masses of photos of the tourist attractions, of Lyndal, Nick and Vicky in various combinations, before handing his camera to a fellow tourist on the boat to take a snapshot of the four of them; happy and smiling as Amsterdam floated by. On that Sunday - with the weekend drawing to a close but still with plenty of time before they had to return to Calais to catch the ferry back to Dover, they agreed to drive further south and possibly stay overnight somewhere in Limburg before the long drive back to the French port. Due to the UK spring bank holiday the following day, they were only due back at work in London on Tuesday and intended to return to the capital on Monday in plenty of time to sleep, unpack and prepare for the short working week. Lawyers Stephen and Nick had recently taken up jobs at McKenney and Company, a law firm in London, where Vicky worked for the NCBC Texas International Bank; the decision to move to London had ostensibly been taken on the grounds of furthering their career prospects back in Australia but also, like most young Australians, to take the chance to travel, to see the cultural sights of Old Europe before returning to Australia to start families. With a few hours of this particular trip to the Continent left, they wanted to wring every last memory out of the long weekend and the foursome set off in their hired grey Citroën BX – with British-registered number plates - in the direction of Roermond.

***

As Stephen, Lyndal, Nick and Vicky slowly made their way south, in The Hague, Pletterijstraat 23 was a hive of activity. Grew ensured that everyone knew their role in the impending operation: Hughes and Hick as drivers, Maguire as intelligence, Grew himself and Harte as gunmen. Quinn and Conlon would be located in The Hague and Hannover to coordinate logistics back at the safe houses in the Netherlands and Germany. Grew and Harte loaded their weapons with ammunition and joined Maguire, Hughes and Hick in the car; the five-strong ASU set off in their hired red Opel Kadett – registration YF-08-UN - in the direction of Limburg.

They drove first to Venlo, a few kilometres north of Roermond to the first planned stop, arriving mid-evening. At around 9.30pm, in a small apartment block just off the main road on Walstraat, a resident heard a car door slam and looked out of his apartment window, which overlooked parking bays outside the block, to see the red Opel parked up in an empty bay next to a neighbour's metallic-brown Mazda 626 car. The resident thought no more of it and busied himself in his apartment preparing his evening meal. A few minutes later, he heard a car drive away at speed and looked out of the window again at the parking bay and noticed that the red Opel, as well as the brown Mazda had both disappeared. Whilst the resident had been tending to his dinner, the Active Service Unit had sprung into action: Hughes had broken into the Mazda 626, hotwiring the ignition as Grew jumped into the passenger seat beside him, Harte taking a seat in the back. As Hughes, Grew and Harte sped off, Hick and Maguire followed in the red Opel Kadett. They drove back in the direction of Eindhoven, before turning south and slipping over the border into Belgium near Valkenswaard. A few miles further they turned off towards Leopoldsburg, before coming to a halt just outside the small town of Hechtel-Eksel; parking the red Opel in woods just off the trunk road, Hick and Maguire joined Harte, Maguire and Grew in the brown Mazda and together they drove back in the direction of the Netherlands.

***

In Roermond, the Australians had spent the early evening looking around the old town, taking pictures – by 10pm they were hungry and began searching for a location to have a late bite to eat. They arrived on the picturesque old cobblestoned market square which housed the *Stadthuis*, the imposing town hall dating back to the early 1700s, a short distance from the railway station, where Dutch, German and British families had mingled earlier in the evening, eating al fresco at the outside tables belonging to the number of restaurants, bars and cafés bordering the cobblestoned square. After parking the Citroën in front of the town hall, they stepped out into the warm summer air, and went on the search for a suitable place to eat on the square. Due to the lateness of the hour, the four were politely turned away from a few restaurants as the kitchens were already closed. They managed to convince the staff of the Tin San Chinese restaurant at the south end of the square to serve them and ordered a couple of beers and a couple of glasses of wine.

***

As the Australian tourists were swapping memories of their long Continental weekend, finishing their meal and preparing themselves to make the journey back to the ferry port at Calais, the ASU had arrived in Roermond. Guiding the Mazda towards the city centre, Hughes drove over the Maas Bridge, right off the main road into the cobbled side street Kraanport, which snaked down towards the north end of the market square. Rolling past the bars at the top of the near deserted square, Hughes parked the car in an empty parking spot and turned the lights off. Surveying the few cars left parked on the square, the Citroën with its British number plates – C

505 GNY - stood out. British-registered number plates indicated off-duty British military personnel; the IRA unit readied themselves. Tense with anticipation, Harte and Grew removed the safety catches from their weapons and waited in the dark for the occupants of the Citroën to appear.

***

At 23:05, the foursome in Tin San made to leave; Stephen Melrose paid the bill and followed his wife, Nick and Vicky who were already on their way to the parked Citroën, laughing and chattering; watched intently by the ASU in the Mazda some eight to ten metres away. The short hair and stocky build of Nick Spanos matched the description of the kind of person the watching IRA team were on the lookout for.

Stephen caught up with his friends at the car and as Nick and Vicki climbed into the back seats; Lyndal walked round to the front passenger seat and began to straighten the seat cover. Stephen marvelled at the old town hall; he shouted to his companions that he wanted to take one last picture of the beautiful square and opened the boot to remove his camera equipment. He set up a camera on a tripod pointing towards the façade of the town hall, and began to fiddle with the exposure settings to accommodate for the poor lighting conditions; unaware of a man moving in his direction in the darkness, weaving between the other cars parked on the square.

Harte had slowly stepped out of the left rear door of the Mazda, pulled a balaclava over his head and walked towards Melrose and the Citroën. Holding an AK-47 in his left hand with the barrel pointing to the floor, Harte weaved through the parked cars and headed towards Melrose at the back of the car. Getting within two to three metres of Melrose, Harte raised the barrel of the automatic rifle with one hand and aimed at the legs of the Australian lawyer; with the safety catch off, Harte squeezed the trigger. The hail of gunfire ripped through Melrose's trousers, causing him to drop immediately to the floor. Having had his back to Harte, Melrose possibly had no idea that he had just been shot; for one to two seconds he lay on the floor screaming in pain, with blood spurting out of his wounds; Harte moved closer and bore down on Melrose lying prostrate on the cobblestones. Harte squeezed the trigger once more, firing a volley of shots into the upper body of Stephen Melrose; the lawyer was killed instantly. Harte quickly moved to the car to where Stephen's wife, Nick and Vicky had turned to see a man firing an automatic rifle at close range at Stephen and were sitting in shock and with nowhere to run. Harte approached the right hand passenger door, took aim at Nick Spanos in the back seat and squeezed the trigger once more.

Vicky Coss, sitting arm in arm in the back seat with Nick describes what happened:

> "I heard a series of loud shots and then more muted noises. Nick pulled me down. I looked at him. I could see that a bullet had entered his head and he was bleeding heavily. It was obvious from the wounds that he had been shot at point blank range. "

The burst of automatic gunfire had hit Nick Spanos in the head and chest multiple times and he died instantaneously. Vicky was uninjured but in shock. In the front seat, Lyndal Melrose was similarly uninjured but frozen with shock and fear. Harte surveyed the inside of the car and looked at Melrose briefly before turning away. As he did so, the Mazda driven by Hughes screeched to a halt a matter of feet away from the body of Stephen Melrose. Dressed in black, face covered by a balaclava and with the Ruger .357 revolver in his right hand, Dessie Grew got out of the Mazda, walked over to the already dead Melrose and putting the barrel of the gun behind Melrose's left ear, coldly fired three shots into his head. Grew then moved around to the side of the Citroën, took aim through the window and emptied the chamber of the revolver into the head of Nick Spanos.

In the car, survival instinct kicked in, Vicky threw open the car door and ran as fast as she could away from the vehicle. She describes the horror of the scene:

> "When I got out of the car, Stephen was lying face downward with the tripod beside him. He had been shot through the side of his head...the bullet had gone through his head and out the other side. I started screaming."

Over in a matter of seconds, the gunfire had naturally attracted the attention of the few people still in the restaurants on the square. Amongst others, Paul Reijngoud, the owner of the De beurs café opposite where the Citroën was parked had come out of the front door of the café to see what the commotion was; Harte noticed him and walked towards him but stood in front of the café owner without saying a word or raising the AK-47. As he eyed Reijngoud up and down and saw that several bullets had missed their target, ripping into the front of the café at head-height, where a few hours earlier a young family had sat with their children, he heard a triumphant battle cry from Grew and a shout from Hughes; Grew got back into the Mazda, Harte turned away from Reijngoud and jumped into the back of the car. Lyndal, who had been crouched in the footwell of the front passenger seat as the shooting had been taking place, finally jumped out of the car and ran to the nearby De Mert restaurant shouting "IRA, IRA, call the police!" as Hughes took off at breakneck speed away from the dead bodies, the bullet-ridden Citroën, Reijngoud, the shocked bystanders, the market place.

The Mazda raced through the now virtually deserted streets of Roermond and back onto the highway. In a matter of minutes they had hit the main A73 road that lead south and drove through the night with the intention of reaching Hechtel-Eksel to where Conlon was waiting. Somewhere along the way, the ASU missed a right turning that would have taken them across the border into Belgium. Half an hour later, at around quarter to midnight, instead of being nearly in Leopoldsburg, they reached the outskirts of Sittard in the southernmost tip of the narrow strip of the Netherlands squashed between Belgium and Germany, from where Gerry McGeough and Gerry Hanratty had two to three years earlier launched Provisional IRA attacks from the area around Geleen. Realising they were travelling in the wrong direction, Hughes turned off the highway into a petrol station. Donna Maguire got out of the back and entered the brightly lit but empty interior. Approaching the lone attendant – John Loofen – she said that she was lost and asked for directions to Belgium. Loofen told her she was travelling in the wrong direction, explained to her how to get back to the border and Maguire returned to the car. Setting off once more, the ASU drove back the way they came and found the correct turning; in the small hours of May 28th, around an hour after leaving Sittard, they finally pulled up just off the motorway between Hechtel-Eksel and Leopoldsburg to where the red Opel Kadett sat waiting. Dousing the Mazda in petrol and setting it alight so as to destroy any forensic evidence, the ASU drove away from the burning wreck, setting off towards the safety of The Hague and Pletterijstraat 23, jubilant that they had carried out a successful attack.

As news reports of the night's events filtered out from Roermond early on Monday morning, and spread via the European news agencies, the IRA team were shocked and shaken by their error. Roermond police chief Kujpers confirmed the attack had led to two fatalities and quickly pointed the finger at the IRA; Alan Patterson, spokesman for the British Army on the Rhine, admitted the Provos were likely to have been the perpetrators, that the attack had been targeted at British military personnel but that the victims had had no military connections. Finally, later that morning the Department of Foreign Affairs in Canberra, Australia revealed that the two victims were in fact innocent Australian citizens and expressed disgust and incomprehension at the crime. Equally dismayed were the IRA's Overseas Department: incredulous that Grew and his team on the Continent had created yet another PR disaster for the organisation, the IRA issued a statement via the Republican Press Centre in Dublin and owned up to the mistake:

> "The IRA accepts responsibility for the deaths...the active service unit involved tragically mistook the men for two British Army personnel. The IRA deeply regrets this tragedy."

As the statement was being issued, Sean Hick was putting the Opel Kadett through the car wash at a Shell petrol station next to the Europcar concession in The Hague. The car was completely filthy and covered in mud from driving through the woods in Hechtel-Eksel and there was no way that Hick could hand back the hire car in that state. After the vehicle had been cleaned, he drove the short distance to Europcar and handed it back to employees, again using his false New Zealand passport in the name of "Stephen Paul Marshall". The employee at Europcar was amazed when he checked the mileage of the much-used Opel: after a return trip to Northern Ireland, trips to various IRA weapons dumps, reconnaissance missions on the other side of the country and the occasional journey to Hanover, it was no wonder that the additional 5,000 kilometres that had been put on the clock within the one-week rental period raised an eyebrow or two. Hick returned to Pletterijstraat and called Ingrid Hijman in Uilenstede, arranging to meet in Amsterdam later that evening. Hijman agreed and at around 21:30 on the night after the killings in Roermond, arrived to meet Hick at the central bus station. Hick disembarked from the bus with no luggage but a dejected look on his face.

On the morning of May 29th, Hijman accompanied Hick to Amsterdam Central Station and said goodbye as Hick boarded a train bound for Breda; Hicks destination was the weapons dump on the Dutch-Belgian border, just south of the city. Donna Maguire was also on the move; she was spotted in Raeren in Belgium shortly after crossing the border from Germany, presumably also heading for the weapons dump. Hughes and Harte drove from Hanover in the red Ford Sierra stolen in Armagh to join them; together they carried out a post-mortem on the disastrous Roermond operation and set about planning their next move. On the same day, Grew was in Amsterdam: the ASU needed another vehicle to replace the returned Opel Kadett. Unwilling to risk using Hicks "Stephen Paul Marshall" passport in case investigators had linked this to the Roermond operation, Grew was tasked with obtaining a new car; rather than hiring a vehicle and risk creating a longer paper trail than necessary, he opted to purchase a red Opel Kadett – with the registration KD-11-LR - almost exactly identical to the one hired in The Hague; he used a different fake passport, this time in the name of "Trevor Paul Holmes", bought the Opel and drove across to the Netherlands in the direction of Germany.

Lyndal Melrose and Vicky Coss were paralysed with shock at witnessing the murder of their partners, as well as surviving the terrifying incident themselves. The Australian embassy helped them to return to London two days after the Roermond attack and on May 30th, accompanied by Australian diplomats, a press conference was held at the Australian High Commission at which Melrose and Coss gave an emotional account of what had happened on the market square three nights before. Lyndal took the lead and explained to the press how the attack had unfolded, how she had taken cover in the front passenger seat when the IRA had started shooting. Clearly still numb and in great shock she said:

> "It was a nightmare. It's just something that doesn't happen to you. It was like something out of a horror movie...(the shooting) sounded like firecrackers and I thought it was just kids...I heard a window smash and realised it was serious...I looked up and saw Nick and Stephen on the ground. I had a blanket in my hand, a car rug, I think. I ran around and nobody came for what

seemed like a long time...I don't think they took any care to avoid us. They happened to be able to kill the boys without touching us. Had we been in the way, they would not have stopped."

Vicki Coss added:

"There was no reason why anybody should have shot at us. It was nothing that we could have foreseen. We were just sitting ducks."

Back on the Continent, after the botched operation, the ASU made a plan to strike again as soon as possible, rather than sit back and mull over their mistake. In addition, the innocent deaths of Melrose and Spanos had the potential to significantly dent the Republican cause – the IRA felt that a quick response was needed to avoid negative propaganda spreading. The message from the Overseas Department was clear: go out and get it right this time. It was too risky to carry out another operation in the Netherlands whilst the country was on high alert after the Roermond murders. In July, the International Four Days Marches - a popular annual event that had been taking place since 1909 and was colloquially known as the Vierdaagse) - was due to take place in Nijmegen. The four day marching event attracted not only crowds of onlookers from across the Netherlands and Western Europe, but also participants from many different military services, including the Royal Air Force and British Army, who were proud of completing the gruelling four day 200 kilometre march in military uniform whilst carrying at least 10 kilogrammes of equipment. Fearful that a new attack on British military targets was being planned, the Dutch domestic intelligence agency *BVD* and Dutch police, in advance of the Vierdaagse, arrested a number of members of the Ierland Komitee Nijmegen - the news of the arrests had naturally reached the ASU. In addition, targeting those who looked like they might be off-duty soldiers, in a public place far enough away from military installations to sow doubts about whether they were a legitimate target brought with it the risk of a further PR catastrophe: the ASU decided to focus once again on the large British Army presence in the North-Rhine-Westphalia region of Germany; carrying out an attack in a Forces married quarter area was more likely to provide a target that the ASU could be sure would be military and it would reduce the possibility of collateral civilian damage. Minimising the amount of time they would have to carry around weapons, the proximity to the local British Army barracks and the ease of escape from the scene, they identified the leafy married quarter estate of Gartenstadt on the outskirts of Dortmund near to a British military garrison as the perfect location to carry out an operation. The area was home to predominantly higher-ranking British Army officers and their families but these lived in a mixed community amongst German families, meaning a lower level of security – in addition Gartenstadt lay on the eastern fringes of Dortmund, directly connected to the Westfalendamm B1 trunk road running in a straight line from Werl to Dortmund – it would be an in-and-out job with little risk involved, at least to the ASU.

On the afternoon of June 1st, Hick, Harte, Hughes and Maguire set off from Heerle in the red Opel Kadett in the direction of Germany, stopping at the quaint roadside petrol station "De Baarlse Witte Pompen" in the border village of Baarle-Hertog to fill up with petrol. From there they crossed from the Netherlands into Germany and headed for Werl, where they once again unearthed the plastic refuse sacks from their underground hiding place, removing two AK-47s and ammunition. They covered the sacks with a thick layer of soil and jumped back into the Opel, setting off for Dortmund. Not wanting to risk sacrificing the red Opel in the operation or to rent a vehicle that could be traced to them, the first task was to acquire an additional vehicle. Heading back in the direction of Dortmund, shortly after 10pm they turned off the main A1 road into the Aplerbeck district in the east of the city. The team cruised slowly round the streets looking for a car to steal – after about fifteen minutes, they found a suitable vehicle on Erbpachtstrasse: a grey coloured Mazda 323, registered in Dortmund under the number DO-UT 693. The ASU had shown a preference to sticking to similar makes and models of cars from operation to operation; familiarity made them easier to handle – and steal. Breaking into the vehicle, Hughes tossed an ICOM radio handset to Hick, who returned to the Opel Kadett; Harte and Maguire - armed with one of the units AK-47 assault rifles and the Browning 9mm taken from Corporal Derek Wood in Andersonstown - got into the Mazda with Hughes and the quartet made their escape. Maintaining radio contact with each other, the vehicles drove circuits around the Gartenstadt looking for potential targets. By now it was well on the way to midnight; soldiers would be returning home from an evening out and the ASU kept a lookout for cars with British registration plates heading either towards Suffolk Barracks or the married quarter estate. Shortly before midnight, as they were driving down the Westfalendamm, the team in the grey Mazda spotted a target: four soldiers in civilian clothes driving westwards in the direction of Suffolk Barracks in a car with British license plates. One of the volunteers readied their AK-47 and Hughes drove up aggressively behind the soldiers' car - the ASU following in hot pursuit at 120 mph. Realising the situation and coming up to a red traffic light, the driver of the soldiers' car panicked, put his foot on the accelerator and sped through the red light. The car turned into the barracks and the ASU following close behind were forced to drive past the barracks and break off the pursuit. Passing the entrance to the Army base, the ASU did a U-turn in the road. Another car was just leaving the barracks and turning left from where the ASU had come; they instantly made out the British registration plate of the dark-green Volvo estate car. The occupants were a couple in their thirties - a thick set man at the wheel with short cropped hair and a woman around the same age in the passenger seat. They indicated to turn off right towards the married quarter estate in Gartenstadt and the ASU made a split-second assessment; British Army. Target. Get them.

Unlike so many other times, the ASU targeting had this time been spot-on. At the wheel of the Volvo was Major Michael Dillon-Lee, battery commander of 32 Heavy Artillery Regiment; based at Suffolk Barracks, and one of the British Army's most accomplished marksmen, Dillon-Lee was looking forward to taking part in the Vierdaagse march in a few short weeks – it was the 10th anniversary of 32 Regiment's association with colleagues from a German Bundeswehr unit and the regiments were planning on completing the Nijmegen march together to mark the event. But this evening, "Mike" was under the weather. Together with his wife Rosalind, he had been at a party at Suffolk Barracks that evening, but as he had been feeling unwell, the couple decided to leave the party early to return to their married quarter in Max-Eyth-Strasse, where their two sons - ten year old James and seven year old Mark – were sleeping. The ASU waited as the Volvo turned off the main road, paused to allow the vehicle to gain some distance, and followed the car. A few minutes later, shortly after midnight and followed at a short distance by the Mazda, the Dillon-Lees arrived in the driveway of their house. The grey Mazda which pulled up on the other side of the road as Mike got out of the car did not cause any undue attention: Dillon-Lee assumed it was a neighbour. Hick in the red Opel had been following both vehicles but too far away to be noticed.

Mike exited the vehicle and went to open the garage door to allow them to park as Rosalind climbed out of the car. As Mike stepped towards the garage door, the ASU pounced; with a balaclava over his head and dressed in black, one of the volunteers sprang out of the Mazda and ran to within a couple of feet of Major Dillon-Lee. The volunteer lifted the barrel of his AK-47 and with his left arm outstretched aimed the rifle at Dillon-Lees head. He squeezed the trigger twice. The two short bursts of gunfire erupted in the dark night; six or seven bullets hit Michael Dillon-Lee in the face, killing him instantly; a brutal execution. One of the other volunteers leaned out of the rear window of the Mazda and fired several shots at the

British soldier from the Browning handgun for good measure. Rosalind Dillon-Lee froze in shock, unable to move as the IRA man aimed the rifle at her. For a fleeting moment frozen in time, she expected him to pull the trigger once more. But the Irishman instead lowered the rifle, turned and raced back to the Mazda, clambering in. At the wheel, Paul Hughes put his foot on the accelerator and as the ASU vehicle slowly picked up speed away from the bloody corpse of the British soldier lying in his front garden, away from a shocked Rosalind Dillon-Lee, the gunman leaned out of the window with rifle aloft and triumphantly shouted *"Tiocfaidh ar la!"* - the battle cry of the Provisional IRA.

As the grey Mazda raced down Max-Eyth-Strasse away from the scene, the team made radio contact with Sean Hick in the red Opel: mission accomplished, target eliminated. Relieved that an operation had finally worked out, Hick gave a whoop of delight and turned the car back in the direction of the Army barracks, where the soldiers who the ASU had followed earlier had still been in the process of reporting the incident in the guardroom when they had heard the crackle of distant automatic rifle fire. High on adrenalin, Hick approached the entry gate to the barracks in the Opel, where two soldiers were on sentry duty. Hick slowed down the vehicle as he came within feet of the entrance, wound down his window and shouted to the guards in his southern Irish brogue "It's been all too fucking easy!" Before the guards had time to react or realise they were being taunted by a member of the IRA unit who had just murdered a colleague of theirs in cold blood, Hick raced off laughing. Less than a kilometre away however, in the grey Mazda, Hughes, Maguire and Harte were not laughing; for as they reached the end of Max-Eyth-Strasse, they realised that they had hit a dead end. Frantically turning the car round they raced back past the murder scene to head back to the main Westfalendamm road. The escape plan was already starting to go wrong; Hughes turned the Mazda left onto Westfalendamm and gathered speed; in the meantime, Dillon-Lee's neighbours had heard the gunfire and had seen the getaway car racing past after its abrupt U-turn; they alerted the police, giving a description of the ASU vehicle and the registration plate. A German patrol car was nearby, spotted the Mazda and gave chase. Hughes piloted the vehicle at top speed down Westfalendamm, the TV tower looming in the distance in the dark. Hughes turned off right towards the city centre and raced through the deserted streets with the police car in hot pursuit.

By 12:28am, the Mazda and the patrol car passed Dortmund's main railway station: the police managed to close down the ASU's car and tried to cut off the escape route; Hughes drove in zigzag lines to prevent the police car from bringing the getaway car to a halt; stopping would have meant arrest and the end of the ASU. The team realised the situation was dire; one of the volunteers aimed the AK-47 out of the window and fired on the patrol car. With Hughes still veering around wildly, only one bullet hit the police car, passing through the door and grazing the ankle of one of the officers. But it was enough to shake off the patrol car: Hughes accelerated away northwards as one of the ASU hurriedly began to dismantle the AK-47 in the back of the car.

The police patrol radioed all units and explained the situation; all exit roads to the north of the city were to be immediately sealed in an attempt to block the IRA's escape. Ten minutes after losing their police pursuers and heading towards Lünen, the ASU were surprised to find a police roadblock had suddenly appeared on the road in front of them; Hughes told everyone in the vehicle to hold tight and accelerated at the police; the Mazda crashed through the roadblock and sped off in the direction of Hamm. As they did so, police fired on the vehicle, a bullet grazing one of the volunteers. Hick meanwhile had adhered to the originally planned escape route, having not been spotted and chased by police. He was keeping in touch with the Mazda via his ICOM handset, frantically trying to keep tabs on their location and work out a possible location where they would be able to meet up, destroy the stolen Mazda and escape together back to the safe house in Cäcilienstrasse in Hanover. Hughes, Harte and Maguire in the Mazda had managed to survive two separate police chases but just before 1am as they approached Pelkum, a small village between Dortmund and Hamm, a police car with plain clothed officers spotted them and once more the ASU was forced to flee through the night. As Hughes, Harte and Maguire gained a large distance advantage on the third police car approaching Unna, Hick finally caught up with the Mazda in the town of Bönen. Still being chased by the police, the trio in the car hurriedly manoeuvred it off the road at an intersection, flung open the doors and hastily jumped into the Opel Kadett as Hick drove full-speed away in the direction of Hanover.

The ASU were relieved to have escaped. They had achieved what they had set out to do: carry out a successful operation, kill a British soldier, deflect attention from the botched operation in Roermond. But the price they had had to pay was potentially high: the chaotic escape, complete with police chases, the blood of at least one member of the Active Service Unit smeared across the interior of the car, the frantic radio calls to Hick - it had been an absolute white-knuckle ride rather than the easy "in-and-out" they had planned. And worse: not only had Hick in the adrenalin rush risked identification or capture in taunting the sentry guards at Suffolk Barracks, but the team in the Mazda had also screwed up badly. For in their haste, they had left behind weapons, important equipment and forensic evidence in the getaway car. When police discovered the abandoned getaway vehicle shortly after 2am in Bönen, they found in it one of the ICOM walkie-talkie handsets, a brown balaclava fashioned from a headrest cover originating from the Opel Kadett, a couple of screwdrivers with green handles, the rifle butt of the AK-47 that had been left behind, ammunition, and three Dutch Komo-brand plastic refuse sacks in which the weapons had been wrapped when the ASU retrieved them from the underground arms depot in Werl. Worst of all for the ASU, they had also left behind the

Browning 9mm on the back seat; the IRA had lost one of its trophy weapons. The handgun that been taken from Corporal Derek Wood in West Belfast on March 19th 1988, as he and colleague Corporal David Howes accidentally drove into the funeral cortége of Kevin Brady, killed by Loyalist gunman Michael Stone at the funeral of the three IRA volunteers killed by the SAS in Gibraltar 13 days previously, was now lost. It was surely a bad omen. DNA testing was not yet far enough advanced to be able to match the bloodstains in the vehicle to known IRA volunteers but there were fingerprints all over the car. Whilst the police did not know exactly where the IRA units were located, the operation had been slapdash enough that when Joachim Rzeniecki and his *SoKo PIRA* team arrived in Dortmund, they would have a whole load of clues to help bring them much closer to apprehending the Active Service Unit.

The Republican Press Centre may not have been aware of just how narrow the escape had been when it released a press statement claiming responsibility the following day for both the murder of Major Dillon-Lee and the gunning down of three off-duty soldiers in Lichfield on the British mainland earlier the same day.

> *"Active Service Units of the Irish Republican Army carried out the two separate operations against British military personnel in England and West Germany. In the first operation in Staffordshire, England, an Active Service Unit opened fire on a number of British soldiers, leaving one dead and two injured. In the second operation a Volunteer opened fire on a major in the Royal Artillery Regiment stationed in Dortmund, West Germany, killing him. While British troops remain in Ireland such attacks will continue."*

If Provisional IRA commanders were likely as yet unaware of how badly the escape from Dortmund had gone, they definitely did not know that German police were about to make an important discovery in the woods outside Werl. A local man reported that he had observed the ASU arriving in a red vehicle to retrieve weapons a few hours before the Dortmund attack, and heard the sounds of digging and weapons being loaded. He alerted the police. Investigators from the SoKo PIRA unit arrived to comb the area and discovered a freshly dug patch of soil. Digging down to a depth of around half a metre, they unearthed four plastic refuse sacks: in three of the sacks was nearly 60 kilogrammes of plastic-wrapped putty-like bricks, each weighing 2.5 kilogrammes and labelled "PLASTIC EXPLOSIVE SEMTEX-H"; enough explosives to make tens of lethal UVBT devices. In another plastic sack they found a disassembled Belgian-made FN machine gun, as well as 750 belted rounds of ammunition for the weapon wrapped in a cloth bag. Both weapon and ammunition had not been wrapped securely and had been exposed to damp conditions: it was likely they had lain there for some time rusting. There were however also a number of newer Belgian-made FN pistols in the arms cache, as well as a small amount of 9mm and AK-47 ammunition. The weapons cache was taken away for forensic examination: crucial to the identification of the source of the underground weapons depot was however the plastic refuse sacks: the blue sacks were stamped with KOMO in yellow letters. The sacks were of the same type found in the Mazda abandoned in Bönen and forensic investigation determined that the perforations of the sacks found in Werl matched exactly the perforations of the sacks found in the getaway car; they had been torn from the same roll, proving that the weapons dump belonged to the Provisional IRA unit that had been on active service in Dortmund. Further forensic and ballistics tests confirmed also that the thirteen bullet cases found outside Major Dillon-Lee's house in Max-Eyth-Str. matched the four cases found outside Langenhagen barracks from the bullets that had been fired during the attack on May 4th. One thing was now clear: corroborating the use of the weapon in both attacks created an indelible link between the two cases and thus it was highly likely that the same team carried out the attacks in both Langenhagen and Dortmund, and possibly also those in Roermond, Unna-Massen and Wildenrath. Information and test results from all cases were pooled and *BKA* investigators set about going through every morsel of evidence piece-by-piece. The discovery of the weapons hide was however not made public: calculating that the ASU might return to retrieve Semtex or, as they had lost at least one weapon in the chase from Dortmund to Bönen – possibly the stashed firearms, Rzeniecki sent two *Mobile Einsatzkommandos* (*MEKs*) - a special forces unit of the *BKA* highly trained in the observation and capture of serious criminals and terrorists - to the spot where the arms cache had been found. The police officers lay hidden in wait in the dirt and awaited the return of the Provisional IRA.

15 HEERLE

On June 3rd 1990, as the *BKA* unearthed the weapons dump in Werl, the Active Service Unit was 250 kilometres away in the Netherlands. They had reconvened at the Dutch weapons dump near Breda to take stock and plan their next move. The feeling was that the next attack should take place as soon as possible to continue momentum but to change tactics to keep one step ahead of the security services. Wanting to move away from close quarter assassinations and the use of firearms, with the inherent security risks posed by physically being present during attacks, they eyed up the plastic-wrapped packages of Semtex in the Click-It rubbish bins. They looked through the maps they had brought with them and identified possible targets for a bomb. During the planning, Maguire was sent to get food and drove to the nearby village of Ulvenhout. On Dorpstraat she found a chip shop and returned to the woods with five portions of *fritten*. It was decided that Maguire as intelligence officer would take the lead in identifying a suitable target and she and Hick headed back across the border to Germany in the red Opel Kadett. Hick dropped off Maguire in the small town of Hamelin – the setting for the story of the Pied Piper - which lies between Hanover and Bielefeld. She checked into a hotel in the town that evening. Hick continued on to Hanover and the safe house in Cäcilienstrasse to join Dessie Grew.

The following day, Maguire began with scouting potential locations for an attack. In the evening, she went out to the club / bar "Crex" on Wehberger Strasse, which was known for being a favourite haunt of younger British soldiers and spent the night there in the company of another woman –it is still unclear whether the second woman was someone Maguire had met during her stay in Hamelin, another hitherto unidentified IRA volunteer or even Ingrid Hijman. Eyewitnesses reported that she looked to be around the same age as Maguire, so the involvement of the considerably younger Hijman is unlikely. Maguire and her companion spent the evening watching the soldiers. The young IRA intelligence officer tried to get a feel for the town, find out where soldiers ate, drank and danced and to try and gather as much information as possible to help plan an attack. Maguire learned that a unit of the British Army – 28 Amphibious Engineer Regiment – had been undergoing training at Upnor Camp, an Army facility on Fischbecker Landstrasse in the northeast of the town, for several weeks. The regiment had completed several tours of Northern Ireland, having been based in Ballykelly, Lurgan, Londonderry and Belfast and near HMP Maze. A possible target had presented itself.

Meanwhile, other members of the ASU concerned themselves with logistics: Hick paid the rent in cash at Cäcilienstrasse on Wednesday June 5th, Hick and Grew being joined the following day by Paul Hughes who arrived from the Netherlands in the stolen red Ford Sierra; unbeknown to him, Hughes had been photographed by chance by an experimental traffic camera in the Ford Sierra on the A20 motorway at the Nieuwekerk aan de Ijssel junction just south of Rotterdam - the camera was triggered by the British registration plate. On June 7th, Maguire and Grew took the car out on another intelligence mission, driving south but had trouble with the vehicle, and had to stop at a garage in Siegen, west of Cologne, to have the car repaired. Maguire returned to Hamelin and spent the weekend dancing in various clubs, whilst Hick, Hughes and Grew scouted other potential locations in North-Rhine Westphalia in the heart of the British Army on the Rhine. On Monday June 11th, Maguire and her female companion spent the evening in the "Casablanca" bar on Pyrmonter Strasse, next to the River Weser. A plan was hatched to plant an explosive device at Upnor Camp: two days later the pair trekked north to the base to take a closer look. The buildings housed a small training facility for two British Army regiments: 35 Engineer Regiment who were based in Paderborn and 28 Amphibious Regiment. Both regiments had been deployed in Northern Ireland several times in the 1970s and 1980s. Maguire and her companion walked unobtrusively around the perimeter fence and found a section near the gate, close enough to a building for their purposes. The following day, dressed in yellow and red anoraks and looking like hikers, the women ambled back to the spot they had identified the following day and left a plastic bag containing an armed Semtex explosive device lying up against the perimeter fence before hastily leaving the area. At 5.15pm the device exploded, gutting the training building, blowing a 1 metre 50 deep crater in the ground and shattering the windows of convenience stores on the other side of the road. For some reason no training was taking place at the time: there was no-one in the facility when the device exploded and there were no casualties but the effect was very much as intended: to unsettle, to confuse the law enforcement agencies chasing the ASU, to make a point about the IRA's intent to hold anyone to account who they held responsible for the situation in Northern Ireland and to underscore the vulnerability of the British Army to such attacks. In short, the IRA wanted to show they had the upper hand.

Maguire returned to The Hague; in Pletterijstraat she joined Harte and Sean Hick – who had arrived the night before from Hanover - back at the safe house to work out their next move. Some of the weapons, including the AK-47 used in the murder of Major Dillon-Lee, were still in Cäcilienstrasse 14, having been stored there after the wild car-chase through Dortmund. The ASU tasked Hughes with bringing the weapons from Hanover to the Heerle arms dump, where they could be hidden with the rest. They arranged to meet on Saturday in the Netherlands, in Chaam, not too far from the border with Belgium, continue on to the woods at Heerle, hide the weapons from Germany and take things from there.

Just after nine a.m. on Saturday morning, June 16th, Hijman received a visit in Uilenstede from Sean Hick and they had a brief chat over a cup of coffee. Hijman was surprised to hear Hick complaining about Martin Conlon; Hick was apparently doing all the hard work and getting no help from Conlon. Hick left again and drove back to The

Hague in the red Opel Kadett; arriving at Pletterijstraat at around 10.30 am, he picked up Maguire and Hick and together they headed south towards Rotterdam. Around an hour later, the trio arrived in Chaam where in a secluded spot in the forest of Chaamse bossen on the north-eastern outskirts of the town, they met up with Hughes who arrived in the red Ford Sierra. Transferring the weapons to the Opel Kadett and leaving the Sierra parked inconspicuously, the quartet continued together to Breda. There they entered a PTT postal agency on Karrestraat and enquired about whether it was possible to send telegrams from there to Sweden in English. From there they drove on to Ulvenhout; at a hardware store on Molenstraat, Hughes and Hick purchased another fifty-litre Click-It bin for using to stash the weapons along with the rest of the arms dump, and finally drove on to Heerle.

In Heerle, the usually deserted manor house close to the woods where the IRA weapons dump was hidden was this weekend uncharacteristically full of life: the owner, retired insurance broker Jean Voortman and his extended family arrived the night before from Brussels with the intention of spending a relaxing weekend to recharge their batteries at the family's country residence. The house had been in the family for generations, having originally been purchased by Voortman's ancestors who were rich textile merchants. 67-year old head of the family Jean had been joined that weekend by his sons – Philippe, 38 and Raoul, 35 - as well as daughter Carla and her husband Amaury, for some fresh air away from the bustle of the Belgian capital to clear their lungs. Voortman was a keen amateur huntsman and the thick bois de Canadas woods bordering the edge of the property provided plenty of opportunity for him to follow his passion. The family spent the morning together before eating a late lunch at the house.

With many different access roads to the bois de Canadas, Hick, Hughes, Maguire and Harte drove into the woods from a different direction to normal, from the main road to the village of Ulicoten and were unaware that the usually empty house on the other side of the woods was occupied. Parking the Opel Kadett in a clearing, the ASU removed the weapons, the Click-It bin, spades and thick gloves from the boot of the car and leaving the car doors and boot open, together traipsed into the undergrowth to where they had hidden their supplies of Semtex, detonators, timers, weapons and ammunition; less than five hundred metres away from the border to the Netherlands. Thirty-five metres into the undergrowth, they set down the Click-It and weapons and began to dig. As Hick and Maguire cleared a hole to accommodate the new Click-It, Harte and Hughes oiled and checked the AK-47 and the Ruger .357 used in the Roermond murders; as they had done several times before, they retrieved ammunition to test-fire the weapons, making sure everything was in good working order before hiding them underground until they were needed again for the next live operation. Hughes aimed at a tree with the Ruger and fired four or five shots. Harte did the same with the AK-47, firing a short burst and listening to the sound of the gunfire echoing through the woods. Happy that the weapons were working properly, Harte began to strip the automatic rifle into its separate parts as Hughes packed away the Ruger.

Back at the house, the ears of amateur huntsman Jean Voortman pricked up at the sound of gunfire in the distance; he was able to tell the difference between different types of weapon, whether rifles, pistols; hunting guns – or machine guns and revolvers; weapons of war. It was clear that the gunfire did not emanate from a hunting weapon. Concerned, Voortman and son Philippe took out their hunting rifles, left the house and jumped into a car, driving slowly in the direction from which they had heard the gunfire.

In the undergrowth, Hick and Maguire had dug the hole and left Harte and Hughes to finish the job of hiding the Click-Its under a thick layer of soil, walking back in the direction of the car.

Voortman and his son came across the red Opel Kadett with Dutch registration plates, just as Hick and Maguire emerged from the woods. Jean Voortman addressed the pair and asked them what they were doing in the woods. Cover story prepared, the pair told them they had borrowed the car from a friend in Amsterdam, were travelling round Belgium on holiday and wanted to take a break in the woods on the way back to the Netherlands; Maguire and Hick offered their passports as identification to back up their story: Maguire was posing as US citizen "Pamela Ann Shaul" from Indiana but working as a secretary in London, Hick as "Andrew Edward Thornton" a professor also living in London. Voortman asked if they had heard gunfire, the pair confirmed they had; Hick told the Voortmans it sounded like it had come from around two hundred metres further away, pointing in the opposite direction from which Jean Voortman thought the sounds of shooting had come. Suspicious, Voortman nevertheless told them they were trespassing on private land and asked them to leave immediately; Hick and Maguire acquiesced and got into the car, driving off in the direction of Meerle, leaving Hick and Hughes behind.

Unconvinced by the story, the Voortmans decided to search the immediate vicinity for any bullet casings; the pair had not had any weapons on them nor visible in the car but Jean Voortman had a strong sense that the pair had had something to do with the gunfire. Philippe Voortman explains what happened:

> "Their story nevertheless seemed unusual. Reason enough for us to search the woods from which they had emerged. Shortly afterwards, we discovered several square metres of disturbed earth. It was obvious: someone had been digging. Footsteps were clearly visible in the soft earth."

Leaving his father to stand watch in case the strangers returned, Philippe went back to the house to fetch a spade and his brother Raoul. When they came back, they began to scrape away the top layer of earth: the top of the refuse bin was revealed. Removing the lid of the bin and feeling inside, they baulked as the barrel of an AK-47 assault rifle became apparent. Unsettled and convinced that the weapons had been hidden there by the strange couple in the Opel Kadett, Jean Voortman immediately decided to call the police. Leaving Philippe guarding the uncovered arms dump, Jean took Raoul with him in the car back to the house and telephoned the police station in the nearest town of Turnhout, who agreed to send out *Rijkswacht* officers to investigate straight away. Back at the unearthed weapons depot, Philippe had the strong suspicion that he was being watched or at least that someone else was close by. Harte had been hidden behind felled trees some distance away and took the sound of the Voortman car driving away to be a sign that he was now alone again. Hughes had earlier headed away through the woods in the direction of the main Ulicoten road, with the intention of somehow finding his way back to Chaam where he had parked the Ford Sierra. Gerard Harte had emerged from his hiding place and was heading towards where the ASU had hidden the weapons a short time before; unaware that Philippe Voortman was standing guard. Philippe explains what happened:

> *"Suddenly, at the edge of the undergrowth, I perceived a shadow. I thought I saw a light-coloured shirt through the branches. Not wanting to take any risks, I shouted "halt! halt! halt!"...then I fired a shot in the air. More to warn the others than to scare the man I could see running away. I was not at ease."*

Harte jumped and turned tail, fleeing further into the dense undergrowth.

At the house, Jean Voortman heard the warning shot being fired; together with Raoul and son-in-law Amaury he drove back to the woods. The Voortmans started searching further into the woods near the clearing where the Kadett had been parked earlier. At the same time, forester Jaak Boudewijn who was patrolling the woods came across the red Opel Kadett of Hick and Maguire, parked a little further away than where the Voortmans had earlier encountered it. Once again there was no sign of the pair, the doors were open and the keys still in the ignition. Boudewijn parked his vehicle side-on in front of the Kadett, blocking any escape route and removed the key. As the Voortmans appeared, Hick and Maguire emerged once more from the undergrowth. Visibly irritated, Jean Voortman asked Hick what on earth he was doing now, to which Hick replied that his girlfriend had left her purse behind and that they had been looking for it. With impeccable timing, a police van sent from Turnhout with two *Rijkswacht* officers appeared. The officers got out to join the group: they began to question Hick and Maguire about events. Hick and Maguire repeated their story and showed their false passports. Unconvinced by their answers and identity papers, the *Rijkswacht* men produced handcuffs and declared they were placing the pair under arrest. To considerable protests and resistance, the officers cuffed Hick and Maguire and guided them into the van for further questioning. Leaving his colleague to guard the prisoners, the other officer headed towards where Philippe Voortman was standing watch over the unearthed weapons dump. Together with Voortman, the officer freed the Click-It from the ground and unpacked the contents; he carefully unwrapped and laid on the ground packets of ammunition, a Webley revolver, a Kalashnikov AK-47 and the second of the IRA's trophy weapons, Michael Stone's Sturm Ruger .357. Very quickly, the officer realised that Pamela Ann Shaul and Andrew Edward Thornton, sitting with his colleague in the back of a police van, were not innocent picnickers, but something more dangerous altogether.

Almost simultaneously, his colleague realised the same thing as he was momentarily dazed by a heavy thump to the side of the head from Sean Hick. Although handcuffed, Hick and Maguire saw a window of opportunity to escape. The shout from the dazed police officer alerted his colleague who ran back and followed the fleeing Maguire and Hick into the undergrowth. A damaged ankle that Maguire had sustained tripping over a broken paving stone back home in Newry in 1985 slowed her down; unable to keep up with Hick, Maguire was quickly overpowered by an officer; Hick however managed to escape through the dense undergrowth. Maguire was led out of the undergrowth and bundled back into the police van, accidentally banging her head on the frame of the door as she did so. Putting out a radio alert to all units to be on the lookout for two English-speaking males - one of whom was wearing handcuffs, both of whom were on the run - the officers closed the van doors and drove Donna Maguire to the police station in Turnhout.

More police officers arrived at the scene and discovered a further patch of dug-over soil a short distance away from the first and found more Click-Its. Hidden in the plastic refuse container was a terrorist treasure chest: a black diplomatic bag was revealed containing a Record air pistol, an HS air pistol, a Reck PK6000 starting pistol, a money belt, a nine-volt battery, a coupling for nine-volt batteries, a soldering iron, rolls of isolated electrical wire, small lamps, a pistol brush, a hacksaw, a Cherry microswitch, a thick elastic band, two large magnets, a variety of time-power-devices, five Canadian-made CIL detonators and a completely assembled UVBT in a cigar box which contained almost two kilos of Semtex-H. The circuit board in the assembled car bomb was identical to those found in Nieuw-Bergen and Bielefeld in 1988, stemming from the bomb factory of Donal Moyna, and the timing device was a Swiss-made Memopark timer from the stockpile accrued by Father Patrick Ryan. It was clear that law enforcement had stumbled onto a major IRA arms depot. Owing to the proximity to the border with the Netherlands, Belgian *Rijkswacht* officers alerted their Dutch colleagues to the escaped Harte, who immediately dispatched a team of detectives and sniffer dogs to Ulicoten, supported by a police helicopter. They started to comb the border area between the villages of Ulicoten and Heerle for signs of the escapers; at around 6pm on the main road they saw a man with dark trousers and a yellow t-shirt carrying a dark object under his arm that he quickly threw away into undergrowth when he spotted the police. A Dutch officer challenged him and told him to lie on the ground; when the man ignored requests, the officer fired a warning shot into the air and he finally complied, lying down in the roadside ditch, calmly waiting to be handcuffed. Arresting him, the police checked the false passport he was carrying – in the name of Peter John Watson – and hauled him off to the police station in Breda to establish his real identity: Gerard Majella Harte, volunteer in the Provisional I.R.A.

Hick - still in handcuffs – stumbled in a panic through the forests straddling the border between Belgium and the Netherlands in the direction of Chaam, where Hughes had earlier parked the Ford Sierra. It took him several hours to reach the town; at 1am, exhausted and panicked he found a phone box and called Hijman in Amstelveen; he told her to go to The Hague and warn their mutual friend "David" and tell him to drive to Chaam to pick Hick up. Hick said he would wait by the church until 4pm in the afternoon. He instructed Hijman to come and get him herself if she wasn't able to reach "David". "David" was the false name used by Paul Hughes. Hijman took a night train to The Hague and walked to the apartment; Quinn and Hughes were nowhere to be seen. Hughes had arrived back at the safe house at Pletterijstraat earlier to meet Dermot Quinn, who had remained in The Hague and told him about the arrests of Hick and Maguire in Heerle; in the Ford Sierra they fled The Hague and drove to Amsterdam. Hijman returned to Amstelveen and the next morning took the train to Breda, from where she got a bus to Chaam. She went to the church but found no sign of Hick; she wandered around the town in the vain hope that she might spot him but Hick had already gone to hide in the relative safety of the Chaamse bossen forest. Finding no sign of Hick, Hijman took the last bus out of Chaam to return back to her student apartment in Uilenstede. She had just arrived back when the phone rang again; it was Hick once more. He had returned into the centre of Chaam to the phone box next to the post office and asked Hijman once again to come and get him. At that time of night there was no way of reaching Chaam. Shortly afterwards the phone rang again; it was Hughes. He told her they no longer needed Pletterijstraat and whether she could come and collect the keys. Hughes explained that he was now in Amsterdam. The exasperated Hijman took a night train to Amsterdam Central Station where, shortly after 2 am, she was met by Quinn and Hughes and took back the keyring with the two keys to Pletterijstraat 23. Quinn and Hughes asked Hijman where Hick was; after Hijman explained where in Chaam Hick might be found, Hughes agreed to drive to the town and go and search for him and set off, leaving Quinn in Amsterdam. Hijman returned to Uilenstede.

Meanwhile around 9am in Chaam, Hick had returned to the centre of the town and sat waiting at the bus shelter next to the church in the centre of the town. Locals had noticed the man walking round the town and had alerted the Dutch police, who arrived to arrest Hick. Hick panicked and jumped into the back garden of a nearby house; hampered by his handcuffs, the police easily caught up with him. Four officers pinned him down and throwing a blanket over him, arrested Hick and took him away.

Shortly afterwards, Hughes arrived in Chaam in the Ford Sierra, unaware that Hick had just been arrested. Police were still on the streets after the operation and noticing the English registration plates of the vehicle, asked Hughes to stop and identify himself. Hughes handed over fake ID in the name of "Michael Collins" and as the officer flicked through the passport, Hughes took the chance to escape, put his foot on the accelerator and sped off in the direction of Ulvenhout and the safety of the Chaamse bossen. A short while later, police found the abandoned Sierra; Hughes had taken his chances and run into the dense forest to hide. Police called for backup from other towns and with sniffer dogs they spent the day and the evening combing the undergrowth in the search for Hughes. Shortly before 2am, sniffer dogs picked up a scent of something and pointed their handlers in the direction of a fallen tree - police advanced on the tree stump with weapons raised. Hughes heard the cocking of the police weapons; there was nowhere to run. He called out "I'll come out, I'll come out!" – Paul Hughes gave himself up to the officers, offering no resistance.

Hughes was handcuffed and taken to Breda to join Sean Hick; with Maguire in a cell in Turnhout and Harte in Baarle-Nassau, not only were police in possession of the contents of two important arms dumps used by the Provos Continental European Active Service Units, but four of the most dangerous members of the Provisional I.R.A. in mainland Europe were in custody. The game was up.

16 THE SURGEON

The rest of the ASU scattered on the arrest of Maguire, Hughes, Harte and Hick. In Amstelveen on the Uilenstede campus, Dermot Quinn sought refuge at Ingrid Hijman's student room. The evening after the arrest of Hughes in the Chaamse Bossen, the pair lounged on the sofa watching the evening news when a report on the roundup of the Active Service Unit flashed on the screen, including photos of the arrested volunteers, as well as Martin Conlon. Hijman told Quinn that she used to go out with Conlon. Quinn feigned incredulity and admitted that he knew Conlon well, prompting Hijman to ask him where Conlon was. Quinn declined to tell her. Instead, he said that he had to leave the Netherlands; Hijman gave him a coach ticket to Paris that she had and Quinn, packing two large bags, departed from Amsterdam Central Station the same night, taking with him the British passports of Gerard Harte and Paul Hughes. Quinn only briefly stayed in the French capital before making his way back to Northern Ireland. A couple of days later, Hijman received an envelope in the post with a Paris postmark: in it, six fifty pound notes – the outstanding rent for the month of July for the apartment in Pletterijstraat – and a message from Quinn: "All the best, Tom."

Three weeks after arriving back in Co. Tyrone, Dermot Quinn was re-arrested by the RUC on July 16th on the attempted murder charges from 1988, after the National Forensic Science Laboratory linked thirty-nine acrylic fibres on a balaclava found in the getaway car used after the attempted murder in Co. Armagh back in 1988, as well as firearms residue in the jacket Quinn had been wearing when arrested that night. In the time intervening between the dismissal of the first case against him and the second arrest, the Criminal Evidence (NI) Order 1988 had come into effect. Upon his arrival at Gough Barracks, he requested to consult with his lawyer. This request was not acted upon until the late morning, after the police had questioned him and he had again invoked his right to remain silent. That same day, he appeared before the court, presented with the original charges.

At trial, in the "Diplock Court", the prosecution's case was based primarily on the new scientific evidence, albeit disputed. Quinn took the stand in his defence and gave evidence of his alibi, which was corroborated by the testimony of his employer. Quinn also explained to the court why he had chosen to exercise his right of silence during police questioning: he knew that the law had changed but didn't know what the changes were; the allegations against him were serious, he had heard of people being forced to make statements during police questioning, and although he had asked to see his lawyer, he was questioned before his lawyer was contacted or arrived. Notwithstanding the statements of alibi made initially at the road-block, the corroboration of his alibi by his employer, his trial testimony, and the fact that the events had taken place before enactment of the Order, the trial judge applied the Order and drew adverse inferences from the fact that Mr Quinn had remained silent during police questioning. Quinn was found guilty and sentenced to a hefty 25 years imprisonment – he was sent to Crumlin Road prison to await a move to the H-blocks of The Maze.

Back in Amstelveen, Hijman was nervous and pining – she had fallen in love with Hick. She found out where he was being held and wrote him a love letter, addressing it to him in Breda, accompanied by a polite note to the police asking to be able to visit Hick in prison. The authorities had ordered all communications with Hick to be monitored and the police read the letter; the decision was taken to carry out a search of Hijman's student apartment in Uilenstede. After sending the letter, Hijman had gone on vacation to Slovenia with friends on June 30th and thus police did not find her at home; they did however find a great wealth of evidence of the close ties between Ingrid Hijman and the IRA's European ASU. Alongside Irish money and a photo of Hick, which had been cut out of a newspaper reporting his arrest, they found an Irish passport in the name of "Kieran James Murphy" – but bearing the photograph of Paul Hughes. In addition, the Irish passport belonging to Gerard Majella Harte was also recovered along with evidence of further fake identities, such as a driving licence in the name of Prescott. Hijman was in big trouble. Aside from the false identification papers, the police found something else of interest: the rental contract for Pletterijstraat 23, signed by Hijman. In the early hours of July 14th, the police stormed the apartment but were too late: realising that the net was closing in on them, Grew and Conlon had left the apartment two days earlier – a doormen confirmed that he had seen them leaving. As Grew and Conlon evaded capture and returned to Northern Ireland, police found a wealth of evidence in the small flat. Fingerprints belonging to Donna Maguire, Gerard Harte, Sean Hick, Paul Hughes, Dessie Grew and Dermot Quinn were secured and corroborated with the fingerprints of the four arrested ASU members, as well as with existing Interpol records for Grew and Quinn. Furthermore there was a load of camping equipment, including new and used tents, tent bags, sleeping bags and rucksacks. Balaclavas and socks were bagged up and sent off for forensic analysis. Maps of Antwerp, Venlo, Limburg, France, Belgium, Europe were found, as well as rail timetables between Dutch cities. False identification papers, oil and a pair of pyjama bottoms with oil stains and gunshot residue were also found and noted. A stamping machine and inkpad, as well as the typewriter lent to the ASU by Hijman were secured. Tools, batteries and foil rounded off the treasure trove of forensic material that would be examined over the following weeks and corroborated with evidence recovered from Heerle. The weapons found at the IRA arms dump were sent away to the Northern Ireland Forensic Science Laboratory, and - when laid next to the material found in Pletterijstraat - allowed investigators to begin to build a very strong case against the ASU members: the AK-47 found in the Click-It buried in the ground in Heerle was subjected to ballistics tests and the results crosschecked with Interpol files; the weapon with the serial number NK-8441 found in Heerle had been used in the attack on Lance-Corporals (name redacted) and (name redacted) in Münster on September 1st 1989, the murder of Heidi Hazell on September 7th 1989 and used to kill Mick Islania at the BP station in Wildenrath on October 26th 1989 – cartridges found in the Heerle weapons dump displayed the same 'ppu 762' stamp as those found on the petrol station forecourt in Wildenrath and on Otto-Holzapfel-Strasse in Unna-Massen. The weapon had also been used to kill Nick Spanos and Stephen Melrose on the market square in Roermond on May 27th 1990; the rifling marks the automatic weapon left on bullet cases matched those found on the sixteen 7.62mm cartridges that had been found in and around the Citroën BX. Tests on the handguns also revealed their history: the Webley - serial number 58311 - had also been used in the attempted murder of the two soldiers in the attack in Münster. The whole gruesome history of the Ruger .357 revolver was unravelled first by the *Zentrale Schusswaffenerkennungsdienst* (Central Firearm Identification Service) of the *BKA* and the Dutch *CRI*: it was the weapon given to Michael Stone the night before the Milltown Cemetery attack in March 1988, killing three including IRA volunteer Kevin Brady. The IRA had recovered the weapon during the struggle with Stone and given to Gerard Harte. The handgun had been used in the murder of Colin Abernethy on September 9th at Finaghy on a train from Lisburn to Belfast. Police suspected that the next time the weapon was used was on October 11th, as IRA gunmen gunned down off-duty RUC officer John Larmour as he worked at Barnam's World Of Ice Cream Parlour on the Lisburn Road in Belfast - but this was not conclusively proven at the time. Grew had taken the weapon to Germany hidden in the side panelling of a car, and on October 26th 1989 had used it to kill Nivruti Islania, after Gerard Harte had killed her father with an AK-47. Finally, it was the weapon that Grew had placed behind the left ear of Stephen Melrose and squeezed the trigger, brutally executing the Australian lawyer on the night of May 27th 1990 in Roermond's picturesque market square.

All the weapons analysed contained fingerprints of the ASU members. Forensic tests also revealed the imprint of the names typed onto false documentation found on various ASU members. A passport found in Pletterijstraat in the name of "Trevor Paul Holmes" was found to match the passport used by Dessie Grew to buy the red Opel Kadett in Amsterdam in May. A plastic mould in the shape of a vehicle registration plate, which corroborated with the D 204 YMY registration of the stolen Ford Sierra found in Chaam, was also discovered. Plastic refuse sacks found in the safe house in The Hague were identical to those found in Heerle, those in the Mazda found abandoned in Bönen after the murder of Major Dillon-Lee, identical to those in which packets of putty-like Semtex-H explosives were found wrapped in a wood near Werl in Germany on June 3rd. The sheer overwhelming amount of evidence tying Hughes, Hick, Maguire and Harte to the murders in Dortmund, Roermond and Wildenrath, as well as the attempted murders in Münster, Hameln, Langenhagen pointed in every respect to the four IRA volunteers sitting in prison in the Netherlands and Belgium. As the case against the four in the Netherlands was being prepared, German authorities were busy building the case against all four for the IRA murders in Germany. Whilst the *BKA* had a lot of evidence and a very good knowledge of how the ASU had operated, they needed witness corroboration of the movements of the four detainees around the time of the incidents in question. With the help of the Special Investigation Branch SIB, as well as other Royal Military Police and RAF Police units, posters were distributed showing the faces of Donna Maguire, Sean Hick, Paul Hughes and Gerard Harte, listing aliases they were known to have used and detailing sightings of the four over the past few months, the posters were displayed at every Army and Royal Air Force base, as well as in local communities close to military installations. Thus the *BKA* hoped to finalise a detailed picture of the movements of the four since they arrived on the Continent and link eyewitness sightings to forensic evidence, in order to be able to build solid grounds for extradition to Germany.

Observing proceedings in Germany and the Netherlands from the relative safety of Northern Ireland, the IRA leadership were nevertheless impelled to act. The Republican community expected the IRA to come to the aid of the incarcerated volunteers, that much was clear; and in particular, to the aid of Paul Hughes. Hughes came from a South Armagh family well known to security forces, the most notorious of all family members being his brother Sean. Sean Hughes was known in the PIRA and to British security forces as 'The Surgeon'. According to many sources, the Provisional IRA South Armagh Brigade commander had responsibility for the deadly "Bomb Alley" area, which had seen the deaths of many British soldiers in previous years, was a member of the IRA's seven-man presiding Army Council, which dictated IRA military policy and was ultimately responsible for the sanctioning of IRA operations in Northern Ireland, Great Britain and on mainland Europe. 'The Surgeon' had a fearsome reputation and had the history to justify it; according to RUC estimates, he was involved in the murder of nearly 70 people. Although arrested by the RUC on numerous occasions, much to the displeasure of the police he had never been convicted. He was first arrested in 1981 following the kidnapping of Ben Dunne, the heir to the Dunnes supermarket chain. Four masked men in Killeen abducted Dunne as he drove to Newry to open a new store. After being held for five days, he was released upon payment of a ransom that filled the coffers of the IRA in South Armagh to the tune of £500,000. In February 1984 he was arrested by the RUC again, after a bomb was detonated next to an RUC vehicle by command wire from a firing point 500 metres from Hughes' farmhouse near Drumintree. Sergeant William Savage and Constable Thomas Bingham were killed in the blast. Hughes stuck to the code of the Green Book and said nothing during seven days of interrogation at Gough Barracks and had to be released without charge. He allegedly directed the mortar attack on the Corry Square RUC station in 1985 that killed 9 police officers which had involved not only his own North Louth-Camlough Brigade but also members of the South Down / North Louth Brigade. A few weeks later he was purported to have been involved in the murder of four RUC officers in a bomb attack in Kileen. Two years later, judge Maurice Gibson and his wife Cecily were killed by a remote-controlled bomb as they crossed the border from the Republic of Ireland into Armagh in the middle of Hughes "patch" – 'The Surgeon' was implicated but never arrested. In November 1988, 'The Surgeon' was back in custody following the murder of the entire Hanna family on a road near Cloghogue Mountain – father Robin, wife Maureen and their six-year-old son were killed in a roadside blast intended to kill judge Ian Higgins. Many have claimed that Hughes was also the mastermind of the IRA ambush in Jonesborough on March 20th 1989 that resulted in the murder of Chief Superintendent Harry Breen and Superintendent Bob Buchanan. 'The Surgeon' was a major IRA player at the top of the target list of British security forces. But in July 1990, Hughes took a break from active service and boarded a plane in Belfast bound for Europe.

Hughes, Hick and Harte had been moved to the top security detention centre Huis van bewaring - Limburg zuid in Beatrixhaven, near Maastricht. Whilst Gerard Harte was visited by wife Elizabeth, Paul Hughes firstly received conjugal visits from his girlfriend as well as two of his stepbrothers, before the imposing figure of Sean Hughes – allegedly one of the most senior and influential military figures in the IRA – appeared and requested to see his brother. Hughes explained that he and the other volunteers were not happy with the lawyers assigned to them and that they weren't up to the job: brother Sean called an old adversary of the Dutch judiciary and the British government: Willem van Bennekom. The Amsterdam lawyer who had successfully helped Patrick Magee to avoid extradition in 1981 and represented IRA volunteers Gerry Kelly and Bik McFarlane in Dutch courts in 1986 took on the case. After receiving the documentation and baulking at the huge amount of evidence against the ASU, he suggested a strategy that could possibly provide a work-around to the evidence problem. The evidence pointed in general to the involvement of the ASU members in various operations but no one single piece of evidence singularly linked an individual volunteer to a murder – due to the nature of the operations, the ASU worked in various combinations with various weapons and no-one had actually been able to identify a particular volunteer in the act of pulling the trigger. If some kind of collective defence could be agreed, the defence would be able to sow seeds of doubt about specific claims in court, and thus when refuting allegations about certain actions by certain people, spread the positive effect of being unable to prove specific individual responsibilities and roles. The four should be tried as a unit in order to cloud the facts and make it more difficult to obtain a conviction against any one of the IRA volunteers. 'The Surgeon' agreed and instructed van Bennekom to proceed.

Even without the help of "The Surgeon" and van Bennekom, there were also problems with the burden of proof on the side of the Dutch authorities in three specific instances: whilst fingerprints of the ASU members were found on the weapons discovered in Heerle, no-one had seen them use the weapons to carry out a murder and it could be argued that the prints occurred when the ASU members re-stashed the weapons in the arms depot, rather than being caused by the weapons being held by the accused in the actual act of murder. Secondly, differences were starting to appear in witness statements from the evening of the Roermond murders. Witness Jos Heitzer and his wife maintained that they had seen Harte drive away from the scene in the Mazda after the killings of Spanos and Melrose and were able to identify him at an identity parade in July. Between his arrest and the ID parade, Harte had lost 22 kilos and looked distinctly different than he would have done on the evening of May 27th; in any effect it was pitch black and the car was driving from the scene at speed – doubts would be cast on whether Harte could be reliably identified under the circumstances. Further witnesses on the market square that night maintained that the driver of the Mazda had red hair, others claimed the driver was blonde. Finally, none of the IRA volunteers had admitted to involvement in any incident that was under discussion; in fact, none of them was speaking at all. The code of the Green Book kept them silent, making it difficult to analyse their words for slips of the tongue, corroboration or any kind of clues that would help pin them to the evidence – which would be needed to help link them conclusively to the murders under the jurisdiction of the Dutch; those of Nick Spanos and Stephen Melrose in Roermond on May 27th 1990.

A key person for the prosecution in unravelling the intricate detail of the cases was Ingrid Hijman, currently on holiday in the former Yugoslavia. After top-level discussions between security forces and the police, the *BVD* were tasked with intercepting her and leading her to the police to be arrested and questioned. A *BVD* operative "Jack" was sent by bus to Slovenia to track down Hijman – arriving at her destination he asked around the resort if they knew where a person matching her description could be found. He finally tracked her down but was not authorised to arrest her; instead he trailed her and her friends around the final days of her holiday and on her departure, took a seat next to her on the coach journey back to the Netherlands on July 18th. He engaged her in conversation on the coach to keep her attention and ensure that she didn't abscond on a motorway stop, whilst keeping in constant contact with police and the security services. The next day, as the coach crossed into the Netherlands, "Jack" radioed to the joint team that they should engineer a stop; under the pretence of a random border check, Dutch police stopped the vehicle and asked to see the passengers' passports. As Hijman presented her identity documents, she was led off the coach and arrested.

Meanwhile in Paris, Düsseldorf and Wiesbaden, the courts and law enforcement in France, Germany and Northern Ireland were preoccupied with other IRA volunteers who had been operating on the European mainland. On July 27th in Paris, the French *cours de cassation, chambre criminelle* upheld the extradition of the members of the "FERMDOWN" unit – pending the outcome of French criminal proceedings, Patrick Murray, Donagh O'Kane and Pauline Drumm would be deported to Germany to face trial for the 1988 bombing of Quebec Barracks in Osnabrück. Ten days later on August 6th, the *BKA* officially requested the extradition of Dessie Grew from Northern Ireland to face trial on charges of being involved in the murder of Mick and Nivruti Islania in Wildenrath, and in the attempted murders in Münster, with the papers once again being resubmitted to the Northern Ireland Office, after the previous request in February had been declined. And in Düsseldorf, the 6th *Strafsenat* (Penal Senate) division finally set the start date for the trial of the two Gerrys – McGeough and Hanratty - for the middle of August. The pair had been indicted on June 15th 1989 for the bomb attacks at JHQ and Duisburg in 1987 and 1988, and up until now had been held in Frankenthal and Kaisheim prisons. In February 1990 they were moved to Wuppertal prison in preparation for the trial, and on August 16th were driven the 35 kilometres down the A4 motorway to be present for the opening day of the trial. The first weeks were spent going through the evidence surrounding the circumstances of the pair's arrests in Waldfeucht on the Dutch / German border in August 1988 and regarding the fatal shooting of RSM Mike Heakin in Ostende in the same month. The Belgian authorities had offered to request extradition for McGeough and Hanratty to stand trial in Brussels for Heakin's murder, and were confident they could achieve convictions: the pair had been caught with the murder weapons, and despite claims from Swedish IRA sympathisers that he had been in Malmö at the time of the shooting, witnesses had had a clear enough view of McGeough as he fired the shots at Mike Heakin that they could positively identify him in court. But the Germans declined and pressed on with the Düsseldorf trial, confident themselves of conviction. They had already lined up two key prosecution witnesses: a leading *MI5* anti-terrorism officer and a high ranking RUC officer who was only too aware of the movements and history of both IRA volunteers – it was shaping up to be an eventful trial.

The IRA had been forced into a corner as regards operations in Germany and the rest of Europe were concerned. The remnants of the Active Service Units had no chance to restarting operations, the bulk of the team had been captured along with most of its firepower, ringleader Dessie Grew was the most wanted man in Europe and would be arrested on sight as soon as he set foot on German soil. It would take a superhuman effort, a lot of money and personnel that the IRA simply did not have to get the show back on the road again. Nevertheless, the Provos had proved time and time again that they were able to surmount such problems and reactivate their campaign - the security services remained wary. However according to several sources, there may have been an unexpected turn of events. No official record seems to exist but the assistants of the architect of the 1988 Duisburg round table talks between Nationalists and Loyalists, Dr. Eberhard Spiecker have indicated that a further attempt to broker peace, at least in Germany, took place in the summer of 1990. Through his extensive network of contacts, Spiecker was supposed to have got in touch with both the German government and – presumably once more via Father Alec Reid - with the Provisional IRA Army Council. Spiecker suggested something unexpected: the leadership of the IRA and the German government should sit round a table and attempt to bring about a negotiated end to the campaign in Germany. Under the utmost secrecy, round table talks were allegedly held in Germany to thrash out the details. If this was the case, the IRA would have had very little with which to bargain, the German government at the time was under extreme pressure to deliver the impending unification of East and West Germany and would have been only too keen to see the back of the Provos, who were taking up time, resources and headlines. Both would have negotiated from a position of weakness and, in secret, are rumoured to have struck a compromise that both could live with: in return for the IRA not recommencing operations in Germany, the German government was to put diplomatic pressure on the UK government to seek a solution to "The Troubles". Both sides would have then taken the deal back to their respective leaderships for sanctioning. Although there seems to be no written confirmation available - such discussions would have been classified to the highest level, even today - the German government allegedly agreed to the deal. Unaware of a secret ceasefire, whilst the British armed forces and the German population were relieved that there was some respite from the murderous attacks of the early summer, both were left with the fear that it was only a matter of time before the next IRA Active Service Unit turned up and started bombing and shooting in Germany. In reality, the Provisional IRA and the government of the Federal Republic of Germany may, unbeknown to anyone, have called an end to the Provisional IRA's campaign in Germany.

17 THE MUSHROOM SHED

As Dutch police questioned Ingrid Hijman in Amsterdam, the state prosecutor overseeing the case against Hughes, Harte, Maguire and Hick - Jo Laumen - was in permanent contact with colleagues in Northern Ireland. The aim was to facilitate corroboration of evidence, glean information on the movements and paramilitary histories of the quartet and the other members of the ASU, in order to flesh out the case against them. Laumen flew to Belfast at the end of July 1990. RUC officers took him on a guided tour of Republican communities and locations important to events in the recent history of "The Troubles". Amongst the places Laumen visited was Crumlin Road prison, where he arranged to meet Dermot Quinn, who had been jailed just a couple of weeks earlier. Laumen found Quinn cold and confrontational when presented with questions pertaining to the activities of the European ASU; Quinn gave no insight into the case and refused to answer specific questions, ending the conversation with Laumen on an unsettling note, giving the Dutch prosecutor a cold stare and telling him he would remember his face for future reference. Despite the lack of forthcoming information, Laumen nevertheless gleaned a lot of insight from his visit to Ulster, had developed an excellent rapport with the RUC, something that was bound to reap benefits in the preparation of the case against the four IRA volunteers detained on the Continent.

Ingrid Hijman was proving to be the key witness in the prosecution case. She gave a detailed statement of her involvement in the role of unwitting facilitator and unknowing participant in the ASU's operations. She described in minute detail events from the moment she had met Martin Conlon at the tram stop in the Hague in October the previous year, the developing relationship with him and her rental of the Pletterijstraat safe house, the subsequent relationship with Hick, and communications and meetings with the other members of the ASU; everything up until the point of the Heerle arrests. It seemed clear to investigators that Hijman had been incredibly naive and gullible in the whole affair – she had been used by Hick, Conlon and the others as an expendable but useful local to help them stay under cover on the Continent. Hijman also gave them clues that the ASU was not only operating out of The Hague but also from the safe house in Hanover, although not having visited there she was unsure exactly where investigators should start looking. After three weeks in custody, Hijman was released and returned to her parent's home in Rijswijk.

After the Heerle arrests, and the return of Quinn and Grew to Northern Ireland, Martin Conlon and Paddy Fox were the last members of the ASU to remain in mainland Europe. They realised it was only a matter of time before the police were to discover the existence of the safe house in Hanover - they fled Cäcilienstrasse, leaving behind masses of evidence. Conlon returned to Armagh City, leaving Fox to travel on to the Netherlands. He stashed a rucksack containing a few possessions, clothes and a selection of false identity papers in a left-luggage locker at Rotterdam Central Station for safekeeping and stayed in a series of guesthouses to await further orders from the Overseas Department, returning occasionally to Rotterdam CS to make untraceable calls to both the IRA and family members. He had returned to the Continent from his native Dungannon shortly after the attacks in Roermond and Dortmund with the intention of assisting the ASU in the preparation of further operations but, after the Heerle arrests and the departure of fellow East Tyrone Brigade comrade Dessie Grew, he was unsure of what to do next. His repeated presence at Rotterdam CS did not however go unnoticed; thinking that Fox was possibly a drug dealer, eagle-eyed members of the public notified police, who carefully observed his movements over a couple of days. The surveillance led them to the left-luggage locker, where they discovered the rucksack and false passports. Lying in wait for Fox to retrieve his possessions, they grabbed him as he returned to the locker on August 22nd and arrested him on charges of possessing false papers. Although the Dutch police made enquiries with British authorities into his real identity, before any confirmation that the man was a wanted IRA suspect, the Dutch made the decision to deport Fox from the Netherlands back to the UK – they put him on a ferry to Harwich and notified British authorities of his impending arrival. Fox was not apprehended on his arrival back in the UK and continued back to Northern Ireland, where it is likely he resumed active service for the Provos in County Tyrone.

Dutch investigators involved in the case of Hick, Harte, Maguire and Hughes had found a key-ring in the possession of Sean Hick on his arrest in June; one which held five keys. The origin of one of the keys was traced to Germany and together with German colleagues, the police carried out extensive and intensive enquiries into the possible location of the door that matched the key. In the first week of September there was a breakthrough: The *BKA* traced the key to Hanover, to the front door of the hitherto unknown IRA safe house in Cäcilienstrasse. Conlon, Fox, Hick, Hughes, Maguire and Grew had long vacated the premises and the flat had been unoccupied for several weeks when the police arrived. But there was enough material left behind to prove that the apartment in Cäcilienstrasse had been used by several - if not indeed all - members of the IRA's ASU during the course of the previous months. Alongside the fingerprints of Hick, Hughes, Maguire and Grew, police investigators discovered maps of Germany, Belgium and Luxemburg, city plans of Hamelin and other towns in British Army of the Rhine territory, as well as three passport photos of Sean Hick. Creating a direct link to the murder of Major Dillon-Lee in Dortmund were a balaclava made from a seat cover matching the one discovered in the Mazda getaway car found abandoned in Bönen and an incomplete set of screwdrivers found in a tin; the two screwdrivers found in the Mazda were identical to the two missing from the set found in Cäcilienstrasse. The police were now certain that whoever had occupied the IRA safe house had been directly involved in the chase with German police through the night-time streets of Dortmund city centre of June 2nd and that at least three of the apartment occupants were now in custody. In addition, another map was found in the apartment covered in fingerprints from members of the ASU, which had been annotated and place names marked along a route that led directly from Cäcilienstrasse to the weapons dump in Werl. This forensic evidence heavily implicated the ASU in the murder and attempted murders in Dortmund and Langenhagen, as well as in conspiracy to illegally possess weapons of war - on this basis, *BKA* investigators prepared documentation to request the extradition of Hick, Hughes from the Netherlands and Maguire from Belgium to Germany. The extradition requests were extremely unlikely to be granted immediately, as any trial in the Netherlands over the murders of Stephen Melrose and Nick Spanos would take precedence, seeing Maguire extradited from Belgium to the Netherlands to stand trial with Hick, Hughes and Harte. In the meantime, information was shared with Dutch and Belgian investigators who were piecing together the cases in the Low Countries; Jo Laumen was becoming increasingly confident that the prosecution had enough material to link the group to the murders of Nick Spanos and Stephen Melrose. One important piece of the whole chain of evidence nevertheless still needed to be found: Laumen needed to provide evidence that the four IRA volunteers were present on the market square in Roermond on the fateful night of May 27th 1990. Eyewitness statements were proving inconclusive.

Key witnesses for the prosecution were Jos Heitzer and his wife, who had seen the getaway car race away from the scene with the gunmen inside; cafe owner Paul Reijngoud who had been confronted by Harte but left unharmed; and Bernard Bähre, who had seen the attack carried out from his attic window overlooking the *marktplein*. Of all of these, the Heitzers were by far the most important; whereas Bähre had seen the attack from a distance and from above, and Reijngoud unable to make a clear identification of Harte due to the black balaclava the gunman had been wearing, Heitzer and his wife had had a five to six second glimpse of the occupants in the getaway car and were sure they had seen Gerard Harte riding as a passenger in the front seat, face visible after having removed his balaclava. In order to prove beyond doubt that Harte was the man they had seen, police invited them to take part in an identity parade. Harte was driven to Maastricht under maximum-security conditions and took his place in the line-up. The Heitzers concurred; Harte was the man they had seen in the passenger seat of the getaway car, the man who seconds before had opened fire on a group of tourists from close range, killing two of them. There was however a major problem for which the prosecution had not bargained: in the intervening time between his arrest in June and the identity parade in September, Harte had barely eaten. Whether due to the stress caused by the realisation that he was likely to be convicted of murder and be sent to prison for 15 to 25 years, or a deliberate callous ploy to deceive; Harte had lost nearly 22 kilos in weight during his time in custody and was barely recognisable from the photo taken a mere three weeks after the murders. The fact that the Heitzers had readily and quickly identified Harte in the identity parade was likely to be contested by defence lawyers as unreliable, especially considering that it had been pitch-black, save for dim street lighting as the Mazda had raced past the Heitzers late that Sunday evening. Laumen was already beginning to doubt whether the Heitzers identification of Harte was going to stand up in court. A further problem presented itself that was also likely to cause difficulties: whilst some witnesses who had seen the Mazda entering or leaving the market square in Roermond claimed the driver had been well-built and dark haired – a description which fitted Paul Hughes - two of them had seen the driver to be red-haired and with an angular face – which fitted more to the appearance of Dessie Grew. None of the witnesses were able to say they were able to positively identify Grew by two tell-tale scars on his temple and the right corner of his mouth – it had been too dark and the view too fleeting. The defence had already picked up on the conflicting witness statements and were preparing to use the argument in court that Grew, who had not been apprehended and who was not on trial - was an important suspect in the case and possibly even the driver. This would weaken the whole prosecution case, which relied on the four being tried as a quartet, rather than individually. If enough doubt could be cast on the participation of one person in the team, it would weaken the defence accusation that the four had acted together as a unit. It was also highly unlikely that Grew would be apprehended in Northern Ireland and extradited to the Netherlands on this basis, especially considering that the Germans had also already applied for Grew's extradition on much stronger grounds over the murders in Wildenrath. In any case, Grew had gone to ground in Ireland; even finding him would be difficult. It was no longer clear to the prosecution that Hughes could be irrefutably identified as the driver of the Mazda in Roermond, moreover there was an indication that the only person who could confirm or deny if in fact Dessie Grew, and not Paul Hughes, had been at the wheel was the man least likely to offer himself as a witness for the defence: Desmond Grew himself.

In fact, Dessie Grew had more pressing tasks to which he had to attend. After having returned to Ireland, he had returned to active service with the Provisional IRA's East Tyrone Brigade and was involved in a number of operations. On July 24th, on Killylea Road in Armagh, a landmine attack on an RUC patrol car killed not only three officers – David Sterritt, William Hanson and Joshua Willis, but also a young Catholic nun – Catherine Dunne – who was travelling in another car past the RUC vehicle as the explosive device was detonated. It was suspected that Dessie Grew was involved in the operation, and - together with another IRA man, Sean McGuiness - he was arrested on August 7th. The news reached New Scotland Yard, where the BKA liaison officer embedded within Special Branch passed the news back to Wiesbaden and the German Foreign Office in Bonn that the ringleader of the IRA Active Service Units in Germany had been apprehended. There was brief hope that the international arrest warrant issued for Grew's involvement in the IRA attacks in Germany might precipitate the possibility of extradition proceedings. But Grew was released without charge and returned once more to active service.

In October, as part of a planned operation, he was tasked with retrieving weapons from an IRA weapons cache on a farm near Loughgall, not far from the scene of the 1987 SAS ambush where the core of the Brigade at that time had been wiped out by British gunfire. He was to travel under cover of darkness together with another IRA volunteer, Martin McCaughey. McCaughey was from the village of Galbally, near Cappagh, a builder by trade and, until two months ago, had sat as a Sinn Fein councillor on Dungannon Council. He was also however a feared IRA gunman and had been seriously injured whilst taking part in a Provo ambush on British forces in Cappagh six months earlier; he had to be whisked away to the Republic for emergency treatment and thus forced to miss several council meetings, which lead to his suspension. Now recovered from his injuries, the task for McCaughey was to drive with Dessie Grew to the farm and remove a pair of AK-47 automatic rifles from their hiding places hidden at the back of a shed used for growing mushrooms. From there they were to take a stolen vehicle parked at the farm and drive on to a planned, but unknown location to carry out an IRA operation, before returning to the mushroom shed, replacing the weapons and escaping in a clean getaway car.

On the night of October 9th 1990, between 11.30pm and midnight, the duo drove to the secluded farm in Lislasly to retrieve the AK-47s, dressed in boiler suits, balaclavas and rubber gloves to prevent any forensic evidence being left at the scene. A bottle of whiskey was stashed in the front of the getaway car to later toast the success of the operation. Grew and McCaughey were unaware that they were being watched. 14 Intelligence Company, known as the "Det" - the former regiment of Corporals Derek Wood and David Howes who had been executed near Milltown Cemetery at the funeral of IRA man Kevin Brady back in March 1988 - had received intelligence that IRA weapons were being stored in one of the mushroom sheds on the farm and had had the area under surveillance for around a week already. The SAS were called in and - heavily armed - had surrounded the shed - even placing men inside the corrugated iron building, hidden right at the back. They noticed the arrival of Grew and his IRA comrade and trained their automatic weapons on the pair. Grew and McCaughey stepped out of the car and entered the shed. The IRA men pulled the AK-47s from their hiding place and emerged once more into the night.

Around 400 metres away, "Mary" – a support officer for the Det - was sat from a vantage point overlooking the mushroom shed and heard the words "Standby, standby" over her radio communications unit.

> *"I was sitting in the van with the doors locked and the windows wound slightly down and just listening. Suddenly there was this thunderous roar of 7.62 fire going down. It's very loud and you feel the jolt..."kerboom", several times, shattering the quietness of the night."*

The SAS opened fire with their own assault rifles on Grew and McCaughey, firing nearly 70 shots at the pair. The two men were hit in the torso, arms and legs and dropped to the floor immediately, dying from their wounds, their AK-47s scattered on the concrete apron before the entrance to the mushroom shed in front of them. A soldier – later referred to as Soldier D – advanced on the bodies quickly. McCaughey was already dead, but Grew, though mortally wounded, moaned in pain and allegedly made a movement: Soldier D quickly fired two further rounds into Grew's head from point blank range.

The Det and SAS teams examined the bodies and called a doctor –

Dr. Brian Cupples - who arrived at 2.30am. On seeing the state of the bodies, Cupples immediately telephoned the local priest – Father Raymond Murray – who arrived at the scene thirty minutes later to administer the last rites to McCaughey and Grew. Father Murray described the scene:

> "The bodies were quite close to each other, maybe four or five yards apart. They were sprawled out, lying face down with arms and legs scattered. I anointed the two men whilst the RUC Inspector shone his light on the bodies. I remember one of them – I think it was Dessie Grew. There was a lot of congealed blood around his head, almost looking like black oil, with a slight sheen of red on it. The brain material out of the head was all mixed up with it. As far as I can remember, there were two [weapons] what I thought was Kalashnikov AK-47s, lying two to three yards from the heads of the men, and I noticed that there was a pistol butt jutting out of Martin McCaughey's pocket."

On the ground, alongside comrade IRA volunteer Martin McCaughey, Desmond Gerard Grew - one of the IRA's most prolific and cold-blooded killers and the de facto commander of the Provisional IRA's Active Service Units in continental Europe - lay dead.

18 CITY OF DIAMONDS

The execution of Dessie Grew – for that is how the SAS operation in Lislasly can surely be described - was a huge blow to the IRA; British security services knew it and took the opportunity to publicly underscore the importance. The RUC issued a two-page press release, detailing the paramilitary activities of the County Tyrone man – an uncommon step and a dubious honour. The news of Dessie's death was received by a crestfallen ASU in Maastricht; the driving force behind the cell, the man who both assembled and directed them, was gone. Nevertheless, it gave defence lawyers some hope - they might be able to pin some of the responsibility for the Roermond attacks on him and attribute the Hughes sighting to Grew, who could no longer speak for himself. For IRA senior commanders, it was a shock to lose such experienced and respected volunteers as Grew and McCaughey, and both Gerry Adams and Martin McGuinness declared themselves willing to travel to Armagh and Tyrone for the funerals. For the Overseas Department, Grew's death brought the European offensive to an abrupt end – however had Grew survived, he was unlikely to have played a major role in any restart of the campaign, with several arrest warrants outstanding for his involvement in IRA activities in the Netherlands and Germany – on Interpol's watchlist, the East Tyrone Brigade volunteer was probably the most hunted man in Europe by the autumn of 1990. As for the rest: Hick, Harte, Maguire and Hughes were imprisoned in the Huis van bewaring Limburg zuid in Beatrixhaven near Maastricht; Quinn was in Crumlin Road prison awaiting transfer to The Maze; Paddy Fox had been deported from the Continent and had returned to Dungannon, where a younger brother had been arrested in the aftermath of the killings of Grew and McCaughey - along with two others - on suspicion of involvement in that foiled IRA attack; Conlon was back in Armagh.

For Joachim Rzeniecki and the *SoKo PIRA* team, the death of Dessie Grew also marked the end of an era. With the main ringleader of the IRA in Continental Europe gone, Rzeniecki sought a new challenge and took up a professorship at the *Fachhochschule des Bundes*, where he would be responsible for teaching criminology, criminalistics and management science to new *BKA* recruits. At the end of October, Rzeniecki threw a leaving party; colleagues flew in from London, Belfast and Paris to pay their respects and wish him well: officers from the RUC, *MI5*, SIB, *DSGE* were also joined by *BVD* and *CRI* colleagues who travelled from the Netherlands. The British Army of the Rhine also sent their best wishes. Rzeniecki received a letter from General Sir Peter Ingle, the commanding officer of British Forces in Germany:

> *"On behalf of British Forces Germany and their families I wish to record my sincere appreciation for your valuable cooperation and assistance to the Royal Military Police Special Investigations Branch in the continuing efforts to counter terrorism. I commend your dedicated professionalism and devotion to our joint aims. We are fortunate to have such a colleague."*

Back in Northern Ireland, although the German government had yet to achieve any diplomatic results to honour their side of the negotiated ceasefire, the IRA felt duty bound to honour their side of the bargain. Yet pressure was on the Army Council to resume operations on the Continent. The Provisional I.R.A.'s Overseas Department decided to reactivate the campaign but concentrate on targets in the Netherlands and Belgium, but after the loss of Grew and the rest of the European ASUs was unsure who should take on the responsibility. Aware that a large proportion of Brigades in the North – particularly South Down and Belfast - had been compromised by informants recruited by the British security forces, the Overseas Department this time looked to the South for reinforcements. In the autumn of 1990, the Overseas Department put together a team to be sent to the Continent, comprising of John "Dollar" Daly, Gerry Roche and Kieran McCarthy.

McCarthy was the IRA logistics officer supporting expert bomb maker Roche and gunman Daly. A native of Cobh in Co. Cork, thirty-year-old McCarthy was a former member of the regular Irish Army who drifted into the Provisional IRA in the early 1980s. He joined the Irish local reserve brigade, the FCÁ, aged 13 and when five of his friends joined the regular Irish army, he wanted to go along with them despite being underage. He produced a fake baptism certificate which proclaimed he was actually 17, 18 months older than he actually was and commenced training at Collins Barracks in Cork. He joined the 4th Infantry Battalion and in spring 1976 was subsequently posted to Co. Monaghan - before long, he was witnessing first-hand the tense situation on the border with Ulster:

> *"I first began to suspect that all was not what it should be, and that this State's role on the border was more than one of peace-keeping and preventing the northern conflict spreading southwards. I knew I wasn't alone as a soldier in feeling, by the experiences we witnessed and the actions we were at times forced to take, that we were in effect nothing more than a southern regiment of the British Army. When we were being lectured and indoctrinated before departing on our tour of the border, the officers were psyching us up to the business of killing."*

That summer, McCarthy began to gradually change his mind about where his loyalties lay. His first inkling of his future path came when he heard Irish Army soldiers openly talking about the killing of an IRA prisoner who had been trying to escape from Portlaoise and how they were gloating about it. Then his Irish Army colleagues and he were humiliated at gunpoint by British troops in front of the locals in Jonesborough, South Armagh, although the British Army troops were well aware they belonged to the Irish Army. Still seething 18 months later he read a newspaper report that the day before the meeting, a British Army helicopter had been shot down by the Provisional IRA and found himself siding with the Provos. Before long, he became a Volunteer. After proving himself on active service in Ireland, he was chosen to travel to the Continent with Dollar Daly and ex-INLA explosives expert Gerry Roche.

Roche, originally from Belfast, was effectively the replacement for Dessie Grew and indeed the pair had close ties to each other, having been on active service together for the INLA and held in the INLA block in Long Kesh in the 1970s. Roche was slightly older than Grew and in his early forties - he had a long history of paramilitary activity. In his early twenties he was one of the driving forces in the formation of the nascent Irish Republican Socialist Party alongside Bernadette Devlin McAliskey and Seamus Costello. During the IRSP wrangles in the mid-1970s, he joined the INLA alongside Desmond Grew and quickly showed himself adept at bomb making. In January 1982, he was asked to supply explosives by Dublin crime boss Martin Cahill. Increasingly aware of the advances in forensic science developed by Dr. James O'Donovan, who had investigated the murder of Lord Mountbatten in 1979, Cahill became worried that these advances would hinder and curtail his criminal activities and ordered the execution of Dr. O'Donovan. Roche supplied the explosive device that was planted under the bonnet of the forensic scientist's car, which was parked outside his home in the Belgard district of Dublin. The device exploded seriously injuring O'Donovan but he survived the blast. Roche was eventually thrown out of the INLA and moved to Shannon in the west of Ireland. In 1985 Roche narrowly survived an assassination attempt in the increasingly violent struggle between warring factions in the INLA and IRSP, at loggerheads over the new Marxist / Leninist ideology of the movement. He subsequently joined the Provisional IRA's Munster Brigade. Completing the trio was John "Dollar" Daly - from Finglas, north of Dublin, Daly was at 25 the youngest and least experienced member of the ASU sent to Europe. The ASU set up base in the

Belgian city of Antwerp and found an apartment in Korte Winkelstraat, a leafy pedestrian zone only a few minutes' walk from the university and the city's fabled Diamond Quarter, the centre of world trade in the precious stone.

As Daly, Roche and McCarthy travelled to the Continent and set up base in the Belgian city of Antwerp, the funerals of Martin McCaughey and Dessie Grew went ahead under tight security in County Tyrone and County Armagh. In Armagh, the home of Grew's sister at Blundell Grange was surrounded by scores of police officers in riot gear. A small crowd had assembled outside the house when the coffin was carried out. The coffin was draped in the Irish tricolour; on top of this Grew's IRA beret and gloves. Pallbearers were Grew's father Pat and one of his brothers Aidan. Aidan Grew – like his brother – was a member of the IRA's East Tyrone Brigade and several years earlier had been convicted and sentenced to 15 years imprisonment for his part in a Provisional IRA landmine attack just outside Armagh in December 1984, in which seven UDR men had been injured. Serving his sentence at HMP The Maze, he had been granted compassionate leave and temporarily released from Long Kesh to help carry the coffin at his brother's funeral. Joining the mourners were IRA top brass: Army Council members Gerry Adams and Martin McGuinness, showing the standing that Grew had in Provisional IRA circles. The funeral cortege began its journey to the church on Grange Blundell Road, a convoy of 10 RUC Landrovers led the procession, with more behind. Three Army helicopters hovered overhead. The coffin was carried into the church, still adorned with the Tyrone man's IRA beret and the Irish flag; Republican paramilitary trappings usually frowned upon by the Catholic church. Several hundred mourners stood outside to pay their last respects to Dessie Grew. Father Peter Kerr told the congregation that Desmond Grew's death was "tragic" and that the circumstances surrounding his death were still unknown, but that questions were being asked. After the ceremony, the coffin was taken to St. Patricks Cemetery in Armagh to be buried in the same grave as Dessie's brother Seamus, who was also killed by British security forces in 1982 whilst on active service with the INLA. The mourners were almost outnumbered by police officers in riot gear, as the RUC and British Army feared that the outpouring of grief could spill over into spontaneous violence. On Grew's gravestone the inscription read

"May my blood serve as a seed for freedom."

Watched by McGuinness and Bernadette McAliskey, at the graveside Gerry Adams gave the oration as the coffin was lowered into the ground and a wreath from the IRA laid on top. Adams pulled no punches with his oration: Desmond Grew, he said, was

"A freedom fighter, a patriot and a decent upstanding Irish citizen. Those left behind will finish unfinished business."

In County Tyrone, after shots were fired by IRA gunmen outside his family home in Galbally as a mark of respect, Martin McCaughey's funeral took place under close surveillance from the RUC and Army, where this time it was the turn of Martin McGuinness to give the oration. Not very far away, Cees Verhaeren, boss of the Dutch security service *BVD* - who were involved in the investigations into the Roermond murders - watched the macabre spectacle of the funerals on TV and wondered where on earth he had landed. Verhaeren had travelled to Armagh to meet with colleague from RUC Special Branch with the intention of gaining important information into the IRA activities of Dessie Grew that might help advance the case against Hughes, Hick, Harte and Maguire in the Netherlands. He returned to the Netherlands empty handed save for his first experience of witnessing a paramilitary funeral and seeing first-hand what standing the IRA commanded within the local community.

In Düsseldorf, the trial of Hanratty and McGeough was in full swing by early November, although the court only sat twice per week. The various *Irlandsolidarität* solidarity groups from around Germany had banded together to put on a show of support for the two Gerrys and denounce the trial. On the first day of proceedings, around one hundred demonstrators lined the streets to the court, waving placards, handing out a self-printed info sheet *Prozessinfo Nr. 1* and shouting vocally for the release of the prisoners on human rights grounds. Similarly, an argument broke out in court itself between the defence lawyers and the federal state prosecutors over the word "terrorist": the defence, along with Hanratty and McGeough themselves went through the charges word by word, denouncing the classification of the pair as "terrorists" and claiming that the pair should not be categorised as such: they were freedom fighters. The press had taken up much of the available seating but by the afternoon, some of the protestors were able to watch proceedings in the courtroom as journalists left to file their stories on the start of the trial. The presence of the left-wing protestors made certain parts of the trial difficult: the various solidarity groups not only supported the IRA but also the anti-capitalist terrorist organisation Rote Armee Fraktion RAF - some of the *BKA* investigators involved in the IRA trial were also involved in investigations into RAF activities, and were unwilling to divulge information such as names and places of residence for fear that the left-wing mob would pass the information on, making the *BKA* personnel easy targets. The court ruled that in such cases *BKA* officers were exempt from giving personal information, which incensed solidarity groups even more.

McGeough and Hanratty held long diatribes about what they saw as the brutal oppression meted out by the British in occupied Northern Ireland, and spoke at length about the Republican cause. Hanratty called the campaign

> "*a justified struggle against colonial oppression*"

McGeough announced on the first day his intentions to turn proceedings into a show trial:

> "We shall tell you about issues ranging from shoot-to-kill plastic bullets that have claimed the lives of at least twelve children. You will hear of death squads, cover-ups, and all the other sordid British activities that rarely come to light. This case is not just about two Irish Republicans being put on trial – it is about Britain being put on trial."

The Republican PR drive in front of the court incensed the British press representatives present: the first days were reported to represent an IRA "propaganda success" as the judge did not stop the IRA men making their political statements, which lasted over an hour apiece. But before long it was the turn of *MI5* and the RUC to have their day in court in an attempt to redress the balance. A high-ranking Security Service officer gave closed testimony before court and gave an insight into what *MI5* knew about the activities of the European ASU, indicating what he believed the roles that McGeough and Hanratty played in the IRA active service unit. RUC Detective Inspector Raymond McClure took the stand on November 15th to give his testimony - background information on previous IRA activities and convictions of the pair on trial – and to give the court an insight into how active service units were set up and operated by the IRA. The prosecution discussed the Ostende murder of Mike Heakin in detail and attempted to link the shooting in Belgium to the activities of McGeough and Hanratty in Germany. McGeough denied IRA membership absolutely and was very dismissive of prosecution attempts to pin it on him:

> "The question that needs to be answered is...what has a shooting in Belgium got to do with a trial in Germany, where the charges are completely different? The answer is quite simply...nothing! The federal state prosecutor is deliberately trying to create a non-existent background to this case by claiming that one of the weapons that were allegedly found at the time of

our arrest was used in the shooting in Belgium. According to this logic, if the weapon had been used in Sarajevo in 1914, the state prosecutor would be trying to attribute the murder of the Austro-Hungarian crown prince on us."

Whilst the attempt of the state prosecutor to create a link in the minds of the jurors to the Belgian murder was – in the eyes of the law – ham-fisted, the facts were nevertheless true. McGeough's dismissal of involvement – or the relevance of involvement in the events of August 12th 1988 was a typical IRA tactic: taking the opportunity to rubbish circumstantial evidence that clearly pointed to involvement in a related case in an attempt to sow seeds of doubt in the mind of the jury, or have the evidence thrown out of court, and thus try to evade justice. McGeough was worried and started to clutch at straws, cynically stoking left-wing political sympathies, stating in a claim to IRA sympathisers from his prison cell in Wuppertal:

"...whilst the newly reunified Germany begins to experience serious budget cuts, growing unemployment and increasing social inequality, millions of Deutschmarks are being wasted on a trial against Irish Republicans, thus supporting the military occupation from the Brits and the forced division of Ireland. The loud and clear message of the federal state prosecution is "England, England, über alles."

McGeough had every reason to be worried. On November 22nd, McGeough's 1983 application to the Migration Board of Sweden for asylum, in which he admitted to membership of the IRA and the attempted murder of postman Sammy Brush, was passed to the Office of the Public Prosecutor in Malmö. From there it was sent via the Swedish Foreign Ministry to British authorities, who began to prepare extradition proceedings. The same application, as well as numerous false identification papers linked to the cases in Germany had been found in the raid on the apartment of McGeough's Swedish girlfriend Pia Maria Håkansson in September 1988 and were to be used in the Düsseldorf trial against him. It is highly possible that McGeough had realised way back in May or June 1990 that the incriminating asylum papers were still lying around – and had instructed visitors, or even his lawyer Rüdiger Decker – to warn Håkansson to get rid of the papers. The information was then possibly passed to sympathisers, and in turn on to Dessie Grew's ASU: for Hick, Hughes, Harte and Maguire had enquired at the PTT post office in Breda about sending a telegram in English to Sweden shortly before they were arrested near the weapons cache in Heerle. Outside of the Düsseldorf courtroom where McGeough and Hanratty were standing trial, the Irish solidarity committees complained that the Swedish evidence was inadmissible and a sign of illegal tactics by "fascist authorities"; but the chance to have the asylum papers destroyed had been unknowingly scuppered by Belgian police 18 months earlier; McGeough was now on the back foot and had a lot of work to do to explain away the self-incriminating evidence.

Meanwhile in Antwerp, Roche and Daly had acquired an arsenal of weaponry that they were itching to use against British military targets. Unlike the previous active service units, they decided against digging holes in the wood to store weapons in underground weapons depots, instead keeping the weapons with them in the apartment. They had carried out surveillance of a number of British military targets in the Netherlands and Germany, including airbases and army camps, as well as pubs and restaurants where military personnel and their families spent their leisure time. Another possible target presented itself: in the second week of December, Prince Charles and Princess Diana were due to travel to Brussels for a brief visit to the Low Countries. Kieran McCarthy maintains that the Royal couple were never a target:

> "We didn't even know they were coming. It was pure coincidence. It wasn't the operation we were planning. We were planning a variety of operations at the time."

Nevertheless the Royal visit presented both an opportunity and a danger to the IRA unit: the impending arrival of the Prince and Princess of Wales inevitably heightened security concerns and precautions in Belgium and the police and security services of Belgium put on high alert. In the course of preparations for the impending Royal visit, Belgian *Rijkswacht* police received a tip-off of suspicious activity in the Korte Winkelstraat apartment - a trio of English-speaking men had regularly been observed arriving and leaving late at night. The *Rijkswacht* put the flat under surveillance and at the beginning of December applied for a search warrant. An operational plan was drawn up together with the state prosecutor's office to storm the apartment, involving dog-handlers, the use of bulletproof vests and police armed with machine guns.

On December 5th, as the ASU were observed to be in the apartment, police blew the front door off its hinges and stormed the apartment, taking McCarthy, Roche and Daly completely by surprise. Their weapons arsenal lying around but not within arm's reach, the ASU were arrested without a struggle. Police recovered from the scene a Browning 9mm pistol, 2 Kalashnikov AK-47s, 2 Belgian-made FN automatic rifles, a revolver and another pistol - a variety of false identification papers were also found; an IRA Active Service Unit, a safe house and arms cache uncovered and neutralised all at the same time. The planned recommencement of the IRA campaign in mainland Europe had been nipped in the bud before a single shot could be fired.

19 „GOOD LUCK"

The day after the arrest of McCarthy, Roche and Daly in Antwerp, there was more bad news for the IRA – this time from the south of Belgium, where Donna Maguire was still on remand in Turnhout. German BKA investigators had requested that she be handed over to Germany on suspicion of being involved in the IRA attacks in Osnabrück in 1989, as well as in those at Langenhagen Barracks in Hanover, Dortmund and Hameln in 1990. At the same time, the Dutch authorities had applied for her extradition to the Netherlands in relation to the murders of Nick Spanos and Stephen Melrose in Roermond. The relative severity of the charges, and the fact that her three co-charged IRA comrades were also facing trial in the Netherlands meant that Belgium acceded to the request from the Dutch. The Belgian Foreign Ministry informed the German Embassy in Brussels of their decision In extradition case 290/90 RK E MAGUIRE, but also noted that the Belgian government had already agreed that defendant would be extradited on to Germany after the Dutch proceedings - on December 6th 1990, Maguire was flown by helicopter to join Sean Hick, Paul Hughes and Gerard Harte in the Huis van bewaring Limburg zuid in Maastricht and prepared to stand trial for the murders of Nick Spanos and Stephen Melrose.

On the morning of May 28th 1990, Limburg regional judge Ed Bakermans heard the news of the Roermond murders and received more details of the night's events as he arrived for work at the regional court in the town. Towards midday he had walked across the market square and seen the bullet-ridden Citroën BX still standing there. Bakermans was not surprised by the attack; everyone in the region knew that there were several large military bases just across the border in Germany – the risk of an attack was ever-present. Bakermans remembers saying to a colleague "If they get the lot that did this, this could end up in our court...I pity the person who has to look after that trial." Little did he know at the time that he would be that person. After the arrival of Maguire in Maastricht and the finalisation of the prosecution papers for the case, Bakermans received the case dossiers and began to read through the hundreds of pages. Before he knew it, it was February 20th 1991 - the first day of the trial.

Bakermans was picked up at his home in Baexem, around 10 kilometres from Roermond, by a fleet of special Volvo 440s and driven via police escort to the courthouse. At around the same time, Hick, Harte, Maguire and Hughes were taken in armoured Mercedes cars from Maastricht to the court; blindfolded and handcuffed to prevent escape and from deducing the route they were taking, for fear of them passing the information to their lawyers, who in turn might pass on the details to the IRA - and try to free them on a subsequent journey to the court. The court in Roermond was subject to maximum security measures - no bags allowed, visitors and press were obliged to pass through metal detectors, shoes had to be removed, even ball-point pens were unscrewed and checked in case they harboured anything sinister. The courtroom itself was protected by bulletproof glass and scores of policemen and women were present. Outside, the centre of Roermond was hermetically sealed off, an evacuation plan in place should one of the regular checks for explosives near the courthouse uncover a device. Above the court building, police helicopters monitored the area. The courthouse in Roermond was an impenetrable fortress.

The ASU members arrived in Roermond to be met by their legal teams: Gerard Harte's lawyer Marie-Jeanne Hegeman, her colleague Ruud Bom who represented Sean Hick, Willem van Bennekom for Paul Hughes and Gerard von Asperen for Donna Maguire. The defendants and their lawyers stood as Bakermans entered the courtroom. Unlike in Britain, the Netherlands legal system does not employ a jury to make the decision whether to convict or acquit; a team of judges preside over the case - on this occasion with Ed

Bakermans at its head. Bakermans took his seat and opened the proceedings. Almost immediately it became apparent that the prosecution had been party to private conversations between the lawyers and their clients and to the families of the accused. The accused had liaised with their families back home, and indirectly with the IRA leadership via a conduit – Pauline Kersten – a Dutch social worker and Republican activist who had moved to Belfast the previous year, and who passed information backwards and forwards and gave updates on the case proceedings to the IRA. One particular call to a man in Northern Ireland calling himself "Mick", who seemed to be directing information directly to the IRA, and may well have been Sean "The Surgeon" Hughes, was intercepted and transcribed and appeared to be arranging for witnesses from Northern Ireland to travel to the Netherlands to give false alibis in the case. Fragments of discussions between Gerard Harte and his lawyer Marie-Jeanne Hegeman were quoted in the initial addresses by the prosecution and worse was to come. Judge Bakermans asked Ruud Bom how many witnesses for the defence he would be cross-examining – he replied "three, maybe six, but nothing like twenty." Prosecutor Jo Laumen remarked "and maybe someone from Paris, right?" – a horrendous slip of the tongue. For Willem van Bennekom and Ruud Bom had had their telephone bugged and the prosecution had picked up a conversation regarding an alleged second ASU in Paris and that it was possible that this ASU could be given the blame for the Roermond attack instead. Ruud Bom suggested that "our lady in Paris should maybe give a statement to a notary" to this effect – the potential witness to whom Laumen had indelicately referred and of whom only Bom and van Bennekom were aware. The defence team was up in arms at having their telephones bugged and protested vociferously to Bakermans; the judge ruled that the phone taps were not admissible as evidence in the trial: the first inkling for the prosecution that securing convictions for Hick, Harte, Hughes and Maguire was not going to be an easy ride.

But the prosecution team had another ace up their sleeve, or so they hoped. Supported by the Dutch Secret Service *BVD*, they were well aware that Pauline Kersten was passing information from Maastricht back to Northern Ireland but they also had their own contact person helping on the ground in Ulster; the impressionable 22-year-old woman had been recruited by the *BVD* from the group of activists surrounding the Ierland Komitee Nederland in mid-1989, given the codename "Iris" and had been sent to London to be interviewed by *MI5*. Returning to the Netherlands, and briefed further by the Dutch Secret Service, she was given a complicated role in the fight against the IRA: the *BVD* wanted her to keep tabs on the troublesome Ierland Komitee Nederland, and *MI5* wanted her to keep them informed of the *IKN*'s involvement in IRA activities in the Netherlands. The two roles went hand-in-hand. "Iris" travelled first to Northern Ireland to get a flavour of the province, take photos of demonstrations and meetings and spend time getting to know Republicans as an innocent, young and Republican-leaning left-wing activist. With the information and contacts, she returned to *IKN* circles with newfound knowledge and networks and ingratiated herself with the leadership. Arian Kuil from the *IKN* asked her if she needed a job; "Iris" became the nanny for the Kuil family and was in an optimum position to report back to *BVD* on *IKN* activities and to *MI5* on the *IKN*'s dealings with IRA members. After the arrests of Hick, Maguire, Harte and Hughes, "Iris" was detailed with the task of making contact with the families of the captured IRA volunteers back in Newry, Lurgan and South Armagh (the family of Sean Hick was a notable exception) and she returned to Northern Ireland. Kersten and "Iris" both kept in regular contact with the families, but whilst Kerstin passed on messages to the defence team for the IRA volunteers, "Iris" passed her information to the security services and the prosecution. Whilst none of the information would be admissible in court, it was a battle of wits to see who could use the information most to their advantage and come out victorious.

The trial schedule was set for three days per week: Monday, Wednesday and Friday. On the other days of the week, both

Bakermans and Laumen would work on other cases, where they would not enjoy the extra security that the IRA case afforded them; although unsettled by the atmosphere, Bakermans and Laumen were not cowed and refused the offer of additional protection in their private lives, reasoning that the IRA were not likely to carry out an attack in the Netherlands on such public targets. And if they did, there would be little that they could do about it. Others due to appear in court for the prosecution were nevertheless intimidated by the extreme security measures and the tense uneasiness surrounding the trial. Paul Reijngoud – the café owner who had been confronted by Harte at the scene of the shooting in Roermond – had received a threatening phone call from a man with an Irish accent – saying that he knew exactly what Reijngoud looked like, where he could be found and if he gave a statement implicating any of the four defendants, the café owner would be kneecapped. Jos Heitzer and his wife were promised that if they gave evidence in court, they would be disguised as a security precaution. However they had previously been promised disguises when travelling to Maastricht for the identity parade and the police had reneged on the promise; Heitzer and his wife were scared stiff and refused to take part in the trial.

On day one, the initial skirmishes after the phone tap episode involved mind games between defence and prosecution lawyers. Van Bennekom knew that it was forbidden for lawyers to touch their clients during a trial but asked for permission to shake the hands of the defendants; Bakermans let them – one of a number of sly attempts by van Bennekom and team to make the prosecution feel that the judge was on the side of the defence. The blatant chicanery by the defence continued in the afternoon as the first witnesses for the defence took the stand. Three of Paul Hughes friends from Newry attested that Hughes had been back in Newry watching a Gaelic football match with them on the night of the shooting in Roermond. All three were staunch IRA supporters who knew full well where Hughes had been that night, but were more than happy to tell lies in court to help out the organisation – and keep in the good books of Hughes influential brother Sean. The prosecution and the judge took the statements with the large pinch of salt they deserved.

The second day of the trial saw the presentation of the statements made by Ingrid Hijman, detailing her involvement with Hick and the rest of the ASU. Whilst she was a key witness, prosecutor Jo Laumen denied that she was to remain immune from prosecution, stating

> "It is still unclear whether a prosecution case can or should be initiated against her."

Hijman's disclosure was followed by statements from those who had witnessed the attack and the aftermath: amongst them John Loofen, the petrol station attendant from Sittard, who had identified Hick, Harte and Maguire as Maguire stopped at the filling station to ask for directions only half an hour after the murders. Also giving evidence was Bernard Bähre who had seen the whole attack take place and whose statement was given under hypnosis by a hypnotherapist from The Hague.

Over the course of the next few days, Laumen presented the case against the four IRA volunteers and detailed the evidence against each of them. Maguire had been arrested very close to two weapons dumps in the woods in Heerle, where the weapons used to murder Stephen Melrose and Nick Spanos were found. Several witnesses had seen Maguire together with Harte and Hick in different locations in the Netherlands. Several witnesses had also seen Maguire between the beginning of June and June 13th in Hamelin, before the detonation of the IRA bomb on June 14th. Maguire's fingerprints were found in the red Opel Kadett sighted at the moment the Mazda used as a getaway vehicle in Roermond was stolen in Venlo. Even more fingerprints were found in the other red Kadett found in

Heerle near the weapons dumps, in the Pletterijstraat apartment, in the other IRA safe house in Cäcilienstrasse and in the campus room belonging to Ingrid Hijman in Uilenstede. Gerard Harte was arrested near to the border with Belgium and presented false ID papers in the name of Peter John Watson that matched those found in the Opel Kadett in Heerle. Witnesses Jos Heitzer and his wife had identified Harte as the passenger in the getaway car that fled the market square after the murders. In addition, Harte's passport was found in Uilenstede, his fingerprints all over the flat in Pletterijstraat and in both the Opel Kadett vehicles used by the killers. Sean Hick was arrested in Heerle close to the weapons caches. Ingrid Hijman had implicated him in IRA activities, his fingerprints were found in both safe houses and in various vehicles used by the ASU. Hughes had been identified by witnesses as the driver of the Opel Kadett used on the night of the murders, been implicated by Ingrid Hijman and given the keys to Pletterijstraat 23 by her. His fingerprints were also found in Hanover and The Hague as well as in the stolen Ford Sierra, and in rental cars used between April and June, in which traces of explosives had been found. Laumen pointed the finger directly at Gerard Harte as the prime suspect in the killings: Harte was the only one of the four who witnesses testified they could identify as having been on the square holding a weapon that night. Nevertheless, Laumen explained, all four were members of the IRA and operated as a team; without the other three the attack would not have been possible. This collective responsibility, he argued, implicated all four in the murders and made them guilty. Laumen pleaded for a 20-year sentence for each of the defendants.

It was now the turn of the defence. Bom, van Asperen, van Bennekom and Hegeman chose an unusual strategy: usually the question of whether or not their client carried out the crime for which they were being charged is irrelevant, the only relevant question is "can it be proved?". The four lawyers addressed the case of each client individually: there was no indication that a woman was seen at the crime scene, so Maguire could not be proved to have been there. Hughes equally should be exonerated from blame; he only came to the aid of Hick after his arrest and admitted only that he had travelled to Chaam via Paris and The Hague. The lawyers however stated they were not actually sure if Hick and Harte could be vouched for. The defence called a psychologist – Willem Wagenaar from Leiden – who cast doubts on the witness testimony of Loofen, Bähre and the Heitzers by referring to the publication of photos of the ASU that appeared in Dutch and international press after their capture. Drawing parallels with the case of Nazi guard John Demanjuk, where it was claimed holocaust survivors had identified Demanjuk from newspaper photographs rather than from memory, the defence lawyers stated that the identification of Hughes as the driver of the getaway car and Harte as the shooter in the identity parade was unreliable and thus the case should be thrown out of court due to lack of evidence. Prosecutor Laumen was apoplectic and had to be brought to order by judge Ed Bakermans.

Bakermans and his co-judges Brouwer and Bruinsma nevertheless brought the depositions of both defence and prosecutions to an end and retired to deliberate the evidence and statements presented to them. It took them two weeks to discuss the intricacies of the case and in the absence of a jury as the Dutch court system dictated, carried the responsibility of trying to differentiate between fact and fiction; truth and conjecture; guilty and not guilty.

On April 2nd 1991, the court reached a verdict in the killings of Nick Spanos and Stephen Melrose and a decision as to whether or not Sean Hick, Paul Hughes, Donna Maguire and Gerard Harte were members of the IRA and guilty of murder. Appearing once more before the court, judge Bakermans read the verdicts: on the charges of membership of a proscribed organisation - namely the Provisional IRA – Sean Hick, Donna Maguire, Paul Hughes and Gerard Harte were found not guilty due to lack of concrete evidence to support the claim. On the charges of the murder of Nick Spanos and Stephen Melrose on May 27th 1990 in Roermond, Sean Hick, Donna Maguire and Paul Hughes were equally found not guilty due to lack of evidence. Gerard Harte – on the basis of the witness testimony and identification of Harte at the identity parade in Maastricht on July 3rd – was found guilty of murder. Gerard Harte was sentenced to eighteen years imprisonment. Defendants, defence and prosecution lawyers, as well as the world press were surprised that Hick, Maguire and Hughes had been acquitted, although they were plainly closely involved in the murders and understandably, the state prosecution team gave notice of their intention to appeal the verdict. Nevertheless, nearly eighteen years after Jim McCann planted a car bomb outside the Globe Cinema at Rheindahlen in 1973 and started the IRA's European campaign, Gerard Majella Harte from Lurgan, Co. Armagh became the first IRA volunteer to be convicted of murder in mainland Europe.

The British press was nevertheless incensed at the acquittals of Hughes, Hick and Maguire and made much of the fact that judge Bakermans had wished "good luck" to Paul Hughes in the courtroom; the judge later defended his choice of words, claiming that it was normal in the Netherlands to wish everyone at the end of a trial all the best, but for those in the UK who had expected the quartet to be convicted, it was a kick in the teeth and added to the feeling that the Dutch court was rather too willing to acquit. The evidence presented by the prosecution was largely circumstantial in the case of Hick, Hughes and Maguire, but then again the defence offered very little to prove that the trio were not involved in the Roermond murders, preferring instead to wave away prosecution evidence with flimsy alibis that went unchecked and get away with casting minimal doubts on witness statements: the strategy of Bom, van Asperen and van Bennekom had worked.

Hick, Hughes and Maguire were however not released; the German authorities had already previously staked a claim to the trio and had requested their extradition to Germany over charges of being involved in several of the attacks in 1989 and 1990. In addition, the Dutch government had been dismayed at the acquittals by their judiciary and incredulous that the trio had not even been found guilty of the lesser offence of being members of the IRA: Advocate-General Frits van Straelen and Attorney-General Rolph Gonsalves appealed the acquittals and the IRA trio remained in custody in Maastricht, pending their appearance before the Court of Appeal in s'Hertogenbosch (Den Bosch), which was scheduled for the end of June. Also scheduled to have his case reassessed by the Court of Appeal - in an attempt to wriggle out of his conviction and eighteen year sentence - was Gerard Harte.

In preparation for the appeal hearing, van Straelen and *BVD* boss Cees Verhaeren travelled to St. Andrews in the north west of Scotland to meet with Professor Paul Wilkinson, head of the Centre for the Study of Terrorism and Political Violence at the University of St. Andrews. As a renowned expert on terrorism, Wilkinson had considerable experience in IRA methodology and had been involved in many IRA trials. After discussing many points of the case with him, Verhaeren and van Straelen convinced Wilkinson to give expert testimony in the impending appeal trial. Also preparing for the trial was Willem Smulders, who was to chair proceedings at the Court of Appeal in Den Bosch as head judge: he procured several books on the Troubles and read up on the history of the conflict, as well as reading through many case notes on previous IRA trials.

On June 5th 1991 proceedings opened in the case against Harte, Hick, Maguire and Hughes. Jo Laumen restated the wish to convict the four on the charges of IRA membership, which had been dismissed by the court in Roermond. Smulders agreed with the prosecution that there was enough evidence to reconsider the acquittals: he referred that part of the case back to the regional court in Roermond. The rest of the appeal proceedings dealt with the testimony of witnesses Heitzer and Loofen; the original case had been acquitted partly on the grounds presented by the psychologist

Wagenaar that their testimony was unreliable The witness testimony was taken apart line by line and descriptions analysed. Another witness for the defence cast doubt about the conviction of Gerard Harte by claiming that they had seen Harte shoot, but with the Ruger and with his right hand: this claim was rebutted by Harte who explained that he was left-handed. At this point, it was erroneously inferred that Harte could therefore not have been the one firing the Ruger – either it was a simple case of mistaken identity and the witness getting Grew (who fired the Ruger right-handed) and Harte (who fired the AK-47 with his left-hand) mixed up or a deliberate ploy to sow seeds of doubt about Harte's involvement at all. The defence team led by Willem van Bennekom introduced a new line of defence and suggested two possible other IRA volunteers for which Jos Heitzer, his wife and other witnesses might have mistaken Gerard Harte in the getaway car on the market square in Roermond that night: Paddy Fox and Dessie Grew. Part of the witness description of Harte matched Grew, who could obviously not be questioned or provide an alibi. Paddy Fox bore more than a passing resemblance to Harte, a proven IRA member and had been proven to be present on the Continent during the IRA campaign of 1989 and 1990. However, the court checked with their colleagues in Northern Ireland: a few weeks before the Roermond attack, Fox had been injured when a bomb he was preparing in Dungannon prematurely exploded, injuring his hand severely. On May 23rd he had been arrested in Dungannon but released a couple of days later; on the day of the shooting and on subsequent days, he had been spotted in Dungannon with his hand heavily bandaged. Although fingerprint and DNA evidence proved that Fox and Grew had been part of the ASU present in the Netherlands around that time: Paddy Fox had not been a passenger in the car in Roermond that night and neither the prosecution nor the defence could prove nor deny that Dessie Grew was the person seen in the passenger seat on the night on May 27th 1990. Grew, despite his absence, cast a dark shadow over the proceedings and prosecutor Laumen quite clearly outlined what role Grew played in the ASU:

> "It was Grew who organised the IRA unit operating on the continent. Grew was getting older. There had to be fresh blood in order to get blood. Grew was the spider in the web".

Van Straelen slowly but surely began to get the feeling that Smulders was being taken in by the show put on by van Bennekom and his team, and reiterated the need for impartiality from head judge Smulders. Paul Hughes protested dramatically at the interjection and stormed out of the courtroom shouting "it's an unfair trial!", before being calmed down and led back into the dock by van Bennekom. The prosecution also contributed to the emotional atmosphere by inviting Vicki Coss and Lyndal Melrose to give evidence for the prosecution. There were a huge amount of psychological factors involved in the final days of the court appeal, which ended on June 19th 1991 with the summing up by the prosecution. At the end of his seven-hour plea, Frits van Straelen reiterated the demand for conviction of Harte, Hughes, Maguire and Harte and eighteen-year sentences for each of them; the demand from Jo Laumen for five years imprisonment for membership of the Provisional IRA would be dealt with by the regional court in Roermond. Smulders and his two co-judges retired to consider their verdict, which was due to be announced on July 5th.

Harte telephoned his wife Elizabeth back in Lurgan the week before the announcement and told her he was fully expecting to be completely acquitted and finally return home – he was so sure he had already renewed his passport earlier in the week in preparation for being allowed to fly back to Ireland. He was to be proved right: Smulders announced that Harte's conviction was to be overturned – the prosecution had failed to prove conclusively that Harte had pulled the trigger on May 27th 1990; for the same reasons, once again Hick, Hughes and Maguire were acquitted of murder. An IRA sympathiser shouted from the gallery "God bless this judge!"

Then things moved quickly: the judges presiding over the case in the regional court in Roermond also announced their decision: they ruled that the prosecution had provided insufficient evidence to prove that the four ASU members had been executing the orders of the Provisionals – as it could not be upheld that they were acting on behalf of the IRA, they could not be convicted of membership of a criminal organisation. Harte, Hick, Maguire and Hughes broke into smiles and shook the hands of their lawyers as they rejoiced in defeating the Dutch justice system. Leaving the courtroom, Hughes yelled with joy and raised his fists high in the air. Hughes' lawyer Willem van Bennekom released an unsurprisingly uncompromising but cautiously worded statement in the wake of the acquittals, saying that he could understand the feelings of grief and anger on the part of the families of the IRA victims, because their murderers had not been found and convicted. He warned that the whole concept of justice was a very delicate thing and that they must realise that the frontier between justice and retaliation and the finding of the truth had to be strictly legal. Van Bennekom was only too aware of Hughes' involvement in the Roermond attack and carefully chose not to proclaim that his client had nothing to do with the murders, but to place emphasis on legal technicalities. He was backed up in his legal assessment of the verdict by Harte's lawyer Marie Jeanne Hegeman, who chose to relay to the press that Harte had told her he had received a fair trial in Holland and that he had believed that would not have been the case had he been tried in England; loosely translated, what she actually meant was the absence of a jury in the Dutch proceedings and the politically charged decision of the Roermond judges to acquit, thus avoiding the potential wrath of the IRA afforded freedom to Gerard Harte that a jury in a country used to dealing with IRA crimes would have rightly denied him. Van Bennekom backed this view, saying there was a big difference in the concept of justice between Great Britain and Holland; the major difference naturally being that it was possible to murder innocent people in cold blood in the Netherlands and still walk free.

For all four though, it was to be only the first victory in a long legal battle to evade justice; the German extradition warrants issued against Donna Maguire, as well as Sean Hick and Paul Hughes came into effect – although van Bennekom played down the chances of Hughes being convicted in Germany either - and the trio were driven back to Maastricht to extradition detention, to await expulsion to Germany. Gerard Harte however had escaped indictment in Germany and was free to leave the Netherlands. He expressed a wish to leave the court building through the front door to freedom, because he had nothing to hide from anyone. He emerged from the regional court in Roermond to a sea of protestors – unlike with many IRA trials, the throng of people were not IRA sympathisers there to support the defendants, but local Dutch people and British military personnel aiming to harangue them; flanked by 20 Dutch policemen; Harte was visibly unsteady on his feet and shocked at the scene. The police officers were unable to prevent a woman breaking through the ranks in an attempt to attack Harte; Leoni Moreland – the Dutch wife of a British serviceman based in Germany, who had made the decision to return to Britain because of the actions of the IRA – flew at the slight 27 year old from Lurgan, swearing and threatening the IRA man and had to be forcibly restrained from punching Harte. Shaken by the unexpected reception, Harte was quickly driven the short distance to Roermond railway station and boarded a train to Amsterdam's Schiphol airport. A ticket had been booked in his name for Aer Lingus flight EI605 back to Dublin and Harte left the Netherlands shortly after 6pm as a free man. Two hours later, he arrived in Dublin to find his short-lived freedom at an end. Upon disembarking from the aircraft, he was arrested by Irish police and held in custody at the airport for questioning over his involvement in IRA activities. He was held overnight in the cells as enquiries were made – including with the authorities in the Netherlands – and was finally released the following morning upon receipt of documentation from the Dutch court showing that he had been acquitted. Gerard Harte returned to the family home, to his wife and children in Lurgan, Co. Armagh, as a known, high-profile, and - above all - free IRA man, which was to solidify his place as a top target for Loyalist paramilitaries. Despite winning his unjust freedom, Harte faced an uncertain, troubling and dangerous future, back home in Northern Ireland.

In the Huis van bewaring Limburg-zuid, Sean Hick, Paul Hughes and Donna Maguire awaited extradition to Germany. Hick and Hughes had been assured by their respective lawyers that that the German authorities did not have enough evidence to convict them on the charges of involvement in the attacks in Langenhagen, Dortmund and Wildenrath awaiting them; as a result they did not contest their extradition and on July 16th 1991, were handed over to officers of the German Federal Office of Investigation *BKA* and flown across the border to Karlsruhe and taken into German custody. The extradition of Donna Maguire was sought by the Germans on the basis of the spring 1990 attacks – she had been on remand in Ireland after her arrest in Rosslare at the time of the murders of Heidi Hazell, Mick and Nivruti Islania and the attempted murders in Münster and Hanover from August to October 1989 – but she was also extraditable on charges of involvement in the partly-foiled bomb attack at Quebec Barracks in Osnabrück in June 1989 and the car bomb murder of Corporal Steven Smith in Hannover in July the same year. Here, the case against Donna Maguire was considerably stronger and she was advised by her lawyers Gerard van Asperen and Hannover barrister Barbara Klawitter in Germany - to fight extradition to avoid a conviction. She lodged an appeal against her extradition and a trial at the Dutch Supreme Court in Den Bosch was scheduled for September 1991.

Away from the courtroom, in August there was some unsettling news: a number of prominent, and experienced IRA volunteers took up jobs as painters and decorators at the soon to be opened Euro Disney Resort on the outskirts of Paris, and resided in living quarters close to the theme park. John Gillen was from a staunchly Republican family - the brother of Belfast Brigade commander and

IRA Army Council member Brian Gillen; a tough Belfast Provo. The second man in Paris was Joe Haughey, also from Belfast from the Carrick Hill area, known as the 'Hawk'. Joe was a hugely experienced IRA volunteer, first convicted in November 1981 for hijacking a car used in the M60 machine-gun murder of a deputy governor of Crumlin Road prison. Haughey, then 28 years old, was given a suspended prison sentence after being found guilty of hijacking and false imprisonment. He was acquitted of IRA membership charges. In June 1986 he was acquitted of involvement in the murder of Mary Travers and the attempted murder of her father, magistrate Tom Travers. Two IRA gunmen ambushed the Travers family in April 1984, as they left Mass at St Brigid's church on Derryvolgie Avenue in south Belfast. Teacher Mary (22) died almost instantly. Her prominent – and Catholic - magistrate father Tom was left fighting for his life having been shot six times - his wife Joan narrowly escaped injury after one of the guns used in the attack jammed. Haughey and IRA volunteer Mary McArdle were charged in connection with the attack. Haughey was originally identified by Mr. Travers as being the man who killed his daughter, however his identification evidence was questioned during trial and Haughey was acquitted, whilst McArdle was sentenced to a life term for the murder. Haughey returned to active service with the IRA before he travelled to Paris. Unbeknown to the other two volunteers and to the IRA, Haughey was allegedly also an informant for British intelligence. A double role as intelligence officer on the IRA's GHQ staff and as a British mole within the IRA would have given him access to useful information that he could pass regularly to RUC Special Branch. The presence of Haughey in Paris in a double-agent role raises eyebrows when viewed alongside the fact that the third member of the Paris ASU was Peter Keeley. It is unclear and indeed unlikely that Keeley and Haughey knew of each other's collaboration with British intelligence. There is no indication that Gillen was an informant. Their presence in France raises a number of questions: did they take the jobs to simply get away from Northern Ireland and earn good money? Many from the North and South of Ireland saw adverts taken out in the Irish press and took the opportunity for some well-paid work. Or was this the nucleus of a new Active Service Unit? It seems possible given the various roles they had each played in previous IRA operations that this was the case – a three man team of such experienced and well-connected volunteers, adept at intelligence, weaponry and logistics, placed in the heart of Europe was sure to set alarm bells ringing within the security services, should they be discovered. Whatever the motivations for being in Paris, Haughey, Gillen and Keeley's stay was not to last long: either thanks to exemplary investigative journalism or acting on a tip-off from the security services, a newspaper publicly revealed their presence at Euro Disney. On the last weekend of September 1991, just a few weeks after Gillen, Haughey and Keeley had started work, the Sunday Express ran a headline story: "I.R.A. INFILTRATE DISNEYLAND", naming the three. The trio were dismissed from their jobs at the theme park and returned to Northern Ireland.

Back in the Netherlands, legal proceedings against Donna Maguire continued. On September 10th, her case was heard before the Hoge Raad in Den Bosch. Maguire and van Asperen were not able to present any pressing reasons why the 24 year old from Newry should not be handed over to German authorities and the Dutch Supreme Court granted the extradition request – Maguire returned to Maastricht where, four weeks later on October 7th, German officials arrived via helicopter, took custody of Donna Maguire and flew her back across the border to Karlsruhe to face trial in Germany.

20 720 DAYS IN THE BUNKER

At the Oberlandesgericht (OLG) regional court in Düsseldorf - a maximum security courthouse that had been refurbished to accommodate high-profile trials involving the Rote Armee Fraktion (RAF), and known colloquially as "The Bunker" - the trial against the two Gerrys - Hanratty and McGeough - was progressing slowly but surely towards an unpredictable, unfavourable but bearable outcome for the IRA men. All charges relating to the bombing of Glamorgan Barracks in 1988 had been dropped on July 31st the previous year due to lack of evidence, leaving McGeough and Hanratty to answer to charges of carrying out the 1987 JHQ bomb in Rheindahlen and the illegal importation of firearms into the Federal Republic of Germany. Whilst the evidence presented by the German prosecution on the latter charge was very much an open-and-shut case, proof of direct involvement in the Rheindahlen explosion was scant - there was very little in the way of useful witness statements or forensic evidence directly linking them to the attack. German law had no provision for convicting foreigners of membership of a foreign terrorist organisation per se, so a prison sentence for being a member of the IRA could not be brought. A conviction on firearms charges McGeough and Hanratty could live with. For McGeough though, there was bad news on September 4th when he received a visitor from Northern Ireland at Wuppertal Prison. The ears of the RUC had pricked up on hearing of the contents of McGeough's asylum application forms in Sweden, corroborated the information contained within and DI Cowen from the RUC was dispatched to Wuppertal to question McGeough. The RUC officer informed McGeough that he was being investigated for his involvement in the attempted murder of postman and off-duty UDR soldier Sammy

Brush in Aughnacloy ten years earlier. Although McGeough was looking at a custodial sentence for firearms and terrorism charges in Germany, by 1991 he had been on remand for nigh-on three years, which would count towards his sentence; there was still a chance however that some evidence would be uncovered that would link him directly to the JHQ attack and put him behind bars for several years; and any British attempt to then have him extradited back to Northern Ireland was looking increasingly likely to succeed. McGeough slept uneasily during the latter stages of the Düsseldorf trial.

Meanwhile in the USA, as Tom King had predicted in his letter to Geoffrey Howe in February 1989, FBI officials had become aware of McGeough's incarceration in Germany and realised that the IRA man was on their "Most Wanted" list, where he had been since he had absconded from justice on June 21st, 1982, when his IRA associate "Skinny Legs" Megahey had been arrested in New York over the pair's attempted purchase of five FIM93 Red-Eye portable missile systems from undercover FBI agents in New Orleans. The US authorities joined the extradition battle and issued a request to Germany for McGeough to be handed over to the United States instead of the United Kingdom. With no formal extradition request from the British in place, the Germans acceded to the US request. Not for the first or last time, McGeough's past caught up with him. On May 28th 1992, he smiled before the court as the judge was informed that the case against McGeough was being abandoned; the US had staked a claim on McGeough. Whilst he was still standing trial for attempted murder in Germany, it was looking like he was instead only likely to be convicted of the lesser charges of firearms possession - the extradition request from the USA involved more serious weaponry. Gerry McGeough was taken from court and driven under armed guard to the US air base at Ramstein, near Frankfurt, where, escorted by US marshals, he was flown overnight, strapped inside a C141 cargo plane, to Dover Air Force Base in Delaware. From there he was transferred to Manhattan Correction

Centre in New York. A little over a week later on June 8th, he appeared before a New York court to make an initial appearance and answer the charges against him – the judge set bond at one million US dollars. The bail was financed by friends and NORAID supporters putting up their houses as security – McGeough was temporarily free but unable to leave the country. He was however now to face a much sterner challenge than the justice apparatus of continental European countries that feared an IRA conviction would bring the Provos knocking at their door – the US court system was not known for being a soft touch.

Five days later, judgement day for comrade Gerry Hanratty arrived. On June 4th he stood before Wolfgang Steffen - leading the five-strong team of judges presiding over the case in Düsseldorf - as he read the verdict. The court found he had shown no resistance upon arrest and was aware that he had grown up in a staunchly Republican area where he had learned early the disadvantages of growing up as a minority Roman Catholic. Whilst it was clear that Hanratty (and McGeough) were Provisional IRA members belonging to an active service unit on the Continent, they found no evidence to suggest he had taken part in the July 1988 bomb attack on Glamorgan Barracks in Duisburg or the March 1987 bomb attack on JHQ in Rheindahlen. He was however found guilty of the illegal import of weapons, including the two Kalashnikov AK-47s and three revolvers found in the white Peugeot 205 at the time of his arrest at Waldfeucht. Although ballistics reports had confirmed that the weapons had been used in the attacks in Duisburg (as well as Ostende and Roermond), Wolfgang Steffen contested the claim that this evidence proved Hanratty had been the person who had pulled the trigger of those weapons in those attacks – they could equally have been used previously by another IRA unit, according to the judge. After 130 sittings at a cost of over £2 million, involving over 180 witnesses and a host of experts from several countries, the court was prepared to give Hanratty the benefit of the doubt and acquitted him of attempted murder. However, on the count of illegal importation of firearms into the Federal Republic of Germany, this could be proven: he was sentenced to two and a half years imprisonment. Hanratty had however already spent nearly three years on remand awaiting the verdict; his sentence already served. But Hanratty was not about to walk to freedom: he had originally been arrested by the RUC in 1984 for his part in a high-speed chase across Belfast resulting in the discovery of the abandoned getaway car full of weapons; as he had absconded bail and not appeared at his trial in 1986, the RUC requested that Gerry Hanratty be held pending the outcome of the extradition request that, after months of diplomacy, had finally been put in by the British government. Hanratty returned to prison in Wuppertal, technically a free man in Germany, but soon to be a prisoner in Northern Ireland. Two months later, the British request was granted by the Germans. On August 14th 1992, Gerry Hanratty was extradited from Germany to the UK and flown back to Aldergrove airport in Belfast, arraigned for a three-minute appearance at Belfast Magistrates Court and sent to Crumlin Road prison to await trial.

By the summer of 1992, three years had already passed since Donagh O'Kane, Patrick Murray and Pauline Drumm had been arrested on the motorway in France after escaping from the French capital. With the legal wrangling between France and Germany finally over, the trio finally stood trial in Paris in the knowledge that, whatever the outcome, they would be handed over to the Germans as soon as the French trial was finished. Although they had made statements at the initial hearing back in 1989 that their actions were in no way directed towards the French state or its citizens, they had admitted to being members of the Provisional IRA. As in Germany, there was however no statute that covered membership of a foreign terrorist group whilst being in France, and thus the case against them was relatively straightforward and based on fact, rather than politics. They were quickly convicted of handling explosives, use and possession of false identification papers and handling stolen goods; all three received sentences of two years each, which, due to the amount of time they had been in custody awaiting trial were declared as served. They returned to prison for a short period of extradition remand, before being handed over to the German authorities in August 1992. There was a modicum of controversy over their extradition however, as three days after their arrival, all charges relating to the car bomb attack on Corporal Steven Smith on July 2nd 1989 in Hanover were suddenly dropped; witness statement had placed them near Saarbrücken on the French / German border at the time of the detonation and thus the German authorities had no choice but to concentrate on building a prosecution case against them for their involvement in the June 1989 oil drum bomb attack at Quebec Barracks foiled by Gunter Kittelmann. Also suspected was Donna Maguire. But first she had to stand trial in Düsseldorf for involvement in the murder of Major Dillon-Lee in Dortmund and the attack at Langenhagen Barracks in the summer of 1990.

By the autumn of 1992, a year had passed since Maguire had been extradited from the Netherlands to Germany, and some fifteen months since Sean Hick and Paul Hughes had also been taken by helicopter from Maastricht to Karlsruhe. Finally on October 26th, the three IRA volunteers filed into "The Bunker" – the concrete-reinforced courtroom in Cäcilienstrasse in Düsseldorf - to stand trial. Each flanked by two lawyers, amongst them Rüdiger Decker - fresh from defending Gerry McGeough in the earlier trial – and Hanover barrister Barbara Klawitter. Presiding over proceedings once more was Wolfgang Steffen, who, four months earlier, had sentenced Gerry Hanratty to two and a half years prison for his role in the IRA's European campaign. The initial hearing saw the prosecution read out the charges, claiming that Hick, Hughes and Maguire were part of an IRA cell set up on the Continent in early 1990, living in Germany and the Netherlands under a host of false identities. The prosecution also said that Hick and Hughes had denied the charges presented to them, but that Donna Maguire had remained silent and made no comment. Wolfgang Steffen read out the names of the IRA volunteers, their dates of birth and their home addresses, which all three volunteers acknowledged. Hick, Hughes and Maguire each indicated that they had nothing further to add and Steffen adjourned the case until November 9th. The trio returned to prison. The trial dates were set; the defendants could expect to travel twice a week for two years to the maximum-security courthouse set up in the 1970s to cope with the Baader-Meinhof terrorist trials. In the background, the German authorities were building up the case against Maguire – and Drumm, O'Kane and Murray – in preparation for the Celle trial. By the middle of November, they had sifted through all the evidence and worked out enough: on November 16th, they were able to formally charge all four over the Quebec Barracks bomb attack and applied to the Oberlandesgericht court in Celle in Lower Saxony for a trial date.

Joachim Rzeniecki was once again called to give a statement on behalf of the *BKA*. On February 4th 1992, he faxed a seven page analysis of the IRA's structure and modus operandi in Germany to the Generalbundesanwaltschaft in Karlsruhe, entitled "Erkenntnisse zur Struktur und Arbeitsweise von terroristischen Gewalttätern der "Provisional Irish Republican Army" (PIRA) in der Bundesrepublik Deutschland". The document contained a psychological profile of the make-up of the Active Service Unit:

> *"A group of violent PIRA terrorists should be understood as a social unit, set up for a certain period of time and hermetically sealed to the outside world. The members of the unit deal with each other exclusively on a face-to-face basis and perceive themselves as a unified team, whose sole purpose is to carry out murders and acts of terrorist aggression against British military personnel or property and operate, plan, and organise themselves on the basis of this common goal."*

Rzeniecki explained that the Active Service Unit was self-sufficient as regards the procurement of accommodation, the creation of false documentation, procurement of explosives and firearms and the settlement of payments to achieve this. He also made reference to the unsuccessful efforts of *MI5*'s Operation WARD to recruit informers from the Irish community in Germany and surmised that the ASU did not receive outside help from the Irish community. The ASU had been given clear instructions from the Overseas Department to avoid Irish communities in Germany, mainly due to the information on Operation WARD that had found its way to IRA senior commanders after being stolen from the *BSSO* office at JHQ. Rzeniecki also made clear that it had been relatively easy to track down the ASU in the early summer of 1990 due, in part, to the activities of the "extroverted" Donna Maguire and used her as an example of the Provisional IRA's inability to recruit volunteers discreet enough to carry out operations whilst remaining invisible to the security services and law enforcement.

As Donna Maguire was still on trial in Düsseldorf, the trial began on April 1st, 1993 without the young IRA volunteer from Newry. Donagh O'Kane, Patrick Murray and Pauline Drumm stood in the dock to answer charges of sabotage, espionage and attempted murder. The prosecution case relied on linking all three to apartments rented in the Osnabrück area around the time of the attack, as well as a hire car rented at the same time, that could be traced back to all three, in which traces of the Semtex were found – the same explosives used in the attack. But as with the Düsseldorf case, the trial was going to take a long time and the ASU prepared themselves for a long wait to find out whether or not they were going to get away with it. In the meantime, O'Kane and Drumm – who had become a couple whilst on active service for the IRA – decided to tie the knot and married in prison in Celle on June 23rd.

In the USA, Gerry McGeough was out on bail on gunrunning charges but campaigning for the Republican cause. He appeared at several NORAID functions across the country to talk about the struggle against British occupation in an attempt to maintain the flow of green dollars into Sinn Fein – and therefore IRA coffers. But he was living on borrowed time: the FBI had videotaped his conversations with their agents pretending to be arms dealers. There was nowhere to run and no chance of pretending that he had not been involved: before his trial at the beginning of 1994 he pleaded guilty to all charges in return for a reduction in prison time. He was convicted and sentenced to three years imprisonment by a court in New York and sent to Federal Correction Institution (FCI) Schuylkill in Pennsylvania.

A considerably large amount of prison time was facing Sean Hick, Paul Hughes and Donna Maguire in Düsseldorf, a great deal more than McGeough. Charged with the brutal murder of Major Dillon-Lee in Dortmund, as well as the lesser charge of attempting to blow up Langenhagen Barracks in Hanover, the trio were looking at life imprisonment if convicted. As with the Roermond case however, there was no solid evidence that the trio had carried out the attacks; merely circumstantial evidence that the vehicles and weapons used in the operations had been used in the same time frame by the defendants. The use of conspiratorial apartments - the two safe houses - and false identification were also not conclusive proof that any of the three were actually physically present on Max-Eyth-Strasse in Dortmund on June 2nd or laying bombs outside Langenhagen Barracks on May 4th 1990. In an attempt to secure the just conviction, the prosecution once again called on Professor Paul Wilkinson from the University of St. Andrews in Scotland, who flew in to Düsseldorf to explain to Wolfgang Steffen how the IRA operated – the same tactic that had failed to work in the Netherlands was about to fail again in Germany. The first bad sign was the release on bail in the spring of 1994 of Paul Hughes; the judge decreed on request that the evidence against him was insufficient to hold him any longer.

The trial drew to a close at the beginning of June 1994. Sean Hick,

Paul Hughes and Donna Maguire stood in the dock as Wolfgang Steffen began his summing up on June 9th. The judge made clear that the three were members of a Provisional IRA active service unit sent to the Continent to carry out "random killings" of members of the British forces. However, despite the huge amount of corroborating evidence – the discovery of fingerprints in the safe houses, the presence of Semtex traces in these apartments, the presence of the remainder of the green-handled screwdriver set in the flat in Cäcilienstrasse in Hanover, that exactly matched the screwdrivers found in the getaway car that the police chased through Dortmund on the night of the Dillon-Lee murder, an identical brown balaclava found in the Hanover safe house that matched the one also found in the Mazda found in Bönen on the night on June 2nd, the links to the weapons found in Werl and Heerle – he said:

"The evidence before us is not enough for conviction. Far-reaching doubts remain."

Hick, Hughes and Maguire were found not guilty of the murder of Mike Dillon-Lee and acquitted of involvement in the attack on the British army barracks in Langenhagen. Friends and IRA sympathisers who had flown to Düsseldorf to attend and were sitting in the courts public gallery waved and cheered, and one man gave a clenched fist salute.

Hick's lawyer Rüdiger Decker gave a brief, scornful statement after the verdicts had been announced:

> "In Germany it is not possible to convict people of being members of a foreign terrorist organisation. If you want to have a verdict delivered for a specific crime, you must find the evidence."

That evening, Hick and Hughes made no comment as they arrived in Dublin on an Aer Lingus flight from Düsseldorf. Punches were thrown as cameramen and reporters pursued them through the airport, and the two men were bundled into a waiting car, which was driven off at high speed. Once again in controversial circumstances, the IRA had beaten the justice system. The names of Paul Hughes, Donna Maguire and Sean Hick were added to the long list of Provisional IRA operatives to be unjustly acquitted of murdering innocent people on the European mainland in the name of Irish Republicanism.

Whilst Hick and Hughes regained their freedom, Donna Maguire was sent to the remand centre in Hanover to await her first appearance before the court in Celle on charges of involvement in the 1989 Osnabrück bombing. In the meantime, the inevitable appeal by the prosecution against the acquittals in Düsseldorf fell as usual on deaf ears – the verdicts were upheld on April 26th 1995 by the Bundesgerichtshof, leaving Maguire to concentrate on the next attempt to beat justice. The case against her co-defendants in Celle had been going on for a year already, so Maguire was tried separately from O'Kane, Drumm and Murray and she was driven every Thursday from Hanover to Celle to the Oberlandesgericht to sit alone in the wood-panelled courtroom, accompanied by lawyer Barbara Klawitter, the five judges, the prosecution and the occasional witness. Evidence was presented before presiding judge Dr. Bernd Völckart; a dapper, bearded, academic lawyer who spoke careful, flawless English and always asked for the translation of all evidence to be consecutive, rather than simultaneous, to prevent errors - thus extending the length of the trial even further. The five judges in Maguire's trial – and that of the other three IRA volunteers – listened, nodded, read or gazed into space as expert witnesses detailed the chemical makeup of Semtex, the precise construction of UVBT switching devices or the text of tenancy agreements that Donna Maguire had signed for the holiday homes she had rented for the Active Service Unit in the Reichshof area way back in spring 1989. The court sat once a week and often adjourned after only three to four hours. The two parallel trials dragged on into 1995 before drawing to a close in June, with all sides exhausted from the mammoth proceedings.

On June 28th 1995, Donna Maguire stood before Dr. Volckärt as he pronounced her guilty on charges of attempted murder, as well as explosives offences and sabotage. She was sentenced to nine years imprisonment. Maguire had however been on remand in the Netherlands, Belgium and Germany since June 1990 for her involvement in the IRA's campaign on the European mainland and was released immediately. She flew back the same night from Frankfurt to Dublin with father Malachy, who had been there to hear the verdict. Around 50 supporters were there to greet here carrying a large banner with the words "Failte abhaile Donna – welcome home Donna". Donna Maguire returned to Northern Ireland for the first time in five years.

Two days later, the verdicts were announced in the same court in the trial against Pauline Drumm, Donagh O'Kane and Patrick Murray: on five counts of attempted murder, sabotage and espionage, the three volunteers were found guilty and – whilst immediately released due to two thirds of their sentences already having been served on remand – were sentenced to imprisonment for periods between nine years and ten years, three months.

Maguire, Drumm, O'Kane and Murray thus became the first volunteers to be convicted of carrying out attacks for the Provisional IRA in Germany.

21 HOLIDAY IN SANDHATTEN

During the long years of legal proceedings on the Continent against Maguire, Murray and the O'Kanes and in the USA against Gerry McGeough, back in Northern Ireland the political and military landscape was showing signs of change. In recent years, discussions with the British government via secret channels had been intensified in an attempt to find a solution to the Troubles. Alongside Derry businessman Brendan Duddy, one of the facilitators for the discussions was Father Alec Reid. The Redemptorist priest from Clonard Monastery in West Belfast had been the person who liaised between security forces and the IRA over arrangements for the funerals of Sean Savage, Mairéad Farrell and Dan McCann, and who subsequently administered the last rites to Corporals Wood and Howes after the pair had been murdered in Andersonstown several days later; over several years Father Reid had become a go-between trusted on all sides; the British and Irish governments and the Provisional IRA communicated with each other via the Catholic clergyman. Father Reid had been the person ferrying secret messages between the IRA Executive – the twelve men elected by the IRA membership with responsibility for selecting the seven man Army Council - British Prime Minister John Major and Irish Taoiseach Albert Reynolds over the past few years in an attempt to find a way to break the deadlock and stop the bloodshed. Slowly coming to the realisation that the IRA could not win the war, the alleged head of the IRA Executive Gerry Adams and former IRA Chief of Staff Martin McGuinness made tentatively positive headway in secret negotiations with Reynolds and Major. However, for the majority of 1993, the IRA Army Council were to some extent kept in the dark over the exact nature of the discussions for fear that the military men would veto any deal – Adams and McGuinness wanted to first make the deal and then sell it to the grass roots volunteers, making it harder for the hard-line militarists on the Army Council to dismiss out of hand a potential solution. Adams and McGuinness told the Army Council they were making promises to the British and Irish governments that they had no intention of keeping and that the focus of the IRA's campaign would remain on armed struggle, not political compromise. Several times Adams and McGuinness had to repeat this mantra to the Army Council to allay fears that the IRA was being sold down the river, unilaterally allowing their arms to be decommissioned and giving up the armed struggle; essentially admitting defeat. Worried that their credibility within the IRA was at stake, they continued to approve IRA atrocities that would cause revulsion and horror in the province and beyond.

On Saturday October 13th 1993, in the final stages of a deal with the Irish and British governments being hammered out, the IRA carried out an operation in Protestant West Belfast, allegedly sanctioned by the same IRA leadership that was negotiating an end to hostilities – an operation which would herald the start of a six-week period that would see some of the worst sectarian violence in the whole of the conflict. The IRA had received intelligence that the flat above a fishmongers on the Shankill Road was used on Saturday afternoons as a meeting place by the Inner Council – the leadership of the Loyalist paramilitary UDA. Sensing a chance to decapitate the UDA in one fell swoop, two IRA volunteers – Sean Kelly and Thomas Begley– and a third IRA man, all from the Ardoyne area were dispatched to the Shankill. They drove to the Shankill Road and headed for Frizzell's, which was packed with customers on a Saturday afternoon. The plan was to plant the bomb, whose fuse would be short to allow enough time for customers to escape but not enough time for UDA leader Johnny Adair and the rest of the senior UDA team in the flat above to evacuate. Provisional IRA volunteer Thomas Begley was the man responsible for trimming the fuse wire, planting the bomb and lighting the fuse. As Kelly held the customers at bay from the door of the shop with a handgun, Begley lifted the device over the counter and preparing to run quickly from the shop, lit the fuse. Begley had however made a critical mistake: he had cut the fuse wire far too short. The bomb exploded nearly instantaneously, blowing Begley to pieces and detonating with such force that the whole building collapsed on top of the shop staff and the customers. Nine innocent people, including two schoolgirls, were killed in the blast – Begley's accomplice Sean Kelly lay seriously injured with scores of customers under the rubble. The UDA leadership had finished their meeting early and had already vacated the premises long before the explosion; they were sitting in a pub not far from Frizzell's when the bomb detonated. Not only was the operation a complete disaster for the IRA but the UDA vowed to avenge the deaths of nine innocent Protestants; a spiral of sectarian violence and tit-for-tat actions in which scores of Protestant and Catholic civilians were caught in the crossfire between the IRA and UDA seriously threatened the peace deal. This backdrop forced the IRA into a corner; had they rejected the brokered peace deal, there would have been uproar in the Catholic community who, like the Protestants, were weary from the sheer unbearable level of violence unleashed by the Shankill bomb.

Against or even due to this backdrop, negotiations between the IRA Executive and the British and Irish governments achieved the unthinkable: an agreement that could potentially end the Troubles. A set of principles which affirmed both the right of the people of Ireland to self-determination, and that Northern Ireland would be transferred to the Republic of Ireland from the United Kingdom only if a majority of its population was in favour of such a move were agreed upon. As part of the prospective of the so-called "Irish dimension", the principle of consent was established, that the people of the island of Ireland had the exclusive right to solve the issues between North and South by mutual consent. On December 15th 1993 at the headquarters of the Government of the United Kingdom and residence of British Prime Minister John Major, the so-called Joint Declaration – to become known as the DSD (Downing Street Declaration) - was made. The introductory words set out the intent of both the British and Irish governments:

"This Joint Declaration is a charter for peace and reconciliation in Ireland. Peace is a very simple, but also a very powerful idea, whose time has come. The Joint Declaration provides from everyone's point of view a noble means of establishing the first step towards lasting peace with justice in Ireland. The central idea behind the Peace Declaration is that the problems of Northern Ireland, however deep and intractable, however difficult to reconcile, have to be resolved exclusively by political and democratic means. Its objective is to heal the divisions among the people of Ireland. The Declaration makes it clear that it is for the people of Ireland, North and South, to achieve agreement without outside impediment. The British Government have also declared that they will encourage, enable and facilitate such agreement, and that they will endorse whatever agreement emerges and take the necessary steps to implement it. The language of the Declaration quite clearly makes both Governments persuaders for agreement between the people of Ireland. The dynamic for future progress must reside in the full use of the democratic political process, in the underlying changes in Irish society, North and South, and in our external environment. Peace is the first essential for better relationships on this island. The Joint Declaration is only the first stage in the Peace Process. There will never be a better opportunity. Peace will allow us to develop a new atmosphere of trust and co-operation and to establish a new era of détente, which is the only way forward."

The statement was positive and there were hopes that the province of Ulster was finally moving towards a long-lasting peace. A key element in the peace process would be the implementation of a ceasefire by the IRA; which could only be called by the IRA Army Council. In his book "A Secret History of the IRA", Ed Moloney gives a fascinatingly detailed insight into the internal political wrangling that took place within the IRA from this point onwards: Gerry Adams and Martin McGuinness began several rounds of meetings with the their fellow Provisional military commanders in an attempt to sell them the deal and get them to agree to a halt to the violence. At an Army Council meeting in January 1994 the deal was presented to the military command of the IRA. By that time, the three most influential members on the seven-man council were Northern Commander Slab Murphy, Chief of Staff Kevin McKenna and Quartermaster General Micky McKevitt – all three IRA hard-line military men. All three opposed the Joint Declaration vehemently: the deal was rejected by the Army Council. Gerry Adams did however manage to convince the Army Council not to openly communicate the rejection of the deal and kill the peace process outright; it would be the wrong signal. He suggested that the IRA keep the rejection a secret and to the outside world, particularly to their own community as well as both British and Irish governments, appear to be considering the deal. As Martin McGuinness used the time to travel round the country talking to grass-roots IRA volunteers and explaining the deal to them, Gerry Adams in his Sinn Fein role asked the Joint Declaration parties for clarification of a number of points; the IRA were playing for time. The pair were trying to appear externally as if they were seriously considering approving the deal, at "troop level" and at "military command level" they were saying that they were just stringing the British and Irish governments along to gain more concessions. The internal message was clear: the deal should be rejected out of hand but that everyone should trust Adams and McGuinness: they had a strategy. Understandably few in the IRA had a clue what to think and were openly suspicious that they were being sold up the river: Adams and McGuinness were forced once again to approve IRA operations to show they were serious about continuing the armed struggle. An

IRA sleeper team in England fired mortars at Heathrow Airport on two consecutive days in March, although apparently the attack had been compromised by an agent working for the British government within the IRA – the mortars were "jarked" and the weapons did not work properly; the last thing Adams and McGuinness wanted was a whole load of civilians being killed in England or on the Continent. That would signal the end of the peace process before it had really got started.

However, Adams and McGuinness came under increasing pressure from Irish Taoiseach Albert Reynolds to show that the IRA were not stringing him along. Adams went to the Army Council with the promise of the lifting of the broadcasting ban on Sinn Fein in the British media, which would put Sinn Fein back on some kind of legitimate footing with the rest of the negotiating parties. The Army Council reluctantly agreed to a small show of willingness to budge, and despite the continuing rejection of the deal as such, announced a temporary three-day ceasefire to run from April 6th to 8th 1994. The ceasefire helped to signal to the British and Irish governments that they were seriously considering the terms of the Downing Street Declaration and intense rounds of diplomacy ensued. Finally in August, the IRA could no longer play for time. At the end of August the ruling IRA Army Council met in South Donegal to decide whether to call a permanent ceasefire and complete the deal or kill it by refusing to lower their weapons even one inch. The Army Council convened: present alongside Gerry Adams and Martin McGuinness were Slab Murphy, Pat Doherty, Joe Cahill, Sean Hughes and Kevin McKenna, all of whom were allowed to vote. They were joined by Micky McKevitt and Gerry Kelly. The two farmers - Chief of Staff Kevin McKenna and Slab Murphy – did not accept the ceasefire, with McKenna voting against, and Murphy abstaining. McKevitt was also against the ceasefire but did not have voting rights. On the other side, Gerry Kelly equally had no official say in proceedings but supported the ceasefire; the votes that counted were cast by Adams, McGuinness, Doherty, Cahill and Hughes. By a count of five to one, the IRA leadership approved a permanent ceasefire; on August 31st 1994, the Provisional IRA announced it was calling an immediate cessation of all military operations – a historic moment in the Troubles.

From then, things started to move very quickly: a week later, Gerry Adams and Albert Reynolds met publicly in Dublin for the first time and took part in an historic handshake – the first sign that the IRA and Sinn Fein were being treated as legitimate partners in the peace process. Ten days later on September 16th, the British government kept the first promise of their side of the deal: British Prime Minister John Major rescinded the broadcasting ban on Gerry Adams and Sinn Fein. Nevertheless there were considerable activities behind the scenes to prevent Gerry Adams from travelling to the USA to allay US Republican fears that Adams was selling out the movement. British officials pleaded to US authorities that Adams was still a terrorist and wary of his motives, asked the Americans to deny him a visa. The US however under direct instruction from President Bill Clinton, issued the visa at the last moment and Adams flew to the USA on September 24th for a two-week tour of cities where Republican sympathisers were focussed. The next big step in the peace process was made by the Loyalist paramilitaries, who on October 13th issued a joint statement that matched that of the IRA: they declared their own ceasefire to allow the peace process to continue. Within six weeks, the conflict between Catholic and Protestant, Republicans and Loyalists had been brought to an end – there was hope for a bright, non-sectarian, peaceful future for Northern Ireland.

December saw the first official talks between Sinn Fein and Great Britain – although discussions had been going on via secret back channels for decades between Martin McGuinness on behalf of the IRA and senior civil servant Michael Oatley on behalf of the Secret Intelligence Service (*MI6*) – and it was McGuinness who led the Sinn Fein delegation to the first meeting at Stormont, joined by Gerry

Adams and his assistant former IRA volunteer Siobhán O'Hanlon. The talks were positive enough for the British to release nine IRA prisoners just before Christmas in a sign of good faith. Early in the new year, there was a further sign that the Troubles were drawing to an end: the British Army stopped daytime patrols in Belfast on January 12th 1995, two months later they also stopped patrolling at night as well. Gerry Adams flew to the US once more and was received by US president Bill Clinton in Washington DC – where in May Adams also met the British Secretary of State for Northern Ireland Sir Patrick Mayhew for talks. Things were going well, although the main sticking point of discussions was the issue of decommissioning. Sinn Fein and the IRA – particularly the Army Council – were not prepared to have their arms unilaterally destroyed before they had achieved their primary objective: the removal of British troops from Irish soil for once and for all. This issue alone was preventing the final agreement, formed on the basis of the Joint Declaration and framework document and marking the official end to the Troubles, from being signed. And it was to contribute to the breakdown of talks between London and Dublin; Albert Reynolds had in the meantime been replaced as Taoiseach by John Bruton, who against the background of faltering talks, rising sectarian tensions through the summer marching season in Londonderry and Portadown and the refusal of the IRA to commit to decommissioning their weapons, cancelled a September 1995 summit with John Major at the last minute. By November 27th, the Irish and British governments were no longer talking to each other. Senator George Mitchell was brought in from the US to moderate and conciliate and try to find a way to defuse the decommissioning row. Meanwhile in South Armagh and Belfast, IRA Army Council members were growing tired of the negotiations and becoming ever more suspicious of Adams and McGuinness motives; they surmised that the pair wanted to be seen as the heroes of the peace process, and only too willing to concede that the IRA had been defeated in order to give up their arms; effectively a surrender. As December 1995 ticked by, with no advance in negotiations to the benefit of the

IRA, Slab Murphy, Kevin McKenna, Sean Hughes and Michael McKevitt put pressure on the Sinn Fein / IRA negotiators to break the ceasefire. Time was running out for Adams, McGuinness and the peace process.

Early January 1996. Toby Harnden's ground-breaking analysis of the IRA in South Armagh, "Bandit Country", details the Brigades involvement in the IRA's preparation for recommencing hostilities. Two hundred yards over the border from South Armagh into County Monaghan, a band of volunteers from the Provisional IRA South Armagh Brigade met in a cattle shed in the dead of night. They had been called there by "The Surgeon" and Micksey Martin, who in turn had been instructed by Slab Murphy to prepare for the resumption of military operations. Alongside Hughes and Martin were members of the feared South Armagh sniper team, veteran IRA activists as well as the younger brother of 'The Surgeon' and ex-Continental Europe ASU member, Paul Hughes. The team set to work grinding down bags of agricultural ammonium nitrate fertiliser into a fine powder, mixing it together with bags of icing sugar and pouring the mixture into sacks. Before long, hundreds of sacks of fertiliser mixture had been filled, some three tons.

One of the team, 27 year old Seamus McArdle, had been chosen by Hughes, Martin and Murphy to drive a white transporter van from the Republic up to Belfast Ferry Terminal on January 15th and cross the Irish Sea to the west coast of Scotland. From Stranraer, he drove the empty transporter down to Carlisle where he stayed overnight at a motel. He had not been checked or followed and so returned the following day to South Armagh in the white transporter to report that the dummy run had been a complete success. The operation could go ahead as planned by Slab Murphy and Sean Hughes way back in November and December the previous year, when the South Armagh military men had decided that the political manoeuvring was getting nowhere. The previously empty transporter van was loaded with the three tons of fertiliser mixture, supplemented by

Semtex and rigged up to detonators, ready for transport back to England. On Wednesday February 7th, McArdle and another volunteer, accompanied by further South Armagh volunteers driving ahead in a scout car, drove the transporter with its deadly payload back to Scotland via the Belfast-Stranraer ferry and drove to Carlisle. This time instead of heading back the next day, they continued to the outskirts of London where they spent the night. The following day, they completed the final part of their journey. On Friday February 9th 1996, the men drove the short distance from Essex to East London, parking the transporter on Marsh Wall, Canary Wharf, a few metres away from South Quay station just after 5pm. McArdle primed the bomb and the two men fled on foot. At 5.30pm, the South Armagh Brigade made a series of telephone warning calls to media establishments including the Irish News and the state TV broadcaster of the Republic of Ireland RTE, using a recognised IRA code word – "Kerrygold – like the butter". Gerry Adams himself was allegedly informed by the Army Council of the impending attack and telephoned Anthony Lake, the US National Security Advisor to President Bill Clinton, to warn him that the ceasefire was about to end. The warnings were communicated to the Metropolitan Police at Scotland Yard but there was confusion and conflicting reports as to the exact location of the transporter. Finally shortly before 7pm, as the timer on the bomb was slowly ticking down, officers found the transporter and hurriedly tried to evacuate the area. There was not enough time to warn everybody. At 6:59pm, a massive blue flash lit up the sky as the ceasefire ended and the three-ton truck bomb detonated in the heart of the Docklands district. Debris was spread over a wide area and the force of the explosion left a ten metre wide, three metre deep crater in the road, causing £ 150 million of damage to some of London's most prestigious commercial property. Worse: over one hundred people who had not been evacuated in time were seriously injured and two men – newsagent Inam Bashir and his assistant John Jefferies were caught in the blast and died of their injuries.

Sinn Fein president Gerry Adams blamed everyone but the IRA for the breakdown in the ceasefire:

> *"An unprecedented opportunity for peace has foundered on the refusal of the British government and Unionist leaders to enter into dialogue and substantive negotiations"*

The Provisional IRA was back in business and in a bad mood.

As the England Department was reactivated and began planning further operations on the UK mainland, it was not long before the Overseas Department, dormant since the arrests of the Antwerp ASU in December 1990, also slowly began to assess its options. The likelihood was that the resumption of military operations by the IRA would either kill the peace process stone dead; or at least put pressure on the British government to accede to IRA demands to take the issue of weapons decommissioning off the table, meaning that the Overseas Department would need to start looking for possible targets on the Continent to communicate to the British that they meant business, that things were going to go back to the way they were before the start of the peace process: a return to the bad old days. Dessie Grew, Sean Savage, Mairéad Farrell, Dan McCann were all dead; Paddy Fox and Dermot Quinn were serving long sentences in prison in Northern Ireland; Donna Maguire, Patrick Murray, Donagh O'Kane and Pauline Drumm had all been convicted of terrorist offences in Germany and were too high-profile to be used; Gerard Harte, Sean Hick and Paul Hughes had escaped conviction in the Netherlands and Germany but also too well-known to be used; Martin Conlon was still an active volunteer in the South Armagh Brigade but was wanted by Dutch and German authorities for his part in the attacks in Continental Europe in 1989 and 1990; Gerry McGeough was languishing in a US state prison; Gerry Hanratty had been released from prison in Northern Ireland in 1995 but had been sent to the UK by the England Department to head up an ASU that was involved in operations there; the Antwerp ASU had been convicted in Belgium and were also of no use. The Overseas Department was faced with creating a brand new team with no European experience, with the obvious problems this might cause. Fortunately for the Overseas Department, an unlikely opportunity and solution presented itself in the form of Michael "Dixie" Dickson.

Dickson had moved from Scotland to London at the end of the 1980s but returned in May 1990 to his native Port Glasgow. In early 1992 he had met and married Ann O'Driscoll, a Roman Catholic from Dundalk, and had reason to travel over the Irish Sea to visit the IRA stronghold on a regular basis. Keeping in touch with Republican contacts in the North, he also appeared every marching season in South Armagh and became heavily involved in protests against the Orange Order marches in Portadown that spilled over into violence in the summer of 1995 during the ceasefire. Finally, Dickson moved from Scotland to Belfast and then on to Portadown: by early 1996, he was a fully-fledged IRA volunteer. The Overseas Department arranged to meet him in Dundalk, telling him to stay away from the marches and to avoid being seen in Portadown with known Republicans; he should not appear on the radar of the security forces, for they had a job for him.

At the meeting, representatives from the Overseas Department asked him all he knew about the British military in Germany. They were keen to find out if and how the British Army could be targeted in Germany. Dickson and the other IRA men spent the night assessing every possible angle and idea, the security implications, where to be based, how to assemble the weapons needed, how to justify an attack afterwards. Dickson explains that the Overseas Department were initially unconvinced:

> "...they believed that attacking a barracks would only have the effect of raising security levels – something that in the end only concerned soldiers. Instead I

argued that there was something else; we had to make sure that every British barracks was besieged as in the Six Counties...for me the aim was to ensure that even in Germany [the soldiers] were scared, so that the barracks had very high security controls and that families lived in terror, so even local traders would have preferred the British to leave."

The Overseas Department concurred with Dickson's strategy and in April 1996, two months after the South Quay bomb, he was sent to Germany on a reconnaissance mission. Travelling with another volunteer, the pair travelled south to the port of Rosslare, from where they spent the ferry crossing to Cherbourg making a list of places to visit. They alighted at Cherbourg and walked into the town to allow them to spot if they were being followed. From Cherbourg railway station they took a slow train to Paris, and from there a fast train to Munich.

Booking into a guesthouse, they first had lunch before renting a car and driving south to Oberstdorf in the southern Allgäu region, on the border with Austria. There, Dickson took his companion around a housing complex which Army soldiers used as weekend retreats and pointed out the absolute lack of security. The following day, they headed back up through Germany and visited around a dozen Army bases, discussing each time the potential each location had as a target – following in the footsteps of several other IRA reconnaissance teams who had carried out the same reconnaissance work over the past few years. After visits to Hamelin and Bielefeld, they took a brief look around Dixie's old base and the target of the "FERMDOWN" ASU in June 1989 – Quebec Barracks in Osnabrück. From there, the IRA men travelled to Oldenburg in the north west of Germany; about forty-five kilometres west of Bremen and around an hour's drive from Osnabrück: there they found a holiday home in Sandhatten, just south of Oldenburg. It fulfilled all the requirements of a safe house from which to plan an attack: three large bedrooms to house the ASU members, a large garage in which weapons and vehicles could be prepared out of sight, close to a road but in a quiet, secluded wooded area. Dixie signed a rental contract in his own name, paid the deposit for two weeks occupancy from June 14th to June 28th and the pair returned to Dublin via Munich the following day. They were met by the same men from the Overseas Department, who told them that the Army Council was going to meet the next day: Dickson sat down to compile a report of the trip and how the IRA should carry out an attack:

> *"What came out was a proposal of coordinated attack between the south and north of Germany. A commando of two men in the north would place explosives in rucksacks inside a barracks at an easily accessible point – within the hydraulic system of a nightclub attended by officers and soldiers, and at the same time make a call to claim the presence of weapons in a residential neighbourhood full of English soldiers. Another commando in the south of the country would have to place a truck loaded with explosives near one of the residences used by the military on a trip, and then run along the highway to Austria. All the bombs were meant to explode by timer, to allow the volunteers time to escape."*

The aim of the parallel attack was many-fold: undermine the feeling of security by calling in fake bomb threats, the device detonating in the nightclub would severely curtail the leisure activities of military personnel in the surrounding German towns, whilst a bomb targeting soldiers in a residential district would make civilians think twice about integrating the military in their local town. The report was submitted: the Army Council responded incredulously and asked if Dickson "wanted a war to break out". The potential extent of civilian loss of life was far too high; the IRA would have scored a very costly own-goal. Dickson was disappointed at the reaction of senior commanders and returned to Portadown.

However a month later, the Overseas Department got back in touch; an operation in Germany had been approved, although the nightclub bomb had been discarded from the report that Dickson had submitted. Dickson travelled to Dundalk at the end of May, where he met four other IRA volunteers in an anonymous house on the outskirts of the town: a 27 year old member of the Belfast Brigade and part-time actor James Corry from the New Lodge area of the city, a further unnamed female volunteer, as well as the 25-year old daughter of long-time Republican activist Bernadette Devlin-McAliskey, Róisín McAliskey from Coalisland, Co. Tyrone. The unnamed fourth man was the most senior volunteer present and took charge of the proceedings.

The senior IRA man gave little away but merely told them they had been selected to carry out an operation - he gave them the opportunity to leave should they no longer be available. Nobody took up the offer; the senior IRA man sent them away and told them to come back for a second meeting a week later, where they were told the newly formed Active Service Unit would need to be away in Europe for a couple of weeks to carry out the operation; again he gave them the chance to pull out. Again no one chose to leave; the ASU was ready. Dickson was given money to rent a car, buy tickets for the ferry to France and pay the outstanding balance of the rental agreement on the holiday home in Sandhatten. Together with Corry and the unnamed female volunteer, Dickson travelled across the Channel and drove to Oldenburg to meet the owner of the Sandhatten holiday home, Manfred Schmidt. Paying Schmidt and taking possession of the keys, Dickson told him that he had to go and pick up the rest of the people who would be spending the holiday with them from France, and leave the Corry's at the house. The following day, Dickson went to Bremen, from where he got the night train to Paris, and from there travelled on to Le Havre. At the port, Dickson awaited arrivals from Ireland: McAliskey, along with three other volunteers, arrived in a Ford Transit, having departed from Cork the previous evening; in the side panels of the Transit van, one of the volunteers had stashed two automatic weapons. Driving in the direction of Paris, Dickson let one of the men out of the vehicle in the open countryside, his delivery task completed; Dickson, the two men and McAliskey continued on to Munich and from there, back up to the house at Sandhatten to rendezvous with James Corry and the female volunteer.

The six-strong ASU still did not know what the plan was and kicked around the holiday home, waiting to hear what exactly they were supposed to be doing. Dickson called contacts back in Northern Ireland and was told to sit tight for a week as the IRA were having difficulty planning how to get the explosives and material needed to carry out the attack and the senior IRA man, the manager of the operation, still needed to travel over to coordinate with the team – the first sign that things were not going to plan. It also did not bode well that not only had various members of the team met Manfred Schmidt, but also his wife and daughter, who regularly came to the house to feed the rabbits and chickens: three witnesses who would likely be able to identify Dickson and members of the ASU should suspicion of their involvement in an IRA attack arise. The day after taking over the holiday home in Sandhatten, there had been a further blow: Gerry Hanratty, and the ASU sent to mainland Britain by the England Department, succeeded in detonating a huge 1,500 kilogramme truck bomb on Corporation Row, right outside the Arndale shopping centre in the heart of Manchester. Made by the same South Armagh team directed by Sean Hughes, Micksey Martin and Slab Murphy, it was a spectacular follow-up to the Docklands bomb and one that injured 212 people and caused nearly a million pounds worth of damage. The UK was hosting the Euro '96 football tournament and security services were jittery enough already; the bomb put them and subsequently law enforcement agencies across Europe on full alert for further IRA attacks; bad news for the Sandhatten ASU, sitting in the middle of Germany with a Ford

Transit van with false number plates, in broad daylight, with no explosives.

The ASU decided to keep themselves busy; they went to a garden centre where they bought two large barrels and spades; in the middle of the night Dickson and two of the other volunteers dug a weapons hide in a nearby wood. Finally the plan was communicated to them; Two of the volunteers and McAliskey were to meet up with a further group of IRA volunteers at a safe house on the Dutch border to pick up a truckload of material to make a makeshift mortar battery; the manager of the operation was also sitting on the Dutch border with the explosives to make the MK15 mortars themselves. The attack in Bavaria had meanwhile been abandoned, so he was going to be delivering too much explosive material. He needed to be relieved of all the explosives, the superfluous amounts to be discreetly disposed of; the truck containing material to make the mortar battery picked up from the other team on the border. The team on the border were all well-known IRA operatives who were supposed to be the ones carrying out the attack, but who all had previous convictions; if they tried to rent a vehicle themselves, they would likely be immediately arrested. Exasperated at a further problem to surmount, Dickson travelled to Cologne and rented another Ford Transit van, drove back to Sandhatten pick up McAliskey and two male volunteers, drove to the border to meet both the senior IRA man and the team arriving from Ireland and transferred the materials from one Transit to the other. The explosives, the rockets, the mortar tubes were all driven back to Sandhatten in one van; the team that had originally been slated to carry out the attack divulged the full plan to Dickson's team; to fire off a salvo of mortars aimed at Quebec Barracks, hitting an accommodation block and killing as many soldiers as possible.

Returning to Sandhatten, the team parked the van in the garage, closed the door and armed with AK-47s took it in turns to guard the valuable contents of the garage. The rest of the team set about tidying and cleaning the holiday home, removing bed sheets and scrubbing walls to remove all traces of DNA and fingerprints. The next morning, June 28th, the operation was ready to be carried out. The team worked through the day to modify the van and construct the mortar tubes, made out of empty red propane gas cylinders: loading the rockets into the tubes, fixing the baseplate to the flatbed floor of the Transit van, preparing the triggers, calculating the inclination angle of the tubes, checking the detonators and connecting the whole shebang to the time-power-unit - a simple wooden box nearly identical to the device used in the Docklands bomb, with a pin that, once removed, triggered the countdown timer. In addition, an explosive charge was primed that would blow up the van to destroy any trace of evidence. The mortars loaded and ready and the launch platform covered from sight by a thick tarpaulin, Dickson and another volunteer then disassembled the AK-47s, covered them with a thin layer of butter, wrapped them in towels and placed them in plastic bags, before hiding the weapons in the underground barrels. Returning to the holiday home, there was a final check that everyone knew what their role was: James Corry was to drive the Ford Transit van equipped with the launch tubes, Dickson was to drive ahead; and the pair were to meet one of the other volunteers, a further advance scout, at a prearranged meeting point at a gas station. The rest of the ASU were to begin their escape back to Ireland via different routes. According to Dickson, the journey to Osnabrück was fraught with problems:

> *"After ten minutes of travel it was already clear that the tarpaulin was useless; it flattered about, did not cover anything and we were on a motorway at risk of being stopped by the police – the van driver didn't have a license on him. I passed the van and stopped it, then went to a service station and bought two more tarps that didn't really work either. All of this and we were late, I was afraid that the others would think we had been arrested. We set off going no more than 50*

kilometres an hour, because the van didn't have a mirror and so was not able to overtake. I was driving and one of the other guys was in front of me in another car. I had the constant worry that the craftsmanship of the explosives might end up causing serious problems...fortunately everything went smoothly, we got to the pre-agreed meeting point where I saw the other vehicles parked."

The ASU finally arrived at a side entrance to Quebec Barracks at around 18:15. The Transit van and the mortar tubes were pointed in the direction of the Mess accommodation block where around 150 soldiers were housed. Corry removed the pin on the time-power-unit, starting the 35-minute countdown timer and made his escape, along with Dickson and the other IRA man. At 18:50 the timer triggered the detonators and launched the three mortars at the Mess; two of the mortars failed to explode and landed harmlessly, failing to clear the perimeter fence of the base, however the third exploded close to a petrol pump at a nearby fuel depot in the barracks. Thankfully it was a close call; the fuel depot was not directly hit and no fire broke out. The Roman Catholic church on the base was damaged, and several cars nearby were demolished in the blast, including the brand new official car of Brigadier Richard Dannatt, who later wryly commented, "I wasn't keen on it anyway". There were no injuries amongst the 150 soldiers in the Mess at the time, but the cost of the damage was later estimated at around €100,000.

Dickson, Corry, McAliskey and the rest of the Active Service Unit escaped back to Ireland without being arrested but the price was high. For not only did the mortars fail to reach their targets or cause any significant physical damage, the explosive charge in the van failed to detonate, leaving behind masses of forensic evidence to be collected, analysed and acted upon by the *Bundeskriminalamt*, Royal Military Police and Interpol. Very quickly, Dickson was identified as the ringleader, after leaving a trail of paperwork behind him; the *BKA* team in Meckenheim near Bonn were able to identify "Mark" and "Beth" as Jim Corry and Róisín McAliskey. Warrants were issued for their arrest.

Politically as well as operationally, the Provisional IRA's first attack in Continental Europe for six years proved to be another in a long line of disasters for the Provos and the Overseas Department. The response of the British and Irish governments was one of scorn. The Irish Deputy Prime Minister condemned the attack.

> "An inane act of violence which will serve no purpose and has no contribution to make to the search for peace."

To make matters worse for the IRA Army Council, the hand of Martin McGuinness and Gerry Adams in the negotiations for peace was also somewhat strengthened, as the British and Irish governments nevertheless refused to close the door on Sinn Fein; a strong signal that no matter what attacks The Overseas Department, Slab Murphy, Sean Hughes and the rest of the Army Council approved in an attempt to block the road to peace, the British and Irish were confident that Adams and McGuinness were the men who would eventually be able to convince the IRA to end the armed struggle for Irish unity. By the summer of the following year, 1997, the peace process reached an important milestone. Negotiations on plans for the future of Northern Ireland advanced to the point that Sinn Fein urged the IRA to call a truce. In quick response the Provisional IRA Army Council agreed to hold a secret vote on the terms of a declaration that would agree to a ceasefire and decommissioning of weapons. As with the ceasefire called in 1994, it was a close run thing. The leadership was split roughly 50/50 on whether to put the deal offered to them to the wider IRA membership or reject it out of hand. Adams and McGuinness lobbied strongly for acceptance and peace; hardliners such as Quartermaster General Mickey McKevitt lobbied for a continuation of the armed struggle. In July 1997, the votes were cast: the peace lobby won the day by one solitary vote. The terms of the deal were agreed to, pending acceptance by the grass roots membership. On July 19th 1997, the Provisional IRA issued a surprise public statement.

> *"We have ordered the unequivocal restoration of the ceasefire of August 1994. All IRA units have been instructed accordingly."*

The terms of the deal were put to the IRA membership in a secret convention in October 1997 in Falcarragh, Co. Donegal. Opinion was extremely divided; the hard-line faction around Quartermaster General Mickey McKevitt and Director of Training Seamus McGrane dramatically stormed out of the meeting and wanted no further part in the peace process; they vowed to continue the armed struggle and immediately began to make plans to form a new radical splinter group, the Real IRA. With the hard-line faction gone, Adams and McGuinness put the peace deal to the vote and strongly recommended that the terms be accepted. The membership of the Provisional IRA concurred.

On Good Friday, April 10th 1998, the British and Irish governments, and the political parties of Northern Ireland, including Gerry Adams and Martin McGuinness leading the Sinn Fein delegation and accompanied by - amongst others - Siobhan O'Hanlon, took a further step towards making the dream of an end to "The Troubles" a reality. In a ceremony at Stormont Castle, all were signatories to The Belfast Agreement - also known as the Good Friday Agreement or GFA – the multi-party agreement that would prove to be the document that would herald the beginning of the end to the conflict in Northern Ireland.

22 EPILOGUE

As I start to write this epilogue, it has been over 20 years since the Good Friday Agreement (GFA) was signed; since 1998, a relative peace has reigned over Northern Ireland. Several minor – and major – incidents involving dissident Republican terrorists have at times threatened this peace – several of these ex-Provisional IRA men and women opposed to the peace deal are some of those IRA volunteers involved in the murder of innocent victims on the European mainland in the name of a united Ireland. These dissident Republicans (DR) operate under various groupings, the most predominant being the New IRA, responsible for the death of journalist Lyra McKee in early 2019, a car bomb that exploded in Londonderry a few weeks earlier and most recently a failed car bomb attack on a senior PSNI officer in East Belfast just two weeks ago as I write. Some of the ex-IRA operatives and commanders are however fully behind the GFA and have either walked away from violence, or actively tried to rein in these dissident factions in an attempt to stop the sporadic outbreaks of violence. Some are now in government and despised by the dissidents they regularly condemn, who have accused them of betraying the Republican cause and putting power over principles. Some of the actors in this book have since passed away; some peacefully, some violently. Most of those incarcerated for terrorist offences have been released from prison under the terms of the Good Friday Agreement, yet some have been unable to come to terms with the end of "The Troubles" and have been convicted of new offences, returning to prison. Some remain on the run.

After his arrest in Düsseldorf in 1991, the man who planted a bomb outside the Globe Cinema at JHQ in 1973, Jim McCann, served around half of the 42 month sentence for narcotics offences he received before moving to the Netherlands where he was involved in scams and financial frauds involving millions of Euros. His drug smuggling activities were partly depicted in the book and film of the life story of Howard Marks "Mr. Nice". He is still wanted for financial crimes in the Netherlands and is on the run, currently living in the south of France.

Maze escaper Tony McAllister, who was involved in the IRA campaign in Germany from 1978 to 1981 went on the run to the Continent after being part of the escape from HMP Maze in 1983. He lived abroad under an assumed identity and started a new life, marrying and having children - McAllister died peacefully of natural causes in 2005.

In 1986, one of the other key members of the Provisional IRA's European ASU in the late 1970s and early 1980s, Belfast Brigade member Patrick Magee, was handed down eight-life sentences for his role in the Brighton bombing two years earlier. Whilst in prison, Magee studied for a PhD examining the representation of Irish Republicans in fiction about "The Troubles" which was later released as a book entitled "Gangsters or Guerrillas?" After marrying for a second time whilst in prison, he was released to much controversy in 1999 under the terms of the Good Friday Agreement after having served 14 years – the Home Office attempted to block his remission, but the attempt was overturned by the High Court. Magee continues to defend his role in the Brighton bombing but has expressed remorse for the loss of life – he has struck up an unlikely friendship with the daughter of victim Sir Anthony Berry, after meeting up in 2000 in an effort to achieve public reconciliation and has taken part in several panels and events with Jo Berry discussing the conflict and the nature of their relationship. He is shortly to release his memoirs entitled "Where Grieving Begins", with a foreword from Jo.

Rita O'Hare remains a fugitive from justice in Great Britain and Northern Ireland. She is still officially wanted for the attempted murder of a British Army officer in Belfast in 1971, having skipped her trial in 1972 and successfully fighting two extradition attempts. She was not a recipient of an OTR letter as part of the 'On The Run' scheme, whereby a number of suspected IRA and Loyalist paramilitary members received letters from the British Government, exempting them from prosecution for crimes committed during "The Troubles". In 2014, Sinn Fein enquired as to whether O'Hare was still being sought by the British authorities: Britain confirmed that she was. After returning from active service with the Provisional IRA in the early 1980s, she became the editor of Dublin-based Republican newspaper An Phoblacht, before succeeding Danny Morrison as the Director of Publicity of Sinn Fein (and the Provisional IRA) in 1990 after Morrison's arrest. She relinquished her Sinn Fein post in 1998 but continued to be a prominent figure in the party, became General Secretary in 2007. Two years later she became Party Treasurer. She now lives in the United States and for the last two decades has acted as Sinn Fein's senior representative in Washington DC, lobbying on behalf of the Republican movement and enjoying close ties with ex-presidents Barack Obama and Bill Clinton. She is planning to leave the US and move back to Dublin.

Another who moved into politics was Gerry Kelly. After the arrest of Hick, Harte, Maguire and Hughes in Europe 1990, Kelly became openly involved in politics for Sinn Fein, whilst, according to many sources, secretly remaining a member of the Provisional IRA's Army Council. Together with Martin McGuinness, Kelly was part of the delegation that held secret talks with the British government on finding a peaceful solution to "The Troubles" in the lead-up to the Good Friday Agreement. In June 1998 he was elected as the MLA for Belfast North in the newly established Northern Irish Assembly, a position he still holds today. Kelly currently also acts as Sinn Fein's Spokesman for Policing and Justice and is a member of the Northern Ireland Policing Board, which oversees the Police Service of Northern Ireland (PSNI).

After his extradition from the Netherlands to Northern Ireland in 1986 to serve the rest of his prison sentence, Bik McFarlane was released on parole in 1997 as part of the prisoner releases agreed in the negotiations leading up to the Good Friday Agreement. He had already become the longest serving prisoner in HMP Maze in 1993. In 1998 however he was charged over his involvement in the kidnapping of Don Tidey, but after a lengthy legal wrangle, the case only came to court in 2008. The case against him however collapsed almost immediately as important Garda evidence was declared inadmissible. He lives openly in Belfast, is a member of *Coiste na n-Iarchimi*, a welfare organisation for Republican ex-prisoners, and also a musician, appearing both with his band Tuan and as a solo performer in the Republican bars of West Belfast.

William "Blue" Kelly, arrested together with Gerry Kelly and Bik McFarlane in Amsterdam in 1986, was released and returned to Northern Ireland, where he became politically active for Sinn Fein. He was a proponent of the Good Friday Agreement and spoke vociferously in support of the GFA at many meetings in the Republican community on behalf of Sinn Fein. "Blue" died in 2009 in Belfast; Gerry Kelly gave the oration at his funeral.

Gerry McGeough was released from prison in the USA in 1996 and deported back to the Republic of Ireland, settling first in Dublin. McGeough was still wanted by the RUC in Northern Ireland for the attempted murder of Sammy Brush in 1981 and thus remained in the Republic for several years to avoid arrest. After a stint as a teacher, the avowed Republican worked as a journalist for the magazines "The Irish Family" and "The Hibernian". After the turn of the millennium, and in the face of the controversial OTR scheme, McGeough decided to risk arrest and return to live in his native Co. Tyrone. In 2003, he made an enquiry to ex-IRA colleague Gerry Kelly to ask if he was himself on the OTR list, to which Kelly as member of Stormont had access. The Northern Ireland Office had previously informed Kelly of a list of six ex-IRA volunteers exempt from the

OTR scheme and who would be arrested on sight in Northern Ireland. It is unlikely that Kelly advised McGeough of this fact – McGeough had left Sinn Fein and was opposed to the peace deal that Kelly, McGuinness and Adams had negotiated - Kelly allegedly saw a chance to have one of the dissident thorns in the side of the new peaceful and politically engaged Republican movement and passed on the current address of McGeough to the authorities, who in 2007, subsequently reopened the investigation in the Aughnacloy attempted murder. In March 2007, McGeough stood as an independent candidate in the Northern Irish elections, running against a Sinn Fein candidate in Fermanagh & Tyrone. As he himself cast his vote on the day of the election, the RUC arrested McGeough as he left the polling station. He was granted bail but, after a protracted court trial, he was found guilty of the attempted murder of Sammy Brush, possession of two firearms with intent and two counts of membership of the Provisional IRA. In April 2011 he was sentenced to twenty years imprisonment for these crimes. After serving only around two years of his sentence, he was released under the terms of the Good Friday Agreement in 2013, which allowed for expedited release of prisoners charged with paramilitary offences. He returned to Dungannon, where he runs a farm and remains a staunch opponent of the Good Friday Agreement.

His co-defendant in the Düsseldorf trial Gerry Hanratty had been released from prison during the first IRA ceasefire between 1994 and 1996. He had returned to active service and had been involved in the Docklands and Manchester bombings; together with several other volunteers, he planned another IRA spectacular. The Active Service Unit based in South London and Birmingham - comprising Martin Murphy, Eoin Morrow, Donal Gannon, Clive Brampton, Patrick Martin and Francis Rafferty, as well as former US marine and convicted IRA man John Crawley – intended to blow up several electricity substations in the South East of England at the same time on July 22nd, 1996, thus causing a blackout and traffic chaos in the capital and home counties. The Security Service received advance warning of the plan, launching Operation AIRLINES. *MI5* placed the ASU under surveillance, following the volunteers on their reconnaissance tour of the electricity substations and watched as they prepared the devices to be used in the attacks. On July 15th, intelligence operatives and anti-terrorist police raided three addresses in Tooting, South London and Birmingham, arresting the ASU. Further information led the authorities to a lockup garage in Wimbledon, where police recovered 37 separate time-power-units, ladders, bolt-cutters and a vast array of false identification papers. Detectives were frustrated not to have located the actual explosives despite a search of a further 7,000 lockups but had enough evidence to convict Hanratty and the rest of the team: a year later, at the trial at the Old Bailey, Hanratty was sentenced to 35 years imprisonment. He spent 18 months in jail in England before being repatriated to Ireland, where he was held in Portlaoise and became the OC of the Provisional prisoners held there. Gerry Hanratty was released under the terms of the Good Friday Agreement and has since lived in Ireland with the occasional further brush with the law - in 2004, he was fined over €17,000 for beating up a former Sinn Fein politician in Co. Wexford.

Following his arrest in Belgium and the extradition affair which saw him return to the Republic of Ireland in late 1988, the man who served as the IRA's quartermaster in Europe, the controversial figure of Father Patrick Ryan awaited the decision of the Irish authorities about what to do with him next. In the meantime, Ryan decided to stand for election in the European Parliament elections in summer 1989, standing as an independent candidate in Munster but with the support of Sinn Fein. He failed to be elected but garnered over 30,000 votes. Ryan continued to help the IRA from Ireland, assisting in drug smuggling operations ran by the Provos to help finance their campaign. Now retired aged 89, the man still known in Republican circles as "The Padre" lives in his native Roscommon. In an interview for the BBC in 2019, he admitted his IRA role and referring to the bombing of the Grand Hotel in Brighton in 1984, he stated his only regret was

> *"I wasn't even more effective...I would have liked to have been more effective, but we didn't do too badly"*

Most of the other members of the Active Service Unit involved in the Gibraltar operation in 1988 have since passed away. After being released from prison for terrorist offences for a final time, Peter Rooney left the IRA. He later went on to study silversmithing and jewellery at the University of Ulster and then pursued a postgraduate degree in Applied Arts. He subsequently became a noted visual artist, focussing on pieces on the theme of "The Troubles". Commissioned Rooney works are dotted around Northern Ireland, including the stained-glass window of Derry-Londonderry's Guildhall commemorating Bloody Sunday. In the past two years, "Pepe" Rooney fought a long battle with cancer but died in April 2019 at his home in West Belfast. A large number of ex-Provisional IRA leaders attended his funeral at Milltown Cemetery on May 1st, including Gerry Kelly and to some controversy, three former comrades from the Belfast Brigade appeared over the coffin with handguns to fire the traditional three volley salute afforded to IRA volunteers, the first time for several years this tradition had been carried out in public.

His former comrade Siobhán O'Hanlon carried out long and dedicated service as Gerry Adams personal assistant and was an architect of the 'On The Run' (OTR) letter scheme negotiated as a side deal part of the Good Friday Agreement with Downing Street Chief of Staff Jonathan Powell. One of the first people to be allowed to return to Northern Ireland under the OTR scheme was another alleged member of the original Gibraltar ASU, Eibhlin Glenholmes: Siobhan O'Hanlon drove to the Republic of Ireland herself to pick up her former Belfast Brigade comrade and drove her back over the border. In 2002, O'Hanlon was diagnosed with breast cancer – and spent the next three and half years as an activist, raising awareness and drawing attention to the availability of mobile breast screening units. Despite treatment, she lost her battle with cancer in April 2006 in Belfast, aged only 43 years old. Glenholmes returned to Belfast for work in an undisclosed capacity for the man her father Dickie had been planning to spring from Brixton Prison in 1979, the then Officer Commanding of the Provisional IRA in Belfast, Brian Keenan, who was also a member of the PIRA Army Council. After the Good Friday Agreement was signed and the arms decommissioning process began, Glenholmes moved to a position on the Sinn Fein Executive before in 2012, she was appointed as the head of the Victims And Survivors Commission, a cross-faith forum representing victims of the Northern Ireland conflict.

Sean Hick, Gerard Harte and Paul Hughes returned to Dublin, Lurgan and Dromintree respectively after their acquittals over the Roermond murders in 1991. Whilst Hick has seemingly vanished off the face of the earth, Harte relocated to Newry, before settling back in Lurgan a few years ago, where he now lives with his wife Elizabeth. In 2016, he mounted an unsuccessful appeal to have his conviction for petrol bombing in 1979 quashed; the Appeal Court ruled that his original conviction had been safe under emergency legislation in place at the time of the offence. Paul Hughes – together with his elder brother Sean "The Surgeon" Hughes – played a prominent role in the Provisional IRA's campaign in England up until the final IRA ceasefire was called in 1997 in preparation for the Good Friday Agreement. Paul was allegedly part of the team that mixed the explosives for the Docklands bomb that exploded in 1996, heralding the end of the ceasefire that had held since 1994. A High Court order was granted against Paul Hughes and his brothers on application by the Serious and Organised Crime Agency SOCA in 2009, freezing a number of properties and other assets held by the family, on suspicion of mortgage fraud, tax evasion and benefit fraud. This was the second time after being convicted of similar offences in 2001. Paul Hughes obtained a fake US passport and fled Ireland to avoid arrest. His brother Sean Hughes was charged with membership of the IRA in 2015 but the case against him and another man, Padraic Wilson, collapsed when key witnesses withdrew evidence and refused to testify against the former Provisional IRA Officer Commanding of South Armagh. Sean Hughes continues to live in South Armagh.

Donna Maguire laid low on her return from Germany to Northern Ireland after her conviction in June 1995, as a legal wrangle broke out over her release. There was confusion as to whether she had served an appropriate proportion of her sentence and the authorities had appealed against her release - the state prosecutor of Lower Saxony argued that she had been released too early. Awaiting a decision, shortly after the failed attack on Quebec Barracks, Leonard Hardy and Maguire married in Co. Louth in July 1996, a few months after a court in Northern Ireland granted her compensation of over £13,000 from Newry City Council as a result of her tripping over a loose paving stone in the city in 1985; the incident that allegedly damaged her knee. In September 1996, the German public prosecutor's appeal against Maguire's release was upheld and Maguire was ordered to return to prison in Germany. Barbara Klawitter and her team appealed against the decision and Maguire remained in Newry with Hardy as legal proceedings continued. The end to the seven year legal process finally came to an end in June 1997 when the highest appeals court in Germany, the Bundesgerichtshof, overturned the decision to return Maguire to prison in Celle. Too high profile to be used for IRA operations and with the "The Troubles" and the Provos slowly moving towards the Good Friday Agreement, the pair no longer had an active role to play in the Provisional IRA. Instead they turned their hand to a different activity: the illegal smuggling of tobacco and alcohol to circumvent taxation. Together with Dessie Grew's brother Aidan, who had been released from prison some time before, they set up a smuggling network, bringing illicit and untaxed cigarettes and alcohol into Ireland from the Far East and laundering the profits by investing the cash in a variety of properties in Spain. As the money rolled in, the pair bought a large, secure house in Dundalk and moved across the border to oversee their smuggling empire from the safety of the Republic. A public break with their former Provo comrades was sealed in November 2000, when Maguire's brother Malachy was seriously injured in an IRA punishment attack, which led to a furious Donna Maguire to call for a top-level enquiry within the Provisional IRA. One of the main players in the rival Continuity IRA, Malachy Maguire was abducted from his car outside his girlfriend's home in Meigh, Co. Armagh, by a number of armed men from the Provisional IRA's South Armagh Brigade and taken to a nearby children's playground, where he was then beaten with iron bars and shot with a handgun through wrists and ankles. The exact identity of the gunmen has never been confirmed but allegedly involved in the punishment attack: Donna Maguire's former comrade Gerard Majella Harte.

The German authorities meanwhile had set their sights on Leonard Hardy. The Germans applied for his extradition for his involvement in the oil drum bomb attack at Quebec Barracks and a Europe-wide warrant was issued for his arrest. In August 2005 whilst in Torremolinos in Spain on a family holiday, Hardy was arrested by Spanish police under the terms of the extradition warrant and remanded in custody in Madrid. After an initial hearing at the Spanish National Criminal Court Audiencia Nacional, he was held at the maximum-security prison at Valdemora, just outside the Spanish capital, to await a full extradition hearing. By January 2006, Hardy could run no more. He flew to Frankfurt and where he handed himself into German police but was released on bail to the tune of €20,000. On February 22nd he was officially charged with attempted murder and with causing explosions at Quebec Barracks on June 18th-19th 1989. The trial began on March 20th, 2006 at the regional *Oberlandesgericht* court in Celle. Hardy, defended by Barbara Klawitter, confessed to all charges presented to him by state prosecutor Wolfgang Hilkert. On April 1st, the prosecution summed up their cases and called for a prison sentence of no less than seven years, as Klawitter pleaded for leniency and a maximum sentence of three years. Judge Wolfgang Siolek found Leonard Hardy guilty on all counts and sentenced him to six years. Although the terms of the Good Friday Agreement did not technically apply in Germany, Siolek agreed that in the new climate of peace, Hardy should not serve his sentence and he was immediately released, leaving the courthouse with wife Donna Maguire, who had flown to Germany to be with her husband. They returned to the Republic of Ireland the same day to continue with the smuggling operation. It wasn't long before Irish Garda police and British customs officials got wind of the network - the Garda intercepted a smuggled stash of tobacco on November 8th 2011, which they attributed to Hardy and tipping off British customs officers, the HMRC opened an investigation into the smuggling racket, Operation Bayweek. Hardy was subsequently arrested on charges emanating from the investigation in 2012 at Stansted Airport but released once more on bail. Claiming that he worked in construction but unable to provide evidence of a legal means of subsistence, back in Ireland Hardy failed to correctly hand in tax returns for the years between 2002 and 2009 and in July 2014, was fined €10,000 by Dublin Circuit Court – the Criminal Assets Bureau (CAB) handed over the further investigations into the smuggling racket to the Director of Public Prosecutions. The investigations took another five months but by December 2014, the HMRC, CAB, Irish and Spanish police had gained enough of an insight and evidence into the illicit activities of Maguire and Hardy to issue European Arrest Warrants (EAW) for their apprehension. Unaware, the Hardy-Maguire family flew to Lanzarote for a Christmas vacation, where they were arrested on suspicion of money laundering and smuggling. On the grounds that money from tobacco and alcohol smuggling was being laundered through the acquisition of properties with estimated value of €10.5 million in different Spanish provinces on the Mediterranean coast and the creation of fake companies. Five other people were arrested with Maguire and Hardy and eleven searches were carried out in the provinces of Las Palmas, Alicante, Malaga and Murcia. Maguire was bailed and allowed to travel back to Ireland straight away to look after their four children, but Hardy was detained for five weeks before being released on a €250,000 bond. Things were getting serious. After returning to Ireland, just a few weeks later, Hardy was in court on charges relating to tax evasion. Pleading guilty, he agreed to pay the CAB €500,000 to settle the outstanding tax bill. Judge Mary Ellen Ring said she was 'slightly baffled' that Hardy was claiming legal aid with the consent of the DPP, when he was able to settle a tax bill of €500,000. The case against them in Spain was prepared and an initial court date set for December 2018. In the meantime, Hardy appeared at Kingston Crown Court in London in June 2018 to face further charges relating to his arrest at Stansted in 2012 but was acquitted due to lack of evidence. Hardy and Maguire flew to Madrid to appear once again before the Audiencia Nacional. The charges were presented to them: between 2005 and 2008, the couple had bought three homes in Orihuela (Alicante), Nerja and Manilva (Malaga) at a total outlay of more than nearly € 1 million. The Public Ministry suspected that Hardy and Maguire were signing purchase contracts and asking for loans that they would have been cancelling with the funds originated by illicit contraband. The couple bought one of the properties – a warehouse worth more than €600,000 - through the company Vinnea Import Export SL, of which Maguire was a majority shareholder. Much of the amount of the loan they requested to pay for properties was paid through cheques or cash in different entities, and nearly €100,000 received by the seller's researchers found to be of "unknown origin". On one occasion, a loan was taken out to cover the cost of property purchase, paid off in full six months later but on the very same day, Hardy and Maguire took out another loan for over €200,000. The case was adjourned until spring of 2019. Upon their return to the Audiencia Nacional, their IRA past was the subject of much discussion. The authorities were all too aware of the PIRA connections of some of the other people involved in the smuggling network, but the judge ruled out any direct paramilitary involvement or funding. Hardy and Maguire were tried on the basis of the laws they had broken in Spain and there was no question that the terms of the political Good Friday Agreement had any relevance to the purely criminal trial, despite accusations from defence lawyer Luis Casaubon Carles that the pair was being victimised for political reasons. The evidence was overwhelming that Maguire and Hardy had made a lot of money out of smuggling the proceeds of which they had laundered through Spain, and there could only be one decision when the trial came to a close in March. The pair was found guilty on all counts; recalling the pair in June 2019, the judge issued Leonard Hardy and Donna Maguire with a fine of nearly €900,000 and sentenced both to two years imprisonment. Hardy is still wanted by British authorities for the bomb attack in Banbridge in 1982 that killed an 11-year-old boy.

Patrick Murray, Donncha O'Kane and Pauline O'Kane (née Drumm) appealed the sentences handed down to them for their involvement in the attack in Osnabrück in 1989, although they had already been released due to the amount of time spent on remand. The appeal was heard in September 1996 but rejected by the *Bundesgerichtshof*. Murray moved back to the Republic of Ireland, whilst Drumm and O'Kane returned to Drumm's home village of Kinawley, near Enniskillen in Co. Fermanagh. Donncha O'Kane rekindled his love for Gaelic football and joined the local club Kinawley GAA, where he is now Vice-Chairman. His wife Pauline (Poilin) became a local councillor, sitting for Sinn Fein but left her post in 2007 in protest at Sinn Fein's decision to support the PSNI for the first time in an historic vote at their annual party conference Ard Fheis. The O'Kanes live and work under the Irish version of their surname "ui Cathain" and remain opposed to the Good Friday Agreement, carrying out voluntary work for organisations that help "those who have been bereaved or been traumatised by British state violence".

After their arrest in December 1990 in Antwerp, John "Dollar" Daly, Gerry Roche and Kieran McCarthy stood trial the following year in Belgium on identity and firearms charges, as well as conspiracy to attack British military targets. John Daly was given a one year suspended sentence and returned to Northern Ireland, remaining an active IRA volunteer whilst working as a taxi-driver and owning a part-share in a local shop in his native Finglas. He joined the Real IRA after the Falcarragh split in 1997 and continued to be involved in paramilitary activities. He was convicted of public order offences in May 2004 and fined. Father-of-three Daly was arrested in 2012 along with another man in the Blanchardstown area of Dublin as a result of a Garda surveillance operation – he was wearing a brown wig, black hat and gloves and driving a vehicle stolen a few weeks earlier and fitted with registration plates that corresponded to a different vehicle. He refused to answer any questions and subsequently stood trial at Dublin's Special Criminal Court in 2013. The judge convicted Daly of membership of the IRA and sentenced him to four years imprisonment. The leader of the Antwerp ASU, Gerry Roche, was given a three-year prison sentence by the Belgian judge. After his release he remained based in Europe but returned to Ireland regularly in secret for talks with Sinn Fein over the peace process and on active service with the Provisional IRA. In 1996, he was allegedly involved in the ambush of two Garda officers in Adare in Co. Limerick: Det Garda Jerry McCabe and his colleague Ben O'Sullivan were escorting an *An Post* truck delivering cash to post offices in County Limerick when they were ambushed. Seconds after they stopped behind the truck, their unmarked squad car was rammed from behind by a stolen Pajero jeep. Masked IRA gunmen Kevin Walsh and Gerry Roche jumped out and fired 15 rounds at the Gardaí, armed with AK-47 rifles, killing Jerry McCabe and leaving his colleague critically injured. Walsh, who was in command of the IRA's Munster brigade, subsequently pleaded guilty to manslaughter and was jailed for 14 years, whilst Roche escaped and remains on the run, living in Spain. Kieran McCarthy served a year of his prison sentence in Belgium before returning to his native Cork. As with other former IRA volunteers he went into politics, serving as a local county councillor for Sinn Fein. In 2015 however, he was first suspended from the party and then expelled as part of an internal enquiry about alleged bullying of the local Cork TD Sandra McLellan. After a long-running feud, Sinn Fein overturned the decision to expel McCarthy, but he refused to return and stood in the following election as an independent candidate, where he retained his seat and continues to sit on the local council. A keen historian and Republican, McCarthy runs guided tours around his native city and is currently in the process of writing a book about his time on active service for the Provisional IRA.

Following the murder of Jerry McCabe, the OC of Southern Command involved in the planning of European (and UK) operations as part of the Overseas Department in the mid 80's and early 90's was unceremoniously relinquished from his position. He left Ireland and moved to Spain. In 1998, AGS issued a warrant for his arrest, but the warrant was rescinded in 2006 on application to the Special Criminal Court in Dublin. It is then alleged he was heavily involved in cigarette smuggling, along with other former Provisional IRA comrades and in 2016, police finally arrested him in Alicante. He was extradited to Ireland to face charges but only a few days before the court case was due to open in June 2017, he absconded and went on the run. He has since been accused on charges of sexually abusing a minor, following revelations from a purported victim, and is still being sought on these and other charges at time of writing.

Dermot Quinn appealed against his twenty-five-year prison sentence for the attempted murder of two RUC officers handed down to him in 1990. The appeal was turned down for the first time in 1993 with the judge stating:

> *"These terrorist crimes arose out of carefully planned ambush of two police officers in which the appellant was an active participant and in which two gunmen armed with rifles fired at point blank range 23 rounds at two police officers in their car. Each of them narrowly escaped death but each was left with very serious injuries. A dastardly crime of this nature calls*

for a long deterrent sentence. "

He took his case to the European Court of Human Rights (ECHR) on the basis of an inference of guilt from his silence when confronted with the charges infringed his human rights, but his appeal there also failed. Although due to be released in 2003, he was given early release in 1999 under the terms of the Good Friday Agreement and returned to Co. Tyrone. He applied once again to the ECHR to have his conviction quashed but in March 2005 the ECHR ruled a final time that the conviction did not infringe the European Convention of Human Rights and dismissed the appeal.

Several of the IRA volunteers involved in active service in Europe remained actively opposed to the Good Friday Agreement and left the Provisional IRA to continue the armed struggle with other dissident Republican organisations. After his return to Northern Ireland, Martin Conlon returned to his unit as a sniper with the Provisional IRA's North Armagh Brigade and was involved in the murders of several British Army soldiers in North and South Armagh in the early 1990's. "Golfball" was unhappy with the decision of Sinn Fein and the Provisional IRA leadership to call a ceasefire and seek peace; he sided with Michael McKevitt and Seamus McGrane when the Provisional IRA split at Falcarragh in 1997 and joined both at the formation of the nascent Real IRA. Used as a firearms officer, Conlon was responsible for training Real IRA recruits in the use of handguns and automatic weapons at secret camps across the Republic of Ireland. At on such camp at Herbertstown, near Stamullen in Co. Meath in October 1999, he was arrested, along with Real IRA leader Alan Ryan, when Garda Special Branch moved in to round up Real IRA members on a tip-off. The Gardai found an RPG18 rocket propelled grenade launcher, a Zastava assault rifle, a CZ-70 pistol and a CZ 9mm machine gun, as well as ammunition. A subsequent search at another location 6 detonators and 8 bombs. Conlon was convicted and sentenced to four years imprisonment in 2001 on charges relating to the

Stamullen raid and served almost three years of his sentence in Portlaoise. He was released in 2004. What happened next is disputed. Some sources say that Conlon had informed on Real IRA colleagues after his arrest, whilst others maintain that he got into a feud with former PIRA colleagues keen to see the end of "The Troubles". Whatever the truth, Conlon was threatened on several occasions. On November 7th, 2005, Conlon was abducted at gunpoint from his home in Railway Street, Armagh City by two armed and masked men. His abductors forced Conlon into his own Silver VW Passat and was made to drive all three to the Madden Estate outside Keady in South Armagh. Arriving on Farnaloy Road, the two men told Conlon to get out of the car and lie on the ground, where they fired two shots into his head at close range, much in the same way that the Nutting Squad executed informers. He was found with severe wounds at 6:30pm by passers-by who called an ambulance; he was taken to Craigavon Area Hospital where doctors could do little but pronounce him dead.

In August 1992, Paddy Fox was sentenced to twelve years imprisonment on charges relating to possession of a 550kg bomb in Dungannon, that was planned to be used to blow up a British Army base. Whilst imprisoned in HMP Maze, just a few weeks later his parents Charles and Tess Fox were shot dead by UVF gunmen in their home. Four years later in August 1996, Paddy Fox was released and returned to active service for the Provisional IRA. As with Conlon, he sided with the hardliners over the vote on the Good Friday Agreement at Falcarragh and joined the Real IRA. In November 1998, his house in Dungannon was searched by former colleagues from the Provisional IRA East Tyrone Brigade, who wanted to stop dissident Republican organisations from continuing the armed struggle. They appeared again just two months later, when Fox escaped an abduction attempt in mid-January 1999. Fox took the unusual step of giving an interview to the press about the harassment, his words appearing in the Observer on January 30th. The day after publication, he was kidnapped and severely beaten by his former Provo colleagues at the Four Seasons Hotel in Co. Monaghan. He was questioned by the Provos for "misappropriation of weapons" – weapons that he and Real IRA leader (and former PIRA Quartermaster) Michael McKevitt had removed from PIRA arms dumps and transferred to the Real IRA after the split – but was released the following day. Fox remained unbowed. He was partly responsible for setting up the 32 County Sovereign Movement (32SCM), the political wing of the Real IRA, together with Bernadette Sands-McKevitt, the sister of hunger striker Bobby Sands and the wife of Mickey McKevitt. In 2012, an internal feud within IRA splinter groups climaxed in the murder of senior Real IRA figure – and gangland boss - Alan Ryan, which precipitated the departure of Paddy Fox from the RIRA and the 32SCM. He joined the newly formed dissident Republican group Oglaigh Na H'Éireann (ONH or "Soldiers of Ireland"), which subsequently joined forces with the remnants of the now disbanded Real IRA to form the so-called "New IRA". Paddy continues to fight vigorously for the UVF Loyalist paramilitary killers of his parents to be brought to justice; naming UVF gunman Alan Oliver as the man who shot dead his parents, allegedly in collusion with British forces. Investigations on the part of the now defunct Historical Enquiries Team (HET), the unit tasked with investigating unsolved paramilitary murders during the "Troubles", have led to further hearings on the deaths of Tess and Charles Fox being scheduled for 2020 and beyond.

What of Ingrid Hijman? The young Dutch woman that had allegedly been tricked by the IRA unit to help them with logistics during the campaign was never charged with any offence. She subsequently moved away from Amsterdam and her parental home in Rijswijk to a central Dutch town, where she completed her studies in 1997. Since then she remained in the academic world, now working as a student advisor and project manager at the same university, where she met her future husband – the couple married a year after she graduated and since her release from custody has declined to discuss her involvement in the events of 1989 and 1990 any further.

The fates of the Sandhatten ASU that carried out the botched mortar attack on Quebec Barracks in 1996 differ considerably. The German TV programme *Aktenzeichen XY ungelöst,* a programme dedicated to presenting unsolved crimes and helping to trace the perpetrators, featured the Sandhatten attack in the episode of July 5th, only a week later. Supported by information from the *BKA* in Meckenheim, near Bonn, photofit pictures and descriptions of "Mark" and "Beth" were shown, as well as pictures and information on both Ford Transit vans used. The programme also stated that Michael Dickson was wanted in connection with the attack and showed his photograph. A warrant had already been issued for his arrest by the *BKA*: Dickson had signed the rental agreement for the holiday home in Sandhatten using his own name and address. "Mark" was soon identified as James Corry, whose fingerprints were found on an empty bottle of whiskey found by *BKA* forensics experts during the search in Sandhatten and matched police records in Northern Ireland. The owners of the holiday home, Manfred Schmidt, his wife and daughter all positively identified Róisín McAliskey from mugshots as the young woman calling herself "Beth". On July 11th, warrants for the arrest of Corry and McAliskey were also issued in Germany. McAliskey was detained a few months later but was four months pregnant. In January 1998 a magistrate cleared her extradition to Germany to stand trial over the Osnabrück operation. After considerable protests from human rights activists, a long and prominent campaign supported by many influential politicians and figures from Ireland, the United Kingdom and the USA, British Home Secretary Jack Straw vetoed the extradition on health grounds. She eventually gave birth to a healthy baby daughter, Loinnir, in England. In May 2007, McAliskey was again arrested under the same warrant, the German authorities having sent it back to the UK for reassessment in October 2006 just as it was due to expire. McAliskey was arrested and released on bail but the bid to extradite her failed once more in November 2007. She has never stood trial for her involvement in the Provisional IRA's European campaign. James Corry returned to Ireland after the Osnabrück attack, where James was arrested under suspicion of being the man calling himself "Mark". He was released four months later, and the couple moved briefly to Dundalk, before settling in Killorgin in Co. Kerry. Investigations into Corry's involvement in the IRA attack in Germany continued but were beset with problems and delays. Finally, the German authorities issued a European Arrest Warrant in 2015 and James Corry's extradition was approved by an Irish court; he was extradited at the end of 2016. He stood trial on explosives charges in August 2017, but at the outset admitted his part in the attack in full and pleaded guilty. In October 2017 he was given a four-year sentence by the regional court in Osnabrück. Although the terms of the Good Friday Agreement did not apply in Germany, Corry was nevertheless released four days later in November 2017 and returned to Co. Kerry. Former British Army engineer Dickson went into hiding. In 2003, he was finally arrested at Prague Airport using a fake passport and extradited to Germany. He stood trial around Christmas the same year and was sentenced to six and a half years imprisonment in Celle. After a botched escape attempt and serving around half of his sentence, he was released at the beginning of March 2006. There to meet him when he left prison in Germany were a handful of German Republican sympathisers, including Sven Brux, the head of security at Hamburg football club FC St. Pauli, well-known for a strong Republican leaning within its supporter base. Dixie was driven back to Hamburg for a small party to celebrate his release - also joining the celebrations in the Jolly Roger pub on the notorious Reeperbahn were former IRA comrades Donna Maguire and Leonard Hardy. Dickson returned to Dublin but after being fined €16,000 by a Dublin court early in 2018 for deliberately avoiding motorway tolls, and his current address being revealed, he moved to Cardiff in 2019.

Aside from Dessie Grew, possibly one of the most key figures in both the Provisional IRA's European campaign and the security services fight to stop them was controversial double agent Peter Keeley. After his return from active service in Germany, Keeley continued to operate on behalf of both sides well into the 1990's. In April 1990, he was involved in the murder of Eoin Morley in Newry, an ex-IRA man who had defected to the IPLO. At the request of Mooch, Keeley was part of an IRA hit squad who called at Morley's home on the evening of Easter Sunday, pulled him into the front garden and shot him dead in front of his girlfriend. He had felt he was unable to decline involvement when asked by Mooch to take part, for fear of being uncovered as a double agent and informed his handlers at the FRU of the incident. He continued active service for the PIRA's South Down Brigade and was later seconded to the "Nutting Squad", the IRA's feared Internal Security Unit, under the leadership of Freddie Scappaticci and involved in the capture, interrogation and murder of suspected IRA informants, whilst all the while knowing that if discovered to be working for the security forces, he himself would be facing the same fate. In 1994, after an IRA operation was botched inadvertently, Keeley was arrested. He said nothing and was released without charge. Yet the "Nutting Squad" wanted to debrief him and started to notice that Keeley was often involved in operations that were thwarted at the last minute. Suspecting the truth, Scappaticci ordered Keeley to a house in North Belfast where he was interrogated by the ISU. He was released unharmed but ordered to return for a second session. After the second interrogation, the ISU was not convinced and ordered him to return for a third time. Realising that he was likely to be executed, he informed his handlers who told him to go to the meeting. Angry that the FRU were sending him to his death, he broke off contact with "Andy" and "Bob", refused to attend the third meeting with the ISU and went into hiding. He moved from the FRU to the RUC's C13 division, dealing with PIRA drug smuggling and racketeering, helping to secure a number of convictions. In the mid 1990's he was involved in an operation to track an Ecstasy tablet press from the UK to the Provisional IRA in Northern Ireland. The press had been sourced by one of Eoin Morley's brothers who lived in Manchester and sent to Northern Ireland, where Keeley was unsurprised to see it being received on behalf of the IRA by none other than Father

Patrick Ryan. The Irish Garda subsequently lost track of the press - whether wilfully or inadvertently - and despite Ryan being photographed taking receipt of the press, no charges were ever pressed. Keeley continued to pass information on PIRA activities to both RUC's SB and CID divisions and by July 1997, he was assigned "participating informant" status, which unofficially allowed him to become involved in crimes in order to access important intelligence, a task he had perversely been carrying out for many years already. A year later in July 1998, RUC's CID Division graded his intelligence work as A1 – the most reliable, whilst Special Branch assigned him B2 status, also generally reliable. Considering his status within the security forces, what followed next was surprising and unexplainable. On August 12th 1998, he received a call from Mooch, who asked to meet Keeley and explained that he needed Keeley's assistance in procuring firearms for the Real IRA. Keeley agreed to meet him at the Claret Bar in Dundalk. Upon arrival, Keeley noted that Mooch exuded the unmistakable smell of diesel and agricultural fertiliser - the main ingredients in a type of improvised explosives. Challenged about the smell, Mooch admitted to Keeley "there's a big one on", meaning that a large bomb was being prepared and was likely to be used in the next 2-3 days; any longer and the mixture would start to separate and render the bomb useless. After the meeting, Keeley immediately informed his superiors, fully expecting the information to lead to the arrest of Mooch and prevention of a possibly devastating explosion, and two days later Keeley flew to Tenerife on holiday. The following day, August 15th 1998 at 3.09pm, a huge fertiliser bomb, made by Mooch and planted by the Real IRA exploded in the centre of market town Omagh, killing 29 innocent bystanders - including a woman pregnant with twins - injuring over 220 and threatening to derail the peace process. The last major IRA bomb attack of "The Troubles" was also the most devastating and came at a time shortly after the Good Friday Agreement, as the people of Northern Ireland were beginning to breathe a sigh of relief that the conflict was finally over. Keeley was incensed that his information had not been acted upon and on his return met with

RUC DCS Eric Andersen in secret in Belfast to find out what had happened. Andersen explained that Keeley's intelligence grading - in the days preceding the Omagh blast – had been inexplicably downgraded and the information classed as unreliable. This error led to the deaths of 31 people (including the two unborn twins) and possibly the most horrific scenes of destruction that the province had ever seen. There was outrage even from the Republican community and the Real IRA were disgraced, actively scorned by their own people. Keeley left Northern Ireland and moved to London, where with the help of ghost-writers began to document his activities for the Provisional IRA. A lot of what he committed to paper was redacted due to legal reasons, but the book "Unsung Hero" nevertheless attracted a lot of attention from both the PIRA and the security services. Shortly after the release of the book in 2006, he was arrested and questioned by the Metropolitan Police over the murder of Eoin Morley but finally released without charge. Further controversy was to come: in 2011, Keeley was called to give evidence on Provisional IRA activities and personnel to the Smithwick Tribunal, set up to investigate the Jonesborough ambush in 1989 and allegations of Garda collusion in the murders of Bob Buchanan and Harry Breen. At the Tribunal, Keeley gave a detailed account of his intelligence work on behalf of the security services, of his time in the IRA, about the activities of several senior figures in the PIRA South Down and Belfast Brigades, including Mooch, Hardbap, Sean Hughes and Freddie Scappaticci, and about the Omagh bombing. Keeley is involved in on-going investigations and court cases relating to a number of murders carried out by the South Down Brigade. He lives under an assumed identity in a secure, secret location in England. His former handler "Bob" from the Force Research Unit apparently followed a different path. According to various sources, if the story is to be believed, he moved to London and joined the Security Service (*MI5*) in 1999, attached to G-Branch, the department of the Security Service dealing with international counter-terrorism, becoming a specialist on the operations and structure of Al-Qaeda and ISIS. Two years later he was made head of

G-Branch (G/0) and in 2007, he took over as Director General of the Security Service, and was chief of *MI5* until "Bob" – allegedly Sir Jonathan Evans – was succeeded by Andrew Parker in 2013.

A story remains to be told about the two Provisional IRA trophy weapons used in the killings on the Continent and likely also in other murders in Northern Ireland: the Ruger Magnum revolver taken from Loyalist murderer Michael Stone after he attacked the funeral of the "Gibraltar Three" at Milltown Cemetery in March 1988, and the Browning 9mm pistol taken by Republicans from Corporal Derek Wood as he and colleague Corporal David Howe accidentally drove into the funeral cortege for Kevin Brady only a few days later. The Browning had been recovered by the *Bundeskriminalamt* from the getaway car used by the IRA on the night of June 1st in Dortmund, when it was abandoned in the vehicle outside the town of Bönen after the murder of Major Dillon-Lee. After being subjected to forensic and ballistics tests as part of the investigation, it remained the property of the BKA for many years. It was subsequently utilised by the BKA for training firearms examination officers. The Ruger confiscated by the IRA from Michael Stone had been recovered by Belgian police when the arms dump near Heerle was discovered and Sean Hick, Donna Maguire, Gerard Harte and Paul Hughes arrested in June 1990 - the weapon was used as forensic evidence in the Roermond trial that began in early 1991. Initial ballistic test results had indicated that the weapons had not only been used in several of the fatal attacks carried out by the Continental European Active Service Units, but had also been used in a number of murders in Northern Ireland, including the unsolved murder of off-duty RUC officer John Larmour in October 1988, shot dead by the IRA as he worked in his brother's ice-cream parlour in Belfast. The Larmour family were understandably eager to find out if the weapons had been used in John's murder, as it would likely be a vital clue in the hunt to bring his killers to justice. Due to the unstinting insistence of the family, the PSNI's Historical Enquiries Team (HET)- set up to investigate the hundreds of open cases after the end of the Troubles - had the Ruger returned to Northern Ireland in August 2008 and subjected it to fresh forensic examination. Eight years later, the LIB (Legacy Investigation Branch) - the successor to the HET - also managed to have the Browning returned by the German BKA for similar testing. In addition the Larmour family requested that LIB seek all relevant forensic and ballistic information from the German, Belgian and Dutch authorities, which was duly carried out. The family was formally advised that investigations would not be continued and that a request for the matter to be fully investigated by an independent tribunal was declined. Undeterred and desperate to find the truth, the Larmour family pushed further for answers and turned to the Police Ombudsman for Northern Ireland OPONI for further clarification. OPONI confirmed the Browning confiscated from Corporal Derek Wood by the IRA, and subsequently recovered in Germany in June 1990, was used in the murder of Roy Butler in August 1988, and fired at customers in the ice cream parlour during the murderous attack on John Larmour in October. They also said the Ruger .357 recovered in Belgium was used to shoot dead Colin Abernethy on the Lisburn to Belfast train in September 1988, John Larmour a few weeks later, and Nick Spanos and Stephen Melrose in Roermond in May 1990. Additionally, an additional Browning 9mm pistol carried by Michael Stone in the Milltown cemetery attack had also been used in the murder of Roy Butler and also in the murder of RUC dog handler Constable Samuel Todd, shot and killed by the IRA on October 15th 1990. Despite the undertakings of the PSNI and OPONI, it has however never been conclusively proven that the Ruger .357 revolver used by Michael Stone was the same weapon that was used to kill Colin Abernethy, John Larmour, Nivruti Islania, Nick Spanos and Stephen Melrose and later recovered by Belgian police in Heerle. More importantly, the real origins of the Ruger used to murder John Larmour and how it came to be in the possession of the European ASU remains unclear even today - relatives of Larmour have been working tirelessly - publicly and privately - to lobby for the full revelation of the history of the weapon that killed

John but have yet to be given the full details. John's brother George carried out his own personal investigations over the years. He had co-operated with the Historical Enquiries Team (HET) and had been disappointed with their report after years of waiting. George had no desire to deal with the Police Ombudsman's office, having little belief in OPONI's ability or willingness to find the hidden truth. He has written to various Northern Ireland Police Chief Constables and found them unwilling to reveal what they know. He has written critical articles that have appeared in numerous newspapers: all with the aim of finding answers, finding the truth. George decided in 2016, before it was too late, to document his own private efforts and his own version of what he believes to be the truth in his book 'They Killed the Ice Cream Man'. In it, he accepts that his version may not be the full truth. The Ruger was almost certainly originally an RUC weapon but there is no clear evidence as to how it became used in the murder of Larmour: in 2018, the OPONI dismissed claims that any element within Special Branch or RUC had anything to do with the procurement of the weapon, the use of informers in the murder or any subsequent cover-up or neglecting to bring the killers to justice. Yet it remains a mystery how no records apparently exist for the RUC weapon - PSNI gave the information that over 7,000 Ruger .357's were issued to RUC officers between 1979 and 1986 but that only 13 of these weapons were reported lost or stolen - none of the serial numbers of these revolvers match the partial serial number of the weapon recovered in Belgium. Where did the Ruger come from, through whose hands did it pass and why was it seemingly untraceable? The conclusive answer to these questions will likely provide an important lead to the killers of John Larmour. Whilst it will not bring him back from the dead, it may possibly bring the justice to his bereaved family that they have long craved and deserved, and help to close just one of the hundreds of cases of unsolved murders of both Protestants and Catholics, that - over twenty years after the Good Friday Agreement - sadly remain a tragic legacy of the Troubles.

And finally: what became of the man who spent two years leading the fight against the IRA in Europe, the head of the *BKA's SoKo PIRA* Joachim Rzeniecki? Herr Rzeniecki took up a professorship at the *Fachhochschule des Bundes*, teaching junior and senior police detectives criminology and criminal psychology, before moving to the *Bundesgrenzschutz* (Federal Border Guard) in 1998, where he headed up the central division responsible for tackling human trafficking. In this role he led German delegations to the UN. Rzeniecki took on responsibility for a variety of projects on behalf of the German Interior Ministry and finally became the boss of the Central Operational Support Unit for the successor to the *Bundesgrenzschutz*, the *Bundespolizei* (Federal Police Force), focussing on forensics, information and communications technology, before retiring in 2011. Since then he has been active in politics at a communal level, and until recently was the mayor of his adopted hometown of Nastätten, not far from the *BKA* headquarters in Wiesbaden, from where he once led the fight against the Provisional IRA.

I will leave it to Herr Rzeniecki to provide the final word to this book.

> *"The PIRA offensive on the Continent can be classed as a failure....the German population viewed the PIRA not as freedom fighters, but as insidious murderers. The PIRA simply copied approaches and methods from Northern Ireland...and thankfully were not capable of adaptation during the offensive. Unlike the Red Army Faction (RAF), the PIRA rarely changed their modus operandi. As soon as a member of an ASU was identified, the German, British, Irish and Northern Irish authorities were able to build a complex persona profile of the entire ASU. A lack of innovation also prevented the Provisional IRA from joining forces with the RAF other terrorist organisations.*

In today's challenging times, people should be made to sit up and take notice of what happened back then, to prevent such senseless murder - whether in Northern Ireland, Britain or on the Continent – from ever being repeated."

BIBLIOGRAPHY

BOOKS

Aan de Wiel, Jerome | East German Intelligence and Ireland 1949-1990

Andrew, Christopher | The Defence of the Realm; The Authorized History of *MI5*

Asher, Michael | The Regiment – The Real Story of the SAS, The First Fifty Years

Bowyer Bell, John | The IRA, 1968 – 2000: analysis of a secret army

Boyne, Sean | Gunrunners: The Covert Arms Trail to Ireland

Collins, Eamon | Killing Rage

Coogan, Tim Pat | The IRA

Coogan, Tim Pat | On The Blanket: The H-Block Story

Davies, Nicholas | Dead Men Talking: Collusion, Cover-Up and Murder in Northern Irelands Dirty War

de Graaf, Beatrice | Theater van de Angst: de strijd tegen terrorisme in Nederland

de Graaf, Beatrice / de Jong, Ben / Platje, Wies | Battleground Western Europe

Dickson, Michael | Renegade Bomber

Dillon, Martin | The Dirty War

Fulton, Kevin (Keeley, Peter) | Unsung Hero

Harnden, Toby | Bandit Country: The IRA in South Armagh

Ingram, Martin & Harkin, Greg | Stakeknife

Kelly, Gerry | Playing My Part

Larmour, George | They Killed the Ice Cream Man

Leahy, Thomas | The Intelligence War Against The I.R.A.

McCrudden, John | A Moral Vendetta

McDonald, Henry INLA | Deadly Divisions

McKittrick, David / Kelters, Seamus / Feeney, Brian / Thornton, Chris / McVea, David | Lost lives: the stories of the men, women, and children who died as a result of the Northern Ireland troubles.

McKittrick David / McVea, David | Making sense of the Troubles

Moloney, Ed | A Secret History of the IRA

Moloney, Ed | Voices from the Grave (Vol.1)

O'Callaghan, Séan | The Informer

O'Driscoll, Sean | The Accidental Spy

Rushbridger, James | The Intelligence Game: The Illusions and Delusions of International Espionage

Sanders, Andrew: | Inside the IRA

Strickstrock, Bodo | Wenn ich so zurückblicke: Geschichten aus 40 Jahren Polizeidienst

Taylor, Peter Provos | The IRA & Sinn Fein

Taylor, Peter | Brits

Taylor, Peter | Loyalists

Taylor, Peter | Families at War

van Gageldonk, Paul | Ruger .357: de IRA in Limburg

Von der Bijl, Nick | Operation Banner: The British Army in Northern Ireland 1969-2007

West, Nigel | Historical Dictionary of British Intelligence

Wharton, Ken | Another Bloody Chapter in an Endless Civil War

Wharton, Ken | A Long Long War: Voices from the British Army in Northern Ireland 1969–1998

PRESS & ONLINE

United Kingdom

THE GUARDIAN

02.05.1988	"Alert after IRA kills 3"
03.05 1988	"Hurt airmen still seriously ill as relatives visit hospital"
03.05.1988	"British police fly to IRA murder scene"
05.05.1988	"BBC in showdown on Gibraltar report"
05.05.1988	"Terrorists timing alarms police"
09.05.1988	"Archbishop condemns IRA as RAF bomb victim is buried"
17.07.1988	"Hunt is on for IRA Germany unit"
13.08.1988	"Soldier killed in Ostend gun attack"
15.08.1988	"Pressure to scrap Army car plates"
	"IRA campaign against troops is the only voice the British understand"
16.08.1988	"Thatcher plans to seize terror cash"
20.08.1988	"'IRA man' denies Gibraltar link"
20.08.1988	"Soldier killed by IRA is buried"
15.06.1989	"Two suspected Provos face BAOR bombing charges"
20.06.1989	"IRA admits third bomb attack on British Rhine

THE OVERSEAS DEPARTEMENT

Army base"

04.07.1989 "Rhine Army fears IRA blitz"

18.07.1989 "Arrests prompt hunt for IRA French connection"

29.08.1989 "British soldier foils car bomb attack in Hanover"

04.09.1989 "Troops will not be confined to base"

09.09.1989 "Anger at killing of Army wife"

09.09.1989 "After the shock, Rhine life goes on"

25.10.1989 "Dublin court remands IRA couple wanted by West German police"

27.10.1989 "Gunmen kill corporal and baby girl"

28.10.1989 "IRA murders anger nationalists"

12.12.1989 "Yard to quiz man on Dutch gun find"

18.01.1990 "Brooke resists deaths enquiry"

08.03.1990 "Suspected IRA bombers to be extradited"

28.05.1990 "Two die in Dutch attack"

29.05.1990 "IRA killed tourists by mistake"

29.05.1990 "IRA ‚regrets' latest gun attack blunder in European offensive"

02.06.1990 "Soldiers killed in twin raids"

02.06.1990 "Shooting may mark new era of violence"

04.06.1990 "No hiding place for soldiers"

11.06.1990 "Adams sees mistakes as hindrance to Sinn Fein"

18.06.1990 "Maguire sought for two IRA attacks in Germany"

19.06.1990 "Maguire escaped extradition attempt"

19.06.1990 "Dutch hold third terrorist suspect"

01.08.1990 "Terror trail stretches back five years"

06.12.1990 "Suspected IRA trio held in Antwerp"

22.02.1991 "Woman who refused IRA job became go-between"

11.09.1991 "Court rejects Maguire appeal against extradition to Germany"

13.05.1992 "Northern Ireland devolution leak hints at Unionist unease"

10.06.1994 "German court frees three ‚clear IRA members'"

10.06.1994 "Killing of ‚spider in web' ended attacks

29.06.1995 "IRA terrorist convicted of bomb attack on army barracks freed by German court"

10.02.1996 "IRA smash ceasefire"

THE OBSERVER

03.09.1989 "IRA admit shooting unarmed soldiers"

29.10.1989 "Bonn offers reward for IRA gang"

03.06.1990 "IRA cells plan mainland gun war"

03.06.1990   "Strategy aimed at spreading terror to mainland"

26.03.1995   "Donna Maguire has been in prison for six years..."

31.01.1999   "I spoke against peace, so now they want to kill me"

SUNDAY TELEGRAPH

10.06.1990   "Hunt for IRA's wounded hit man"

24.06.1990   "Germany is closing the net on IRA murderers of major"

THE INDEPENDENT

07.09.1992   "Murder of Ulster couple fuels fears over future targets"

29.06.1995   "German court frees IRA bomber Maguire"

APNEWS

28.03.1987   "IRA claim responsibility for car bombing at British base"

14.07.1988   "Two IRA bombs injure nine British soldiers"

03.07.1989   "Suspected IRA car bomb kills one, injures three"

02.09.1989   "Two British soldiers seriously wounded in suspected IRA attack"

08.09.1989   "British soldiers wife killed in attack claimed by

	IRA"
27.10.1989	"Gunmen slay British soldier and six-month old daughter"
28.10.1989	"IRA claims responsibility for slayings"
05.05.1990	"IRA claim responsibility for failed bomb attack in Germany"
28.05.1990	"IRA says it mistakenly killed two Australian tourists"
02.06.1990	"IRA kills British soldier in West Germany; another in England"
15.06.1990	"Explosion Causes Damage at British Military Area"
17.06.1990	"Two suspected IRA members arrested in Belgium, Netherlands"
18.06.1990	"Dutch police arrest second alleged IRA runaway"

HERALD SCOTLAND

20.07.1989	"Three linked to car bomb death tell court they are IRA"
29.06.1990	"Heroine's return for IRA terrorist after six years on European tour of jails"
05.05.1990	"Bomb attack on army barracks"

NEW STATESMAN

THE OVERSEAS DEPARTEMENT

20.10.1989   "Carry on spying...and dying?"

UPI

04.05.1990   "Gunmen try to blow up British army barracks"

BELFAST TELEGRAPH

19.08.2005   "Sinn Fein call on Spanish to release

20.08.2005   "Army base bomb suspect vows to fight against extradition charges"

22.03.2019   "IRA bombers deny money-laundering charges"

29.03.2019   "Longer jail term call at money-laundering trial of IRA bombers"

Irish Republican news sources

Innumerous articles from An Phoblacht / Republican News

Republic of Ireland

IRISH TIMES

02.05.1988 „Three RAF men killed in IRA attacks in Holland"

02.05.1988 „Dutch towns frequented by British servicemen"

06.05.1988 „RAF to fly bodies of soldiers"

02.09.1988 „Search for IRA Dutch cell"

19.07.1989 „IRA suspects charged in Paris court"

08.09.1989 „Soldiers wife shot dead in Germany"

09.09.1989 „Murder of army wife in Germany is condemned"

09.09.1989 „Now we have joined the war, says Minister"

28.10.1989 „Killing of soldier and baby girl condemned"

28.10.1989 "Three IRA men sought over killings"

28.10.1989 „Haughey condemns 'callous' IRA killings in West Germany"

28.10.1989 „English ghettos offer little safety"

05.05.1990 „Police seek IRA gang for bomb attack in Germany"

29.05.1990 „The price of terror"

02.06.1990 „British officer shot dead in West Germany"

13.06.1990 „The implications for law enforcement of opening borders"

10.10.1990 „Killing of SAS men may have resulted from SAS

operation"

10.10.1990 „Armagh killings fit pattern of SAS operations"

11.10.1990 „IRA men to be buried today"

12.10.1990 „Adams pledge at IRA funeral"

12.10.1990 „Grew fingerprint link"

13.10.1990 „Priest questions morality of SAS role"

13.10.1990 „The life and death of a paramilitary"

15.10.1990 „Corrections and clarifications"

20.02.1991 „The thinking behind IRA terror tactics"

22.02.1991 „Woman says IRA asked her to lure soldiers into trap"

23.02.1991 „Three arrested near arms dump, court told"

01.03.1991 „Screams haunt Roermond witness"

08.03.1991 „Balancing the scales of justice in Dutch style"

15.03.1991 „Witness should be tried, court told"

16.03.1991 „Acquittals call in Roermond trial"

20.03.91 „Alleged IRA man decries civilian killings"

03.04.1991 „IRA strategy outlined in evidence"

06.07.1991 „Dutch court clears four of murdering Australians"

28.08.1992 „Over 200 killed in incidents outside NI"

10.06.1994 „British army targeted in two continental campaigns"

29.06.1996 „Attack may signal IRA campaign in Europe"

Irish News

08.05.2017 „IRA man tells inside story of the Loughgall attack and SAS ambush"

Netherlands

Nieuwsblad van het noorden

22.11.1988 "Speciaal IRA-commando in Duitsland?"

12.12.1989 "Verboden IRA al tien jaar actief in ons land"

Limburgsche Dagblad

06.05.1988 "Aanslagen IRA op vasteland voorspeld"

06.05.1988 „Een dramatisch nacht na konigenndag"

06.05.1988 „Nog veel vragen over IRA-aanslagen"

11.10.1990 "Doodgeschoten Ira-verdachte gezocht voor moord Wildenrath"

Digibron

02.05.1988 „Drie britse militairen gedood bij IRA aanslag"

03.05.1988 „Aanslagen moegelijk gevolg uitwijzing twee IRA-leden"

07.12.1990 „Drie IRA-leden in Belgie opgepakt"

11.06.1991 "Boetekleed voor verdeding IRA-proces"

02.07.1991 „Vijf jaar geeist"

Reformatorisch Dagblad

22.11.1988 „IRA-team ‚onderzoekt' zwee Geleense wijken"

27.07.1990 „Studente Ingrid H. will andere advocaat"

11.08.1990 „IRA-verdachte Hughes zegt alibi te hebben"

18.02.1991 „IRA-leden morgen voor de rechter"

23.02.1991 „IRA-verdachten mogen bij verhoor getuigen zijn"

12.03.1991 „Verdachten IRA waren in opleiding"

16.03.1991 „IRA-lid wordt getrained om te doden"

26.04.1991 „Verzoek tot opheffing uitleveringshectenis Hughes in IRA-zaak"

12.06.1991 „Verdachte Hughes will rechtszaal verlaten"

16.07.1991 „Hick en Hughes uitgeleverd aan Duitsland"

19.07.1991 „OM stopt met IRA-zaak"

NRC HANDELSBLAD

28.03.1987 "Aanslag IRA in Nederland beraamd"

11.01.1989 "IRA-onderzoek vastgelopen"

28.05.1990 "Aanslag in Roermond: twee Australiers dood"

22.06.1990 "Aangehouden IRA-lid was in Roermond"

12.03.1991 "Gedood IRA-lid was brein achter aanslagen"

10.06.1991 „IRA-advocaten: nader onderzoek"

16.07.1991 „Zwee Ieren na vrijspraak uitgeleverd aan Duitsland.

19.07.1991 „OM: geen hoger beroep IRA-proces"

Provinciale Zeeuwse Courant

16.06.1990 „Politie arresteerd lid IRA; jacht op vierde"

DE TELEGRAAF

22.11.1988 "IRA-terrorist schuilde in Geleen"

BND STEM

27.04.2013 „Nederland laat terroristen gaan"

Germany

TAZ

16.02.1989 „IRA-Sympathisanten festgenommen"

18.02.1989 „Berichtigung zum Beitrag vom 16.02"

12.10.1989 „Briten bespitzeln Iren in der BRD"

14.08.1990 „Erstmal IRA-Prozeß vor deutschem Gericht"

03.06.1991 „IRA-Prozess mit stumpfer "Waffe"

31.03.1992 „Anklagen im IRA-Prozess unhaltbar"

Die Zeit

39/1989   „Belfast liegt im Münsterland"

Oberbergische Anzeiger

01.08.1989 „Verschiedenes"

Spiegel der Zeit

08.09.1989 „Entsetzen über IRA-Mord in Unna"

Bild Zeitung

09.09.1989 „Im Sterben druckte Heidi das Gaspedal durch"

STERN MAGAZIN

14.09.1989 "In jedem Krieg gibt es zivile Opfer"

HESSISCHE ALLGEMEINE

27.10.89 „Britischer Soldat mit Kind getötet"

BONNER GENERALANZEIGER

27.10.1989 „Britischer Soldat und sein Kind in Mönchengladbach erschossen"

02.06.1990 „Terroristen entkamen trotz Verfolgung"

14.08.1990 „Das Kalaschnikow-Sturmgewehr ist ein Indiz"

DEWEZET

16.06.1990 „Explosion war doch ein Terroranschlag"

18.06.1990 „Die blutige Spur nach Hameln"

19.06.1990 „Mutmaßliche Terroristin war in Hameln"

DER SPIEGEL

17.03.1980 „Brutaler Gangart"

14.03.1988 „Teuflische Ungeheuer"

19.09.1988 „Gesetz des Dschungels"

07.08.1989 „Bombe zum Dinner"

04.06.1990 „Streit um IRA-Prozeß"

25.06.1990 „Größere Schlagzeilen"

01.06.1992 „Ein Mann, ein Gewehr"

25.10.2017 „Ex-IRA Mitglied in Osnabrück zu Haft verurteilt"

Belgium

Le Soir

26.11.1988 „AMI DE L'IRA"

29.11.1988 „PATRICK RYAN ENTRE MAGGY ET MARTENS"

30.11.1988 „L'AFFAIRE RYAN"

15.12.1988 „UN BUREAU DU SINN FEIN"

18.06.1990 „Terroristes presumés arretes: ils s'entrainemaient au tir á Hoogstraaten"

19.06.1990 „LE MEMBRE DE L'IRA TROP SUSPECT AVEC SES MENOTTES"

20.06.1990 „LA BELGIQUE VEUT LES TERRORISTES DE L'IRA EXPORTER LA VIOLENCE POUR SOUTENIR LE MORAL DES MILITANTS"

22.06.1990 „IRA: FILIERE DE ROERMOND CONFIRMEE DES EMPREINTES A CHARGE DU TERRORISTE P.HUGHES"

06.12.1990 „TROIS MEMBRES PRESUMES DE L'IRA ARRETES A

ANVERS.

07.12.1990 „LES MILITANTS PRESUMES DE L'IRA REFUSENT DE PARLER TROIS ANONYMES LOURDEMENT ARMES"

France

Le Monde

20.07.1989 „Interpellés par la *DST* á Saint-Avolde"

USA

Albany Democrat

27.10.1989 "IRA gunmen slay British soldier, 6 month old baby"

Santa Maria Times

14.11.1989 "Irish activist bail set at $25.000"

New York Times

03.09.1989 „British soldiers wounded by gunman in West

LA Times

14.11.1989 „Irish activist granted release on $25,000 bail"

The Odessa American

27.10.1989 "Soldier and daughter killed by gunmen"

The Morning Call – Pennsylvania

30.10.1989 "Activist looks for violence to bring peace to N.Ireland"

Australia

The Sydney Morning Herald

31.05.1990 "Dutch police were told: keep your eyes open"

Daily Journal

08.03.1990 "Suspected IRA bombers to be extradited"

Canada

The Ottawa Citizen

19.07.1989 "Suspected IRA terrorists face trial"

THE OVERSEAS DEPARTEMENT

LEGAL & SECURITY SERVICES DOCUMENTS

LEGAL DOCUMENTS

Workshop notes 23.03.2015 „Lethal force, policing and the ECHR: McCann and others vs United Kingdom"

European Court of Human Rights Application 03.09.1993 McCann and others vs United Kingdom

Ref# 18984/91

NI Supreme Court judgement 08.09.2017 in Patrick Anthony Guiness v The Queen

Ref# STE 10372

United Kingdom Court of Appeal judgement 17.12.1998

R v McNamee

Ref#: 9704481 S2

German Bundesgerichtshof judgement 26.04.1995

against Sean Hick, Paul Hughes, Donna Maguire

Ref# 3Str 30/95

THE OVERSEAS DEPARTEMENT

German Bundesgerichtshof judgement 20.08.1996

against Patrick Murray, Donogh O'Kane, Pauline Drumm

Ref# 3Str 258/96

The Queen vs Terence Gerard McGeough 07.05.2013

Ref# MOR8859

French Court of Appeal Cours de cassation chambre criminelle

- Extradition request 90-82883
- Extradition request 90-82884
- Extradition request 90-82885

European Court of Human Rights Final Judgement 16.10.2013 on MCaughey and others vs United Kingdom

Ref# 43098/909

Smithwick Tribunal, Dublin

- November 2011: Testimony Patrick Joseph Blair
- December 2011: Testimony Peter Keeley (Kevin Fulton)
- 29.11.2013 Final report

AUSWÄRTIGES AMT (GERMAN FOREIGN OFFICE) DOCUMENTS

Considerable assistance was given by the team at the Political Archive of the *Auswärtiges Amt* in Berlin in locating and making available relevant documents, for which I am eternally grateful. Here an overview of the documents used as source material in the writing of this book:

Referat 301 Counter Terrorism

PA/AA B46-ZA / 195691

PA/AA B46-ZA / 195731

PA/AA B46-ZA / 195734

PA/AA B46-ZA / 195843

Großbritannien / GRO, GRB

PA/AA B31-ZA / 135425

PA/AA B31-ZA / 160037

PA/AA B31-ZA / 160042

SECURITY SERVICE DOCUMENTS

During the research for this book, documents generated and / or disseminated by the following intelligences services were accessed; individual documents are not listed.

Binnenlandse Veiligheidsdienst (*BVD*)
(since 2002 „Allgemene Inlichtingen- en Veiligheidsdienst" (AIVD)
(Domestic intelligence agency of the Netherlands)

Bundesnachrichtendienst (BND)
(International intelligence agency of Federal Republic of Germany)

Bundesamt für Verfassungsschutz (BfV)
(Domestic intelligence agency of the Federal Republic of Germany)

Ministerium für Staatssicherheit (MfS or "Stasi")
(Domestic intelligence agency of the former German Democratic Republic – Department HAXXII "Terrorabwehr" / "Prevention of terrorism")

TV & MISCELLANEOUS

Journal of Strategic Security Vol. 9 Number 1

„The Provisional Irish Republican Army and the Developement of Mortars"

Gary A. Ackerman

Ierland Bulletin (Journal of Ierland Komitee Nederland / NL)

"A long way home"

23-04 // 2002

Kameradschaft 248 German Security Unit e. V.

Guard Report 2015

„Scharfer Wind in den Kasernen"

THE OVERSEAS DEPARTEMENT

„The IRA & Sinn Fein: Inside the IRA": PBS, USA

„Brits" | „Provos" | „Loyalists": BBC, UK

„The Funeral Murders" BBC, UK

„Death on the Rock": THAMES TELEVISION, UK

„Collateral Damage" CHANNEL 7, AUSTRALIA

„The Shankill Bomb": BBC, UK

„Stakeknife: The Spy in the IRA": BBC, UK

"Spotlight: A Secret History of The Troubles": BBC Northern Ireland, UK

THE OVERSEAS DEPARTEMENT

INDEX

Adams, Gerry · 31, 47, 82, 123, 126, 264, 335, 339, 340, 374, 378, 379, 380, 381, 383, 384, 393, 394, 399, 401, 428, 433
AK47 automatic rifle · 8, 57, 103, 139, 148, 154, 155, 157, 164, 171, 184, 191, 209, 210, 237, 238, 251, 258, 271, 276, 281, 286, 288, 294, 295, 297, 298, 304, 306, 308, 309, 316, 332, 356, 408
Andersonstown · 59, 61, 83, 86, 93, 121, 126, 129, 170, 263
Antwerp · 262, 316, 339, 344, 346, 384, 407, 428

B

Bakermans, Ed · 346, 347, 350, 353, 354
Baxter, SAC John · 15, 139, 141, 142, 143
Belfast · 21, 22, 23, 24, 26, 30, 33, 37, 49, 50, 51, 55, 56, 59, 60, 61, 62, 65, 67, 68, 69, 82, 83, 84, 85, 86, 87, 88, 92, 93, 95, 96, 98, 99, 101, 116, 118, 120, 121, 122, 123, 124, 125, 126, 127, 129, 131, 135, 142, 144, 147, 149, 152, 153, 157, 161, 162, 169, 170, 174, 175, 195, 208, 222, 223, 227, 228, 243, 255, 258, 262, 264, 271, 303, 320, 326, 336, 338, 348, 360, 366, 374, 375, 381, 382, 385, 388, 394, 395, 396, 397, 398, 401, 415, 437

Berlin · 7, 18, 25, 74, 76, 77, 150, 152, 172, 173, 195, 237, 259, 444
Blair, Patrick Joseph ‚Mooch' · 149, 443
Bom, Ruud · 347
Brady, Kevin · 24, 83, 86, 93, 123, 124, 126, 131, 170, 299, 317, 332
Breda · 38, 135, 139, 145, 205, 274, 290, 302, 305, 311, 313, 315, 344
Breen, RUC Chief Superintendent Harry · 197, 198, 200, 320, 417
Brussels · 34, 35, 54, 87, 91, 94, 97, 101, 102, 135, 146, 152, 185, 186, 305, 323, 344
BSSO · 10, 11, 39, 70, 74, 94, 143, 156, 159, 174, 176, 235, 258, 369
Buchanan, RUC Superintendent Robert · 197, 198, 199, 200, 201, 320, 417
Bundesnachrichtendienst (BND) · 76, 94, 436, 445

C

Cahill, Joe · 22, 53, 65, 77, 338, 379
Canepa, Joseph · 97, 112
Co. Antrim · 150
Co. Armagh · 30, 35, 39, 42, 44, 55, 62, 63, 64, 78, 83, 95, 135, 148, 149, 168, 171, 175, 197, 198, 199, 201, 222, 225, 244, 245, 257, 260, 263, 275, 280, 291, 314, 319, 327, 335, 337, 339, 340, 349, 354, 359, 381, 382, 384, 385, 389, 403, 404, 410, 424, 433
Co. Fermanagh · 39, 90, 135, 399, 407

Co. Louth · 42, 47, 147, 148, 150, 151, 197, 320, 403
Co. Monaghan · 43, 168, 337, 382, 412
Co. Tyrone · 39, 41, 42, 43, 78, 79, 82, 168, 170, 196, 224, 233, 260, 274, 275, 314, 327, 331, 335, 339, 340, 388, 398, 410, 411
Collins, Michael · 151, 174, 226, 312, 337, 423
Cols, Serge · 35
Conlon, Martin · 171, 225, 228, 229, 234, 245, 250, 251, 252, 253, 257, 263, 264, 268, 269, 272, 273, 274, 275, 280, 284, 289, 304, 314, 316, 326, 327, 328, 335, 384, 410, 411
Cork · 18, 153, 161, 337, 389, 408
Corry, James · 150, 320, 388, 391, 392, 413
Coss, Vicky · iii, 283, 287, 291, 292, 357

D

Daly, John ‚Dollar' · 337, 338, 339, 344, 345, 346, 407
Decker, Rüdiger · 344, 367, 371
Derry / Londonderry · 21, 22, 24, 30, 31, 47, 243, 303, 374, 381, 395
Dickson, Michael ‚Dixie' · 206, 234, 235, 237, 385, 386, 387, 388, 389, 390, 391, 392, 413, 423
Dillon-Lee, Major Michael · iii, 15, 295, 297, 299, 304, 318, 328, 367, 370, 371
Doherty, Pat · 28, 53, 62, 379
Dortmund · 35, 169, 190, 229, 231, 233, 234, 237, 239, 240, 251, 259, 269, 273, 293, 297, 298, 299, 304, 318, 327, 328, 346, 360, 367, 370, 371
Drumm, Pauline · 135, 145, 153, 154, 158, 168, 203, 204, 209, 211, 217,
219, 220, 221, 223, 248, 268, 323, 366, 368, 369, 372, 373, 384, 407, 443
Dublin · 30, 31, 36, 43, 48, 52, 53, 56, 66, 68, 73, 77, 88, 101, 102, 118, 121, 134, 152, 157, 161, 173, 182, 185, 186, 188, 223, 227, 228, 232, 239, 266, 275, 290, 338, 359, 371, 373, 380, 381, 387, 397, 398, 402, 405, 408, 414, 427, 443
Duisburg · 31, 75, 154, 155, 157, 159, 163, 165, 182, 183, 184, 185, 191, 192, 194, 205, 218, 223, 269, 323, 324, 365
Dundalk · 68, 135, 144, 147, 148, 149, 150, 151, 170, 197, 198, 199, 226, 385, 388, 404, 414, 416
Dungannon · 41, 79, 168, 170, 196, 244, 327, 332, 335, 356, 399, 411

E

Eckenhagen · 203

F

Farrell, Mairéad · 61, 62, 64, 65, 67, 69, 78, 82, 86, 91, 93, 100, 101, 103, 104, 107, 109, 110, 113, 114, 115, 116, 117, 118, 120, 121, 124, 131, 137, 151, 161, 168, 170, 195, 374, 384
Farrell, Niall · 65, 78, 170
Fox, Patrick · 170, 196, 224, 225, 257, 269, 275, 327, 328, 335, 356, 384, 411

G

Geleen · 135, 136, 164, 218, 289, 436
Gibraltar · 16, 87, 88, 89, 90, 91, 93, 95, 97, 98, 99, 102, 103, 104, 105, 106, 107, 108, 109, 112, 113, 114, 116, 117, 118, 119, 120, 129, 131, 135, 137, 142, 151, 152, 153, 195, 222, 299, 401, 426
Glenholmes, Evelyn · 66, 67, 89, 96, 401
Göttingen · 7, 257, 269, 274
Grew, Desmond · 137, 168, 170, 171, 195, 196, 224, 225, 226, 227, 228, 231, 234, 237, 238, 243, 245, 251, 253, 257, 260, 262, 265, 267, 269, 274, 275, 279, 281, 284, 286, 287, 288, 290, 291, 302, 303, 316, 318, 323, 324, 327, 328, 330, 331, 332, 333, 334, 335, 336, 338, 339, 340, 356, 357, 384, 403, 414, 433

H

Hakansson, Pia Maria · 47, 58, 71, 136, 161, 165, 344
Hamelin · 74, 205, 218, 302, 303, 328, 351, 386
Hanover · 7, 28, 205, 206, 211, 216, 218, 220, 223, 229, 231, 237, 239, 259, 266, 268, 269, 275, 278, 279, 280, 284, 290, 291, 298, 302, 304, 327, 328, 346, 352, 360, 367, 370, 371, 372, 427
Hanratty, Gerard · 59, 60, 61, 65, 69, 70, 71, 73, 76, 87, 89, 91, 93, 98, 119, 132, 135, 138, 154, 158, 160, 161, 163, 164, 165, 166, 167, 168, 184, 190, 191, 192, 193, 194, 195, 202, 215, 253, 289, 323, 340, 341, 342, 344, 363, 365, 367, 384, 389, 399
Hardy, Leonard · 147, 148, 149, 152, 170, 173, 174, 175, 196, 198, 201, 203, 209, 217, 219, 223, 225, 226, 227, 248, 259, 266, 403, 404, 414
Harte, Gerard · 225, 226, 227, 237, 238, 251, 253, 256, 274, 275, 276, 279, 280, 284, 286, 287, 288, 291, 293, 296, 297, 304, 305, 306, 308, 310, 313, 314, 316, 318, 320, 321, 326, 328, 329, 335, 340, 344, 346, 347, 349, 350, 351, 353, 355, 357, 358, 359, 384, 397, 402, 404
Haughey, Charles · 118, 188, 189, 190, 254, 361, 432
Hazell, Heidi · iii, 15, 237, 243, 244, 249, 258, 271, 317, 360
Heakin, Regimental Sergeant-Major Michael · iii, 15, 160, 161, 162, 165, 180, 191, 323, 342
Heerle · 274, 293, 304, 305, 310, 311, 316, 318, 321, 327, 344, 351, 371
Hegeman, Marie-Jeanne · 347, 352, 358
Hick, Sean · 225, 227, 237, 238, 257, 269, 270, 274, 275, 276, 279, 280, 284, 290, 293, 295, 296, 297, 298, 302, 303, 304, 305, 306, 307, 308, 309, 311, 312, 313, 314, 315, 318, 320, 326, 328, 335, 340, 344, 346, 347, 349, 351, 353, 354, 355, 357, 358, 359, 360, 367, 370, 371, 372, 384, 397, 402, 435, 442
Hijman, Ingrid · 245, 250, 257, 264, 268, 272, 273, 274, 281, 290, 302, 304, 311, 314, 315, 322, 326, 351, 352, 412
Hughes, Paul · 75, 80, 171, 198, 225, 228, 257, 275, 276, 280, 284, 285, 287, 288, 289, 291, 293, 296, 297, 303, 304, 305, 306, 307, 308, 311, 312, 313, 314, 316, 318, 319, 320,

326, 328, 330, 335, 340, 344, 346, 347, 349, 350, 352, 353, 354, 355, 357, 358, 359, 360, 367, 370, 371, 372, 379, 382, 384, 397, 402, 435, 442
Hughes, Sean · 171, 198, 199, 225, 275, 319, 320, 321, 348, 379, 382, 389, 393, 402, 417

I

Islania, Mick · iii, 11, 13, 15, 254, 258, 260, 281, 317, 323, 360

J

JHQ Rheindahlen · 25, 27, 69, 72, 74, 77, 87, 99, 156, 177, 191, 205, 249, 323, 363, 365, 369, 395
Jonesborough · 199, 200, 201, 203, 320, 337, 417

K

Keeley, Peter · 147, 150, 152, 172, 173, 174, 226, 234, 235, 236, 237, 246, 251, 256, 260, 361, 414, 423, 443
Kelly, Gerard · 24, 47, 48, 51, 52, 55, 56, 57, 69, 77, 79, 140, 141, 163, 193, 215, 222, 223, 224, 240, 320, 375, 379, 397, 398, 401, 424
Kelly, SAC Andrew · iii, 139
Kersten, Pauline · 348, 349
Kinawley · 135, 407
Kittelmann, Gunter · 209, 210, 367
Klawitter, Barbara · 360, 367, 372, 403, 404

L

Langenhagen · 275, 278, 281, 300, 318, 329, 346, 360, 367, 370, 371
Laumen, Jo · 326, 329, 330, 348, 350, 351, 353, 355, 357
Le Havre · 52, 172, 203, 218, 388
Loughgall · 78, 79, 82, 170, 197, 200, 332, 434
Lurgan · 55, 175, 225, 226, 227, 303, 349, 354, 357, 359, 402

M

Maastricht · 7, 60, 320, 330, 335, 346, 347, 349, 350, 354, 355, 359, 362, 367
Magee, Patrick · 37, 38, 39, 49, 50, 56, 58, 119, 121, 132, 133, 134, 174, 217, 320, 396
Maguire, Donna · 39, 129, 133, 170, 196, 203, 205, 209, 217, 219, 223, 225, 227, 231, 248, 259, 261, 262, 266, 267, 268, 269, 274, 275, 280, 284, 289, 291, 293, 298, 302, 303, 304, 305, 306, 307, 308, 309, 311, 313, 314, 316, 318, 326, 328, 335, 340, 344, 346, 347, 349,351, 352, 353, 354, 355, 357, 358, 359, 360, 362, 367, 369, 370, 371, 372, 373, 374, 384, 397, 403, 405, 414, 428, 429, 442
Maguire, Malachy · 170, 373, 404
Mainz · 7, 87, 158, 163
Malmö · 47, 58, 60, 71, 136, 163, 165, 191, 323, 343
McAliskey, Roisin · 92, 338, 340, 388, 390, 392, 413
McAllister, Tony · 49, 123, 145, 396
McCann, Daniel · 26, 83, 84, 85, 86, 88, 90, 91, 93, 95, 96, 98, 99, 101, 102,

103, 104, 107, 109, 110, 113, 114, 115, 117, 118, 120, 121, 122, 123, 124, 131, 137, 151, 161, 168, 170, 191, 195, 354, 374, 384, 395, 442
McCarthy, Kieran · 337, 339, 344, 345, 346, 407
McCaughey, Martin · 332, 333, 334, 335, 339
McFarlane, Brendan ‚Bik' · 49, 51, 55, 56, 57, 163, 193, 215, 320, 398
McGeough, Terence · 41, 43, 44, 45, 46, 58, 59, 60, 61, 65, 69, 70, 71, 73, 75, 78, 87, 89, 91, 93, 98, 119, 132, 135, 136, 138, 154, 158, 160, 161, 163, 164, 165, 166, 167, 168, 184, 190, 191, 192, 193, 194, 195, 202, 215, 253, 289, 323, 340, 341, 342, 343, 363, 364, 365,367, 369, 370, 374, 384, 398, 443
McKevitt, Michael · 77, 223, 378, 379, 382, 393, 394, 410, 412
Melrose, Stephen · iii, 15, 283, 286, 287, 291, 292, 317, 321, 329, 346, 351, 353, 357
Memopark timers · 54, 90, 91, 103, 104, 107, 138, 143, 144, 145, 146, 159, 208, 212, 213, 219, 310
MI5 · 29, 32, 57, 69, 74, 78, 88, 89, 93, 94, 96, 97, 108, 110, 119, 143, 145, 147, 153, 170, 174, 176, 195, 235, 260, 271, 323, 336, 342, 349, 369, 400, 417, 423
MI6 · 29, 32, 36, 53, 54, 172, 176, 380
Michaux, André · 15, 34, 35
Millar Reid, SAC John · 15, 121, 129, 130, 139, 141, 142, 143, 184, 192, 194, 324, 374
Milltown Cemetary · 118, 121, 123, 126, 127, 131, 142, 228, 251, 294, 299, 317, 332, 374, 401
Mönchengladbach · 25, 27, 31, 69, 72, 74, 75, 77, 87, 99, 156, 177, 191, 205, 219, 249, 323, 363, 365, 369, 395, 438
Morré, Peter · 176
Moy · 168
Münster · 37, 60, 183, 205, 219, 220, 229, 231, 234, 235, 258, 271, 281, 317, 318, 323, 360
Murphy, Thomas ‚Slab' · 42, 44, 45, 95, 129, 149, 171, 197, 198, 222, 223, 225, 316, 378, 379, 382, 389, 393, 399
Murray, Patrick · 124, 132, 133, 134, 135, 138, 154, 158, 168, 169, 189, 203, 208, 209, 212, 217, 219, 220, 221, 223, 248, 268, 323, 334, 366, 368, 369, 372, 373, 374, 384, 407, 443

N

Newry · 148, 149, 150, 151, 152, 170, 173, 201, 256, 275, 310, 319, 349, 350, 362, 369, 402, 403, 415

O

Osnabrück · 37, 205, 207, 208, 210, 217, 220, 259, 261, 266, 268, 278, 323, 346, 360, 369, 372, 386, 391, 407, 413, 439
Ostende · 160, 161, 162, 165, 191, 323, 342, 365
OTR · 397, 398, 399, 401

P

Paris · 53, 55, 56, 57, 69, 101, 172, 173, 174, 195, 204, 217, 219, 220, 223, 268, 280, 314, 322, 336, 348, 353,

360, 366, 386, 388, 432

211, 213, 215, 220, 221, 232, 249, 253, 258, 260, 265, 270, 277, 299, 301, 336, 368, 420, 421

Q

Quinn, Dermot · 170, 196, 224, 225, 257, 269, 275, 284, 311, 314, 315, 316, 326, 327, 335, 384, 409

S

Saarbrücken · 204, 276, 367
Savage, Sean · 83, 84, 86, 88, 90, 91, 92, 93, 98, 99, 101, 102, 103, 104, 107, 108, 109, 110, 111, 113, 115, 117, 118, 120, 121, 122, 124, 131, 137, 151, 161, 168, 195, 319, 374, 384
Scappaticci, Freddie · 119, 121, 149, 174, 415
Semtex · 71, 91, 98, 103, 107, 138, 143, 170, 208, 212, 213, 216, 220, 230, 251, 261, 265, 273, 274, 276, 278, 300, 302, 304, 306, 310, 318, 369, 371, 372, 383
Shinner, SAC Ian · 15, 138, 142, 143, 155, 163, 191
Smith, Cpl. Steven · iii, 15, 102, 107, 112, 113, 114, 116, 212, 213, 217, 223, 229, 230, 266, 268, 360, 367
Spanos, Nick · 15, 283, 286, 287, 292, 317, 321, 329, 346, 351, 353
Spiecker, Dr. Eberhard · 182, 184, 192, 194, 324
Staatspolizei (StaPo) · 66
Sykes, Sir Richard (UK Ambassador to the Netherlands) · 15, 32, 35, 36

R

Reichshof · 203, 221, 231, 373
Reid, Father Alec · 121, 129, 184, 192, 324, 374
Rheindahlen · 25, 26, 69, 71, 74, 78, 87, 94, 177, 191, 205, 354, 363, 365
Roche, Gerry · 337, 338, 339, 344, 345, 346, 407
Roermond · 60, 71, 136, 138, 141, 142, 145, 155, 159, 163, 190, 206, 223, 251, 257, 279, 281, 284, 285, 288, 289, 290, 291, 292, 298, 301, 306, 317, 318, 321, 327, 329, 330, 335, 340, 346, 347, 350, 351, 354, 355, 357, 358, 359, 365, 370, 402, 433, 435
Rooney, Peter · 83, 84, 86, 98, 153, 161, 168, 170, 401
Rosslare · 133, 172, 203, 218, 224, 225, 231, 360, 386
Ruger · 8, 123, 125, 128, 131, 171, 228, 237, 251, 281, 287, 306, 309, 317, 356, 425
Ryan, Father Patrick · 51, 52, 53, 54, 55, 56, 60, 65, 66, 71, 76, 77, 82, 90, 91, 104, 119, 132, 135, 138, 144, 145, 146, 147, 152, 168, 169, 170, 185, 186, 187, 188, 189, 193, 208, 212, 310, 400, 410, 412, 416
Rzeniecki, Jochen · 17, 155, 156, 157, 159, 166, 167, 180, 190, 195, 210,

T

Thatcher, Margaret · 40, 50, 82, 91, 97, 98, 119, 131, 132, 134, 142, 143, 159, 186, 187, 188, 189, 217, 219, 243, 426
Thornberry, Patrick · 35

U

Unna · 234, 239, 240, 249, 258, 271, 298, 437

V

Van Asperen, Gerard · 347, 352, 354, 360, 362
Van Bennekom, Willem · 38, 58, 320, 321, 347, 350, 352, 354, 356, 357, 358, 359
Van Straelen, Frits · 355, 357

Verhaeren, Cees · 340, 355

W

Webley .38 revolver · 160, 163, 165, 191, 232, 309, 317
Werl · 169, 208, 273, 274, 276, 293, 299, 300, 302, 318, 329, 371
Wildenrath · 10, 11, 13, 14, 15, 25, 60, 136, 139, 142, 163, 205, 218, 229, 246, 248, 250, 251, 253, 255, 256, 258, 260, 271, 281, 301, 317, 318, 323, 331, 360, 434

Printed in Great Britain
by Amazon